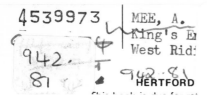

Please renew/return this item by the last date shown.

So that your telephone call is charged at local rate, please call the numbers as set out below:

	From Area codes 01923 or 0208:	From the rest of Herts:
Renewals:	01923 471373	01438 737373
Enquiries:	01923 471333	01438 737333
Minicom:	01923 471599	01438 737599

YORKSHIRE
WEST RIDING

THE KING'S ENGLAND

Edited by Arthur Mee

In 41 Volumes

THE KING'S ENGLAND

YORKSHIRE
WEST RIDING

By
ARTHUR MEE

fully revised and edited by
FRANK BECKWITH Jr.

Illustrated with new photographs by
A. F. KERSTING

HODDER AND STOUGHTON

Printed in Great Britain
for Hodder and Stoughton Limited,
St. Paul's House, Warwick Lane, London, E.C.4,
by Richard Clay (The Chaucer Press), Ltd.,
Bungay, Suffolk

INTRODUCTION TO REVISED EDITION

In preparing the new edition of THE KING'S ENGLAND care has been taken to bring the books up to date as far as possible within the changes which have taken place since the series was originally planned. In addition the editor has made his revisions both in text and illustrations with a view to keeping the price of the books within reasonable limits, in spite of greatly increased production costs. But throughout the book, it has been the editor's special care to preserve Mr Arthur Mee's original intention of providing something more than just another guide book giving archaeological, ecclesiastical, and topographical information.

In the case of every town and village mentioned in the King's England Series, it has been the intention not only to indicate its position on the map, but to convey something of its atmosphere. And the biographical selections about people who are ever associated with that part of the country in which they lived, or who are commemorated in the parish church—which was such a popular feature of the former edition—have been retained and in some cases supplemented.

For this new edition of *Yorkshire—West Riding* the editor is most grateful for the assistance he has received from his father, Mr Frank Beckwith, Sr, of Leeds.

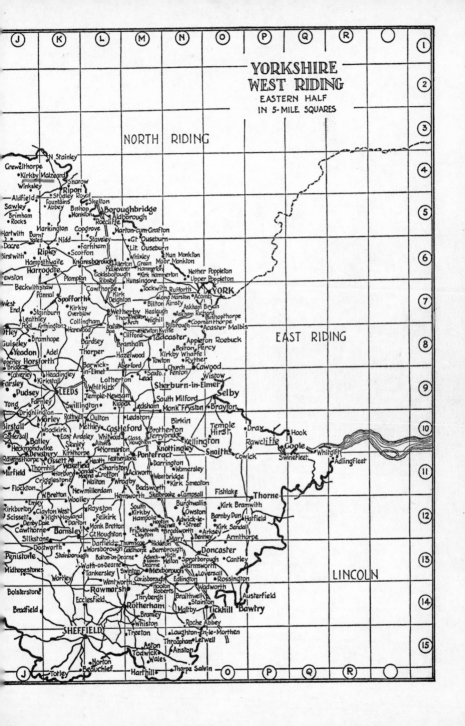

YORKSHIRE
WEST RIDING
EASTERN HALF
IN 5-MILE SQUARES

LIST OF ILLUSTRATIONS

YORKSHIRE
WEST RIDING

INTRODUCTION

THE West Riding of Yorkshire is an area of immense diversity; and this is not to be indicated by any mere enumeration of acreage, nor by a computation of how many other counties could be fitted into its bounds. Several possible divisions suggest themselves—proceeding from West to East there are, one might say, the high hills, among them some of the highest peaks in the Pennine range—Ingleborough, Penyghent, and Whernside for instance, which together constitute the great endurance challenge to Northern walkers, the "Three Peaks" walk; next the industrial spread, great conurbations on the edge of the hills—Leeds, Bradford, Huddersfield, Halifax, Dewsbury, and Wakefield; this part merges into the minefields centred on Barnsley and Doncaster, with the Steel City, Sheffield, on its own to the South; and finally the pastoral lowlands of the plain of York, a long band of farmland, for the most part unrelievedly flat. High versus low; ugliness versus beauty; the picturesque and the wild of Nature versus the artificial and often sordid of Man. All of this has a measure of truth; it is indeed difficult to realise, standing among the mineshafts of the Dearne valley, or in the back streets of Batley, that one is in the same administrative region which contains the wild grandeur of Gordale Scar, or the rolling moors above Pateley Bridge, or, for that matter, the peaceful quiet of Nun Monkton. But yet there is a measure of truth only; the divisions are not so simple; the contrasts are not so absolute. The high hills are cut by valleys—the much advertised Yorkshire Dales, with their charming villages, unchanged for the most part for generations; the area around Halifax in particular contains hidden valleys and hidden treasures from Yorkshire's past. (A museum in Halifax contains a map listing over 100 houses of the 17th century and earlier within a small radius.) There is beauty even in the blackest part of the mining district—old churches which are in themselves oases, reminding us of times when there were no mines or mills or factories and very little human habitation. Nor are all the creations of Man ugly; one remembers the superb Fountains Abbey, Ripon Cathedral, Selby Abbey, and Harewood House for instance. The truth is, there are many divisions and subdivisions to be made, each with its own unique interest.

Man has long inhabited the region, and there is evidence remaining of Stone Age, Iron Age, and Bronze Age settlements; of Roman camps and roads—and even a complete town at Aldborough; of magnificent mediaeval church buildings and of Elizabethan halls; of great mansions of the 17th and 18th centuries; of the horrors and ugliness of the Industrial Revolution and of the new exciting developments of the mid-20th century, especially in the vast rebuilding of the larger industrial cities.

Indeed the character of much of the industrial West Riding is undergoing drastic change. At the time of writing such an amount of demolition and rebuilding is going on that one hesitates to commit oneself to any definite statement. To take Bradford as an example; in the centre no less than in the suburbs vast areas and large buildings have fallen before demolition squads, so that large cranes, and lorries carrying away piles of rubble, have become accepted parts of the landscape, and at the same time new panoramas have been revealed—such as have not been seen for many years. One regrets the passing of such buildings of character as Horton Old Hall and the Swan Arcade, where J. B. Priestley worked, and one hears the terms "vandalism" and "wanton destruction" used all too often; but one waits with anticipation to see the new city rise. And the pattern is being repeated in Huddersfield, in Wakefield, in Leeds, and in Sheffield. This is all part of the changing of the character of the whole region—the old "where there's muck, there's money" image is going, and going quickly. There has been, in addition to the rebuilding, a vast enthusiasm for cleaning buildings, and many are now seen, scoured of the coating of industrial grime, as they have not been seen since they were erected—and alongside are the new white towers of flats and offices. The coming of smokeless zones, the closing of many railway stations and the change-over on the part of British Rail to diesel power, all will help to ensure that the predominant darkness of the buildings of the Riding in many of its areas will not return in anything like its previous ugliness.

In the wool and clothing towns especially there has been another change that has helped to remove much of the parochialism that one has been led to associate with the region in many a novel and play. Such towns have seen a large influx of coloured immigrant people. Walking the streets of many northern towns one sees considerable numbers of dark faces; and integration has happened for the most part quite peaceably—there are now, for instance, Indian and Pakistani cinemas, columns in the local newspapers, instructions in phone boxes, and even representatives on local

2

councils. The night shift at many a mill is composed almost entirely of coloured workers, the contents of shops, and indeed the shopkeepers and stallholders themselves reflect the coming into the area of new blood—and many a northern worker eats his midday meal in a Chinese restaurant, as opposed to the traditional fish and chip shop. All this is not to say that rows of squalid, back-to-back houses, men in cloth caps, gaunt factories, mills and warehouses, and hard Yorkshire dialect do not still exist—but they become increasingly hard to find.

If one finds such developments not to one's taste, then one may take refuge in the Dales; they in particular constitute havens of peacefulness—although in these days of greater accessibility and the "affluent society" where everyone has some means of transport, overcrowding becomes a serious problem. With such vast numbers, of people congregated in so comparatively small an area, there have been set up extensive provisions for the recreation of the thousands who seek some sort of escape from the towns. Here are ample opportunities for watching and taking part in football (soccer, Rugby Union, and Rugby League) cricket, motor-racing, golf, and many other sports: parks provide open spaces for these and other pursuits —and indeed the Dales themselves constitute in part a "National Park". Many also find a sort of refuge in the great number of amateur dramatic and musical societies and art clubs, to be found in almost every town.

Truly, this is a region which it would take many years to explore, and a lifetime to know.

Aberford. In a richly wooded country of rolling hills, it has old houses, and an old bridge over a tributary of the Wharfe, the Cock Beck. There are traces of a ford said to have been paid for by a Saxon lady, a mill with a silent waterwheel, and an old windmill quickly falling into ruin. Facing the War Memorial on the edge of the village are the almshouses of 1844, an unusual piece of architecture with a great show of gables, domed turrets, and a central tower with a clock and fine canopied niches.

The church of St Ricarius, a French missionary of the 7th century, has been almost rebuilt except for the Norman tower, with quaint corbels old and new. The chancel has a Norman and a 13th century window; fragments of a Saxon cross are on a windowsill; and a Jacobean table stands by the modern font. There is rich woodwork, delicately carved, in the screenwork and panelling of the chancel, the altar, and the reredos. The stalls are adorned with tiny faces and angels, and other small faces peep from quatrefoils of the altar rails. Round the arch to the chancel is a huge painting of the three crosses on Calvary, with the crowds below.

The porch has a sundial of 1806, and a stone coffin is in the churchyard. An old cross has come back to its place near the gate after being carried off during the Civil War.

Acaster Malbis. Aloof from the village, the pretty little aisleless church with low gabled walls looks over the meadows to Naburn, nestling in trees on the other bank of the Ouse. John Sharp, Archbishop of York in 1691, would often come from his palace at Bishopthorpe to pray at this quiet shrine.

Shaped like a cross, with a wooden turret and a small spire, it was built in the 14th century, and within it lies a stone knight of the Malbys family who may have been its founder, though a Norman capital built into the east wall tells of an earlier church. There are old coffin lids perhaps belonging to this family. The windows are curious for their outside splays, and two in the chancel are barely five inches wide. There are old glass fragments showing shields, Our Lord in Majesty, St Peter, St Alban, St Julia, St Bartholomew with his own skin hanging over his arm, and St James with shells on his garment. There are many brackets and several piscinas, an old font and an old chest, and a pulpit carved by an ancient craftsman. The bells are said to have belonged to York Minster long ago.

5

Ackworth. It is High and Low Ackworth, near the source of the River Went, and has long been famous for the Quaker school founded in 1779 by Dr John Fothergill. The original school-house, once a foundling hospital, is still here, though almost lost among the handsome new buildings. Among the portraits in the fine library is one of Dr Fothergill, the astonishing Wensleydale Quaker, one of the greatest doctors and naturalists of his day. He was a friend of Benjamin Franklin, and assisted him in drawing up a scheme for the reconstruction of the American colonies, and was never weary in well-doing, but his founding of the school here was probably the best thing he did.

We were told that in the first 67 years the school was all work and no play. There were no Christmas holidays till 1878. Till recent times the boys wore long-tailed coats and buckled shoes, the girls little white caps, dark frocks, and mittens. But they grew up fine men and women, and the school roll call includes Sir James Reckitt, one of the merchant princes of last century; Henry Tennant, a power in the railway world; James Wilson, who helped on the great idea of Free Trade; Henry Clerk and his sister, who went to the far corners of the world as missionaries; William Howitt, the author, and (most famous of all) John Bright, who was here for a year and hated it, for Ackworth was truly spartan then. But we may be sure that it was at Ackworth that the great Apostle of Peace received some of the inspiration which made him an ennobling figure in our national life.

The church at High Ackworth is buried in trees above a sloping green with an old cross, and near by is Mary Lowther's Hospital, founded in 1741. Most of the church is modern, but its tower is 15th century. An old floorstone is engraved with shields by the stem of a cross, and on the porch is a statue of St Cuthbert, linked with an ancient custom, still observed, of giving a sheaf of corn to the birds. Twice a year a sheaf of corn is tied to St Cuthbert's staff, in memory of the fact that his body is said to have rested here in its long wanderings before finding a resting place in Durham Cathedral.

The church has two fonts, on one of which is the name of a chaplain to Charles I. There is an old chest with three ornamental panels, a gravestone of 1506, and an inscription which tells us that Robert Gully was wrecked on the Island of Formosa, where he was murdered by Chinese in 1842. He was the son of John Gully, an extraordinary man who lies here.

John Gully was born at an inn near Bristol, and lived through 80 years of queer life. Starting as a butcher's boy, he found himself at 21 in a London prison, and, regaining his freedom, became a pugilist, being driven round Newmarket racecourse as a hero. Soon after this Gully gave up the ring for the turf, but fell out with his gambling partner, whom he horsewhipped, paying £500 for the pleasure of doing it. He bought Ackworth Park (a grand place now with old oaks and sycamores), and paid his way into Parliament. Having grown rich by horse-racing, he invested his money in coal-fields and died among them in Durham, but was brought to rest at Ackworth. He had two wives, and a dozen children by each.

Acomb. York has stretched out its wings to the old village swallowed up in the new. There is a windmill with five great arms, and the rebuilt church has odd tapering buttresses, a tower and spire, and two old carved chairs. In a field hereabouts was found a jar of yellow beads thought to have been brought from Egypt by a Roman soldier. The jar was clearly 14th century, and antiquarians believe that the beads were first buried by the Romans, found a thousand years after, and hidden again till someone brought them to light in our own day.

Addingham. It is a grey village near Ilkley, the hills and moors rising finely above it, and the church standing apart on a green bank above the River Wharfe, not far from the site of an ancient camp. It is said that when the Vikings attacked York in 876 the archbishop found refuge here. It comes into the ballad of the Shepherd Lord, who led its men to Flodden Field. A round-arched stone bridge over a stream flowing to the river brings us to the prim little church. Though it was made partly new in the 18th century, and again from 1947 to 1959, it has remains of over 400 years ago in the north aisle and its arcade, the north chapel, and the chancel arch; and on one of the pillars is the shield of the Vavasour family who helped to build York Minster. A prized possession is a Late Saxon cross.

Here in the family vault sleeps Samuel Cunliffe Lister, first Baron Masham, his memorial a marble tablet with a shield of arms in enamel. He was born in 1815 and lived until 1906, his 90 years being as crowded with industry as any man's years have been. He gave his life to invention and took out over 150 patents, his first valuable one being for mechanical woolcombing, so as to separate long hairs from short ones. His invention clashed with others, but in ten years he was head of the woolcombing industry and was bringing great prosperity to Bradford and to the wool trade of Australia. He then turned his attention to silk-waste, and almost ruined himself with his experiments. He lost on one machine a quarter of a million, but in the end established himself and made a

7

fortune by buying silk-waste and making it into velvet and carpets. He became enormously rich and bought three estates in Yorkshire which cost him a million, Swinton Park, Middleham Castle, and Jervaulx. He bought a colliery and multiplied its output by twelve. He was made a peer, and had a statue set up to him in his lifetime; it is by Matthew Noble, and is in a park at Bradford.

Adel. On the high ground between the Wharfe and the Aire, it was old when the ancient church was new, for the Romans were here and the Britons before them. Now city folk come here to play golf, and new houses are creeping up in sight of the church, but Adel is still a village looking over a fair scene of fields and wooded hills. There are fine views from the big churchyard, which is like a clearing in the trees. It has a sundial of 1628.

The tiny church is one of Yorkshire's gems, much as the Normans built it in the 12th century. It has an aisleless nave and chancel of charming simplicity, relieved by an exceedingly rich south doorway and the chancel arch—its two outstanding features.

There are still nine small Norman windows, but those in the east and west walls are modern. The nave has two Tudor windows, and the chancel a low window of the 14th century; one of 1681, now in the vestry after being the east window of the chancel, still has its original heraldic glass. There are flat Norman buttresses, and Norman corbels under the eaves, though some of the fine array of heads supporting it are renewed.

The doorway through which we come and go is one of the loveliest the Normans left in England, and is like a shallow gabled porch projecting from the south wall. Its two outer orders of zigzag and roll moulding rest on shafts, but the others (of zigzag enriched with flowers and beak-heads) are continued to the ground. On the worn capitals are still recognisable animals, and in the gable over the arch are stone panels showing Our Lord in Majesty, and a holy lamb. The space between the panels is filled with a curious pattern like interwoven snakes. The arch is a splendid frame for the massive oak door with its fine old hinges and bronze closing ring, which is one of the church's treasures; from the round plate projects the head of a beast, holding the ring in its mouth and a man's head between its lips.

The chancel arch is a triumph of Norman building, fascinating us with its sculpture. Its innermost order is of rich zigzag; the second is like a stone ladder running round the arch; and the third has the quaintest of beaked and bearded heads, among them an imp playing a fiddle as if to set the tune for the antics of the rest—men with

8

tongues out, a demon eating a child, one eating two people at once, others with animals in their jaws. On the capitals of the north side of the arch are two dragons fighting, a centaur shooting with bow and arrow at a monster with fiery breath, and St John the Baptist baptising Jesus, while David and an angel with a robe stand by, and an animal tries to drink the water. Fighting dragons come again on the south side, with scenes showing a vigorous knight on horseback fighting a dragon, and the Crucifixion with the sun and moon above the Cross and Joseph of Arimathea drawing the nails from Our Lord's feet with his long pincers.

The bowl of a Norman piscina rests on a pillar, and the font (looking old enough to be Norman) has a striking modern cover with panels showing scenes of the Crucifixion with the two theives, the Upper Room, and the Sacraments of the Church, Marriage represented in Georgian setting, and Baptism in the days when men wore armour. Two chairs are Jacobean. Beautiful craftsmanship of modern days is in the pulpit and the screen, which has dainty iron gates. Very dainty are five brass candelabra, and pleasing is a window with modern glass showing a knight, a bishop, and another knight with a white rose on his red tabard. On the walls are paintings by Vanderbank dating from 1748: the nearby rectory is also of the 18th century.

Adlingfleet. It lies in rich marshland, seeing the small green hills of Lincolnshire beyond the Trent, which joins the Ouse a mile away. Its old brick houses are clustered about the weatherworn church, and in the barn facing the church is an old doorway which may once have belonged to this interesting village shrine. Most of it is 13th century, but there is a 14th century window in a kind of transept, and from the 15th come the top of the tower, its west window, and the clerestory. The doorway through which we enter the church has a pointed arch enriched with zigzag, and its old door has traceried panels. The porch is modern, but over its arch are three battered old sculptures of the Annunciation, the Coronation, and the Assumption.

The cream-walled interior is striking with fine clustered pillars and the sides of the tower arch, their shafts detached and banded; the pillars lean this way and that, and the arches, including the chancel arch, are all askew. The bowl of the font, a piscina with projecting drain, part of a coffin lid with leaves of the shaft of a cross, and the stone figure of a woman with two angels at her head, are all mediaeval.

Francis Haldenby's monument of 1587 shows him in armour,

9

his figure curious for the very long face and very short thighs. On the front of the tomb is a splendid group of 11 sons, like a regiment of soldiers with their swords, wearing cloaks and ruffs; three daughters kneel behind their mother, and below all the children are their names. A floorstone with crosses and shields is said to mark the resting-place of Robert Haldenby of 1399. The name of the family lives in that of a neighbouring hamlet, where the Elizabethan Haldenby Hall is now a farmhouse. Another monument has the white marble figure of Mary Ramsden, who left a fortune to her father's college, St Catherine's at Cambridge, when she died in 1745.

Adwick-le-Street. Its name is a link with the Romans, telling us of its place near their old road from Doncaster to Castleford. Its church takes us back to the Normans, and shelters a tomb which makes this place a magnet for Americans, for it keeps green the memory of the Washingtons, who lived here the best part of two centuries, though their old home is no more.

Engraved on the tomb are the portraits of James Washington in Elizabethan armour and elaborate collar, his wife in a fashionable dress with a small ruff, and their 12 kneeling children. On the knight's breast is the Washington shield with the stars and stripes, which were thus in this place long before they were on the American flag. There are tombs of the Fitzwilliams who lived here before the Washingtons, and an inscription to Joseph Elmsall, who fought at Waterloo.

Remains of the Norman church are the south doorway, part of a window in the chancel (with one of the 14th century under it), and perhaps the sedilia. The north chapel is chiefly 13th century; a curious effect is given by the chancel arch extending beyond the chapel arcade. The tower is 15th century, and from its close comes the north aisle and perhaps the arcade dividing it from the nave.

There are remains of an old cross in the churchyard, and near by is a charming wayside garden in a park with fine chestnuts and elms.

Adwick-upon-Dearne. Its neat bellcot church has the same plan as in Norman days, and is entered by a Norman doorway within an old porch. Piercing the old walls are three Norman windows. The old pulpit has a star and stripe on the shield of the Washingtons, a family said to have lived in the neighbourhood, and to have been linked with America's first president.

Airton. Here in a deep hollow the sparkling little River Aire dashes over its rocky bed to the old mill, founded originally by the

Canons of Bolton Priory, and bridge, with no suggestion of the squalid miles it must journey before its 70-mile course is run. Into the magnificent view of the moors and fells rising to the north comes Gordale Scar, a remarkable gorge where a rapid stream from the slopes of High Mark falls in cascades. The posts of the stone stocks are on the green, and with the houses gathered round it is the charming little Quaker chapel of 1700, with a low stone seat enclosing the tiny court in the graveyard. Attached to the chapel is a cottage with a pretty porch. One house comes from 1696, the old manor house is now an inn, and at one end of the village is a fine 18th century house with three balls crowning the gable of its two-storeyed porch.

Aldborough. Here comes to mind the glory that was Rome, for this astonishing village stands on the foundations of a Roman city probably as splendid in its day as Roman York; and it has a rich store of treasure for all to see.

A charming neighbour of Boroughbridge, it has fine old houses great and small. The green has a tall maypole and ruined courthouse. On a little green by the church and a pretty timbered cottage is a tall old cross (like a slender clustered pillar supporting an unusual top) which may commemorate the Battle of Boroughbridge, when Edward II defeated the Earl of Lancaster.

The long church with a low 15th century tower is said to have in its walls some of the materials from the Roman city. Built into the west wall of the north aisle is a stone panel with a figure of the god Mercury (the work of a Roman sculptor of the first century), and below it are two small carved pillars, and a capital adorned with acanthus leaves. Spacious and light, the church has a 14th century nave with two fine arcades, the arches on the north side having between them three big faces, quaint and with eyes wide open. The clerestory and the long chancel are 15th century, and the south aisle is made almost new. The fine old roof of the nave has bosses of lions, cherubs, and grotesques, and among other old woodwork are five handsome chairs, the altar rails, the reredos, panelling on the sanctuary walls, the vestry door with old ironwork, a table, a mediaeval panel showing Daniel with the lions, and the inscribed pulpit, which is chiefly 17th century but has older tracery from a mediaeval screen, and a base of much interest because it was probably made from a pile of a Roman bridge. In the lovely old glass of the north aisle are oak leaves and acorns, canopy-work, and borders with castles and cups. Two bells date from the 15th century and the clock was made by an Aldborough man in 1783.

There is a wall-monument to William Aldborough of Charles Stuart's day. The mediaeval gravestone of a namesake of his was long used as a table for counting votes at election times, and a third William Aldborough, who died about 1360, is remembered by a big and fine brass portrait: standing on a bracket engraved with his name, he is shown as a knight with a shield, his armour showing the change in style from chain mail to plate. A mediaeval stone in the churchyard has the head and shoulders of a man in a circle.

But it is Roman Aldborough (proud Isurium) that most of us come to see. We have read that this may have been the stronghold of Queen Cartismundua who betrayed Caractacus to the Romans, but we do not know. That the Romans found Isurium a little town of huts behind wooden walls and left it a magnificent city we know, for some of its splendour remains.

Covering 60 acres and protected by walls 20 feet high, Isurium had noble houses, a hall of justice, a forum, and a temple where sacrifices were made. We can still trace the city walls and the four gates, one leading to the Great North Road. Here are foundations of the watch-towers, and near the south gate is an earthwork 70 yards long and 10 yards wide, perhaps a sort of stadium for the races. Studforth Hill close by was a fortified outpost, and Chapel Hill was a Roman cemetery.

For nearly 400 years Isurium was a proud place, the home of rich and powerful Romans, including the consuls and governors of York. The west end was the fashionable quarter where most of the wealthy people lived in fine villas with central heating and frescoed walls. Many of the mosaic pavements in their houses have been lost, and some have been taken into our museums. One showing Romulus and Remus is in a Leeds museum, but some remain where the Romans laid them one having a Greek-key pattern, plaitwork, and a star in the middle, the other (13 feet long and 11 wide) having in the middle what appears to be a lion under a tree.

In the garden of a cottage is part of the basilica, originally 52 feet long and 24 wide, with an apse. About half of it remains, with the vestibule and fragments of the tessellated pavement. Worked into the pattern are part of a figure in flowing robes and a Greek word meaning, "Have pity". A hole in the floor marks the place where a skull was found.

One of the most fascinating corners is near Aldborough Manor. Here is all the charm of an old-world English garden and something of the wonder of a fallen empire, with huge elms and chestnuts and ancient yews shading fragments of Roman walls and houses, Roman milestones, and Roman altars among the roses. It is thrilling to walk here amid a grandeur which was rising when Christians were being martyred in Rome; and perhaps the strangest thing of all is to come to the quarry from which the Romans hewed stone for their city. In its walls are curious little niches for urns and in one of the niches is a stone god, now barely distinguishable, forsaken by his worshippers over 50 generations since.

Many of the treasures of Isurium have been gathered into a museum, where we may see sculptures of Castor and Pollux (or are they Romulus and Remus?) and a battered Mercury with winged sandals. There are remains of mosaic pavements, fragments of Roman glass and Roman concrete, a gravestone with an inscription to the wife of a Roman soldier, an altar to Jupiter, coins of four centuries from Claudius and Nero to Valentinian, a flower-pot, and bits of pottery, one with a lion jumping over a child. There are keys and chains, rings with keys attached, oyster spoons, brooches, lamps, tear bottles, ivory counters dice, needles, rings, hairpins, enamelled scent bottles, and two very fine seals—one with the Three Graces and one with a hare on a chariot drawn by a cock, its detail so amazingly minute that we need a magnifying glass to reveal it. It is a masterpiece of the craftsmanship of the days of Caesar, the rarest of the small treasures in this treasure-house.

Aldfield. Its small group of houses and its quaint 18th century chapel look from a green hill to the towers of Fountains Abbey and the spire of Studley Royal. Facing a noble company of beeches, the chapel is shaped like three arms of a cross, with a door (invitingly open) in the middle of the long side. It is filled with box-pews and has a three-decker pulpit with a canopy, and the oak vaulting of the roofs springs from corbels. The old font has a bowl like a quatrefoil, carved with leaves.

It was at Aldfield that William Powell Frith was born in 1819. His first pictures were illustrations for editions of Shakespeare, Scott, and Dickens. His Derby Day and his picture of a Railway Station were among the most popular paintings of his time.

Allerton Mauleverer. A long avenue and a string of lakes enrich the deer park of over 400 acres, enclosed by a wall three miles round.

Looking up to the house from outside the park is the quaint village church, shaped like a cross with a central tower and mediaeval arcades, the tower having simple round arches to the chancel and the nave. The aisles are curious for having the western bays cut off by walling in which are small archways, similar ones leading to the transepts. Cream walls reflect the sunshine inside. The nave has a striking hammerbeam roof of elaborate construction, old poppy-head benches, and some Jacobean box-pews from which rises the three-decker pulpit. There are two Jacobean chairs, old altar rails, and a big painting of Moses and Aaron with the Tables of the Law. The Mauleverer shield is in old glass, and among fragments perhaps 200 years old are two pictures of the church after its restoration, a Crucifixion, and figures of Moses and a saint.

Rare for being carved in oak are two cross-legged knights, both worn and perished but still solid. They may be Mauleverers, and it is thought that two battered alabaster figures of a man and woman are also of the family. None the worse for wear are the fine little portraits (engraved on a brass plate) of Sir John Mauleverer of 1400 and his wife, the knight in armour enriched with the greyhound of his shield. The movable vizor attached to his headpiece is an uncommon thing to find on a brass.

Almondbury. This old parish from which a dozen others were formed last century has now been swallowed up by Huddersfield, but is still finely set among trees round the top of a hill above the Colne. It looks its best as we come from Fenay Bridge, and on this wooded eastern slope of the hill is one of many old houses hereabouts, Woodsome Hall. Though used by golfers now, and stripped of much of its beauty, this Tudor home of the Kayes was partly rebuilt in 1600, and was in the old days all that a great house should be, with its barn, terrace, courtyard, and the quaint riding-steps below the lawn. The hall has a minstrel gallery, a fireplace with stone seats, and a host of carved beams. Whitley Hall, begun in Elizabeth's day, was long the home of the Beaumonts; and Longley Old Hall, now a school, was the home of the Ramsdens. Fenay Hall has been very much restored, but the timbered front is beautiful 17th century work, and on a door are the words, "Let Fidelity enter, let Deception pass out"; while in one of the rooms we read the old inscription: "Fear God, honour the King, obey the laws, repay a kindness, think of death."

In the old part of the village by the church is a fine house with a black and white storey overhanging one of stone, its doorway dated 1631; it is now a club. The grammar school was founded in 1608 and received from James I a charter which can be seen in the school library. Woodsome Mill, said to have been grinding corn since 1100, was still working when we called. King's Mill has lost its ancient wheel, but the water flows through sluices built 900 years ago.

The stately church is attractive outside, with a tower rising above long lines of battlements and pinnacles. Most of it comes from late in the 15th century, though the chancel has remains of the 13th. The chancel is unusual in having three windows (as well as a tiny slit) in the east wall, a tall one of the 15th century between two double lancets of the earlier church. In the restored old glass filling two windows in the Kaye chapel we see some of the family who built it—a man kneeling on a purple cushion, his wife in green, his children with golden hair. There are shields and canopies, and figures of saints: Elizabeth holding an open book, the Baptist clothed in camel hair, Helena with cross and book, Barbara with castle and chalice, Anne teaching Mary to read, and Margaret with a crown.

The glory of the bright clerestoried nave is its old roof, looking down on tall arcades. The bosses are carved with instruments of the Passion, a half moon and a face, a face with two tongues, and a head with three eyes and two noses (two faces in one). The inscription round it is thought to have been composed by John Skelton, one of our 16th century poet laureates.

The aisles have black and white panelled roofs, the north adorned with shields, the south with quaint corbel heads. In the screens of the chancel and chapels are remains of 15th century work, and the fine tall cover of the old font is the work of the 16th and 17th centuries. Two massive oak chests may be 16th century, and four staves are of Queen Anne's day. A crucifix came from Rheims Cathedral. A floorstone of 1574 has the portrait of one of the Kayes.

In the churchyard are the old stocks, and on a stone to a child of seven months we read this variant of familiar lines:

> *This world's an inn, man think of that,*
> *Some call for breakfast and go quickly back:*
> *A many dine, and some to supper stay,*
> *But those who early go will have the least to pay.*

High as Almondbury is, Castle Hill is higher, and is crowned with a lofty tower, a striking landmark of the Victorian era. Folk love to come here for the magnificent view of the Holme valley with Huddersfield in the hollow and the moors above. Below the tower are traces of an Iron Age hill fort destroyed by the Romans about AD 70. A castle was built here in the 12th century, but all that now remains of it is a square sectioned ditch.

Altofts. Crowning a knoll in this mining village is a stone cross with gold mosaic shining above the pits from which over 70 men

15

went to their death in the Great War. In the modern church are inscriptions to Thomas Mellor, killed in the war at 18, and Tom Ibbeson who was 17 when he lost his life in the pit.

Martin Frobisher was born near by, he was married at Whitwood across the fields in 1591, but his happiness here was cut short when Sir Walter Raleigh sent him to fight the Spaniards. The Altofts he would know was a grey village among green fields and woods near the River Calder. He must have loved it as a child to have come back to it after many an adventure on the high seas.

Anston. Built for the most part over six centuries ago, with a tower and spire 100 years younger, the attractive church looks from a hill to the mines of Yorkshire and Notts. Its oldest work is the north arcade with pointed arches of the 12th century, its heavy style contrasting with the daintier arcade to the other aisle. An old arch leads to a chancel made almost new. There are old sedilia and a double piscina, and in one of two old recesses rests an unusual sculptured stone showing a man at prayer, an angel touching the head of the tiny woman at his side. It may be 14th century.

This village has paid great homage to Methodism, beginning in an old room now transformed into a Garden of Remembrance and ending in a noble church which is known hereabouts as the Cathedral of Methodism. It goes back 100 years, when James Turner, a working mason in the Anston quarries, joined the Methodists in the old room, helped them to build a small chapel, and set his heart on giving the people a worthy temple of their faith. In 1924 Mr Turner died, but he had left the land for a new church and his four sons built it as his memorial. It is an impressive place, designed by Mr B. D. Thompson and built in Norman style because it was the Norman Minster at Southwell which led the Westminster Commissioners to the Anston quarries in looking for stone. It has a fine rugged tower, a pointed porch with a round doorway of three orders, an apse, Norman arches, and three glowing east windows given by James Turner's daughters.

Apperley Bridge. The old bridge of two arches over the River Aire still takes a little of the traffic between Harrogate and Bradford, but a 20th century bridge is close by. Mills have come into the green valley, and a 1930 bridge crosses the canal where barges are for ever passing between Leeds and Liverpool.

Woodhouse Grove school here, a Wesleyan foundation, is housed in a late 18th century mansion. Patrick Brontë visited the school and his daughter Charlotte was once a governess near by.

Appleton Roebuck. Here are green pastures and fine trees, a few houses, and a 19th century church with a clock in its lofty bellcot, the works seen in a glass case inside.

Hereabouts are great earthworks, and a mile and a half away, in a spacious park going down to the Wharfe, is the great house, Nun Appleton Hall. Much of it is 17th century, but its story goes back to Norman days, when a nunnery was founded in this lonely spot. There was an older house built by the Fairfaxes from the ruins of the nunnery, and remains of stone cloisters were unearthed about 20 years ago.

It was from the nunnery that Sir William Fairfax of Steeton carried off the rich and beautiful Isobel Thwaites of Denton, who might have become a nun had not her bold Lochinvar ridden off with her on his saddle. They were married in Bolton Percy church, where they sleep, and from them was descended the man who gave the name of Fairfax a proud place in our annals.

For Thomas Lord Fairfax, the famous Parliament General in the Civil War, Nun Appleton was all the world he wished for in his later years. One of the noblest figures in the story of our land, he was soldier, writer, poet, antiquarian, and lover of all things good and true. Here he wrote his books, among them a collection of 170 epigrams, and walked in the garden with Andrew Marvell, the tutor of his daughter Mary. The joy of her father's life, Mary had been with him in the fight at Selby when she was only five, and in 1657 she married the Duke of Buckingham in Bolton Percy church. Black Tom, as the villagers called Lord Fairfax, had the finest stables in Europe, and it was from Nun Appleton that at the Restoration he sent a horse for Charles II to ride in his triumphal entry to London.

Few Englishmen of his century lived more nobly or died more cheerfully. He sleeps in Bilbrough church.

Appletreewick. Looking up to the fells and down to the Wharfe, this quaint little place, a mile or two from Barden Tower, where lived Wordsworth's Shepherd Lord, has gay garden borders, an old barn, and low stone houses by the steep road. Monks Hall has a projecting wing and carvings on its walls. Low Hall, the last house in the village, restored in the 17th century, has a huge stone trough beside it. High Hall has stables, a heavily studded door, an old oak screen, and a dining-hall with a minstrel gallery. At Skyreholme hamlet is the beautiful Parcevall Hall in lovely gardens, a surprising house to find in its lonely moorland setting. It was a rest house for the monks of Fountains, has associations

17

with Nevinson, the 17th century highwayman, and was restored by Sir William Milner in 1928. It now belongs to the Bradford Diocesan authority, but its beautiful gardens are occasionally open to the public. Half a mile beyond it is Trollers Ghyll, a dark glen with crags 60 feet high.

The village stocks may be seen by the Craven Arms.

Facing High Hall is the simple church with small windows, and 1635 over the doorway. Looking much like the houses about it, it is said to have been converted from two cottages in which Yorkshire's Dick Whittington was born. He was Sir William Craven.

It is four centuries since a carrier's cart carried a boy of 13 away from Appletreewick and packed him off to London to earn his fortune. He became a tailor's boy, and by the time the Armada had been and gone he had bought a fine house, and become Warden of the Mercers Company and an Alderman of the City. He was one of the last Sheriffs under Queen Elizabeth. King James made him a knight, and in 1611 he was Lord Mayor of London. He founded a grammar school at Burnsall, a mile or so from Appletreewick, and helped to build a college at Ripon.

Arksey. Though the collieries are not far away, Arksey remains an attractive village in the fields near the River Don. The imposing old church stands in company with a fine old school, old dwellings with red walls and stone roofs, and the almshouses (founded in the 17th century) gathered round a green quadrangle. Hereabouts are the earthworks known as the Roundabout, perhaps once a Roman camp. The church has memories of the Normans and those who followed till Tudor days. Charming inside and out, it has embattled walls of tinted stone, a fine porch over 400 years old, and a central tower built at the close of the 12th century and crowned by a short spire. A primitive form of tracery is seen in the belfry windows, each consisting of two lancets with a shaft between them and an oval piercing the round arch above them.

The north aisle was added when the tower was built, the north chapel is 14th century, the south aisle and the south chapel are Tudor. Between the north aisle and the transept are a Norman arch and window. The chancel has three much restored Norman windows in the east wall, with a round one above them, and a 13th century lancet in each side wall. The font may be 12th century, there is a mediaeval piscina, and in old glass are shields, a face, and a crown. From the 17th century come the pews with bobbin ends and the canopied pulpit, and an old screen has a band of quatrefoil tracery.

18

Armthorpe. Industry has brought many new houses here, and the simple old church of nave and chancel is now part of a bigger place. A plain 12th century doorway frames an old door, the small chancel arch was built by the Normans, and by a big pointed arch at the west end of the nave is a flat Norman buttress that was once outside. Some windows are 14th and 15th century, one is Norman, and there is a mass dial from the days before clocks.

Arncliffe. It is the chief of the four villages evenly spaced in Littondale, a mountain valley through which the River Skirfare runs to the Wharfe near Kilnsey. The little river is one of Yorkshire's most enchanting streams, and Arncliffe has an exquisite share of its valley. The houses are round a green, and the Cowside Beck falls into the stream before it flows under a beautiful bow bridge and cascades by the churchyard.

It would be hard to imagine a lovelier setting for the church, a simple place with a grey mediaeval tower peeping over a mantle of trees. All but the tower was refashioned in 1841. The fine black and white roof has six tiebeams with traceried gables. There are two old chairs, a bell of 1350, and inscriptions to 68 men of the dale who went to the wars; of 34 who went to Flodden Field 400 years earlier, we read that two were from Hawkswick, 22 from Littondale, and from Arncliffe 9 bow and billmen and "one with able horse and harness". Kingsley was a frequent visitor here and wrote part of his Water Babies in the village.

We pass Hawkswick on our way from Wharfedale, along the road which threads Littondale to Halton Gill. If we take the longer way from Stainforth the journey over the fells is magnificent, climbing to 1430 feet, rising under Penyghent and dropping down to Littondale, where the road swings round at Halton Gill. Seen from the heights, this tiny place is a charming huddlement of grey farms and cottages and little church, alone in a silent world, sheltering under the steep slope of Horse Head Moor. Its own stream tumbles into the hurrying Skirfare near a bridge. The church is only a nave and chancel, joined to a school with 1626 over the doorway; they share the bellcot between them.

Litton village lies between Halton Gill and Arncliffe, and gives the dale the name we know. Its older name of Amerdale lives in Wordsworth's *White Doe of Rylstone:*

> *The White Doe followed up the Vale*
> *In the deep fork of Amerdale.*

Arthington. A Wharfedale village, it lies between the hills and a stretch of the river with an old mill and a weir and delightful woods. From Bank Top, 500 feet up, there is a magnificent view of the valley and the moors beyond. One of the fine houses in the view is Arthington Hall, built in the Italian style in a small park. From Norman days till the 18th century it was the home of the Arthingtons. One of the Sheepshanks who followed them gave the village its cross-shaped church of 1864, its high tower and spire rising from a lawn by the busy road. One of the stained windows dimming the interior has Capronnier's brilliant glass showing scenes in the lives of Joseph and Jacob.

A mile along the road to Harewood is Nunnery Farm, attractive with its big chimneys, small windows, and a porch older than the Spanish Armada. It is thought to have been built from the ruins of Arthington Nunnery, a small house of nuns founded in the 12th century, with Alice de Romilly as its benefactor. There are remains of its mound and moat, and the spring known as the Nun's Well can still be seen. Above Nunnery Farm is Rawden Hill among the trees.

A mile west of the town in Creskeld Hall among beeches and clipped yews, a fine manor house with some remains of mediaeval days, standing where there has been a settlement since Saxon times. The old moat can still be traced. Not far from the hall the railway comes out of the great Bramhope tunnel, crossing the valley on a viaduct of over twenty arches.

Askham Bryan. Copper beeches, chestnuts, and elms are among its grand old trees, of which some are round the trim churchyard facing a willow-bordered duck-pond. It is a charming setting for the small Norman church, with ivied walls and a bellcot with a bell over 300 years old. The old porch has a splendid entrance arch built by the Normans, the rich zigzag arch resting on shafts with capitals of stiff leaves. Three Norman slits deeply splayed in the east wall are enriched with arches and shafts, and over them is an oval window. In the black and white roof are six old tiebeams, the pulpit is 17th century, and there are Roman tiles in the masonry.

Askham Richard. Delightful from a distance if we come from Healaugh by Sandwich Lane, it is charming when we arrive. The cottages have bright red roofs, the green has a big pond, and the stately avenue of trees bordering one side of it leads to the gates of a great house whose walls of brick and timber are crowned with a turret and spire, and a tower with a pyramid cap. In the trees

20

Bolton Abbey.

Bradford Town Hall.

beside this modern house is the small 12th century church, made partly new, its companion in the churchyard a stone coffin (with a coped lid) in which a Roman is believed to have lain; it was found in a field. The shafts of the modern porch are more worn than the doorway it shelters, a fine fragment of the Norman church, with roll mouldings in the arch, and capitals carved with leaves and scallop. A flat stone in the porch, carved with a wavy pattern on the edges, may be as old. There are oak panels of three centuries ago, and the altar rails are made from ancient roof timbers.

Aston. It is near the Derbyshire border and has collieries close by, but it keeps its rural charm, with a fine little church at a green corner where the great house stands in a hundred acres of woodland. There are still a few stones of the older house where lived Archbishop Melton who fought the Scots, restored St William's tomb in the Minster, and died six centuries ago.

The oldest work is in the nave arcades, built by the last of the Normans, one pointed arch showing the English style. The south aisle is two centuries later, the north aisle is made largely new, and the tower is 15th century. The weathered porch has an angel carved on a niche, and guarding the windows of the south aisle are demons and grotesques. There are shields in old glass, an old stone altar, and a fine 15th century font remarkable for two quaint carvings at the base—a fierce-looking man with a spear and an angel with a scroll.

There is a monument of Sir Francis Fane of 1680, and another to Lord Darcy whose widow Sir Francis married. It shows the baron in a fine doublet, kneeling with his first three wives.

One of the rectors here was William Mason, whose 43 years' service ended with his death in 1797. His medallion is in the church, where he sleeps, and in the vestry is a copy of a poem he wrote when six years old. It was Mason who built the big square rectory and planned the garden in the style he advocated in his book, *The English Garden*.

The most notable thing he ever did was to give us a life of his best friend, Thomas Gray, who often came to stay with him here. Gray called him Scroddles, and the two loved to sit in the summerhouse, where we sat when we called.

Austerfield. Its name is at least 1200 years old, and its fame has reached the western world, for in this red-roofed village, hiding from the Great North Road and seeing the great expanse of the Carr lowlands, was born William Bradford, whose memory has made the place a shrine for our American visitors.

His modest brick birthplace has an attic where he must have played, and curious stairs in what is really a chimney. After being imprisoned for his faith he found refuge in Holland, and in 1620 he sailed in the *Mayflower*, keeping a log of the journey which is now one of America's great possessions.

Bradford was only 32 when the Pilgrims chose him as the second governor of Plymouth in New England, and it was no doubt his foresight and energy which enabled them to succeed. Unlike many Puritans, he had the grace of tolerance, and when he died in 1657 he was mourned by Red Indians and Englishmen alike.

The register tells of his baptism in 1589, and the font is still here for us to see, a relic of the church which has come down from the Normans. It is simple and cared-for, crowned by a bellcot, the rubble walls pierced with some 14th century windows, and a 13th century lancet at the west end, where there is a Norman buttress. In the porch is a leaning Norman doorway, its arch carved with beakheads and zigzag, and the tympanum with a quaint dragon. Two faces peep from the capitals of the Norman chancel arch, and a hooded man is on a capital of the stout Norman arcade leading to the aisle, which was rebuilt by Americans in 1897, as a memorial to Austerfield's Pilgrim Father.

A brass inscription tells us that the aisle was rebuilt by the Society of Mayflower Descendants and other citizens of the United States in memory of William Bradford, "first American citizen of the English race who bore rule by the free choice of his brethren".

Bradford was one of the little group of extreme Puritans who met at the house of William Brewster at Scrooby, and called themselves the Brownists. Having to flee to Holland, he was betrayed by the Dutch captain with whom he sailed and was thrown into prison, but by the time he was 20 he was free again, and soon sold all his property and sailed in the *Mayflower*.

Austwick. The stern grandeur of mountain scenery is all about us if we come from Horton-in-Ribblesdale to Austwick, where a stream is flowing to the Wenning. The church is new, but old houses are huddled closely on the village road and round the little green with its quaint old cross, and grouped among the trees on the hillside are an Elizabethan house, an old ivied cottage, and the hall, a fine old house with some of the stout walling of an ancient tower in its entrance hall. Near by is the very attractive hamlet of Wharfe.

Badsworth. Not far from Upton Beacon, from where we see the Derbyshire hills and the Lincolnshire wolds, Badsworth is charming with old houses and trees, a church made new in the 15th century, and a stately hall in beautiful grounds with poplars, copper beeches, and old oaks.

The massive west tower stands between aisles with tall arcades separating them from the nave, and a lower arcade leads from the chancel to the chapel. There are a few shields of old glass, a handsome font 500 years old, and two carved Norman stones set like brackets at the end of the south aisle.

A wall-monument pays tribute to Sir John Bright, who lived at the great house and died in 1688. He fought for Cromwell, won distinction as a prudent and capable soldier, commanded a brigade at the battle of Selby, and was at the siege of Pontefract.

Baildon. Some of its houses are one above another instead of side by side, so steep is the hill on which the village is built. Below is one of the busiest industrial centres in Yorkshire, and above is Baildon Common with its reservoirs and golf course, leading on to miles of lonely moor. There are modern houses in gardens, and old houses in the shadow of bare crags. The Old Hall, a fine gabled house, has been repaired and is now used as a club, with new dwellings all about it. In the little square below the church are the posts of the stocks, and an old cross with a new top.

There was a church here in the 12th century, but the one we see was made almost new in 1848. Edmund Hodgkinson, the parson who had watched its transformation, died the day after its reopening. The arcade, the arch to the chancel and the one to the south chapel, and a group of lancets in the east wall, appear to be remains of the mediaeval church. The old font has a new base; the pedestal pulpit is Jacobean. Near the church is a house from whose upper window it is said Wesley preached in 1786.

Barden. Amid some of the most enchanting scenery in Wharfedale, it looks up to the heights, with Simon's Seat less than three miles away. Over Barden's fine old stone bridge, with three arches, scheduled to be preserved for all time, rode the Appletreewick boy who became Lord Mayor of London.

The road from the bridge winds steeply up to the ruined Barden Tower, with doorways and windows in the roofless walls. Said to have been a hunting lodge of the Cliffords of Skipton, it was rebuilt about 1485 by the Shepherd Lord, and after falling into decay was restored in the 17th century by the famous Lady Anne Clifford.

23

Attached to the little retainer's cottage at its side is the tiny old chapel, now in a sad state of neglect, with an outside stairway on the wall of the sturdy low tower. It was this place which the Shepherd Lord loved most of all. From the windows he watched the stars, and here, with crucibles and retorts, he searched for the Philosopher's Stone. Wordsworth pictures him "standing on this old church tower in many a calm propitious hour". The Lister family have lived here for many years and in the main room of the cottage (where one can enjoy a genuine Yorkshire tea) is a halberd used by one of them at Flodden.

Bardsey. New Bardsey has attractive modern houses on the hillside; old Bardsey is tucked away in a glen. The road by the timbered cottages brings us uphill to a house which was the vicarage till the middle of last century, and higher still to the tithe barn, its massive arches impressive, its walls fast falling into decay. Above the church is a green mound on which a castle stood. Some of its stones, and others from a granary of the monks at Kirkstall, are said to be in the walls of Bardsey Grange, where was born William Congreve, the Bardsey boy who sleeps with kings in Westminster Abbey. The church, on a lovely hillside among trees, began as a Saxon shrine, and has become a captivating place through Norman, mediaeval, and later building.

The slender west tower is chiefly Saxon, and oblong in shape. The lower part (earlier than the rest) is thought to have been a porch on which later Saxons raised a tower for their simple nave and chancel. In its north and south walls are small round doorways with windows above them, the one on the north side having an old latticed door.

The Normans built the tower arch and the arch to the chancel, the south doorway with zigzag and beak-heads, the deeply-splayed window in the west wall of each aisle, and the fine north arcade with arches on round pillars with scalloped capitals. The pointed south arcade shows the passing of the Norman style, and over it are 19th century clerestory windows. During the 14th century the aisles were widened and the chancel enlarged; two of its fine lancets look now into chapels instead of to the churchyard. The sedilia and the piscina are 15th century. Among a collection of ancient stones are fragments of a Norman font with bead ornament, and part of the head of a cross. One of several coffin lids has shears, and another has a chalice and a book by the stem of a beautiful cross; it may commemorate a 13th century priest, and on it are initials and the date 1644. A stone pillar and sundial in the churchyard is 1751.

The record of Congreve's baptism is given as on 10 February, 1669–70 in the register, which is itself interesting as dating from 1538.

Barkisland. Swept by wind and clouds, busy with spinning cotton and making woollens and paper, it has marvellous views from its hill, old stone houses, two halls of much charm, and a simple 19th century church. Barkisland Hall, built in 1640, has a porch with a round window and admirable plaster ceilings. Howroyd Hall, only two years younger, is hidden by trees. The village stocks remain and the village inn dates back to the 17th century.

Barnborough. Long the home of the wealthy Cresacres, whose fine hall (which has a priests hiding chamber) has stood since the 16th century, it is by the pits of industrial Yorkshire. Tradition tells of a Cresacre who was attacked by a wild cat, both man and beast being killed in the church porch; a wild cat is on the family shield, and carved in stone on the church tower. The lower part of the tower and the north arcade are part of the church of the 12th century. The south aisle and the arcade are 14th century. The stone-ribbed porch has pinnacles and panelled buttresses. Mediaeval relics are gravestones serving as lintels in the clerestory, several piscinas, and the font. There are fine old roofs, and some 15th century screenwork. There was much scaffolding about when we called—a sign of the ever-present danger of subsidence.

In the nave is the tall shaft of a Norman cross remarkable for its carving of two figures. A rare possession is the marvellously preserved oak figure of Sir Percival Cresacre of 1477, said to be the knight who fought the wild cat in the porch; he lies under the arched canopy of a tomb adorned with shields and rosaries, a badge of his family. He is in armour and helmet, with a heart between his hands and a cat at his feet. On his wife's stone are rosaries arranged like a cross.

A link with a famous Englishman is a brass inscription to Anne Cresacre, for she married the idiot son of Sir Thomas More.

Barnby Dun. Here the canal and the River Don are so close that we could throw a stone across both. There are many old red houses with pantile roofs, and in some of the gardens are fine elms, beeches, and cedars, and one weeping beech like a green waterfall.

The fine church with quaint gargoyles is chiefly 14th century, but the tower is a century younger, and the beautiful nave arcades with slender clustered pillars may be 700 years old. In the sides

25

of a north aisle window are two brackets with angels under them, and close by in the wall is a big 14th century niche. Lovely glass in the east window of this aisle has Peter with his nets, an old sailing ship (the Ark of Christ's Church), and a red-roofed church on a rocky pinnacle in the sea. The chancel, partly rebuilt, has still part of the old walling, the priest's doorway, buttresses enriched with niches, and the sedilia and piscina with angels between their richly moulded arches. Under the piscina is carved a man's head and outstretched arms. A little man is under a big niche in a buttress of the north aisle. Projecting into the nave between the south arcade and the chancel arch is a turret stairway to the roof, once opening to a roodloft. The old font has tracery and flowers.

An inscription tells of James Bruce, son of the Earl of Elgin, who was drowned in 1798 when trying to cross the river here on horseback. Another is to Roger Portington who suffered much for his loyalty to Charles Stuart. He raised a company of soldiers at his own expense, lost over £10,000 in the king's service, and spent years in prison.

Barnoldswick. Known hereabouts as Barlick, this cotton town near the Lancashire border has an old church over a mile from the busy streets. It is at the end of a long lane, standing in trees above a lovely glen where a stream flows on its way to the Earby Beck. There are fine yews by the gate, and a flower-bordered path leads to the quaint low porch. The porch has a restored old roof, and shelters a battered stoup which may be Norman; it is crudely carved and has an odd face at one corner. The chancel is partly 13th century, but the tower and the rest of the church are two centuries later. A small door in the middle of the south wall opens to the surprising interior, where, soaring above the old bobbin-ended pews, is a three-decker pulpit. There is no chancel arch, and the fine old roofs go east to west without a break. The altar table is Jacobean. The font, shaped like an egg-cup, is probably Norman, and near it is a stone coffin. Attached to a bracket is a roundel with the arms of Kirkstall Abbey, which was founded in 1152 by monks of the monastery which existed here.

We were interested to find in the Roman Catholic church here two pieces of work by a local craftsman, John Pickles. One is a public clock and one a perpetual calendar. Near by a stretch of Roman road is visible.

Barnsley. It was mentioned in the Domesday Book, but there is little old here now. The coal and iron which gave it fame gave it also the name of Black Barnsley. It was a smoky place even when Daniel Defoe saw it in 1727, but the Barnsley of today is relieving its industrial dress with the dignity of fine new buildings.

In a commanding place on a hill is the Town Hall, an imposing classical building completed in 1933. Over the entrance are Corinthian columns, and rising from the roof is a fine tower of diminishing stages. The hall is of travertine—floor, walls, pillars, and staircase. The fine council chamber is of panelled walnut, its rich ceiling supported by fluted columns with capitals of blue and silver.

Next to the Town Hall is the fine new building of the Mining and Technical College, and by the college is the parish church of St Mary, encircled by trees. On the other side of Church Street is the grammar school, founded in 1660 by Thamas Keresforth: the scholars are now in a new school in Shaw Lane, and this old stone building with a new porch and arms over the doorway houses the Cooper Art Gallery. It was Samuel J. Cooper who bought the old place in 1912 and endowed it for the use of the public, and here is the collection of paintings and sculpture he made. Here are also paintings and etchings by Lord Leighton, Corot, Millet, Rousseau, and others, and Sir Michael Sadler made a generous gift of 85 English drawings from Gainsborough's time to ours.

The old church of St Mary was made new last century, except for the 15th century tower. The best of its modern screens divides the south aisle from a chapel in which is an unusual War Memorial, a tall pillar enriched with pinnacled buttress and canopied saints, all painted in mediaeval colour. Among the heroes recorded is a woman, Dorothy Fox. There are two old carved chairs, plain old pews are in the north chapel, and among the poppyheads of the chancel seats is a pelican with her young. The organ goes back in parts to the 18th century, and is attributed to Snetzler.

On the edge of the town, at Kingstone, is St Edward's church, built this century in mediaeval style, and sheltering some beautiful glass. The striking east window has an unusual Crucifixion. Very charming is the west window, symbolising the "ship of the church" approaching the New Jerusalem.

Near this church is Locke Park, with forty lovely acres of trees, green banks, and gardens. The tower is a memorial to Mrs Locke. The park was her gift in 1861 in memory of her husband Joseph Locke, the famous engineer who was a scholar at Barnsley Grammar School. Here is the bronze figure of this man remembered today as one who found an opportunity in every difficulty. Apprenticed to George Stephenson, he became one of the greatest railway builders of last century.

By the Doncaster road is an obelisk with a bronze angel carrying a wounded man, recalling a pit disaster of 1866. We read that it is a tribute to "Parkin Jeffcock and other heroes of rescue parties who lost their lives in further explosions, and also to commemorate the signal bravery of John Mammatt and Thomas Embleton, who rescued the sole survivor". In the churchyard sleeps old John Hallifax, a gentleman and clockmaker whose son, a grocer's apprentice, was Lord Mayor of London in the 18th century and died worth £100,000.

The most famous son of Barnsley is James Hudson Taylor, the missionary, who sailed for China when he was 21, and after a voyage of 11 months arrived at Shanghai with a barrowload of New Testaments. The May Day green market, established by Royal Charter in 1249, is held on a Monday, and is the largest in the North of England: the stall holders will keep the visitor amused for many an hour. Pitt Street still contains some old buildings (although it is undergoing change rapidly) including the Methodist Church, outside which are some stone steps from which John Wesley preached in 1786. Some street names here intrigued us, "Graham's Orchard" and "Gas Nook" being two.

Barwick-in-Elmet. Every three years the Maypole is given new finery, a May Queen is chosen, and old games are revived. On the old steps near the maypole is a new cross carved in the style of long ago, a tribute to men who fell in the Great War.

By the Leeds road is an old windmill, and west of the village are great earthworks unlike anything else of their kind in England. One, known as Wendel Hill, covers ten acres and was perhaps a British camp, a Celtic stockade, and a Norman fortress; the other, Hall Tower Hill, was a meeting place of the Saxon Council, and is said to have been the site of King Edwin's palace, a royal house amid forests of elms and oaks of which there are traces even yet. Long before Paulinus baptised him in the little church which was to become York Minster, Edwin hunted the wolf and the wild boar hereabouts.

The church has a fine 15th century tower with an overhanging parapet, and in a niche on its west wall is a figure of Henry Vavasour, who helped to build the tower, holding a block of stone. The spacious nave and narrow aisles are also 15th century; the chancel is 14th and has a Norman window. The oldest possessions of the church are two fragments of Saxon stone, both carved with strapwork, one with three quaint figures.

A big stone with a cross has an inscription to John Gascoigne, one of the Nova Scotia baronets created by Charles Stuart; their motto, Honesty is the glory of the mind, is with the coloured coat-of-arms above John's stone. A north aisle window is bright with heraldry and kneeling figures of Gascoignes of the 17th and 18th centuries.

North of the village, by the road from Leeds to Tadcaster, stands Kiddall Hall, now a farmhouse but once the home of the Ellis family. Their arms, with an inscription to a 16th century couple, Thomas Ellis and his wife, are carved round a lovely projecting window.

Batley. A busy town in Yorkshire's woollen district, it is not without touches of beauty.

The grammar school was founded in Shakespeare's day, and the museum has much to show of the past in and about Batley, including letters from Charlotte Brontë to her friend Ellen Nussey, who lived a mile or two away; the Art Gallery can boast of at least one famous painting: Francis Bacon's *Magdalene*. Oldest of all things hereabouts is what is left of Howley Hall, a great house of the Saviles of the 16th century. Battered in the Civil War, its stones were sold in 1730, and today only two piles of masonry and a few fragments stand forlornly on a hill far above the mills, in the middle of a golf course.

We think of the house when we come to the church of All Saints, for the Savile who built the hall has this inscription:

> Here rest, thou hast been glorious in thy days,
> There can no more be said for Caesar's praise.

On an alabaster tomb lies a knight of the Mirfield family, three rings on his fingers. His wife, who lies by him, was one of the Saviles of Howley Hall, and we see her wearing a headdress like a garland, a robe falling in long folds over her feet.

The quaint church is long and low, the sturdy 15th century tower having an overhanging crown on battlements and pinnacles. Most of the building is as old as the tower, but the south arcade and the chancel arch are 14th century. The porch has an old door, the nave slopes down to the chancel, and fine old screenwork encloses the two chapels, that of the south chapel specially rich with its linenfold base, carved pillars, and a cornice band with shields, dragons, and mermen. The font is 1662, and in 14th century glass we see part of a Crucifixion and a figure of the Madonna.

Bawtry. It is the South Gate to Yorkshire, a small market town on a bit of the country dipping into Notts. Here the Great North

29

Road enters the biggest shire in England; here in the old days it was the custom for the sheriff to welcome kings and queens, and the town long continued a stop for coaches. Sir Robert Bowes, in company with 200 gentlemen in velvet and 4000 yeomen on horseback, met Henry VIII here, and in the name of Yorkshire gave him a purse with £900 in gold.

It stands on the River Idle, which comes through an old bridge and touches the town before turning east to the Trent. The road is wide and pleasant, and on a spacious square are remains of an old cross. Tucked away among small houses is a church built in the 12th century as a chapel of Blyth. The tower was made partly new in the 18th century, perhaps with stone from Roche Abbey, but its belfry windows are mediaeval. One of two blocked doorways is Norman, and of the arcades running the length of the church the north is mainly 13th century, and part of the south is 15th. The 13th century east window, with a carved hood outside, is remarkable for its time, having two mullions going up to the pointed arch without a break; it is said to be one of only two of its kind in the country. The 15th century chapel has a piscina, and the red and gold altar in memory of men who died for peace has figures of St George and St Michael, and of soldiers by the Cross. On the arm-rests of a splendid chair of 1595 are winged lions.

Beamsley. Nestling between Beamsley Beacon and the Kex Beck are its stone-walled fields, old houses of mottled grey stone, and gay flower gardens, sharing the lovely countryside with Bolton Abbey. The Beck tumbles over rocks and under trees to meet the Wharfe near a fine stone bridge. The Beacon, a moorland peak rising over 1300 feet, is a magnificent viewpoint, overlooking a wide range of the valley. On the Blubberhouses road is the famous Beamsley Hospital, an almshouse founded in 1593 and restored by Lady Anne Clifford about 1660. It is a circular building, some thirty feet in diameter, with a tiny chapel in the centre.

Beauchief. A Derbyshire village now drawn into Sheffield, it lies in the valley of the Sheaf, with high land about it stretching to the moorland country of the Peak. In the time of Charles II Edward Pegge built the great house from the ruins of a Norman abbey, and with what was left of the stone he refashioned the church, which has a monument to him. He kept the old tower, fine and stately still though some of its height is gone; most of it is 600 years old, with a big west doorway a century older. Joining the tower are two doorways from other parts of the church, one Norman, one 13th century. The old refectory table is now under the altar, there is a two-decker pulpit and some old box-pews. A beautiful monument showing a lady coming down the steps of her house, with food for a poor old bent woman in distress, is the work of Henry Weekes, Chantrey's assistant. It is in memory of Elizabeth Pegge Burnell.

Beckwithshaw. A trim stone-built village among the green hills, sheltered by woods and 250 acres of Moor Park, it has Harlow Car Springs and Harrogate on one side, and on the other the wide stretch of moorland with heather and rocks known as Haverah Park. It is a fine ride across this moor, passing the pile of gritstone rocks called Little Arms Cliff, to the few remains of John of Gaunt's Castle, built probably as a lodge to guard the park. The stream near by fills a reservoir, and not far away are the mounds known as Pippin's Castle. There is another reservoir near the village, which has an old inn facing a modern church, an attractive structure with an embattled tower serving as a porch.

Ben Rhydding. From its high place on the slopes of Ilkley Moor it looks out on scenery worthy of Scotland to which its name seems to belong. Below is the valley of the Wharfe, and beyond is the splendour of the high peaks of the Pennines. There are beautiful houses and gardens, and the fine 20th century church is in the style of five centuries ago. Its butressed tower with corner turrets is at the end of the aisle, and the chancel is raised. There is much oak panelling, and the font, striking in itself and in its setting within an arched recess, is like an octagonal cone on a buttressed stem.

Bentley. On the fringe of Doncaster, it has the ugly slag heaps of a mining town, but has given itself a touch of beauty in a wayside park of 30 acres, with lawns and bushes and flowers, and a rockery of Alpine plants. The church of 1891 is imposing outside, and at the crossroads is a monument to Joseph Walker, a doctor of our time. He gave fine service to St John's Ambulance Brigade, and in the stone to his memory is a cabinet with First Aid appliances, so that we may say that his good work lives after him.

Bewerley. A neighbour of Pateley Bridge, with the River Nidd flowing between them, it is charming in autumn when the woods are brown and gold. Here a stream comes down from Ravensgill, a romantic wooded glen with waterfalls and ferns. Beyond it Guise

Cliff stands out boldly above the dale, with the mock ruins known as Yorke's Folly rising 1000 feet above the sea, nearly as high as the top of Heyshaw Moor. In the wood below the cliff is a charming little lake, and near the Nidd is the site of a Roman camp.

The round tower of Bewerley Old Hall still stands, and its buildings have become cottages. Close by is the low building which Marmaduke Huby (Abbot of Fountains in early Tudor days) built for a small chapel and priest's house. They are under one roof, and the priest's house is still a dwelling. In a lovely setting where the stream comes from the glen is the restored Tudor manor house, delightful with its porch, and its high-walled old-world gardens. It is reached by a little stone bridge, and has a glorious view of the hills rising from the dale.

Bilbrough. Here in the little village church lies one of the noblest Englishmen of the most stirring hundred years of our history, Thomas Fairfax. Bilbrough Manor, a modern house on old foundations, was one of the family homes in our time, but it was at Nun Appleton Hall that Thomas Fairfax died in 1671. They laid him here to rest, in the church which was made new last century except for the sunken chapel divided from the nave by a mediaeval arcade of two bays. Here is a huge 15th century tomb that has lost its brasses but keeps some of its tracery, but the chief possession of the church is the handsome tomb of Fairfax and his wife. It has a black marble top, and panels rich with heraldic carvings and trappings of war. In this tomb lies that renowned soldier, statesman, and English gentleman of whom Milton wrote:

Fairfax, whose name in arms through Europe rings.

Bilton Ainsty. A small place on the road from York to Wetherby, it has Bilton Hall in a park of 100 acres, a house much loved by Annie Keary who was born in it in 1825. Well known in her day, she is remembered for the fairy tales she has given us, and for her splendid collection of Scandinavian myths. She died at Eastbourne in 1879.

In a churchyard with a mounting-stone is the charming little towerless church, rich in remains of the church the Normans left. Here are their tall arcades of two bays, their chancel arch with zigzag carved on roll moulding, their plain font, and their gallery of corbels, some carved with a tiger, a mermaid, and a man with a pig on his shoulder. The nave has a Norman window. The porch has a Norman entrance arch on shafts with carved capitals, and we enter the church through a plain Norman doorway and a door of 1633. The oldest part of the church is the west end of the south aisle, where a round-headed window with a stepped sill may be Saxon.

One of a small collection of Saxon stones is the fine head of a wheel cross, carved with four little men holding hands, their heads towards a central boss, their feet in knotwork. Another has Moses striking the rock, and Abraham about to slay Isaac with a Viking sword. A third is a block of stone with traces of knotwork. Quaintest of all is one whose carving is said to represent Shadrach, Meshach, and Abednego in the fiery furnace, the amusing little trio arm in arm, their legs astride. There is a broken pillar piscina. A chair, a chest, and the altar rails are old. A rare treasure is the lectern with an oak eagle carved in mediaeval days, though its legs are new. It has had an adventure, for it is said to have served as a block on which wood was chopped.

In one of the mediaeval chapels lies a woman carved in stone six centuries ago. She was perhaps an abbess of Syningthwaite Nunnery, a house of Cistercian nuns founded in the 12th century. What is left of it (including an original doorway) is in a farmhouse a mile from the village, near a Roman road.

Bingley. It lies on the edge of industrial Yorkshire, and its new town has grown round what was old. It had ancient memories when it came into the Conqueror's Domesday Book, for the Romans were here, and a chest with coins of Nero has been found. Yet even the Romans found this place old, for before them came a people setting up a stone circle among the heather, and up on the edge of the moor are huge stones at which men are supposed to have worshipped strange gods before the world had heard of the Caesars. We come down to the river with its mills and find woods reflected in the water. It is rich in fine houses and lovely parks. To the north is Ryshworth Hall, almost hidden by a majestic lime over 30 feet round; it has an 18th century wing, and parts older, and now it is made into several houses. Marley Hall not far away comes from the 17th century, and has the three owls of Savile on its gateway. What is left of Old Harden Grange, now a school, adjoins the great house known as St Ives, standing in hundreds of acres of park, wood, and moorland on the west bank of the river. It is now a centre for the study of sports' turf, with a golf course near by. Above the canal is the many-gabled Gawthorpe Hall, the home of the lord of the manor in Tudor days.

Myrtle Grove, the fine Georgian house now used as the Town Hall, is in a park which has the charm of the valley and John Wesley

33

called it a little paradise, but the Prince of Wales Park on the other side of the town has the glory of the hilltop. Steep paths wind through the trees to an open space at the foot of lofty crags, and here, in a strange and silent region after the bustle of the town, have been preserved the fine market house with its stone pillars, the old stocks, and the splendid village cross, its restored shafts peeping through the sheltering roof.

By an 18th century footbridge near where the Harden Beck falls into the Aire is an old farm with stone lanterns on the gables, and a cross on a stone lintel, reminding us that the Knights of St John once had property here. Few industrial towns in Yorkshire have kept their old-world corners with more charm. Here we come upon a stone bridge, there a cobbled street, and now a group of houses which have long been neighbours of the church of All Saints, some with yellow walls and small gables. There is a fine old inn near the churchyard, where it is good to see the gravestones laid flat and separated by tufts of flowers, making a bright show below the road to Keighley.

The church we see comes largely from early Tudor days, though the tower was raised 200 years ago. The mediaeval church was destroyed after Bannockburn, and of its Norman predecessor there are fragments in the bases of some of the pillars. The Saxons are believed to have built here, and in the church are a fragment of a Saxon cross and a curious battered rune stone carved on two sides with knotwork, having on a third side an illegible inscription believed to include the words Eadbergh King, dating it 8th century. Its use in Saxon days is uncertain. It may have been a font, the base of a cross, or even a relic chest; now it is set up like a bowl, companion for a modern font with a lofty steeple cover.

Three angels in a window designed by Burne-Jones and executed by William Morris are now hidden by a screen. A window in the south chapel, designed by George Cooper, has Our Lord in Glory, with saints and tiny kneeling figures of Richard Wilson (Bishop of Meath and builder of the chancel, thought to have been born at Bingley); William Paganel, who gave the church to Drax Priory; John Wesley, and the Abbot of Drax. In the border of the window are quaint little pictures.

A curfew was rung here for many years but was stopped in 1945; a "pancake bell" however is rung on Shrove Tuesday. In the churchyard lies a villager, William Shaw, who died in 1726 of whom we read that "sober, laborious and faithfull at 2s per week for above 40 years in 1 family he maintained a wife and numerous issue". There is also a grave of a sexton Hezekiah Briggs who interred upwards of 7000 corpses; and in the cemetery sleeps the poet John Nicholson, in the heart of the countryside he loved. He lay in the churchyard till the new road was made through it. Disraeli brought Bingley into his novels, John Wesley fell in love with it; but the chief singer of its praise is its own poet John Nicholson.

On the Leeds–Liverpool Canal near here is the famous Five Rise Lock, which raises barges 59 feet.

Birkin. Time brings little change to this place, where the stream known as Old Eye comes winding through green fields to join the River Aire. The few farms and houses are dotted about the wonderful little church, which strikes the keynote of the village, for it stands much as the builders left it eight centuries ago.

The 14th century gave it an aisle and the top of the tower; but so sturdy and strong is the Norman part of the structure that it carries its years better than the later work. We enter through a lovely Norman doorway of four orders (reset in the aisle), enriched with zigzag, beak-heads, and 24 roundels with quaint ornaments of figures and scenes.

Between the nave and the delightful chancel is an arch with rich carving of zigzag, only a little lower than the two huge arches of the nave arcade, which reaches the modern roof. A simpler arch frames the fine apse, whose vaulting springs from tall pilasters. The windows of the apse are charming outside with shafts, scalloped capitals, and imposts carved with interlacing, and arches with zigzag, beak-heads, and carved medallions. Under the original arch of the east window is 14th century tracery. There are two taller Norman windows, and under one of the 14th century is a crude alcove serving as sedilia. A Norman stringcourse runs round the chancel and the nave.

One of a host of old corbels has a quaint little man with a bow, a horn, and a bundle of faggots on his back, his dog beside him. A crude wooden stairway climbs to the belfry. The bowl of the font is 1663, old glass shows angels and shields, and the Georgian pulpit has an inlaid canopy.

In a niche in the nave lies a stone man with long curled hair, wearing a garment like a smock with long cuffs, and holding a heart. His feet, which rest on a dog, are in thin leather shoes, the lacing-together of the skins cleverly shown by the sculptor. A fine little bronze memorial is to George Dixon Todd, a doctor who died in 1929, showing him in his top hat on horseback, as if setting out on his round.

One of the rectors here was Robert Thornton, on whose inscription

35

we read that he suffered much for his loyalty in the Civil War, was robbed of his goods, and was dragged from Birkin to Cawood Castle tied to a horse's tail. He lived to see better times, was restored to his church, and was followed as rector by his son and grandson.

Birstall. It is a grey town among the hills and mills of industrial Yorkshire, much loved by Charlotte Brontë, for here lived her friend Ellen Nussey, and she brought it into two of her books. Here also sleeps her schoolmistress, Margaret Wooler, who outlived her pupil and delighted in her fame.

Charlotte Brontë was charmed with the Tudor Oakwell Hall, described in *Shirley*. Here are the lawns on which she watched the pigeons, and the tiny bridge over the moat bringing up to the porch she knew so well, with the stone seats and a great door barred by a heavy beam. The most remarkable room of this fine Elizabethan house (which is now owned by Batley Corporation) has a balcony, massive oak pillars, a stairway with small wooden gates, and a window of 30 lights with two transoms, nine mullions, and over a thousand pieces of glass. Looking down on the mills from among the fields and trees is another fine house known as the Rydings, believed to be the Thornfield Hall in *Jane Eyre*. It was Ellen Nussey's home, and here she and Charlotte would sit and talk for hours in a room where we sat and talked with an old lady who knew Miss Nussey well. Charlotte and Ellen were at school together, life-long friends, and Charlotte wrote her about everything until she died.

Ellen Nussey has been sleeping in the churchyard here since 1857, and in a grave not far away sleeps Margaret Wooler, the kindly teacher whom Charlotte loved. It was at her school at Roe Head that Charlotte met Ellen, and the three remained close friends. When Patrick Brontë failed his daughter at her wedding it was Margaret Wooler who gave the bride away.

The churchyard is a charming corner of a plain town. The church, rebuilt last century except for its Norman and 15th century tower, is a clerestoried, embattled, pinnacled pile, with a surprising interior of over 30 arches, for it has six aisles, two north and two south and two in the chancel. There are two fine vaulted porches, many stained windows (so that the only clear light is from the clerestory), and a rich chancel roof adorned with angels, resting on stone saints in niches. The stone pulpit has apostles in niches, there are a few old bench-ends and three old coffin lids, an old font was altered last century, and a rough-hewn one may be Norman. A stone with crude diamond pattern may also be Norman, and one with scroll and interlacing work may be the base of a Saxon cross.

Here in brass is Elizabeth Popeley of 1632, in an open shroud with her daughters kneeling by her; one is holding a handkerchief. There is a modern portrait brass of John Kemp, who was vicar for 45 years last century. There is a curious old gravestone here of Old Amos who died in 1777 and was huntsman to Mr Fearnley of Oakwell Hall for many years.

The church has an inscription to a mason of Birstall who gave up shaping stones to help John Wesley to shape men's lives. He was John Nelson, one of the greatest preachers of his day, discovered by Wesley in a cottage here. By the Methodist Chapel is a little building known as John Nelson's study, in which this man would presumably prepare his sermons. He faced angry mobs and suffered much ill-treatment, and his inscription in the south aisle of the church describes him as a noble and fearless man.

But most famous of all the men at Birstall is the immortal Joseph Priestley, Father of Modern Chemistry. As a boy he would tramp this countryside and look in at the woollen mills with their clumsy machinery driven by water-wheels. The stone house in which he was born in 1733 (Fieldhead) is much as he knew it, but the road he tramped to Batley Grammar School is much changed, for the drab hillside has become a park. In the marketplace is a statue showing Priestley performing an experiment; the sculptor has shown him with a candle in one hand and a jar in the other.

Birstwith. A charming spot with splendid trees, it lies in the valley of the Nidd, where the river falls over a weir. The houses shelter in the wooded folds of the hillside, and away from the rest is Birstwith Hall, its creepered walls rising from fine banks of lawn above a stream flowing to the river. Swarcliffe Hall, with gables and a tower, was rebuilt in the mid-19th century, and looks down from its mantle of trees on fine views of the dale. Below it stands the 19th century church with a soaring spire, one of its glorious trees a giant Wellingtonia guarding the gate. It has windows in memory of two adventurers: Thomas Oxley, who was drowned in South America in 1868, and Harry Denison, who died from his wounds at Lucknow. The striking feature of the church is the carving of the great corbels of the chancel arch, with Passion flowers, vines, and corn.

Bishop Monkton. It is in the green pastures between Ripon and Knaresborough. A stream with fern and flowered banks flows under the churchyard wall and along the street, crossed by many little bridges and making waterfalls. The neat 19th century church stands finely on a bank. The tower has an octagonal belfry with a spire, and its base with a vaulted roof serves as the porch.

Bishopthorpe. New houses have descended on it like a wave of suburban York, but there are still delightful corners and glorious trees. It has no more charming picture than the group of the fine church tower, the noble gatehouse, and the palace of the archbishops rising from a courtyard.

Three miles from the Minster, Bishopthorpe has been the home of the archbishops for seven centuries but little is left of the mediaeval palace except the charming 13th century chapel and some of the walling. Most of what we see comes from rebuilding of the 18th century. Standing in a green bay of the road, the gatehouse is adorned with battlements, pinnacles, and gargoyles; its upper room has a pyramid canopy, and through the rich entrance arch we see a fine picture of the palace flanked by limes, eagles surmounting the open parapet of the creepered walls, and a splendid flight of steps climbing to a lovely three-arched porch with a fan-vaulted roof.

The long dining-room was the work of Archbishop Frewen in Charles II's day. The plaster ceiling and cornice are exceedingly rich, the grand old table is over 20 feet long, the windows look out on the river where barges and tugs are for ever passing, and the walls are hung with portraits of archbishops. We meet here Tobias Matthews in black hat and ruff, Richard Sterne wearing a mortar board, and Thomas Lamplugh, archbishop in the memorable year when James II ran away. John Sharpe is looking like Bunyan, and Edwyn Sandys is the only archbishop shown with his wife. A sketch of Wolsey is said to be the only full-face portrait we have of him, and there is a portrait of the unfortunate Archbishop Scrope, whose trial was held in the earlier room on this spot.

The exquisite little 13th century chapel, opening from the hall, has three east windows, and a north door to all that is left of a stair which once led to the river gate. The lancet windows in the south wall are under alternate arches on slender shafts; and at the west end is the richly canopied archbishop's seat, and oak panelling with a great company of angels carved by a craftsman from Oberammergau.

A narrow aisle of Irish yews leads to the remains of Bishopthorpe's old church on the wooded bank of the river. There is a cross on the site of the high altar, and the beautiful west front still stands finely, enriched with leafy niches, pinnacles, and buttresses with faces and finials. A bellcot crowns its gable.

The fine church which took the place of the old one in the last year of last century is reached by an avenue of limes and Irish yews. Built in 15th century style, it has a 13th century piscina from the old church, a 15th century font said to have come from a destroyed church in York, a table probably over 300 years old, and statues of St Peter and St Andrew on each side of the east window. Tributes to two men who fell in the Great War are the richly traceried oak panelling of the chancel, and the beautiful oak reredos, which has a rich canopy with vine and grape, sheltering a Crucifixion with Mary and John and a soldier. An inscription keeps green the memory of William Thomson, Archbishop of York, who died here in 1890.

Blubberhouses. Every motorist from Harrogate to Skipton knows this tiny village so much prettier than its name, its grey houses dotted sparsely about a lovely bit of the Washburn valley between the heather moors. Over a mile away, above a stream from Kex Gill Moor, are Brandreth Crags, a range of rocks among which is a great rocking stone said to weigh 24 tons. From a steep bank the last-century church looks down on the old stone bridge where the Washburn is flowing to one of the great reservoirs it fills for Leeds before joining the Wharfe. It is a charming picture outside, with a tiny tower and spire, and a quaint porch nestling as if for shelter by the tower's big buttresses.

Bolsterstone. Its beautiful approach is from Bradfield. Its few houses are round a modern church on a hill of the windswept moors, between the romantic valley of the Ewden and the industrial valley of the Little Don. So high is it that from here we can see miles of moorland in Yorkshire and Derbyshire. By the church are the stocks and two big stones which were perhaps part of an ancient monument. Within is a fine old carved chair and a desk made of old bench-ends. A doorway and part of an archway near the church are probably part of the castle built about 1250 by the Sheffields, who were here till the 14th century.

Bolton Abbey. We may think Yorkshire has little to show more fair. In a superb setting of woods and meadows by the River Wharfe, the grassy moors and fells rising majestically above, are the ruins of a famous priory painted by Turner and immortalised in Wordsworth. The gentlest ruin in Yorkshire, it has long been linked with the

39

tradition of the Boy of Egremond, whose mother is said to have founded the priory on the spot near where her son was drowned. Wordsworth tells us that,

> *Wharfe, as he moved along*
> *To matins joined a mournful voice,*
> *Nor failed at evensong.*

The village has its own charm. A hole in a wall—one of the most romantic peepholes imaginable—frames a delightful view of the ruins, and the wall itself has grown lovelier with the years, its crannies half-hidden by creeper. The road here is shaded by trees, and round a green is a lovely group of creepered cottages with stone roofs, set in gay gardens. One of the cottages has a carved beam with an inscription asking us to say an Ave Maria as we pass by, and there is a barn with a roof resting on grand old timbers. Rising like a castle by the wayside are the embattled walls of Bolton Hall, home of the Duke of Devonshire, a striking modern house built on two sides of the old priory gatehouse. A quaint sight here is the rugged stone aqueduct with three arches across the road, once used for carrying water to the flour mill of the monks.

There are two fine memorials to Lord Frederick Cavendish who was assassinated in Phoenix Park, Dublin, in 1882. One memorial is a fountain, an ornate stone structure of six sides, with elegant buttresses, shields, and a lantern with a spire 40 feet above the ground; the other is a cross 17 feet high in the churchyard. In this churchyard is the gravestone of William Carr, who was rector 54 years and died in 1843 after making nearly fifty miles of paths in the beautiful valley. Who could not spend days following in his steps? One path from the churchyard goes down to a bridge, where 57 stepping stones cross the river. A lovely sight it is when the banks are glorious with bluebells and wild campion in spring and summer, and in autumn glow with crimson and gold.

Coming to the ruins we pass the rectory, a house with a fine porch on the south side of the site of the cloister, and low shattered walls reach up to it. From it we have a view of the great house, with the delicate foliage of two trees hugging its walls and reaching the battlements.

Little is left of the ancient priory except the church, itself a ruin except for the nave, which has continued to be the parish church. Of the domestic buildings on its south side there are only a few fragments of walls and foundations, but these are enough to help us to see their plan. The plan is in the shape of a cross, with an aisleless choir, transepts with eastern aisles, a nave with a north aisle only, and a west tower which was never completed. Most of the walling of the three eastern arms is still upstanding and it is in the ruined eastern portion of the church that the loveliest work is to be found.

Of the 12th century church, begun after the establishment of the priory on this site, are left the lower parts of the walls of the choir and nave, and the piers of a central crossing. In the 13th century the nave was given the fine line of tracery windows in its south wall, and the lovely west front—charming with its central doorway, its ornamental arcading, and fine windows enriched with moulding. The pity is that this front is hidden by the tower which Richard Moone, the last prior, began to build, little dreaming that before he could complete it the King of England would sweep away every monastery in the land. Had the prior finished his work he would have taken down the west wall of the nave to reveal his soaring tower arch, which serves now as a frame for the earlier front. The prior's tower is only as high as the tip of its fine west window, which has below it a handsome doorway under canopied niches and a display of shields. Two bands of beautiful tracery run round the base of the tower. Three of the buttresses have dogs sitting on pedestals, and another has a statue of a pilgrim with a shield and a staff, a 17th century sundial above him. Richard wrote his name on his tower with the letter R and a crescent moon.

The north aisle was added in the 13th century (though its windows are from the beginning of the 15th), and the sturdy arcade is impressive. Above it is a clerestory. The roof was restored last century, but some of its timbers are mediaeval and some of the bosses have queer carvings, one showing a man's head with a snake creeping through his ear and coming out of his mouth. There are a few old glass fragments, an altar stone with five crosses and a hollow where relics were kept, and a fragment of a gravestone thought to have been in memory of John Clifford, a Knight of the Garter buried here 500 years ago.

In the 14th century the transepts and parts of the choir were rebuilt, the choir being lengthened. The single wall of the south transept is pierced by two windows, and has a pinnacle standing like a sentinel. The north transept has lofty walls, and through the two bays of its aisle arcade we see the river. The 12th century walling of the choir at each side is enriched with lovely arcading, and one of the 14th century windows above has its tracery still perfect. Beautiful indeed must have been the great east window, now only a stone frame for the woods and waterfall beyond. Here are the steps of the sanctuary, traces of seats for the priests, and a recess thought

41

to have been the resting-place of Lady Margaret Neville. In the south wall is part of a lovely doorway which led to a chapel, perhaps the spot where tradition says the coffins stand upright:

> Face to face, and hand to hand,
> The Claphams and Mauleverers stand.

The home of old romance is the choir of Bolton Abbey, where legend says Alice Romilly came to pray for the soul of Egremond, and where the Shepherd Lord loved to come from Barden Tower five miles away. It is said that he studied alchemy here, and that when his strange life ran out he was buried within the shadow of these walls.

The Shepherd Lord was Henry Clifford, whose father, called Butcher Clifford because he was a brute, died in battle fighting for the Red Rose, and left two sons alive when Edward IV came to the crown. They were hidden, and nothing was heard of them until after eight years, when the rumour was spread that Lord Clifford's heir was alive, hiding in Yorkshire. As he was dangerous to the plotters for the crown spies searched the moors and dales, but no trace of a Clifford was found. Fifteen years later came the Battle of Bosworth Field, and Henry of the Red Rose became Henry VII of England. Exiles came home. Banished men threw off their disguises. Lady Clifford announced that her eldest son lived, and one day there walked up the floor of the House of Lords a man looking like a ploughman, his great hands horny with toil. He was the Good Lord Clifford, come to claim the barony of Westmorland and the castle of Skipton. He was a man of only simple learning. He had been brought up in a cottage, and had been used to wearing rags, walking barefoot, and sleeping on straw. He had lived a shepherd's life.

Now he was one of the lords of England, standing among his peers, and he came to live near Bolton Abbey, studying the stars. The boy condemned to die at seven lived to be seventy; he who had obeyed a shepherd now commanded knights and yeomen.

Somewhere here also sleeps Francis Norton, whose story we read in Wordsworth's *White Doe of Rylstone*. We are told that his sister came to weep over his grave and that when her spirit fled the Doe which had long been her companion came along by hight. The story greatly impressed the poet.

From the park, extending over 700 acres, we may climb to Standard Hill, where Francis Norton is said to have met his end, or we may follow the river up the valley where the hills come nearer and the trees crowd to the riverside, the banks closing in till the water roars along a channel only a few feet wide but very deep; it is known as the Strid, and has claimed many would-be jumpers.

Bolton-by-Bowland. The Bond Beck winds by this charming village on its way to the Ribble, which comes through the park with its lovely trees and storied hall. Trees shade the roads. There are quaint old stone houses, and a green with remains of a mediaeval cross and the old stocks.

At the great house a king found refuge in the 15th century, poor Henry VI, half mad and almost friendless. When most doors were shut in his face after his defeat at the Battle of Hexham, when it was a crime to give him a cup of cold water, Sir Ralph Pudsey of Bolton gave him the shelter of his roof.

We meet this kindly man in the church, where he has an amazing memorial. It is a huge marble stone 10 feet long and half as wide, showing 29 portraits of Sir Ralph himself, his three wives, and their 25 children, all carved in low relief. Sir Ralph is a knightly figure in armour. Each wife has the number of her children carved on the hem of her dress, and over the children are their names. The wives and daughters wear long graceful gowns and horned headdress. The parents are under fine leafy canopies, and dainty canopies cover the sons and daughters. Some of the sons have swords and spears, and others are armed to the teeth, even with a battleaxe; two are priests. This remarkable monument is almost a record for its number of children.

Another of the Pudseys was Henry, who died in 1509. His brass shows him kneeling with his wife, he wearing a tabard and she a kennel headdress and a gown with rich girdle. Henry Pudsey is said to have built the south chapel which contains a hagioscope. The unusual font, shaped like a star, has eight shields of Pudsey and their alliances, and an inscription with the name of the Pudsey who gave it over 400 years ago.

Typical of the Craven churches is this which comes chiefly from the 15th century but stands on earlier foundations—in fact there has been a church here since 1190. It has a handsome tower, fine roofs, arcades running from east to west, and an old porch with coffin lids in its walls. On the lintel of the doorway within it a 13th century craftsman left his carving unfinished. Below it is a door of 1705, studded with about 600 iron nails and still secured with the old bar fastening. Adding to the simple charm of the interior (where the walls are of lovely mottled grey stone) are the low 17th century pews, every end adorned with what remind us of door-knobs. There is a tiny coffin lid in one of the altar steps, and in a niche near by is part of another stone with roses on its edge. The altar rails are 1704. The modern pulpit, resting on an old carved oak block, has two ancient panels carved with the Annunciation and the Nativity. Three bells date from about 1520.

Bolton Percy. A gem among Yorkshire villages, greatly has it grown in grace since the Conqueror put its church into his Domesday Book and the Percys came. It was probably old when they found it, for excavation has revealed a Roman road.

Charmingly grouped in a frame of fine old trees, and with a peep of the Foss running to the Wharfe, are the noble 15th century church with its imposing tower, the rectory of 1698 with a huge copper beech on its lawn, and a Tudor barn with massive beams, a great door, and an overhanging storey; unfortunately it is now in a sad state of disrepair. More ancient and more dramatic is a boulder of Shap granite, brought here by a glacier and now a companion for the beautiful lychgate, which has a charming canopied figure of St Oswald carved in one of the oak posts. On a pillar in the churchyard is a Tudor sundial with four faces.

Except for the 19th century porch, the church stands almost as Thomas Parker designed it 500 years ago. He was rector from 1411 till 1423, and the building was not completed till after his death. Of the church he replaced there are many stones in the churchyard walls, and two mass dials found in this wall, believed to be Saxon, are now inside the church, no more telling the time as they did in the days before clocks.

The church is a stately casket for much treasure. The chancel arch is so high that it merges into the grand old roof sweeping over the nave and the narrow aisles, and continuing through the chancel, where two of the corbels are thought to represent Thomas Parker and the Archbishop of York of his time. There are lovely sedilia and a piscina with leafy hoods and finials, a 12th century font with a Jacobean cover like a traceried lantern, a mediaeval altar stone with five crosses (beneath the present altar), and part of an old altar stone with three crosses in the north aisle.

From the 17th century come the fine bobbin-ended pews (with some of the oak of earlier benches worked into them), a prayer desk which may have been a pulpit, a table in the vestry, and chairs in the chancel. The stalls facing the altar were part of the mediaeval chancel screen, and the handsome pulpit (1715) has a canopy enriched with carving of cherubs. The north door has 15th century timbers and a great lock and key of the 18th century, and near it is a cannon ball which was dug up by the tower and probably left here by

44

soldiers quartered in the church during the Civil War. Three bells were cast in Elizabethan days and the lovely chalice is from the same time.

Full of tinted light from seven windows, the chancel has a price-less possession in wonderful glass, the east window shining with a rich medley of red, blue, green, and gold, and showing ten lifesize figures of saints and archbishops, with shields, cherubs, and angels in the tracery. The amazing thing is that about half the glass filling this window is 15th century, the rest an excellent restoration. The five figures in the upper row are St Peter, St Anne, the Madonna, St Elizabeth, and St John, and above each of them is a tiny face with its tongue out. The identity of the five archbishops is not certain, but they are probably Paulinus, Chad, Oswald, Wilfrid, and William. The tracery of a north and south windows is filled with mediaeval glass, and other fragments are in some of the canopies. Above the east window outside is a stone carved on two sides with Our Lord on the Cross and the Madonna and Child; it lay for a long time in the rectory garden.

Two brothers of the Fairfax family have memorials here—a floorstone to Henry, who was rector during the Commonwealth, and an elaborate wall-monument to Lord Ferdinando, a commander at Marston Moor and father of one of our greatest generals. The church register records the surprising marriage here of Thomas's daughter Mary with George Villiers, second Duke of Buckingham, a king's man marrying a Cromwellian's daughter.

In the chapel at the east end of the north aisle (where part of the mediaeval screen remains) sleep some of the Fairfaxes of Steeton, among them Sir William and Isobel Thwaites, whom he married in this church after carrying her off from Appleton Nunnery. They were the founders of that branch of the house which gave us the great Parliamentary soldiers. The gravestone of Agnes Ryther, a prioress of the nunnery, lies in the nave, its inscription almost gone; it was brought here in the 18th century from Appleton.

Bolton-on-Dearne. The churchyard of this small colliery town is like a garden, kept as we should like to see all our churchyards kept, and three gravestones are against the wall of a house near by. The plain church is chiefly 15th century, the time of the tower; but some windows are 14th century and one is Norman. The pointed arches of the nave arcade are on Norman pillars and capitals, and there is a Norman stone with crude carving in an outside wall.

Boroughbridge. Here, like sentinels guarding the little town from the west, are the three biggest arrows in England, three upright stones varying in height from 16 to 22 feet, worn by centuries of wind and weather perhaps from the time of the Ancient Britons. Standing in fields by the road to Roecliffe, they are known as the Devil's Arrows, and had for ages a fourth companion, which is said to have been broken up over 300 years ago to make a bridge over the little River Tutt. They are known as menhirs, the Celtic word for long stone, and are found chiefly in Cornwall, Dartmoor, Northumberland, and Wales, often in the neighbourhood of stone circles or the burial chambers of Stone Age men.

The town keeps its old-world air since it is now by-passed by the main road. The river divides the North and West Ridings, and falls over a weir. There are red-roofed old houses, quaint courtyards, big coaching inns, noble trees, and a cobbled marketplace with a well 250 feet deep, covered by a pillared canopy with a cupola.

The old church was pulled down last century, but fragments of it built in the walls of the new one include part of the head of a Norman doorway and a Crucifixion; a fine font enriched with tracery has taken the place of the old one standing by the porch. It was in the old church that the rebel Earl of Lancaster sought refuge and found none in 1322. Defeated after terrible fighting, he ran into the church and fell before the altar, from which his enemies dragged him unmercifully, carrying him off to his own castle at Pontefract, where after a mock trial he was executed with his face towards Scotland.

Boston Spa. The Wharfe flows majestically here as a broad deep river in a beautiful valley, and is best seen from the fine bridge, where the rocks are hidden by trees and there are peeps of lovely houses and gardens. Thorp Arch is over the bridge. On the bank rising from the river, this tiny trim town, with wayside trees and a pump room, is growing in favour, having begun its life as a spa when John Shires found a mineral spring here in 1744. The imposing 19th century church has a big tower, lofty arcades with capitals of overhanging foliage, and 36 stone angels supporting the roofs of the nave and aisles. A small cross in the church was made from a piece of timber from Ypres Cathedral after the Great War.

Bracewell. The little green hills rise in a tumult about this small place, and on two of them, north of the church, Prince Rupert is said to have encamped. In the grounds of the hall (a modern house with gables, battlements, and turrets) is a barn, all that is left of an old manor house where poor Henry VI found a friend after the Battle of Hexham, his host being one of the Tempests.

Some of the Tempests sleep in the church they made partly new over four centuries ago. It is lowly and quaint, among lofty trees by the wayside. There is 13th century work in the squat tower, and fine old black and white roofs look down on walls touched with gold. The south doorway and the plain chancel arch are Norman, and so probably is the font. Fragments of 16th century glass include shields of Tempests and Cliffords. The pulpit is about 200 years old.

Bradfield. It is among the Pennines, a charming neighbour of Sheffield with the city's lake-like reservoirs for company. High Bradfield, in a lovely setting on the steep hillside, has a fine church with some treasures; Low Bradfield in the valley has its own tragic tale.

There is a fine panorama of the moors from the churchyard, and the curious stone house at its gate once sheltered the watchers for body-snatchers; it is one of the few watch-houses still left in our churchyards. As beautiful within as without, the church is chiefly 15th century, though the chancel arch and the nave arcades were built when the Norman style was passing. There is much old work in the fine roofs, with moulded beams and carved bosses resting on crude stone heads. The reredos has old carved panels, a fine old chest has two lids and much ironwork, and in ancient glass are two bishops and a saint. Brass portraits of 1647 show John Morewood and his wife kneeling at a desk, John with nine boys behind him, his wife in a broad-brimmed hat with seven girls in pretty hoods. There is a sunken chapel, the font is old, and an 11th century cross, four feet high and enriched with five bosses, is one of the most perfect in the county.

Low Bradfield's old houses are by the pleasant River Loxley, which was once a river of death. Here in 1864 a reservoir of 76 acres above the village burst its banks, and 700 million gallons of water roared down the Loxley valley. It was midnight when the retaining wall gave way, and the immense volume of water went thundering through the darkness. Surging with irresistible power through Low Bradfield and the tiny villages of Loxley, Little Matlock, Malin Bridge, Hillsborough, and on to Sheffield, it destroyed houses and mills, uprooted trees, carried away bridges, and took toll of 240 people. The Bar Dike, a prehistoric entrenchment, runs near to the villages.

Bradford. It thrives on foundations of wool and steam, and has steam to thank for its prosperity. Before steam came Bradford was a little town in a hollow of the hills, busy raising sheep, marketing the homegrown fleeces, and making cloth on handlooms. From the beginning of the power loom Bradford's story is one of astonishing progress. It trades with every land under the sun.

It is the world's central market for wool and wool products, the chief centre for the sorting of fleeces produced in England and brought from abroad, and for the process of combing which separates the long fibres from the short—the long fibres to be used for worsted cloth, the short for woollen cloth. It is said that five-sixths of England's business in wool is carried on at Bradford, and it has a great trade also in other fabrics; cotton and silk have become an important part of its industry, and the Manningham Mills, where silk and velvet are made, are the biggest of their kind in the world. The city's other industries are legion, among them being dyeing and finishing, engineering, machine-tools, motor cycles, and quarrying.

Yet Bradford has not been entirely absorbed in its business. It was a Bradford MP, William Edward Forster, who laid the foundation of our free education system, and the city has been a pioneer in such social work as hospitals and clinics, school doctors, and cheap meals at poor schools.

The central area of the city has been reconstructed and modernised, resulting in a great deal of transition, including the replacing of the old Swan Arcade, where J. B. Priestley worked as a young man. Morley Street, a fine road running south-west from Town Hall Square, has been cut through some of the oldest parts of Bradford, as has the more recent Broadway. The Exchange Station is notable for a roof with two spans of 100 feet. Near this station is St George's Hall, the home of political and musical Bradford in Victorian days. Facing it is Britannia House, a handsome new business block with a fine copper dome. Near by, just off Leeds Road, is the Bradford Playhouse, formerly known as the Bradford "Civic", the best known amateur theatre in the North of England.

The most striking of the city's central buildings is the Town Hall, built last century after the fashion of a building in Florence, and since greatly extended. Its imposing façade has a tower, a fine array of windows, open parapets, gables, and a remarkable sculpture gallery of kings and queens. The entrance is charming, with an archway between statues of two queens, an oriel window above, flanking turrets, and broad steps leading to a fine hall with marble stairs and balcony and a domed roof of stained glass. There are scores of rooms. The splendid banqueting hall has windows aglow with shields and walls hung with pictures. The fireplace is magnificent with a stone frieze representing the city's industries, and a rich grate of ornate ironwork. The council chamber has mahogany panelling, pillars of coloured marble supporting a gallery, and a domed roof of heraldic glass. It has recently been cleaned, restoring to us its previous stone colour.

The Exchange, near the Town Hall, is a fine building with a tower and a slender spire 150 feet high, an open parapet, and a statue of the patron of woolcombers, St Blaise. In the great hall where crowds of merchants meet twice a week to buy and sell wool for the world is a noble statue of Richard Cobden, unveiled by his best friend, John Bright. Prominent also in the centre of the town is the massive tower of the new library.

Another impressive building is Commerce House, headquarters of the Chamber of Commerce. The post office is a handsome building of 1887, in the Italian style. In Great Horton Road are the College of Art and the new University buildings; the University, the latest in Yorkshire, received the right to grant its own degrees recently, and has Prime Minister Harold Wilson as its Chancellor.

The Royal Infirmary, established in 1824, has housed itself on a site of 23 acres at Daisy Hill. Proud to remember that its MP was the author of the historic education bill which established popular schools all over England, the city has today many secondary schools, and its grammar school, carrying on after more than 300 years since its founding, has fine new buildings near Lister Park; they have long low roofs, mullioned windows, and a low embattled tower in a setting of terrace gardens and playing fields.

Lister Park and Bowling Park are on opposite sides of the city, each with over fifty acres. Bradford Moor Park and Horton Park lie east and west, and Peel Park, the biggest of all with 56 acres, lies east of Lister Park. Three miles north of the city centre are 750 acres of Baildon Moor, where the workers can lose sight of the industrial world and breathe the air blowing over 900 feet above the level of the sea.

Lister Park is a great possession, a delight to see with its lawns and flowers and trees, spacious drives, and a Botanical Garden which boasts of being the biggest outside London. There are shady walks, a boating lake, and a splendid open-air swimming pool, which form a noble setting for Bradford's Art Gallery and Museum, housed in the Cartwright Memorial Hall—a tribute to Edmund Cartwright, to whose inventions Bradford owes its rise in fortune. The hall is also a tribute to Samuel Cunliffe Lister, first Lord Masham, who spent his busy life at Bradford and founded the Manningham Silk Mills. The hall stands on the site of his old home in the park, and just within the gates is his statue, with panels showing sheep in their

49

rocky homes, handworkers dealing with the wool in their cottages, and machinery in the mills. The statue of another prince of industry, Sir Titus Salt, founder of Saltaire, also stands in Lister Park.

A regal building in classical style is the Cartwright Hall, its imposing three-arched entrance under a balcony crowned with a domed lantern, round which are four statues. With its fine stone staircases, pillars, domed roofs, spacious corridors, and splendid rooms filled with light, it is a noble shrine for treasures of art and collections of natural history and archaeology. The oil paintings and water colours are mostly by artists of the British School, and there are many drawings and studies which show us how the pictures have been evolved. Many of the pictures are by Yorkshire artists, and some are of Yorkshire scenes, one being George Graham's *Bolton Castle*. It is privileged to have many travelling exhibitions of first-rate pictures and sculpture. The museum part has a fine collection of model trams, a vehicle until recently much used in the North.

In the fine show of marble sculpture are busts by John Adams Acton of Sir Titus Salt, Queen Victoria, and Prince Albert. A Derwent Wood group represents Humanity overcoming War, and there are busts of George V, Queen Mary, and Lord Masham by Alfred Drury.

A rare possession of the gallery is a group of stained glass windows on exhibition, illustrating the story of Tristram and Isolde as told by Sir Thomas Malory. They were made for Harden Grange near Bingley, and were designed by William Morris, Sir Edward Burne-Jones, Ford Madox Brown, Rossetti, Val Prinsep, and Arthur Hughes.

Looking over the city so often veiled in smoke from its tall chimneys, Bowling Park has sloping lawns and a fine show of rhododendrons in due season. Facing it are four broad flights of steps climbing to the terraced gardens of Bolling Hall, a beautiful old house with two sturdy towers. It is one of Bradford's two surviving links with days long gone by, and is now a museum illustrating the history of Bradford and its neighbourhood, and the conditions of life since the 14th century, when the old house was begun. The house grew with the years, and a tour of its rooms is a journey down five centuries. It has been the home of the Bollings, the Tempests, the Saviles, the Lindleys, and the Woods, but its glory declined till it was actually divided into tenements. Splendid restoration, however, has made it a fascinating place of which Bradford may well be proud.

The manor of Bolling came into Domesday Book, and an interesting link with the Bollings and our own day is that Edith Bolling, who married Woodrow Wilson, was a descendant of Robert Bolling who went to Virginia when he was 14 and married Jan Rolfe, granddaughter of that Pocahontas who saved the life of Captain John Smith and lies by the Thames at Gravesend.

The oldest part of the house is the south-west tower, believed to have been built by Robert Bolling six centuries ago, though the windows are probably 17th century. This tower, with its undercroft, hall, and drawing-room, was almost the whole of the original dwelling. Of the old kitchen there still remain the chimney stack and the arch of the fireplace, now part of the Tudor wing. The rest of the house (including the other tower) comes chiefly from the first 30 years of the 17th century, but the drawing-room by the mediaeval tower was panelled and given its beautiful fireplace about 1700, and the wing by the newer tower was modelled in Adam style after a fire in the 18th century.

In the mediaeval tower are chests of the 15th and 17th centuries, and an 18th century fire-engine. The Tudor kitchen is most attractive with its oak rafters, and the low fireplace. In the larder are wooden churns and grain measures, a flail for threshing corn on the barn floor, man-traps, and a big wooden box mangle.

A fine room in the 17th century part of the house is the hall, with a balcony and a three-tiered window which must have been a magnificent sight with the old glass in its 30 panels. Today there are only a few old fragments left; the restored glass shows the arms of Bradford and the families living here. The stone mantelpiece is about 1700, and the beautiful Jacobean furniture includes a massive table, two benches, handsome court cupboards, and a chest over seven feet long. Two other 17th century rooms are one at the north entrance with a fresco telling the story of the Bradford crest, and the room next to it, in which are fine pieces of 18th century furniture, water-colours of Bolling Hall, and engraved portraits of people who knew Bradford long ago.

The rooms remodelled in Adam style are notable for their plaster ceilings, cornices, and woodwork: and for their collection of swords, rapiers, daggers, watchman's rattles, musical instruments, brass and copper and pewter ware, fire-making appliances, snuff boxes, clay pipes, 18th century watches, and Old Bradford pictures. Elsewhere are fine examples of English glass and earthenware, local pottery, toys, samplers, needlework pictures, and old combing and weaving tools. Most interesting is the collection of 300 water-colour drawings by John Sowdem, showing local worthies and a group of street characters including ragmen, Cockle Sarah, Trotter Bill, Quiet John (a coachman in long coat and top hat), Pot Mary with

51

her pot, Fish David with his fish baskets and rabbits, and Blind Jim playing his fiddle in his top hat and frock coat.

Exceedingly rich is the 17th century bedroom above the drawing-room. It has a plaster frieze patterned with heads and grotesques among foliage, and the plaster ceiling, one of the finest in the county, is a mass of ornament with strapwork, flowers, fruit, birds, and a lion's head. The sumptuous fireplace has fluted and carved pillars, oak and vine carving, and paintings of a man and a woman. It is said that the Duke of Newcastle slept here during the Civil War, on the night before the soldiers were to carry out his order to kill every man, woman, and child, and that as he lay asleep an apparition appealed to him to "Pity Poor Bradford". Legend it may be, but the duke changed his mind when morning came, and only those who resisted were slain. In the room next to this is a series of oak panels carved with linenfold, found during restoration and now part of a Tudor screen. The remains of Bradford's old market cross are in the grounds, which are laid out in harmony with the fine old house.

Bradford takes pride in honouring great men. We have seen Lord Masham and Sir Titus Salt in Lister Park. We come upon Sir Robert Peel in Peel Place; William Edward Forster (the Yorkshire-man who made education the birthright of every child) in the square bearing his name; and (in Darley Street) the bronze figure of Richard Oastler with a boy and a girl. He was the Yorkshire man who did so much for the children in the mills, making himself un-popular by advocating a ten-hour day and laws to control the factories. The imposing memorial to Bradford men who fell in the Great War (a cenotaph with bronze figures of a soldier and a sailor) is in Victoria Square, near a bronze statue of Queen Victoria guarded by stone lions. A tablet at the Theatre Royal (now a cine-ma) tells us that there in 1905 Sir Henry Irving made his last stage appearance; he had been playing Becket, and died at his hotel an hour after speaking his last words, "Into Thy hands, O Lord, into Thy hands".

Other men remembered in the city are John Cousen, the finest engraver of Turner's pictures; John Sharp, Archbishop of York in Queen Anne's day; and John Fawcett, an 18th century hymn-writer. It was at the grammar school that Sir Frank Dyson, Astro-nomer Royal, was educated, and Bradford gave Australia Sir Douglas Mawson, the Antarctic explorer, who was born here in 1882 and sailed with Shackleton in 1908. A house by the Technical College, sheltered by a thorn tree and a sycamore, was the home of Frederick Delius, born here in 1863. His place in music is fixed for

Bramham Park.

Bramhope Chapel.

The farmhouse and gateway at Cawood.

Drax Church.

ever by his power to express the magic of the English countryside. His birthplace was recently demolished to make room for a garage.

Bradford became a cathedral city in 1920 when the parish church of St Peter became the cathedral. It is for the most part a link with the 14th and 15th centuries, and stands on the steep hillside, a noble pile with a massive embattled and pinnacled tower. The chancel and the long clerestoried nave of nine bays are chiefly 14th century, but the west bay of the nave was added when the tower was built in the 15th century, and some of the capitals of the slender four-clustered pillars may belong to the earlier church. Most of the windows are mediaeval, and the Bowling Chapel is about 500 years old. The site of the church is believed to be Saxon, and built into a wall on the north side is a stone carved with knotwork before the Conqueror came. There are traces of the old roodloft stairs. The chancel has its old piscina, and a peephole high in the north wall. The modern font has a splendid 15th century cover like a spire, adorned with tracery and pinnacles. There are old moulded beams in the roofs, and the nave roof, resting on 20 angels, has traceried gables and richly coloured bosses shining with gold. It has had considerable extensions added this century, notably by Sir E. Maufe.

The bishop's throne is enriched with linenfold, figures of a lion and a lamb, fish behind a net in the cornice, and a statue of St Peter with his fishing net. The south porch shelters a mediaeval gravestone with a flowered cross, and another stone with engravings of two queer little people wearing ruffs and dresses trimmed with bows.

There is sculpture of a woman mourning over a pedestal with a portrait of William Sharp, a surgeon who died in 1833; and a marble monument with a quaint carving of the Leeds-to-Liverpool Canal is in memory of Bradford's son Joseph Priestley, who died in 1817 after half a century of engineering. Among the names of vicars is that of William Scoresby, the Arctic explorer who made many voyages to Polar seas and captured hundreds of whales before settling down to preach here in 1839. Another vicar, John Crosse, who preached here 30 years, is remembered as the blind parson who was a great friend of Patrick Brontë. A Flaxman sculpture showing Age instructing Youth is a memorial to Abraham Balme.

There is an inscription to Thomas Wood of 1712, headmaster of the grammar school, and a memorial with compasses, a ruler, and other instruments is to Abraham Sharp, a scholar at the old school who became a notable mathematician and made astronomical appliances for John Flamsteed. He died at 91, having been born in 1651 at Horton Old Hall, a gracious old house in a pleasant setting

C

of trees and lawns, now in a sad state of dilapidation (as is the so-called Paper Hall (of 1643) near the Cathedral).

Facing this hall is one of Bradford's many modern churches, a cross-shaped building with a fine tower and spire. At Little Horton near by is the fine church of St Oswald, its high tower having a spire with dormer windows. Built in 14th century style, it is a spacious place with arcades running from east to west, a font richly carved with tracery and leaves, and a low stone screen with the pulpit at one end and the reading desk at the other. The east window has a rich riot of purple and red. In the tracery is the head of Our Lord surrounded by angels; at the base are tiny pictures of the Madonna, the boy Jesus, and the Crucifixion.

Braithwell. Where four roads meet stands an old cross, with an inscription unreadable now for most of us. It has been thought to be a memorial to one of the lords of Conisborough Castle, or a thank-offering for the safe return of Richard Lionheart.

The church, among beeches and sycamores, was begun by the Normans, and the tympanum over the south doorway is one of the few they left in the county, carved with rings, stars, and lattice. The original shape of a cross was lost when the aisle was added in the 14th century, and of the old central tower there are only three pointed and leaning arches, built when the Norman style was passing. Now there is a 15th century west tower. The 19th century chancel has a recess of the 14th, and the aisle its old piscina.

Round the pulpit are old inscriptions, one dated 1574, and its three old panels are carved with foliage and flowers and a quaint scene of a man in a long robe kneeling at a prayer desk in a church.

Bramham. There is much to charm us in Bramham, where the Great North Road and a stream flowing to the River Wharfe are crossed by one of many Roman roads hereabouts. It has a fine bridge, an old windmill looking down, and houses great and small in a lovely green setting.

South of the village are four fine houses not far apart: Bramham House, Bramham Lodge, Bramham Biggin (which began as a chantry to Nostell Priory), and Bramham Hall, a house in classic style with an entrance crowned by a pediment on six pillars. Shading its beautiful gardens are cedars, beeches, chestnuts, and ancient yews. Off the Roman road running through rich woodland west of the village is Hope Hall, where Sir Thomas Fairfax lived, now the kennels of the Bramham Moor Hunt. Between the village and Newton Kyme is Oglethorpe Hall (now a farmhouse), the birthplace of Bishop Oglethorpe, who saw Latimer and Ridley burned, and lived to crown Queen Elizabeth.

The finest of all these parks is Bramham, with miles of woods (devastated by gales in 1962), gardens which Queen Anne declared to be the most delightful she had seen, and a great house in classic style where lived one of Yorkshire's most famous squires, George Lane-Fox, who loved the old ways and hated new ideas. The house, which is often open to the public, has a fine collection of paintings, including a portrait of Queen Anne by Kneller, presented to Lord Bingley when she stayed here.

Through a richly carved oak lychgate we come to the church, which still has much of its old work and is an exceedingly lofty place. The tower is chiefly 12th century, with its old corbel table of crude heads under the overhanging parapet, some Norman windows, and a fine Norman arch to the nave; the battlements and the small spire are later. A Norman arcade leads to the north aisle. From the 13th century come the south arcade, the south doorway with a rich arch resting on shafts, and the chancel with its lofty arch and lancet windows. The east window is 14th century. We come in by an old studded door.

A black and white roof covers the nave and aisles. The chancel has rich modern screenwork with unusual tracery, and cornices carved with vines, trailing foliage, flowers, and a snake in the branches of an apple tree. The benches in the nave have leaves and flowers on their edges, and the modern font is carved in the old style with rich rows of leaves.

Still remembered here is old Levi Whitehead, the swiftest runner in the England of his day. He ran four miles in 19 minutes, and even when he was 96 he walked four miles an hour. He was 100 when he took his last step in 1787.

Roman roads are still traced on Bramham Moor, a high plain where bones and weapons are sometimes dug up, relics of a terrible battle fought in the snow of 1408. Henry Percy, first Earl of Northumberland, who with other nobles had rebelled against Henry IV, was met here by Sir Thomas Rokeby; the rebels were cut to pieces and Percy was killed, his head, with its silver locks, being carried off and set on a stake on London Bridge.

Bramhope. It is a small place between Leeds and Otley, but it has a treasure worth coming many miles to see. In the grounds of the now demolished Bramhope Hall is a Puritan Chapel, built between 1646 and 1649 by the then Lord of the Manor, Robert Dyneley—and is therefore one of the only two chapels of this type and age in the country. The Puritan preacher, Oliver Heywood, often preached there, and the building retains its box-pews and three-decker pulpit of his day. The Wharfedale Rural District Council has restored it with great care and it is open to the public frequently.

Bramley. A small place near Rotherham, it has only two things to show, a chapel where John Wesley preached in 1786, and the simplest church we could wish to find. Only 32 feet long, it looks like a white cottage, centuries old.

Brayton. It has a small green, and many willows, oaks, and sycamores, with a venerable elm; but it is for its church that we come. It is one of the best of the fine group round Selby, and is notable for the richness of some of its Norman remains.

In the 14th century the Norman nave was given its aisles, and the chancel was made the long and stately place we see with its east window of flowing tracery. From the 15th century come the aisles and clerestory windows, and at the same time the Norman tower was given its lantern top and a short stone spire, rising above the churchyard trees. The belfry windows have shafts and capitals between the lights, and the arch to the nave is tall and massive.

The splendid Norman chancel arch is adorned with zigzag, and in the carving of the exceptionally fine capitals are heads and animals among leaves, and dragons over interlacing foliage. The south doorway is a Norman masterpiece, magnificent with wonderful carving of zigzag, beak-heads, and medallions of quaint figures and scenes—animals fighting, two eating leaves springing from a man's mouth, a tournament, one man riding a lion and another a horse, a hunter, a woman with a palm, and Sagittarius. On the capitals crowning the three shafts on each side are a hunter and falcon, with dogs among branches; another hunter carrying an animal, and a dragon in the branchwork; and four canopied saints.

Two fonts are ancient and modern, the old one keeping the iron staples for locking it against witches. The south aisle has its old piscina, and there is a fine old chest. On a tomb in the chancel are the battered Tudor figures of Sir George Darcy and his wife, their heads, arms, and feet gone. The knight's father was Lord Darcy of Templehurst close by, who lost his head for joining in the Pilgrimage of Grace rebellion.

On the old churchyard cross is an 18th century sundial.

Brighouse. An industrial town bristling with chimneys, it has given its parish church a commanding place on a steep hillside. A cenotaph crowned with Victory is in the park, and here too is the art gallery and the library. It has an inn with timbers from an old battleship, Smith House where John Wesley preached, and a bridge over the Calder. The fine views from Harry Castle Hill are worth the climb, and Freeman's Wood and Waterclough Valley are charming spots. Two churches here have fine stained glass by William Morris, St Martin's and St James.

Brimham Rocks. Nearly a thousand feet above the sea, Brimham Moor is a wilderness of heather and bracken, so high that we can see over miles of Nidderdale and the Plain of York. From the Rocks is a majestic panorama giving on to the dark swelling lines of the fells. The fantastic rocks jut out from a vast carpet of bracken and heather; one is so lightly poised that it seems as if a touch would topple it over.

Scattered over sixty acres, these great rocks have been shaped by thousands of years of wind and rain. Some are huge grotesques, some look like prehistoric monsters turned to stone, and some seem to have been sculptured by giants. Four are known as Rocking Stones, the biggest weighing 100 tons. The Idol, a huge mass twice as heavy, rests on a pedestal only about 12 inches wide. The rocks known as Lover's Leap have a natural arch locked by a keystone. There are what are known as the Druids' Caves, the Cannon Rocks with curious round windows, and rocks fancifully named a dog, a rhinoceros, a rabbit, a tiger, and a tortoise. Two are known as a yoke of oxen; and perhaps the most remarkable of all the creatures in this strange zoo are a dancing bear and a baboon weighing 40 tons.

Brodsworth. Though the collieries are not far away, Brodsworth is fair and unspoiled, lying in a peaceful little valley between two busy roads from Doncaster. Perched among trees on the hill is the neat and cared-for church, and near by, in the lovely gardens of the great park, is the home of the Thellussons, the French family of bankers and merchants who escaped the Massacre of St Bartholomew. Peter Thellusson, who bought lands here and died in 1797, made a curious will by which about £800,000 was to be left to accumulate till it became 140 million pounds; but an Act of Parliament prevented his estate from lying idle to make money after he was dead.

The Thellusson memorials are in the church they restored last century, giving it the south aisle and chapel, and the porch. Its old work dates from the 12th to the 15th century. There is a Norman window, and the passing of the Norman style is seen in the stout arcade leading to the old north aisle, its western bay later than the rest. Coming mainly from the 12th century, the tower has two-light belfry windows with crude carving in their heads, a stringcourse of diamond pattern, and a low massive arch to the nave. The font, and the arcade leading to the chancel's north chapel, are mediaeval. A carved chair, and the pulpit adorned with cherubs and foliage, are 17th century. In the walls of the porch are two coffin lids carved in relief, one with a serpent twisted round a sword, and others are in the floor of the nave. The church looked sad when we visited it, being swathed inside and out with scaffolding—owing to the permanent threat of subsidence.

Brotherton. It is now overshadowed by vast cooling towers of a Power Station. On one side is the River Aire, bounding Fryston Park, and on the other is Byram Park with its trees, lake, and fine house. It came into history for giving its name to a prince who was born here in 1300. He was Thomas of Brotherton, eldest son of Edward I and his second wife Margaret, who came into the world while his parents were guests of the Archbishop of York. Thomas was made Duke of Norfolk when he was 12 and Marshal of England at 16, and he died at 38.

The mediaeval church was made new in 1842, and looks from its hill to the church of Ferrybridge, standing in the marshes where was fought the battle in which Butcher Clifford (father of Wordsworth's Shepherd Lord) lost his life in 1461. The interest of the church is in its unusual appearance within, where the great stone pulpit and reading desk stand on each side of the steps up to the chancel; a second flight of steps mounts to the altar, and a third to the chapel, the floor of which is on a level with the gallery. The east end of each aisle is all window. An ancient altar stone has five crosses, and mediaeval gravestones have traces of inscriptions.

Among the monuments is one to poor Charles Daubuz, a French Protestant who saw his father buried by lamplight in a garden at Calais in 1685, and escaped to England the day after. A great scholar, he left Cambridge to become master of Sheffield Grammar School, and spent his last years as vicar here.

Broughton. On the banks of the Earby Beck flowing to the River Aire near by, Broughton is altogether charming. Its cottages with creepered walls are bedecked with flowers, and the hall, mantled in trees, is seen from the road which runs with the stream, the moors rising behind it. It is a stone house in classical style, on a different site from the older one it replaced. The Tempests, whose home it has long been, are said to have made the church new at the close of the 15th century. A lonely building between the village and Elslack, reached by a rough lane over the fields, it has a squat, massive tower, and an arcade with a niche on a pillar which is said to be typical of the churches restored by the Tempests. There are two Norman doorways and a Norman font. The chancel has a blocked priest's doorway, and a stone with a tiny round arch which may be the head of a Norman window. One of two fragments of alabaster sculpture has the Madonna and Child, and in a glass case is a 17th century almsdish of blue porcelain, said to be one of only two of its kind in England.

Buckden. The grandeur of green hills and the sombre dignity of purple fells and mountains is about this small village far up Wharfedale. Across the valley the fells rise 2000 feet above the sea, and deer roam the wooded slopes coming down to the river. On its own side the village is sheltered by the rock-strewn slopes known as The Rake and East Side, with a stream flowing between them from Buckden Pike, 2300 feet up. We can climb this towering hill from Buckden, Starbotton, and Cray in Wharfedale. The place was formerly the residence of the Forest officials for Langstrothdale Chase; and wool sales used to take place in the local inn which still has some weighing equipment.

Burghwallis. We think of Robin Hood hereabouts, for Burghwallis is in Barnsdale Forest, where he and his merry men are said to have waylaid travellers on the Great North Road. Robin Hood's Well, under an arch designed by Sir John Vanbrugh, is by the roadside, where John Evelyn found a stone chair and an iron ladle with it. It is a small place buried in trees, its roads like green tunnels. The cottages are among great sycamores and beeches, the hall (with a Roman Catholic chapel) has yews and cedars for company, and the simple aisleless church is one of the most secluded we have found.

There are fine masses of herringbone in the walls of nave and chancel. The tower is a patchwork of big and little stones, and, though it has some semblance of Saxon or early Norman days, it is thought to be mainly 12th century, with a later parapet. There are round-headed windows in the base, a bull's-eye window cut from a single stone, and belfry windows with shafts between their pointed lights showing the passing of the Norman style. The font and the massive chancel arch are also from the close of the 12th century. Within the fine stone-ribbed porch is a doorway with a Norman

59

arch, and under it is a shallow arch of only two stones. The door has been turning on its hinges for centuries. A stone bench serves as sedilia, and many of the windows are renewed. The lovely vaulted chancel screen is a great possession; made in mediaeval days and restored last century, it has flowers and leaves in a rich cornice, and vine carving under the traceried bays.

Thomas Gascoign's brass portrait shows him as a Tudor knight in armour. In the churchyard sleeps the Abbé Leroux, who escaped from the Revolution in France and ended his days in this peaceful spot; and by the porch are remains of an old cross.

Burley-in-Wharfedale. Traffic streams through this growing place, busy with bleaching and worsted spinning, but these cannot rob it of its fine setting in Wharfedale. It has come into Ilkley, but it remains a place to visit, if only as the birthplace of a poet and the home of a statesman. The poet is William Watson, who gave his heart to the Lake Country; the statesman is William Forster, who was born in Dorset but always regarded this as Home, and has been sleeping in the cemetery since 1886.

A post of the old stocks is still by the gate of the 19th century church, which has a tower and a spire, panelling from the Fairfax pew in the old church, and an inscription to Thomas Clark, schoolmaster here for 40 years, to whom the village has dedicated a fountain in the recreation ground. In the church porch is a tablet to Mr Forster, and on a wayside lawn are two crosses, tributes to the statesman and his lifelong partner in business, William Fison.

Mr Fison was one of the most successful manufacturers in Yorkshire woollen mills, and William Forster was associated with him for many years. Becoming keenly interested in politics, Forster went into Parliament as a Liberal, and his chief work was the piloting of the first great Education Bill through the Commons.

Burnsall. Burnsall lies in a richly wooded stretch of Wharfedale with the fells and grassy moors rising on each side.

Over the river is a fine 19th century stone bridge of five arches with cut-water piers. There are houses in gardens ablaze with colour in summer, a green with a maypole among old elms, Thor's Well said to be a thousand years old, a church with a fine tower and a charming grammar school of 1602, founded by Sir William Craven who was born at Appletreewick near by. Sir William "repaired and butified" (as an old document in the church puts it) Burnsall's church, which had been rebuilt about 1520.

The nave, high and narrow, has leaning arcades continuing from the western tower and resting on massive arches. There are still a few fragments of an older building, including 14th century windows in the south chapel, and a Norman capital in the north arcade; and a rare collection of ancient stones telling of days before the Conquest. A fine fragment of a Saxon cross, covered with interlacing, is about five feet high. There are parts of other Saxon crosses, and a wheel-head with a cross carved in the middle. Two hogbacks and part of a third (found in the churchyard) are very narrow, with crude carving of animal heads at the ends; the finest of them (in two parts) has scalework on its sides.

Extraordinarily crude is the font, coming from the second half of the 11th century. Shaped like a tub, with an old cover like the lid of a copper, it has rough carving of birds and beasts and cable pattern on the rim. In striking contrast is the exquisite sculpture of an alabaster panel of about 1350, still with traces of colour, and showing the Wise Men, one holding his crown as he offers his gift to the Child on the Madonna's knee, while Joseph tends the ox and the ass. There are old screens, an old chest, old panelling in bench-ends, and a Jacobean pulpit from which two John Alcocks preached from 1733 to 1810, one for nearly 60 years. The church has four Church-wardens reminding us of the days when there were two Rectors in the parish each with his own parsonage, pulpit, and reading desk in the church.

We come to the church through a curious lychgate turning on a centre pivot and closed automatically by a heavy stone weight.

The village attracts many vistors to its Sports, held in August on the Feast of St Wilfred.

Burnt Yates. A hamlet high in the world, catching every wind that blows, it has a fine view of the hills and moors round it. Its stone houses, the creepered school, the church, and the inn are strung along the road from Ripley to Pateley Bridge, the school having been built and endowed in 1760 by Admiral Robert Long. We read in the 19th century church that the church and the village itself were partly rebuilt by Charles Frederick Taylor.

Burton-in-Lonsdale. A few miles from Ingleton, it looks out to the grandeur of the mountains, and has many old houses clustered on the green hillside above the River Greta, which is spanned by an old humped bridge. Standing by the maypole (a rare sight in these times) is the 19th century church, a fine spacious place with rich arches, capitals with overhanging foliage, a vaulted chancel, and a vaulted tower serving also as a vestry. Unusual and lovely are two

61

old chairs with brass studs and seats of leather, richly embossed. A chest is Jacobean, and a fine chest of drawers may be Elizabethan. The pewter chalice and paten are from an older church. On the big grassy mound above the church stood an old castle of the Mowbrays.

Calton. Near the Foss Gill, where a stream from the moors makes lovely waterfalls before joining the Aire, Calton's pretty group of old houses and farms is perched on top of the hill. Sharing in the magnificent view is the old hall (now a farmhouse) with a mounting stone by the pillared gateway.

We remember this tiny place for having given England Honest John Lambert, who fought for the Parliament at Marston Moor, went on to fight in Scotland (where he had command of the army at Dunbar), and was captured and wounded at Musselburgh. He helped to win the crowning victory of the Civil War at Worcester, and had a horse shot under him. During the Commonwealth he was the Army's representative in Parliament, and his dealings were so fair that friend and foe alike knew him as Honest John. He was the Army's darling. A man of independent spirit and fearless honesty, he stood so high that a Royalist said he had it in his power "to raise Oliver higher or to set up in his place". He parted from Cromwell over the question of kingship, but not long before he died Cromwell asked Lambert to see him, and fell on his neck and kissed him. After the Restoration he remained true to the memory of Cromwell, but his life was spared; he was made a prisoner and died in captivity. He was fond of gardens, and is said to have brought the Guernsey lily to England; he was also an art-lover and bought some of Charles I's pictures.

Calverley. It was the scene of a tragic deed in Shakespeare's day and came into a play which was printed in Shakespeare's name during his own life. Nearer our own time it was the birthplace of Frederick William Faber, whose grandfather was vicar here for 52 years. Faber became a Roman Catholic and is remembered chiefly for his hymns, which are sung today all over the English-speaking world.

There is much that is new in this pleasant place, on high ground above the River Aire, with Bradford only four miles away, and there is a delightful walk through Calverley Woods to Apperley Bridge. The church stands finely on the hill, looking over the valley to a countryside of woods, towns, and villages.

Most of the old work in the church is 14th century, but the clerestory and the top of the tower are a century younger, and an arch of the south arcade breaks into a Norman window. The porch has a vaulted roof, the tower arch is oddly askew, and the much-restored chancel has three sedilia and a piscina. Its east window with flowing tracery has much old glass, in which are roundels and shields, a Crucifixion almost complete, and heads and figures in a medley. The font has a fine 17th century cover, the altar table is Elizabethan, and the reredos of 1877 has the Last Supper carved in relief.

In the north wall outside are two stones carved with crosses, one 12th and the other 13th century, said to be memorials of the Calverleys. More of their stones lie in the churchyard, some with swords and crosses, and there are many stones of the 17th and 18th centuries. Here too are the graves of a Royalist who fell in the Civil War and of a giant of last century, Benjamin Cromach, who was so tall that he needed eight feet of English earth when he died, at only 25.

The Calverleys lived here for about six centuries. Their old house, now a few cottages with some remains of 500 years ago, is interesting as the home of that Sir Walter Calverley who was a friend of Addison and may have been his model for Sir Roger de Coverley; and of that other Walter at whose hands two children met a tragic fate. His story is the theme of a poignant 17th century play, *A Yorkshire Tragedy*.

Campsall. It is Robin Hood country; hereabouts is Barnsdale Forest, with almost as many memories of Robin as Sherwood has. Huge elms and beeches make a living stockade round the village, and every road takes us through the forest. Tradition says that travellers on the Great North Road (two miles away) often went on their way with heavy hearts and light purses after falling in with Robin Hood, and that the Bishop of Hereford had to dance in his boots near the village.

A forest village of rare charm, Campsall has beautiful stone houses, fine old barns, and a hall in a magnificent park with a grand array of cedars near the lake. Charmingly grouped with the old buildings at an entrance to the park is the lovely church, its walls of light-coloured stone gleaming against the rich green of the village. Facing it is the stately vicarage, buried in trees.

Except for its battlements, the lovely tower is a monument to the Normans who built it. Fine arcading frames the windows, those of the belfry being especially striking. Its original arch still opens to the nave, but the doorway, rich with zigzag, is made new except for the outer moulding. The door is covered with lovely ironwork in circles, and similar ornament is on the south door. Other remains of the Norman church are traces of windows in the north transept, its arch to the aisle, a chancel window with carved imposts and hood, the buttresses beside it, and carved fragments in the south aisle. From the 12th century come the pointed arches (carved with zigzag) leading from the nave to the transepts and the plainer arch to the chancel. The baptistery has a 700-year-old vaulted roof. The aisles were added in the 14th century—the time of the doorway, adorned with flowers and sheltered by a handsome porch.

The chancel has stone benches, and the south transept a recess with a piscina in the ledge. There are old coffin lids, old wooden figures supporting the north transept roof, a 17th century chest and an older one, and a pulpit partly Jacobean. A great possession is the 15th century chancel screen with traceried vaulting and an inscription in which we read "Beware of the Devil when he blows his horn". In a room over the baptistry is a library of 180 books collected by an 18th century vicar.

Cantley. Woods are all about this attractive spot, and its big house is in a park of a hundred acres. Half a mile away the church has stood 700 years, but its tower is 15th century and its north aisle is new. The 13th century doorway with a carved arch is in a porch perhaps as old as itself, and over the original east window is a small kneeling figure, with part of a mediaeval gravestone showing a man with praying hands. There is an old almsbox. The striking modern screenwork of the chancel and the chapels is glowing with colour; that of the chancel has fine vaulting and a loft. Over the altar is a great canopy, and the reredos has the Crucifixion and saints shining with gold.

Carlecotes. A thousand feet high, it is a charming spot in the heart of the moors, looking away to the Peak. By the pretty garden of an old house made partly new is the tiny modern church whose rich woodwork includes eight canopied stalls.

Carleton. It is the Carleton near Skipton, a village of old and new, where cotton mills find work for most of the folk. On its own side of the River Aire is Carleton Moor, with Pinhaw rising 1274 feet above the sea. Embsay Moor is part of the great mass across the valley.

The first church was a Norman chapel-of-ease to Skipton. The second was built in its place about 1500 by the monks of Bolton, and on its ruins the church we see was raised in 1859. The clock in the tower was made by a villager. Built in 1584 by William Ferrand (chief steward to the Cliffords of Skipton Castle), Carleton Hall is now used as a cowshed and a barn, the ground on which it stands still providing money and flour which are given to the poor at Christmas and Easter, and also the ten shillings for the parson to preach a sermon on mortality every Good Friday. The almshouses were founded in 1698, the school was founded early in the 18th century, and the youngest children have lessons in the tithe barn which has old oak beams.

Trapps Hall is a beautiful Elizabethan building formed now into several houses, Biggin Farm still has something of the shooting box of the Cliffords, and Yellison is an old farmhouse which once belonged to a daughter of the Tempests. Attached to the rectory of 1821 is a brewery, where in olden days the parson brewed his beer.

Castleford. An old rhyme says that Castleford lasses must needs be fair, for they bathe in Calder and wash in Aire. That was in the days when the countryside was green and these rivers were sparkling here; today Castleford is under its own smoke cloud, and looks out on little that is beautiful, though fragments of the famous forest of Elmet are close by. Long famous for its manufacture of glass, it is said to give the world 20 million bottles a year.

This way came the Romans, and here was found one of their milestones set up about the time Roman pottery was being made in the neighbourhood. Fragments of the pottery, together with Roman coins and an altar dedicated to the goddess of victory, have been brought to light, and antiquarians think the modern church stands on the site of the Roman camp. The church took the place of a 13th century one last century. It has a central tower and arcades with foliage capitals. The sculptor, Henry Moore, was born here, although the town has none of his work.

Cawood. It has been called the Windsor of the North, and time was when it deserved the name, for it was the scene of royal splendour and its ruined walls are instinct with the thrill of history. Today it is a small town round a sharp bend of the River Ouse, with something of the old world clinging to its narrow streets. Some of the houses are charming, one having ivied walls and Dutch gables. The Romans had a camp by the river and their gilded barges came to and fro. Here came the Saxons and the Vikings, and in the Middle Ages the place was famous for its tournaments. It is for the old church and what is left of the palace of the archbishops that we come now.

The church, high on the river bank near the old toll bridge, has a fine tower from the 15th century, but the chancel, the nave, and the

65

south aisle were built at the end of Norman days, the chancel keeping its original pointed arch with traces of painting, the nave its original west doorway with a round arch, and the lovely south arcade its delicate clustered shafts. Both arcades are leaning. A pillar piscina, the font, and two stoups are mediaeval, and there is an ancient stone used for holding candles. A bell is probably from the old palace, and the fine chest and the pulpit were carved in Jacobean days.

Under an alabaster canopy is the bust of George Mountain, showing him as if he were preaching, his fingers in the leaves of a book. It stirs us to think that he sang as a chorister in this charming little church, and that as a boy he made up his mind to be Archbishop of York. A poor farmer's son, he worked hard and rose to be Bishop of Durham, and Archbishop, but his high ambition was broken by a bitter stroke of fate, for he was enthroned at York one day and died that night.

The palace in which he had hoped to live is believed to stand on the site of a castle built by Athelstan, first King of all England. Made into a palace in the 14th century, it was a magnificent building to which bishops and kings came for centuries. Seven archbishops of York died here, and here Edward I held some of his parliaments. Cawood saw all the glory of a royal court in those days. In 1465 George Neville, brother of Warwick the Kingmaker, celebrated his appointment as Archbishop of York by giving what was perhaps the biggest banquet ever known in England, employing 2000 cooks who used over 100 oxen, 500 deer, and 1000 sheep. At length the palace passed to Cardinal Wolsey, who made it his great house, and in the Civil War it was taken for the Parliament and almost destroyed. The 15th century gatehouse still stands, like a sturdy tower, with two lovely oriels, balconies looking on the lawn, and a vaulted archway through which Henry VIII rode in splendour and Cardinal Wolsey in disgrace. Built of gleaming stone, it is sandwiched between a brick house with dormers in its pantiled roof, and a long barn draped with ivy; and enshrined within its walls is the memory of one of the most dramatic days in our Tudor Age, for here was the Fall of Wolsey.

Cawthorne. It is part of an unspoiled countryside, a surprisingly lovely spot to come upon four miles from Barnsley. To the west is the imposing Cannon Hall in its fine park of over 170 acres, where a stream falls in cascades and flows on to join the River Dearne. Bought by Barnsley in 1951 it is now a Country House museum and art gallery. It has pleasant collections of furniture, pictures, and glass. A popular exhibit is *Little John's Bow*. Some of the village's quaint and charming houses have old carved stones in the walls. Prettily perched on a ledge above the road is the village museum, which began life as two cottages and was for a time a chapel. Attractive outside with black and white walls, and keeping its fine old timbered roof within, it is like a pocket museum, with a 17th century fireplace from the old vicarage, stone weights dug up in a garden, a bomb dropped at Dodworth not far off, and a varied collection of coal fossils, coins, birds, and butterflies.

Cawthorne has an extraordinary drinking fountain no longer used, a big stone cross with dragons on the shaft, and on the base a writhing mass of dragons entwined. We turn by the fountain to the church, or may reach it by an avenue of trees.

In the churchyard is the massive mausoleum where sleeps Sir Walter Spencer-Stanhope of Cannon Hall. Fragments of old coffin lids are in the churchyard wall, and by one of the gates is a tall cross of which the head and part of the shaft have Saxon carving. The head of another Saxon cross is built into an outside wall of the church. The church has been much altered since the time of the Norman window in the north aisle, and its chancel is made new, but the tower is 15th century, and the north chapel is 14th or 15th with some earlier windows; in it is a tomb enriched with quatrefoils. There is a square bowl probably from a Norman font, and an old one like a chalice is carved with tracery and shields, faces and lettering. An inlaid desk and a carved chest are old. Rich modern carving is in the chancel screen and stalls, and the pulpit has paintings of two angels and Our Risen Lord.

Chapel-le-Dale. It is a tiny place of a few grey houses and a stolid little church, tucked away in a hollow and looking up to the heights. The upland valley in which it lies, carved out by a glacier, is wild and desolate; through it runs the River Greta on its way to Ingleton, and at each side rise two of Yorkshire's highest mountains —Whernside, and Ingleborough with its top like a table a mile round, linked by a narrow neck to its satellite, Simon Fell.

A ridge of limestone like an immense earthwork looks down on the old church, which is less than 50 feet long, with a bellcot, a stone roof, and great beams and kingposts within. Those who lost their lives during the construction of the Settle–Carlisle railway have a wall plaque to their memory here. Southey, wrote of the village in his story of *The Doctor*, and the visitors' book of the Hill Inn contains many famous names.

Some of the caves and waterfalls for which the valley is famed are here. Jingle Pot and Hurtle Pot are deep holes by which we hear a sound as of many waters; and 300 yards away is Weathercote Cave, the finest of all Yorkshire's pot-holes, with sycamores and firs, ferns and wild flowers about it. It is a roofless rift in the limestone, divided into two caverns, and from a hole in one of them a stream falls in a cascade of over 70 feet before being swallowed up to flow underground. Douk Caves are half a mile away.

Church Fenton. Set in green fields, it has an attractive church shaped like a cross, built for the most part in the 13th century. The sturdy central tower, rising above gabled stone roofs and resting on arches which spring without capitals from the piers, is 15th century. The east window of the chancel has the flowing tracery of the 14th century, framing glass which may be as old as itself. More old fragments are in the north transept. The doorway in the modern porch is 13th century, the time of a piscina. The bowl of an ancient font is on a windowsill, an altar stone with five crosses is in the chancel floor, and there is a child's stone coffin. Two carved chairs are Jacobean. Lying in the chancel is a woman sculptured in stone, a dainty mediaeval figure in her graceful headdress and a gown with pointd sleeves and long cuffs. Her hair, bunched at the sides, is held by plaits, and at her feet are a lion and a dragon, fighting for an animal's head. There is a sundial on an old pedestal in the churchyard, and in the village is a fragment of an old cross. The local airfield, so busy during World War II, now comes to life once a year for a large Air Show.

Clapham. With Ingleborough high above it, and the Clapham Beck running through it on its way to the River Wenning, it is a village of rare delight, with old stone houses and white cottages. At one end of the bridge carrying the highway over the stream is a fine stone seat; at the other side is the old cross on a wall. Close by stands the old manor house built in the early 18th century with what look like pigeon-holes in the gable of the two-storeyed porch, and by it is one of the shaded ways to the church.

By the bridge towering beeches grow, and below it is one of the waterfalls. Passing a footbridge up stream we come to another bridge which helps to make what is perhaps the village's most enchanting scene. Yew trees trimmed like a table top reach the parapet of the bridge; on a high bank stands the pretty embattled church with its low tower, and just above the bridge is an exquisite waterfall like snow-white lace, cascading down the rocks.

The Beck fills a lake in the grounds of the imposing Ingleborough Hall, now a special school for children, the lovely wooded glen extending for about a mile beyond the lake to the famous Ingleborough Cave, which penetrates for 900 yards into the flank of one of York-shire's three highest hills, second only in this Riding to Whernside, which rises a few miles away to a height of 2414 feet. From the top of Ingleborough, where there are traces of Celtic fortifications 2373 feet above the sea, is a panorama of some of the wildest and grandest scenery in all England. Hiding from the world in the cave below are chambers glittering with stalactites and stalagmites, pools fringed with lacework, and rocks of fantastic shapes. The stream runs into the cave after being swallowed a mile away by Gaping Gill Hole, a famous pot-hole 340 feet deep (which one can descend nowadays, at certain times, with the aid of a winch, in 90 seconds!) at the base of Ingleborough. Another of these remarkable gulfs in the limestone is Alum Pot on the lower slope of Simon Fell not far away. Nature has been lavish in her gifts to this neighbourhood, where geologists come to study the rocks and botanists to find rare plants, among them rosewort, marsh stonecrop, and wrinkled willow. The botanist Reginald Farrer lived here, as did the father of Michael Faraday.

Except for the 15th century tower, the church was made new last century. Its striking features are the lofty arcades running from east to west and reaching the roof. There is 17th century oak panelling round the walls, and the handsome pulpit has carved panels of Our Lord and two saints.

Clayton West. The neat stone church of 1875 is at the top of a hill, its interior dimmed by good glass showing the Nativity, the Crucifixion, and a gallery of saints. A fine oak monument, with a carving of a destroyer, is in memory of Charles John Wintour, com-mander of a flotilla which fought at Jutland in 1916. He was killed on the bridge.

Cleckheaton. Its big 19th century church of St John has a fine 20th century oak screen with a vine cornice and the Twelve Disciples in niches. Away on the hill is a simple building with a turret and spire, still known as the old White Chapel, but many times rebuilt since its beginning in Norman or perhaps Saxon days. Its chief possession is a font with crude carving of cable moulding and five quaint little figures in arcading. It comes from the close of Norman days, and there is a gravestone about as old in the porch.

Cleckheaton will not soon forget Richard Richardson, who has been sleeping in the White Chapel since 1741. He was a doctor who would not practise for money but was ever ready to attend the poor.

He became famous as a botanist, travelled over England in search of specimens, and had a garden with many curious plants.

Clifford. A mile from Boston Spa, and less from the Great North Road, it has an attractive 17th century house and two churches. The Roman Catholic church, in Norman style, is by a row of beeches; its massive tower, wearing a pyramid cap and resting on three open arches, dominates the village. The impressive interior has great arcades with some pillars carved, one capital having in its foliage the Evangelistic symbols, and scenes of the Nativity, the Baptism, the Crucifixion, and the Ascension. Over the arches behind the altar are one wheel and two oval windows, and in a chapel filled with golden light is a sculpture of the Madonna. The door through which we enter has an enormous closing ring.

Crowning the hill at the other side of the village is the church of St Luke, in 13th century style, its oldest things a fine Jacobean bench and several chairs.

Coley. The people of the hamlets round about come to this modern church with a lofty tower, standing like a sentinel on the hill, looking down on Halifax. Beyond the church is the old stone gabled hall, with worn heads and two dogs on its gateway.

Collingham. Here the Collingham Beck flows to the River Wharfe and there are spacious views down the wooded valley. The church has a 15th century tower with eight bells, 13th century pillars in the nave, and a chancel only ten feet wide, but its chief interest is in its ancient stones. Two Anglo-Saxon cross fragments are the most interesting: the oldest, of about AD 800, has figures of the Apostles, and the other has a Runic inscription and dragon interlacing, and one of the very old cresset stones, which has eight hollows for lights.

Conisborough. Its fame is a ruined castle, now cared for by the National Trust, which lives in Scott's *Ivanhoe*, a remarkable sight in its green setting above the River Don, in a countryside scarred with industry. A majestic pile believed to rise on Saxon earthworks, it crowns the end of a ridge which dips between it and the old church in a small town of steep streets.

Covering three acres and protected by a deep moat below a wall 60 feet high, it was strengthened with round towers and must have been one of the strongest fortresses in the north. The old bridge has gone, and only a few walls are left of the buildings in the courtyard, but the keep stands supremely above all lesser ruins. It is thought to have been built by Hameline Warrenne, who saw Richard I crowned and was treasurer for his ransom.

Of about twenty round keeps in England, this is the oldest, yet in spite of over 700 years it looks almost new. Like an immense stone cylinder, it rises 90 feet and is 52 feet across. Its six huge buttresses are nine feet thick. Not till we have climbed 20 feet up steps which have taken the place of the original drawbridge do we come to the doorway, astonishingly small for so great a place. It brings us along a narrow passage in a wall 15 feet thick to a great circular room with a hole in the middle to the cellar which once had a well over 100 feet deep. Another stair with a vaulted roof brings us to a circular room with a window which keeps its stone seat, and a beautiful fireplace under an arch with keyed stones resting on finely carved shafts. Higher still is another circular room, and a flight of steps to the roof where we see Yorkshire, Lincolnshire, Notts, and Derbyshire, and the river below.

The most thrilling room of all is a tiny oratory in the thickness of the wall. Only 12 feet long, it has three peepholes, a deep moulding over the arch, a vaulted roof with carved bosses, and two piscinas. This curious little chapel, over 60 feet above the ground, delighted Sir Walter Scott so much that he made it the scene of one of the most dramatic incidents in *Ivanhoe*.

It was probably Hameline Warrenne who built the church, which still has much work of Norman days, some showing the old style changing to the new. The tower is 12th and 15th century, with new stone outside; it opens to the aisles with Norman arches and to the nave with one of mediaeval days. The porch has a restored front in 13th century style; a worn figure in its wall may be Norman, the time of the doorway. The old arcades have round and pointed arches, and a fine capital is carved with men in foliage. There are two Norman windows, and a Norman chancel arch leads to a chancel made partly new.

From the 15th century come the clerestory and the font with carvings of a Resurrection and a man in a long robe. There are two old piscinas, an old niche, old glass with a saint and a bishop, and a chalice made before Elizabeth's day. A coffin lid and a stone altar are mediaeval, a Saxon stone has knotwork, a worn stone shows a bird like a raven, and a magnificent Norman gravestone has carvings of Adam and Eve under a tree, a bishop with a staff, a man fighting a dragon with a branching tail, and a splendid tournament scene of two knights on horseback.

Coniston Cold. It lies in the little hills among the moors and fells, the group of grey houses in a green hollow, their trim 20th century church up a lane, looking away to the rugged line of Flasby Fell and the tower on Rylstone Fell. There are neat panelled pews, a stolid three-decker pulpit, and two old carved chairs. One has a quaint scene of Our Lord's baptism, John seeming to be kneeling in the air, and three men looking on from an archway by a mediaeval street. The other has the disciples with Our Lord, who is laying hands on a kneeling woman in the shade of a fig tree growing from a rock. Just above the village we have a peep of Coniston Hall, a modern house looking down on the 25-acre lake in its densely-wooded park.

Conistone. Lonely and impressive is this stretch of the valley of the Wharfe, striking in its perfect harmony of green fields and hills, grey walls and rocky crags. Sheltering under Conistone Beacon are the houses and barns and church, the tiny square, and the maypole. The lowly church has been made almost new, but the nave arcade has two Norman and two mediaeval bays, and the crude font may be Norman. It is claimed that this is the oldest church in Wharfedale. There is an old almsbox, and an old bell stands on the floor. The doorway has been rebuilt in Norman style.

Copgrove. A charming spot with beautiful trees, it lies off the beaten track, with golden cornfields and green meadows about it. The road to Burton Leonard crosses one end of the big lake in the park, and from the stone bridge we see the creepered house on its high bank reflected in the placid water. Facing each other at a pretty corner are the church (in a lovely mantle of trees), and the fine old rectory, with a magnificent copper beech sheltering a patch of lawn about 90 yards round, and a stone pedestal in the garden given by a Belgian who found refuge here in the Great War.

Restoration has not spoiled the simple church begun by the Normans. Their chancel arch is still here, and the old painting round the mediaeval east window may possibly be their work. A Norman window in the chancel has part of a mediaeval coffin lid for a lintel, and what may be part of a stone altar for a sill. The font has a Norman base, and an old bowl lies on the floor. Older than anything else here is a stone in the vestry wall outside, with carving of a Tau cross and a quaint little man with one arm akimbo. Over the pulpit from which he preached for 57 years of last century is an inscription to John Charge who died in 1870. A tribute to Brigadier Malise Graham is the fine glass in a window showing two saints— Francis of Assisi with a horse, a cow, a goose, a dog, a cockerel, an otter, a fox, a squirrel, and a pheasant; and St Mungo blessing two children at the old well which supplies water for the great house.

Copmanthorpe. The Knights Templars held much of the land here centuries ago, and stones from their buildings are still to be seen in house and garden walls.

Older than their story is that of the lowly church, a plain oblong under one long roof, crowned with a double bellcot and sheltered by three big trees. It comes from Norman days (though much of it is made new in the old style), and keeps some of its original work in the group of three windows in the east wall, the interior arch of the west doorway, the window above it, and the walling. The nave has an old black and white roof, and a broken old font is in the churchyard.

Cowick. The church is modern, but traces of a moated tower said to have been built by John of Gaunt are still in the park, where there has been a hall since Tudor times. The house we see reconstructed, it is said, by Paine in 1752 is imposing, but its great days are gone. In the park are old beeches and great elms, and a magnificent chestnut said to be one of the biggest in England.

Cowling. High above its houses is Crag Side with rocks like steps, and higher still are the moors, with what is known as the Hitching Stone, a great boulder said to have been left by a glacier which shaped these winding valleys. Above a deep glen is the 19th century church, with an inscription to George Bayldon, vicar for 40 years. In the churchyard lie the parents and sister of Philip Snowden, three times Chancellor of the Exchequer, who was born in a cottage at Middleton close by and has a memorial cairn at Pad Cote on the moor above. His father died in 1889, but his mother, living to be 90 and dying in 1922, saw her son's rise to fame. The school at Middleton where he was a scholar has become a Sunday school; at Cowling school he was a pupil teacher.

Cowthorpe. A tree has brought fame to this tiny village in the byways, looking to Hunsingore on the other side of the Nidd. It is the Cowthorpe Oak; it was long past its prime when John Evelyn saw it, but even then it stood 85 ft high and was so majestic that he gave it a place in his book of trees. Said to have covered half an acre with its immense spread of branches, and to have sheltered 95 children in its cavernous trunk, it is certainly over a thousand years old, and may be half as old again. It is just possible that it was growing here as a sapling when the Romans were masters of Britain. It is now completely dead and has collapsed.

Perched on a steep bank above the river, the quaint little 15th century church stands by a farmyard. Its singular feature is the tower, which projects on each side of the nave's west wall. The outside recess so formed has a big open arch flanked by buttresses, and a roof with two massive ribs. At each side of the window in the east wall of the recess is a great corbel, supporting the overhanging portion of the tower within the church. The walls of the striking interior are an extraordinary medley of rough stones of all shapes and sizes, some red, some golden. Among the old glass in the windows is the shield of the Roucliffes, seen also on the old font. It is to Brian Roucliffe that Cowthorpe owes this church. He died in 1494, and his brass portrait, mounted on white marble, shows him in his robes as Baron of the Exchequer, holding what is left of a church. An old door is barred with a great beam, and there are rough-hewn timbers in the roof. A rare possession is an extraordinary 15th century chest, five feet long and panelled on every side; it has a gabled canopy enriched with Tudor cresting, resting on four posts.

Crofton. It hides on a hill near Wakefield, the church at the top having wide views of the countryside. An aisleless place like a cross with a central tower, it is said to have been built five centuries ago by Richard Fleming, an Archbishop of York believed to have been born here.

The older church was on another site, and two fragments of a Saxon cross from the old churchyard are in the church we see, carved with strange beasts and a bishop with staring eyes. The font and a piscina are mediaeval, and a stone table rests on a bracket with a bunch of grapes carved under it. Most of the windows are restored. There are two odd-looking doors from the belfry to the roofs, and a stone coffin by the stone-ribbed porch. The old stocks are near the lychgate, which was made by the men who came back from the war in memory of those who did not. In the churchyard is a huge domed canopy resting on many pillars, a memorial to the Byngs of Crofton Hall.

Here also lies a forgotten woman whose school book was once almost as widely known as Euclid's *Geometry*. Every child learned history from it, and everyone knew it as Mangnall's Questions. Richmal Mangnall came as a pupil to a school at Crofton Hall, stayed on as a teacher, and at last took the school over, running it till she died in 1820.

74

Cullingworth. A grey moorland village with worsted mills and stone quarries, it has low stone houses, a massive cenotaph to those who fell in the Great War, and a modern cross-shaped church, a quaint spire crowning the tower, which serves as a porch. Its handsome clock has a pendulum swinging in a glass case.

South of the village the railway crosses the valley by a great viaduct 120 feet high, its 17 arches each having a span of 50 feet. On nearby Cullingworth Moor is an Iron Age earthwork.

Dacre. It is on a slope of lovely Nidderdale, with Hayshaw Moor rising 1100 feet above it. The church is at Dacre Bank, where a fine bridge spans the river, and a bill announcing the opening services in 1837 hangs on the wall inside. It has two old chairs.

Between the two hamlets is Low Hall, said to have stones from Fountains Abbey in its walls. It was the home of the Bensons, who gave us the Archbishop of Canterbury who collapsed in Mr Gladstone's pew at Hawarden and died at the castle. A disused school here was modified to become one of the first Youth Hostels in Yorkshire.

Darfield. The mines round about have taken their toll, for in the churchyard are monuments to 189 men and boys who were buried alive in the Lundhill Colliery in 1857, and to ten miners to whom death came swiftly in the pit at Houghton Main in 1886.

The rectory garden was famous in the early 17th century, when the rector (Walter Stonehouse) was a sort of Gilbert White. He completed the first garden list known in Yorkshire and the third in all England, the manuscript giving a most detailed plan of his garden.

Darfield's great possession is its church—a huge oblong with a noble west tower of Norman and 15th century days. There is Norman walling at the eastern ends of the chancel arcades. The rest of the chancel, its arch, the nave aisles, and the south chapel, are mainly 15th century. An old painted roof looks down on the south aisle and chapel, and fine Jacobean pews with carved bobbin ends are continued under the tower. A box-pew in a chapel was perhaps carved 500 years ago for one of the Bosviles, to which family may have belonged the battered knight in armour and collar of SS, lying with his wife on an alabaster tomb. Katherine Willoughby's monument of 1658 has many shields.

There are two big peepholes and old altar rails, and old panelling is on the wall by the mediaeval font whose cover may be Jacobean, the time of two chairs. The canopied pulpit is a fine modern copy of that style, and the chest is mediaeval.

One of Darfield's sons was Obadiah Walker, a great preacher and a friend of James II. He published notable books on religion, was imprisoned in the Tower after the king ran away, and was so poor in his last years that he was glad to wear the clothes one of his old scholars gave him.

To many pilgrims the chief interest of this place will be that Ebenezer Elliott lies in the churchyard. He was the poet of the poor, and his own lines suit well as his epitaph:

> Stop, Mortal! Here thy brother lies,
> The Poet of the Poor.
> His books were rivers, woods, and skies,
> The meadow and the moor.
> His teachers were the torn heart's wail,
> The tyrant and the slave,
> The street, the factory, the gaol,
> The palace and the grave!

He was known as the Corn Law Rhymer, and had a large share in abolishing the tax on corn which made bread so dear when wages were so low. He lived all his life in South Yorkshire, and died at Great Houghton near Barnsley on December 1, 1849, having lived to see the corn taxes repealed.

Darrington. It lies in a fold of the hills, the lovely old church looking from its green slope upon the village's red roofs. The 12th century tower stands at the west end of the nave, opening to it by a Norman arch, and to the aisles by a low round arch and a high pointed one. The high arcades were built with the aisles in the 13th century. There are windows of the three mediaeval centuries, with a little old glass and a lovely modern picture of the Transfiguration. A Norman doorway is blocked in the north aisle, and the long chancel has a priest's doorway and some buttresses only a little younger. The vaulted north chapel, the font, a beautiful piscina, and a bracket in the south aisle are all mediaeval. So is the porch, sheltering the loveliest possession of this place—a recessed 13th century doorway with three shafts on each side and a mass of exquisite mouldings in the arch. There are a dozen bench-ends with 15th century tracery, four old stalls with heads and foliage carved on the misericord seats and arm-rests, and an old pulpit.

A rare relic is a stone carved with a small Crucifixion, the cross unusual for having double arms. It is thought to be over 700 years old, and was found at Cridling Park last century. Very curious is a stone gallery over the arch leading from the north aisle to the chapel;

it has an arcade of three arches on each side, and is reached by a winding stair in a turret. It may once have had some connection with a roodloft.

There are two ancient figures; a mediaeval lady lies in stone in an aisle, and a knight lies in chain armour as he probably wore it in one of our famous wars, for he is thought to be Sir Warin de Scargil, who fought at Bannockburn. A quaint tomb like a table has a border of fruit and flowers, and arms showing three horseshoes; it is to William Farrer of 1684.

Darton. Famous for its nails, this mining town near Barnsley has a church which comes chiefly from the 15th century, an inscription on a wall-plate telling us that by 1517 the monks of Monk Bretton had finished the rebuilding of the chancel. Crowned by a high tower outside, it is attractive within, where the light stone contrasts with the black timbering of the fine old roofs, their bosses carved with shields and heads, flowers and foliage. There are old screens and old rails, a rood stairway, a figure of Mary Magdalen among old glass fragments, and mediaeval gravestones with engraved crosses. Posing on his big wall-monument is John Silvester who lived at Birthwaite Hall, 18th century benefactor of Kexborough school.

Delph. The big village and the mills are in the deep hollow, looking up to the plain church a mile away at Friarmere. Built in the 18th century, and reached by a winding road, it is on a wind-swept height over 1000 feet above the sea, with the great hills all about. There is Castleshaw Moor with a Roman road which can still be traced, and a Roman camp where fragments of beautiful pottery and other treasures have come to light. The village still has interesting old weavers' cottages, as has the near-by village of Dobcross.

Denby Dale. It is a small place which would not particularly attract the eye of the passer-by, but here periodically since 1788 colossal pies have been baked. The first Denby Dale Pie was made in 1788 to commemorate George III's recovery from "mental affliction"; subsequently pies were made in Waterloo year, 1846, 1896 and 1928. The Great Jubilee Pie of 1887 went bad, and the immense job of accumulating ingredients and baking them had to be redone; the latest pie, of 1964, weighed over six tons.

Denholme. From its high place midway between Halifax and Keighley, this tiny town has a magnificent view of a moorland

77

world. In Foster Park is an old cross, and here too stands a soldier on a pedestal, reminding us of men who fell in the Great War. Built in 1846 in the style of the 13th century, the church looks from the hill to the grey cluster of houses and spinning mills on the other slope. It has a good tower and spire, and is surprisingly attractive within. The fine clerestoried nave has splendid arcades of clustered pillars and capitals with rich mouldings, and between their arches is a gallery of stone faces. Other pleasant faces of mediaeval people are in the arcaded walls of the chancel, and floral bosses enrich the vaulted roofs.

An evening's walk takes us over the hills and far away, for hereabouts we come upon the quarrymen's hamlet of Egypt.

Dent. A delectable place, famed in past times for its "terrible knitters" it is in the heart of one of Yorkshire's loveliest valleys, hemmed in on both sides by the moors and fells and mountain heights. It lies four miles from its railway station, which stands 1150 feet above the sea.

North of Dent (the valley which shares the name of the town) the long ridge of Rise Hill climbs up to 1825 feet. To the south are Yorkshire's second highest mountain (Whernside), and table-topped and torrent-scarred Dent Crag, and between them comes the Deepdale Beck to join the Dee. The splendid view from the top of the Crag, 2250 feet above the sea, embraces the Yorkshire fells, the valley of the Lune, and the Lakeland heights. Below the summit, on its southern side, is a great stone marking the spot where three counties meet, Lancashire, Westmorland, and Yorkshire.

Cars and pedestrians alike must squeeze their way through the village street, for it is narrow and crooked and has no pavements; but it is clean and bright and fascinating with white walls shining in the sun. At the wall of one of the houses is a curious fountain shaped from a solid block of Shap granite, set here in memory of Dent's greatest son, Adam Sedgwick, who was born at Dent in 1785. He was a scholar at the old grammar school still standing in the churchyard, but the only relic of his day is the master's chair. Afterwards he was the pupil of John Dawson, the Yorkshire surgeon and mathematician who had helped to bring him into the world, and he went on to become Professor of Geology at Cambridge, where his lectures inspired a new interest in the story of the rocks. A typical Dalesman with a fine, strong face, he was one of the pioneers of geology.

There is a marble tablet to him in the church where he was baptised, and where his father, brother, and nephew preached; and a brass inscription pays tribute to his great-nephew and namesake, Adam Sedgwick, Professor of Zoology at Cambridge in our own century.

The spacious church, in a churchyard with a fine view up and down the Dale, comes chiefly from 15th century rebuilding, and was restored in memory of the great geologist. The tower was made new at the close of the 18th century, and the clerestory is modern, but the two western pillars of the nave arcades are 13th century, and a doorway built up in the north wall is older still, its round arch under a hood. The two pillars without capitals in the arcades may once have supported a chancel arch. The pulpit is Jacobean, and an unused font has a tiny Jacobean cover; there are Jacobean pews in the aisles, and later box-pews. The modern roof has 13 beams with queen-posts, and the best glass has a fine medley of colour in portraits of St Nicholas, St Margaret, and St Hilda.

Half a mile below Dent is the hamlet of Gawthrop. Two miles up stream is the pretty waterfall known as Hell Cauldron, near Gib's Hall, which comes into Mary Howitt's *Hope on, Hope Ever*. Two miles farther up the Dale is the hamlet of Cowgill, where the Dee makes waterfalls by the wayside, and the Cowgill Beck comes down to two little bridges and a cluster of cottages among flowers. The small lancet church, dating from the early 19th century, stands by a charming old bridge, and all round is fine scenery. Higher up the dale still are the remains of the once renowned Stone House marble works.

Denton. A small secluded place on the lovely wooded hillside above the River Wharfe, it has a church buried among fine trees near the park gates, and a queer round stone from which the villagers used to draw water.

Built in 1776 as a private chapel, the church has a slender tower with a lantern top, the base serving as a porch, and in glass painted in 1700 by Henry Giles of York is a king playing a harp, cherubs about him.

From the beginning of the 16th century Denton was one of the homes of the Fairfaxes. Of the old house, burned down in 1734, fragments can still be seen near the house which took its place, looking out on a magnificent view of Ilkley Moor, and of the river hurrying through the valley. From the windows of the old house the Fairfaxes looked out on the park of 300 acres, where many of the old trees still stand. Here lived old Ferdinando Fairfax, who was a child in Elizabeth I's day and liked anything better than fighting, though he put a manly courage on at last and fought at Marston

Moor. Here in Armada year was born Henry Fairfax, educated by his scholarly uncle Brian Fairfax, a lifelong friend of George Herbert. When the Civil War broke out Henry was a parson at Newton Kyme near Tadcaster, and his house there was a refuge for many of his friends, Royalists and Roundheads alike. Sir Charles Fairfax walked by the green banks of the Wharfe about 1600; and another Charles, who was born in 1597, was a man of peace, loving his quiet home at Menston more than the din of war.

They were a scholarly family, and Thomas, who finished his busy days in 1640 after settling in the old house here in the first years of the Stuarts, was a fine English gentleman. He sleeps with his wife in Otley church. Most famous of all was another Thomas, who was born in the old home of the Fairfaxes in 1612, a very perfect knight who fought with his sword for the Parliament but loved old books.

It is a thousand pities that the old house and church have gone, but the hall we see, built about 1770 by Carr, is one of the noblest in Yorkshire, imposing outside with its fine stonework, its handsome terrace, and its perfect lawns, and inside beautiful with treasures of inestimable price. Here is china, silver, exquisite furniture, rooms gorgeously panelled, ceilings richly patterned. Some of the Fairfaxes may have admired the treasures which were once in the church —a 15th century screen, a carved chest, and rare old benches with tiny figures shaped 500 years ago. There is a stone mantelpiece with panels of the Madonna, an archbishop, and a monk, and in the spacious entrance hall is a lofty ceiling resting on massive columns.

Dewsbury. A busy town in a deep hollow of the Pennines, it appears in Domesday Book as the head of a parish covering 400 square miles. Long before then, it is said, Paulinus preached on this site to the Saxons, having come north from Kent with the daughter of Queen Bertha on her marriage to King Edwin.

The Town Hall, with an imposing tower, stands in the market-place. On the hillside west of the town is the fine Crow Nest Park of 70 acres, with lawns and ponds, flowers and avenues.

The churchyard, spacious with lawn and trees, has some walling with fragments from a mediaeval vicarage, and a 13th century door-way. East of the church lies the flat stone to Hannah Scott of 1812, who by some queer chance has her age set down as 814. Here every Christmas Eve the "Devil's Knell" is rung—the bell of the Parish church being tolled once for every year since Christ was born.

The church itself has changed so much that little of it is old. The tower and the north aisle were made new in the 18th century, the rest in the 19th, including the unusual oak arcades of the transepts.

Now it is a long, spacious place with nearly 30 arches, keeping its south arcade from the close of the 12th century, and the north arcade of the 13th century, charming with its pillars of delicate banded shafts detached from the central column. The chancel arch and the font are also 13th century. The roof beams of the nave have golden bosses.

There are stone screens and an iron one, a reading desk made of wood from the roof of the old chancel, a silver processional cross, and a splendid reredos extending across the east wall, with Our Lord and the Twelve Disciples over the altar and six saints each side. Two modern brass portraits are of Henry Tilson of 1655 (Chaplain to the Earl of Strafford) who died at Dewsbury; and Patrick Brontë, who preached here in his young days before going to Haworth.

Old glass and old stones are the great treasures of the church. The glass, in a north transept window, is chiefly 14th century, showing five coats-of-arms, headless figures of Thomas Becket and St Jude, three roundels apparently illustrating summer, autumn, and winter, and faded quarries with leaves and birds, snails, a porcupine, and a lion. One of a group of Norman coffin lids is exceptionally fine, a dragon on each side of its raised cross. Among the Saxon stones is part of a coped tomb. Others are parts of crosses, some carved with figures and lettering. A curious survival here from Luddite days is the firing each night of the "10 o'clock gun" in a local millyard: it used to let the millowner know that all was well, and is now used by Dewsbury folk to check their watches!

Dodworth. We came to this place in a drab mining area and found a man creating things of beauty in a converted barn. The work of the artist, Ashley Jackson, is well known in the North, for in lively water-colour he can make us see beauty not only in scenes of the Dales and moors of Yorkshire, but also in mining and industrial landscapes. The church dates from 1845 and is remarkable chiefly for its strange pinnacles.

Doncaster. It stands on the River Don, a busy town with little left to tell of its ancient story. There is evidence of settlement here in Roman times, and a well and some brick kilns were discovered in the suburbs as recently as 1954–5. The Romans called it Danum. Kings had a palace here before the Conqueror came, and the town was sacked more than once by the Danes. The charter granted to the citizens in 1194 by Richard Lionheart is still in existence. The town comes into Shakespeare, for here it was that Henry Bolingbroke swore he came to claim only his rightful estates from Richard

81

the Second, and the breaking of his oath brought Doncaster into history and gave it a place in Henry IV:

> *You swore to us,*
> *And you did swear that oath at Doncaster,*
> *That you did nothing purpose 'gainst the State.*

To Doncaster came our first Tudor princess, Henry VII's daughter Margaret, and here came the proud Cardinal Wolsey in a sadder hour, for he had fallen low and was a miserable man as he arrived by torchlight.

Doncaster is now the headquarters of the Northern Division of the National Coal Board, centre of the Yorkshire coalfield, which is the biggest in Britain. With a vast store of coal in the neighbourhood, and half a hundred industries, this market town is one of our commercial and manufacturing centres, notably among other things for butterscotch, iron foundries, and agricultural machines. It is best known for being the seat of the engineering works of the LNER, the birthplace of the Flying Scotsman type of locomotive, and, of course, for its races, which go back to 1703. Here the St Leger has been run longer than the Derby at Epsom, being first run in 1776.

We should come to it from Bawtry, the planes and the Dutch elms making a fine show. There are dignified houses of the 18th and 19th centuries, with bay windows and iron balconies, and crowning Hall Cross Hill is an 18th century pillar on a massive base, said to have some stones of a 13th century cross in memory of Ote de Tilli.

The town is rightly proud of its 18th century Mansion House, designed by James Paine. It has a handsome entrance, and a noble staircase with rich plasterwork and a beautiful hand-wrought iron balustrade. There is a splendid banqueting hall, and the reception room has much valuable furniture. The strong-room has a collection of plate, and the ballroom a gorgeous plaster ceiling and a beautiful fireplace. Among the fine portraits are those of the Marquis of Rockingham, Earl Fitzwilliam, Sir Frank Lockwood, and the Earl of Lonsdale. There is also a rare Parliament clock, made when Parliament taxed the small clocks in 1797.

The town has a fine new museum and art gallery, opened in 1964, with many good collections. There are fragments of Roman pottery and ornaments, Saxon spear-heads, and mediaeval pottery; one good collection is of birds of this county, another is of fossils and minerals. Of special interest are the fossil forms from the collieries round about, showing trees and ferns of 300 million years ago. That was the beginning of the coal. We see it as the miner hacks it for our fires, and what it becomes in the shape of dyes, saccharine, baking powder, and many other products. In the art section we found a good collection of modern pictures.

Doncaster's two notable churches are St George's (the parish church) and Christ Church, built over a century ago except for a later chancel. The best feature of Christ Church is the steeple, which has an eight-sided lantern of two stages on a square base. There is some Belgian glass.

The town's imposing landmark is the glorious central tower of St George's church, one of the highest of any parish church in England. Rising 170 feet above the lawns, with fine windows, canopied buttresses, and parapets with a great array of pinnacles, it is the crowning beauty of a beautiful church Sir Gilbert Scott raised on the foundations of one destroyed by fire in 1853. The mediaeval church was one of the finest in the West Riding; the new one is a worthy successor, a spacious place in the shape of a cross, adorned with rich parapets and pinnacles, and having long lines of clerestory windows, a fine vaulted porch, and a lovely doorway.

The dim light of stained glass fills the interior, the great west window showing a Jesse tree and the east window having wheel tracery. Lofty arches rest on clustered pillars, their capitals carved with strawberry, maple, buttercup, and vine. Below the clerestory are medallions of Old Testament kings and prophets. The four massive pillars of the tower are each 28 feet round and have elaborate capitals, and the stone pulpit is one of the biggest in Yorkshire. The Seaton chapel has a vaulted roof and a fine marble font, the chalice is Elizabethan, and a table top is made from the sounding board of the old pulpit. An inscription tells of William Pickering, a hero of the mines killed while leading a rescue party.

The organ was built by Edmund Schulze in 1862. One of the finest in England, it came too late for Edward Miller, the organist of the old church, who played here for over 50 years, wrote many tunes which are still sung, and was greatly admired by Southey. It was his proud boast that he discovered the young German musician who was afterwards organist at Halifax and was later to be known as William Herschel, discoverer of the planet Uranus.

Drax. It is a pleasant place among the cornfields and the meadows between the Ouse and the Aire. The Normans gave it a castle, a priory, and a church. The castle has vanished, and only a few stones are left where the priory stood near the Ouse, but the church we see is the Norman one, altered through the centuries.

The Norman tower has a 15th century top with a short ribbed spire. Its wide arch and the narrower one to the chancel are

Norman, and a massive Norman arcade (with zigzag on the arches and four-leaved flowers on two of the hoods) leads to the north aisle, which keeps a Norman window. The south arcade may be 700 years old, and both are leaning. On each side of the chancel arch is a square-headed opening, with another above it. The chancel itself is 13th century, charming with seven lancets in the side walls, a group of three and an oval window in the east wall, and an arch leading to the 14th century north chapel; the arch rests on dainty corbels of graceful foliage, the head of a man under one of them.

The striking feature of the church is the 15th century clerestory of the nave, like a continuous arcade with eight three-light windows each side, adorned outside with a great show of gargoyles and fine battlements. Under the windows inside is a fine sculpture gallery of saints and apostles, abbots, bishops and kings, relics of the priory.

The beautiful new roofs of the nave and aisles shine with gold and colour, the bosses in the nave carved with flowers and shields. The Tudor bench-ends in the nave are enriched with conventional ornament, and with such things as a pig playing bagpipes to a dancer, a kneeling figure upside down with a sheep's head above it, and a giant in a crown with three feathers, leading a boy by a chain. There are old glass fragments, a battered font and a modern copy of it, and an old coffin lid. Part of the old cross is in the churchyard.

A bigger school has grown out of the one founded here in 1667 by Charles Read, who made a fortune as a shipper. He founded others at Tuxford and Corby, a rule of them all being that the boys should take turns at sweeping out the schoolhouse every Saturday afternoon, or else be fined sixpence.

Drighlington. Busy with spinning and manufactures, it lies about the crossing of two highways, from Bradford to Wakefield and from Leeds to Halifax. One of the few old houses is Lumb Hall, with nursery gardens about it now; ivy grows on its stone walls with mullioned windows and gables, and the upper room of its porch is lit by a rose window.

People would probably look out of this window one June day in 1643 and see Lord Fairfax and his men riding over the hills to meet the Royalists from Wakefield. Hodgson lane is named after a Parliamentary captain who marshalled his men here and made a bold stand before being scattered. The battle was fought on Adwalton Moor, and the Roundheads had good reason to remember it, for of their 4000 men about 700 were slain.

One who suffered much in the unhappy days of the Civil War was James Margetson, who was born at Drighlington in 1600 and

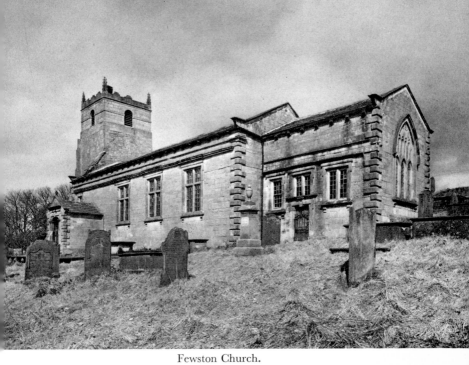

Fewston Church.

Fountains Abbey, from the west.

The Chapel of the Nine Altars, Fountains Abbey.

became Bishop of Armagh. The 19th century church has a massive tower, and its stone pulpit has a striking band of relief carving of scenes in the life of Paul. Another famous son of this village is J. L. Hammond, the economic historian, whose father was vicar here.

Earby. We should come to it from the east, over the moors, seeing a magnificent panorama of endless hills and fells and valleys. For long it was a village, near the Lancashire border; now it is a busy little cotton town. Its quaint 17th century grammar school has become a clinic, and the church of 1910, exceedingly lofty and light, is waiting for a north aisle and a tower. Its best thing is the stone pulpit, growing from a low stone screen. There is vine carving on the chapel screen and on the reredos, which has panels of linenfold.

East Ardsley. It has little that is old, and its green countryside is less beautiful since the ironworks came, but it remembers two notable sons. One was James Nayler, who came into the world the year Shakespeare went out. He fought for the Parliament, became a Quaker, and began preaching. His preaching was declared to be blasphemous, and after being whipped and pilloried in London he had his tongue bored and his forehead branded. He was then whipped again and imprisoned for two years, and in 1660 he was set upon by highwaymen who robbed him of his money and cudgelled him so that he died soon after.

The other man of note at East Ardsley was John Field, who was born here about 1520 and was the first man to make the discoveries of Copernicus known in England. He is said to have ended his days here a year before the Armada came, and to lie under the porch of the old church. The church he knew was rebuilt in 1881, but the restored doorway through which we come has a Norman arch and capitals, the arch enriched with two rows of zigzag with two beak-heads set in the top. The font and two carved chairs are 17th century and there is an old chest.

Ecclesfield. It lies by the city of steel, but looks out on a wooded countryside. In a lovely glen is Whitley Hall of Queen Elizabeth's day. In a house by the church are remains of the ancient priory.

Over the way is the memorial hall which brings to mind a lady whose name is still beloved by children and older folk, Mrs Gatty, and behind the church is the vicarage where the Gattys wrote their books. They were a wonderful couple, Alfred Gatty, vicar for 63 years, writing books on Sheffield, Margaret writing her famous

D

books for children and carrying on in spite of much suffering. She would write illuminated manuscripts on vellum in the old style of monks. She wrote on seaweeds and zoophytes and sundials, and took such interest in chloroform that she allowed herself to be chloroformed as an example to the parish.

But it is for her books for children, for her fairies and parables and legends and Aunt Judy's Tales, that she is most remembered.

It was Alexander Scott, her father, who sat up night after night by Lord Nelson's coffin as it lay in state at Greenwich. He was with him when he died and saw all the horror of the cockpit, with men dying about him in scores.

In the churchyard lies Joseph Hunter, who asked to be buried under a spreading willow. A Yorkshire historian, he began studying churches as a boy, copying epitaphs in the churchyard here. His monumental books on Yorkshire are greatly valued, and his marvellous collection of notes is treasured in the British Museum. America owes him a debt of gratitude for discovering the names of the Pilgrim Fathers who sailed in the *Mayflower*, and for showing that William Bradford and other settlers came from the neighbourhood of Scrooby and Austerfield. He died in London but lies where he longed to be, his beloved Yorkshire all about him.

The church where Alfred Gatty preached till he was 90 is the pride of Ecclesfield. Known as the Minster of the Moors, it is chiefly 15th century, a spacious and beautiful place with a score of arches, and a handsome tower begun in the 14th century. Fragments of the 13th century are a pillar at the west end of the north arcade, and part of an arch built into the porch, where is also an old beam with three carved bosses. There are mediaeval coffin lids, a fragment of a Saxon cross enriched with circles, and an old altar stone with five crosses. In a bright medley of old glass are shields and portraits, and in the old roofs of the aisles are bosses carved with faces. The fine array of old woodwork includes 15th century screens; stalls with 15 poppyheads of saints, angels, and the Madonna; and a chest. The lectern has two lovely figures, and the pulpit has scenes from the life of Christ.

Richard Scott of 1638 reclines in armour on his imposing marble monument. These are banners and bugles and swords of the Ecclesfield Volunteers of 1803, and a wooden cross from Flanders. Alfred Gatty has an inscription, and his wife's memorial window has scenes from her best-known book, *Parables from Nature*.

Edlington. The old village's grey walls, red roofs, dovecot, and rare little church are on a hill, and not far away are the lovely acres of Edlington Wood, where Lord Molesworth set up a monument to his favourite greyhound.

There is much Norman masonry in the nave, the base of the tower, and the chancel. The rest of the tower is 15th century. A Norman corbel table with heads and grotesques runs along the south side of the church, and another is seen inside, between the nave and aisle, which are divided by a 13th century arcade.

Three lovely fragments of the Norman church are a window with carved pillars and capitals and an arch of zigzag; a doorway within the ancient porch, with zigzag and beak-heads carved all round and a hood of medallions; and the arch to the chancel, its zigzag mouldings resting on short shafts set shoulder-high from the floor and crowned with capitals of leaves and band-work.

There is a little old glass, and old panelling in the pulpit and in some pews. The mediaeval chapel has a 15th century screen, and the font is Elizabethan.

Elland. There are mills in the valley, a park above the River Calder, Elland Hall of which only a little is old, and New Hall of which only a little is new. Now a farmhouse, New Hall has timbered gables, a rose window, a studded Tudor door, and a porch.

Standing high in the narrow streets of the old part of the town, the church is chiefly 15th century, with a chancel arch probably 13th. It has a sanctus bellcot, a tower with two arches in line with the nave arcades, and beautiful modern woodwork. The chancel screen, gleaming with gold, has a cornice with three rows of carving, and is in memory of Ernest Winter who died in the church. The sanctuary has a fine low screen, and in the rich dark oak panelling round its walls (with coloured and gilded cresting) are two seats. The font is old, and there are old beams in the roofs. Old glass is the treasure here. The west windows of the aisles are filled with a medley of it, and among much that is modern in the east window are old pictures of the Resurrection, the Ascension, and Pentecost; the Annunciation, the Visitation, the Nativity, with Joachim and Anna. The disappearance, in 1966, of Grace Ramsden's school ended an unique chapter in Elland history—the school was founded in 1734 for poor boys. The Fleece Inn in Westgate is a fine old building thought to be Elizabethan.

Elslack. Near the Earby Beck flowing to the River Aire, it is a quiet spot among the hills. There are trim grass verges and wayside flowers, and the small group of houses and farms are by a tiny green. One of the farms is the old hall. Here is the site of a Roman camp, excavated in 1908, and traces still remain of the Roman road from Ilkley to Ribchester in Lancashire. If we come over the heather moors by Standrise Plantation (where there is the site of another camp) we have what must be one of the most glorious views in the county.

Emley. Now dominated by the TV mast on Jagger Hill, it is a grey village on a lofty plain near Flockton Moor, which has remains of a mediaeval market cross, and a church seen from afar with a high tower over 400 years old. Over a piscina in the nave is a rather battered Norman tympanum carved with a dragon and a holy lamb with a cross. The nave and the porch have old roofs, the pulpit has an inlaid sounding board, there are two old chests, and the old font is like a fluted egg-cup. A fine brass candelabra for 24 lights is one of the biggest we know.

In the old glass filling the east window are shields of arms, a Crucifixion, and kneeling figures of a man and his wife and two knights. Another window has an old panel with St George and an angel in a medley.

There are 17th century graves, and in the porch is a photostat of a charter granted in 1253 to Sir Thomas Fitzwilliam, Lord of the Manor of Emmeley.

In the churchyard wall are fragments of the old school, and a stone saying:

> *If fortune keep thee warm*
> *Thy friends about thee swarm*
> *Like bees about a honey-pot;*
> *But if she frown*
> *And cast thee down:*
> Lie there and rot.

Esholt. It hides in the Aire valley, an enchanting spot reached from Shipley by a road winding with the river. A pretty village group is the 16th century Old Hall (now a farmhouse), the century-old church, and the vicarage, which has from its lovely garden a fine view of Baildon on the hill. The church is on the edge of a tree-bowered bank where a stream flows through a charming glen, bounding the churchyard by the Nuns Walk. A small nunnery stood where the 18th century hall now stands in its park of 100 acres, and a cellar of the ancient place remains.

The neat village memorial hall was built by village men. The church has a panel of old glass with a figure of Paul, and a pulpit with three panels carved by an Italian craftsman 400 years ago, one showing the Madonna and Child.

Farnham. Its fine little church, on a high bank, has a magnificent Norman chancel. The nave, not so high and not so wide as the chancel, is the work of the builders who followed. Between the western arches the 15th century tower stands oddly detached, resting on three massive, narrow arches and climbing through the nave roof. Entered by a modern arch, the ancient chancel is like a lantern, with nine Norman windows in wide splays, framed by continuous arcading. Over the three arches in the east wall are two smaller original windows, and a mediaeval window has old fragments of glass. A piscina in the north aisle may be over 700 years old. A curiosity here is a large barrel organ, given in 1831, which has three barrels each playing nine psalms.

Farnley. It has a house John Ruskin fell in love with, and we do not wonder, for he found it full of his beloved Turners. Standing in a park of 200 acres, Farnley Hall is finely set among grand old trees and beautiful gardens, and from its terrace the view looks far down Wharfedale, with the river shining below the moors. Here the hall is everything, for there is nothing else but the 17th century stone lodge where the gate opens to a shaded pool by a pretty row of cottages with clematis and roses creeping over them. A little farther along the road we have a view of the great house which, though partly 18th century, has much remaining from Tudor days. There is a spacious room with a Tudor chimneypiece said to have been made from a four-poster bed in which slept our first Stuart king, and a dining-room with 80 hunting scenes in its panels, and with an oak mantelpiece on which are figures of Adam and Eve, Cain and Abel, Abraham and Isaac. Part of the hall has now been converted into flats.

Among the treasures that have long been kept at the hall are Cromwell's watch and sword, and the broad-brimmed hat he wore at Marston Moor; a table at which he dined, a pair of brass candlesticks belonging to Sir Thomas Fairfax, and a letter from Charles Stuart asking Thomas Fawkes for a loan of £13.

It was a descendant of Thomas Fawkes who brought Turner to the hall; he was one of the few men the artist really loved, and for 17 years Farnley was his second home. He would stand by the window or walk on the terraces for hours together, watching the changing sky and the light and shade in the valley. It was after gazing on this scene that he painted his picture of Hannibal crossing the Alps. Turner came for the first time to Farnley in 1797, and his friendship with Squire Fawkes lasted till the squire died in 1825. Once the artist strode into Farnley Hall straight back from the

Rhine, where he had been for a month. He fumbled for a moment in the tail pocket of his coat and pulled out a roll of paper, tied with a shabby piece of string, with 51 drawings. It was the beginning of the squire's collection of Turners, which were the treasure of this great house for over 100 years. In less than five months Fawkes had offered to buy them all, and the delighted artist turned on his heel, marched down to the nearest shop, bought some brown paper, and mounted the sketches. The squire paid him £500 for them, and by the time he died his collection of Turners numbered 200, for which he had paid about £3000. In another 70 years about 50 of them were sent to Christie's and sold for £20,000.

Farsley. A small town with a workaday air, busy with spinning and making cloth, it has several things to remind us of one of its sons who won fame.

Its famous son was Samuel Marsden, born here in 1764. His house has gone, but on the lawn where it stood is a wall tablet with his portrait in bronze. He was the first missionary to the Maoris, and he landed in the Bay of Islands, New Zealand, and preached the first sermon ever heard there, on Christmas Day in 1814. He is remembered, however, not as a missionary but as the first man to bring New Zealand wool to England, the first cargo being stored in a warehouse at Farsley and manufactured into cloth at Rawdon. The inscription here tells us how George III gave him five Spanish sheep to take back with him, after visiting London in 1807, and even this far-seeing wool-gatherer can never have dreamed that this was the beginning of the vast trade which sprang up between Australasia with its great sheep farms and the Yorkshire woollen mills. There is an obelisk in the churchyard in memory of him, and a window in the 19th century church. The richly carved oak pulpit, with canopied figures of disciples and prophets, is in memory of a vicar for 45 years. The chancel is panelled with linenfold and the reredos, with folding doors and rich tracery, has a fine copy of an Old Master's Descent from the Cross.

Featherstone. The old village is on the hilltop, its pleasantest bit where the church stands near a wood, looking down on the colliery's great slag-heaps. Reached by a path charming with flowers, it is long, low, and embattled, and has a stone-ribbed porch leading to the attractive interior with golden-tinted walls. Some of it has stood about 400 years, but much of the walling outside and many of the windows are new. The tower is much restored, but its arch is mediaeval. Like the nave, the charming chancel has an arcade of three bays, and its splendid old roof has bosses gleaming with colour and gold, some floral, some with quaint heads, one with three faces. The font, said to have been brought from Pontefract in the Civil War, has the name and arms of John de Baghill. Sleeping in the church are many Fairfaxes, and Langdale Sunderland, who raised a company of soldiers for Charles and was heavily fined by Cromwell. He lived at Ackton Hall within a mile of the church, the old home of the Featherstones, now past its great days.

Felkirk. The old church and the small Tudor schoolhouse are companions in the churchyard, looking over fields to mountainous slag-heaps and smoking pits. Much of the church is 13th century, but in the 15th the fine tower and the north aisle with its arcade were largely rebuilt. A little later the chapels were added and some of the windows made new. Carved stones in the tower walls tell of the Norman church, and its arresting arch into the nave has the old Norman clusters of shafts and richly carved capitals. A pillar in the north arcade has the original 13th century capital under one 200 years younger, and in the south aisle wall is the head of a Norman window. The stout little ribbed porch has a 700-year-old entrance, and is a fine shelter for a doorway as old as itself. The font is ancient, there is a chained Prayer Book, a stone coffin is under the tower, there are old roof beams, and in a seat by the door is old inlaid panelling with carved borders. A battered fragment is all that is left of an old stone knight.

Ferrybridge. Here was a ford in Norman times and a bridge when the wearers of Red and White Roses fought close by on the eve of the Battle of Towton. In that skirmish John de Clifford, called the Butcher, was killed. Here, riding to his doom, Cardinal Wolsey dismounted by a cross on the green and confirmed 200 children. There is an inn where 30 coaches would draw up in a day in the 18th and 19th centuries, and on a hill is a windmill that has lost its sails. A ceaseless stream of traffic pours over the stone bridge across the Aire, and the electric power station close by becomes an impressive mass when floodlit at night. Then this bridge corner is a fascinating picture, glowing with red light reflected in the dark river.

Lonely and forlorn, the church stands on the edge of the marshes, compassed about with the railway and the network of wires of the great transformer. It is a lowly place of the 12th century, with an aisle and chapel added perhaps in the 15th, when the chancel and its arch were made new. The tower has a plain Norman arch and

13th century lancets, and a few other windows are old. The curious font, with vertical lines cut on the bowl, may be 800 years old, and we come and go by a doorway only a century younger.

A fine company of people gathered in the church one day in 1885, for Lord Houghton was being laid to rest in the churchyard. He had died at his great house Fryston Park, which has since vanished. There he gathered about him a host of friends, artists, poets, authors, scientists, for he knew everybody, and everybody liked him.

Born in Mayfair as Richard Monckton Milnes, he became a popular speaker at the Cambridge Union, travelled much in Europe, and was back in London at 26, a welcome figure in society, and a frequent guest at Samuel Rogers's breakfast parties. He went into Parliament as a Conservative but soon joined the Liberals, and took a deep interest in the rise of Liberalism on the Continent. Carlyle came to vist him at Fryston, and so did Lord Palmerston, who made him a peer. He represented the Royal Geographical Society at the opening of the Suez Canal.

Fewston. Deeply wooded hills and purple moors enfold this hillside village, its setting made more lovely still by two great reservoirs like beautiful lakes filled by the River Washburn to give water to Leeds: the valley is much beloved by local walkers.

Across the Swinsty Reservoir we see Swinsty Hall buried in trees. Sheltering together are the vicarage and the church, which was rebuilt in 1697 after an adventurous career. The east window and the greater part of the tower belong to a 15th century church which was burned down after replacing a Norman one also destroyed by fire. It is attractive outside with its bold windows and moulded cornices, and a quaint porch reached by a three-sided flight of steps, and has a mediaeval font with a Jacobean cover.

Christopher Ramshaw was vicar here from 1790 till 1844, and here sleeps Edward Fairfax, who died in 1635, little dreaming that his house and garden were to be drowned in a reservoir. A notable poet, he published a translation of Tasso which Dryden praised, and a book on witchcraft which is one of the most curious volumes in our literature.

Fishlake. Old windmills and willows, dykes and a network of waterways, make up this village of the lowlands. Three centuries ago Cornelius Vermuyden, the Dutchman, was brought over to reclaim the marshes of this countryside, but the people would have none of him, and the great scheme he began was not finished till long after his day.

On a bank of the River Don, it has cottages decked with roses, remains of old crosses, an old vicarage, and a lovely grey church rising above the rich red pantiles of the roofs. It has one of the finest doorways in England.

Built by the Normans and refashioned in the three mediaeval centuries, the church has splendid 15th century work to show in the high tower (with strange gargoyles looking down and a statue of St Cuthbert over the west window), and in the fine clerestory of the nave and chancel, adorned with heads of men and women, a king and a bishop by the windows. The chancel has 14th century windows and a Norman one; and the east window has seven lights. There are a few fragments of old glass, the rest of the windows allowing the light to stream through unhindered. From the 13th century come the nave arcades, with pointed arches on round pillars, and the pointed chancel arch with rich mouldings.

The lofty tower arch reaches the nave roof, one of the simple old roofs remaining everywhere here. There are 15th century screens, a 14th century font with eight canopied statues and a Jacobean cover with a dove, an old chest, and part of a pew made in the year Shakespeare died. A curious notice in the belfry forbids anyone to ring the bells (one of the finest peals for miles round) in hat or spurs.

There are 17th century gravestones, and an inscription to Thomas Simpson of 1740 in a frame with foliage, cross-bones, a chalice, a skull, a face, and a dove. The figure brasses are gone from the tomb of Robert Marshall, a vicar who died in 1505, but its sides are enriched with inscriptions and symbols, among them a chalice and paten, bells, books, skulls, and a balance.

There are two old porches. The south porch (with a modern front) shelters the architectural glory of this place, a Norman doorway projecting from the wall in great splendour. Its arch is of four orders, resting on shafts at each side with capitals of foliage in which we see dragons fighting, knights tilting, a monk rowing, a griffin, an angel, and a demon. The inner side of the arch has formal carving, including honeysuckle pattern, which comes again in the second order with an array of 35 grotesque heads and two figures. Then come a hunting scene, men carrying a coffin, a demon with a rake, and a canopied figure holding a staff. On the outside of the arch are many roundels with figures in scenes almost worn away. The door for which all this is so beautiful a frame has worn carving of stars and leaves and band-work, and looks old enough to be Norman too. We understand that it was brought from Roche Abbey.

Flockton. On the hillside rising to Flockton Moor, it has a view far over the Pennines, an attractive inn with timbers 400 years old and two pokers chained to the floor, and a simple church made new last century. Low stone pillars support its brick arches, the tall screen is painted in mediaeval colours, and the pulpit has paintings of Gabriel and Mary. On the road to Emley is Kirkby Hall, a gabled house of the 17th century, now a farmhouse.

Fountains Abbey. It is unsurpassed in loveliness among all the ruins of England, and no ruined abbey surpasses it in the completeness of its survival. In Yorkshire, which has the biggest number and the finest examples of monastic ruins in any county, Fountains is approached only by Kirkstall. These two Cistercian houses are without compare. Here the scene of enchantment is in the narrow wooded valley of the little River Skell. It is now possible to experience Fountains in quite a new way, for occasionally evening "Son et Lumière" performances are arranged.

Fountains was a wilderness in those early years of the 12th century when Archbishop Thurstan gave the site to a band of 12 Benedictine monks who with their prior had left the Abbey of St Mary's in York to live under the severe rule of the Cistercians. For two years they endured privation, with little more than trees for shelter, bread for food, and the river water to drink. From this simple foundation by 12 poor monks grew the mighty abbey which Marmaduke Bradley surrendered to the insatiable greed of Henry VIII.

It is an unforgettable experience to approach the abbey through the park of Studley Royal, glorious with avenues of limes and beeches, then through the pleasure grounds, laid out in the 18th century by John Aislabie, by the river, with temples and statues and lakes. One delightful spot is called Surprise View because here we see an incomparable picture of the ruins reflected in the water, and Robin Hood's Well in the mediaeval arch of a recess 700 years old.

This approach to Fountains brings us to the remains of the gatehouse by way of the abbey mill and a lovely bridge across the river. The gatehouse is 12th century, the mill and bridge 13th. Tradition says that the old yews above the mill gave the monks their first shelter.

As we reach the gatehouse the ruins spread before us beyond a broad green expanse, the west front of the church facing us with its great window, the lordly tower, 168 feet high, rising at the northern end of the transept. The tower, the most striking feature of the ruins as we come to them, was new when the rest of the abbey was old, for it was built by Abbot Huby in Tudor days and almost all else comes from between the years 1134 and 1247. Opening from the transept with a mighty arch, the tower has bands of inscriptions with shields; the buttresses are enriched with niches and leafy gables; and there is a statue thought to be of Abbot Huby himself.

The walls of the magnificent church and the splendid buildings round the cloister are still standing, and east and west are scanty remains of groups of buildings, some of which were erected astride the river, which the monks made to run through four parallel tunnels. The church has the shape of a cross 370 feet long, with a central transept of 150 feet, and a wonderful chapel at the east end forming another transept of equal length. Most of the windows in the clerestoried nave and transept are round. The great west window (now only a frame), was built by Abbot Darnton, whose emblem and the date 1494 are between the window and a headless statue of the Madonna. Below the window is a weathered Norman doorway. The Galilee once extended right across this west front, and a fragment of its lovely arcade has been rebuilt with the old materials. It was a place of burial, and has fragments of stone coffins and lids.

Entering by the west doorway, we are held spellbound by the spectacle of this impressive place, the vista of 370 feet ending with the great 15th century east window 60 feet high. The nave arcades are like an avenue of stone, the pointed arches resting on pillars which look as if the 12th century builders meant them to stand for all time; they are 23 feet high, and all these years of wind and rain have failed to bring one down. The narrow aisles, like corridors, are still spanned by the Norman arches which divided the vanished vaulting into bays.

The building of the presbytery and its chapel was completed in the first half of the 13th century, in the time of three abbots named John—John of York, John Pherd, and John of Kent who gave it its crowning glory, the chapel. The presbytery has only a few traces of its arcades, but the walls of its aisles still stand, and below their lancets, set in rich frames, is fine trefoiled arcading. A stone coffin nine feet long was probably the resting-place of Henry, Lord Percy, buried here in the 14th century.

The chapel must have been a peerless place seven centuries ago, with vaulting for its roof instead of the open sky. Lighted chiefly by exquisite lancets, it is divided into three compartments by soaring arches resting on slender pillars. Its name, the Chapel of the Nine Altars, is not misleading, for there were walls dividing the chapel into nine compartments, each with an altar; the bases of seven altars remain. The most graceful feature of the ruins, this chapel is famous as one of only two transepts at the east end of an English church, the other being at Durham.

The cloister itself has gone, but its site, a square of 120 feet, is a charming picture with a fine cedar shading the lawn, on which is a great stone trough probably brought from the cellarium. The buildings round the cloister are almost entirely from the 12th century, some of the work being as the Normans built, and some showing the changing of Norman style to English.

Separated from the south transept by a vaulted passage, and entered from the east side of the cloister by three lovely Norman arches, is the chapter house, a striking apartment 84 feet long and half as wide, with traces of the arcades which divided it into nave and aisles, and of three tiers of stone seats. About a score of the abbots were buried here, and there are still many gravestones and a stone coffin. On the south of the chapter house is the parlour, a fine room in which the monks were allowed to talk. Above this eastern range was the dormitory, and here still is the grand flight of steps by which they entered the cloister.

As was usual in a Cistercian house, the kitchen, the refectory, and the warming-house are on the south of the cloister, the refectory between the smaller rooms, and extending in length from north to south. The small kitchen has fireplaces and a hatch for serving food, and there are fireplaces in the warming-house, a fine chamber vaulted from a central pillar. Above the warming-house is another vaulted room with a central pillar. Entered from the cloister by a beautiful Norman doorway, the refectory is a noble apartment, 109 feet long and 46 wide, lighted by lancet windows, and keeping on its west wall a bracket like a lily, which once supported a stone lectern where one of the monks read to the brethren at meals. There were once lofty marble pillars down the middle of this room.

But not yet is the wonder of this mighty monument exhausted for us. On the west side of the cloister, extending southward over the river, is the cellarium, one of the remarkable survivals of the 12th and 13th centuries. There is no sight in all England like these two vast tunnels side by side, 300 feet long. With its earth floor, and its long line of 19 central pillars from which the ribs of the vaulting spread like the branches of a mighty tree and dip to the ground on both sides, this immense hall, lighted by small windows, is something we can hardly forget once we have seen it. Among all our ruins is no vista of ancient arches to equal it. Massive enough to shelter a battalion, it was built in three compartments, of which one may have been a refectory. To the west of the cellarium are remains of an infirmary built over the river, which is crossed here by a 12th century bridge, and there are remains of the guest houses beyond the bridge.

East of the cloister buildings are traces of what was once a splendid group of buildings erected over the river, consisting of the infirmary hall, its cellar, its chapel, and its kitchen. Built by John of Kent, this 13th century hall was a magnificent chamber 171 feet long and 70 wide, like a church with two long arcades dividing it into nave and aisles. Now there is little more than foundations.

A small museum containing a model reconstruction of the abbey and fragments of mediaeval pottery and other objects, has been established recently in the grounds of the abbey itself.

Retracing our way to the gatehouse, it is only a step from Norman and mediaeval England to Stuart England, for here stands the lovely Fountains Hall built by Sir Stephen Proctor in 1611. He is said to have used the stone of the old infirmary buildings for this wonderful many-windowed house. With projecting wings and towers, battlements and gables, it is Jacobean without and within, where the furniture is true to its time. The doorway, between pairs of pillars and with a sundial over it, is ornamented with stone figures, and the balustraded balcony is enriched with a company of stone knights in armour. The spacious banqueting hall has a minstrel gallery, a grand old door, a big fireplace, and much beautiful furniture—old pewter, a pair of iron candelabra, an Italian chest with half a dozen portraits in panels, and on a curious writing desk (perhaps in the abbey 500 years ago) a pair of iron candlesticks in the shape of women wearing what look like Welsh hats, both women holding torches. There is a bedroom with a secret panel, an Elizabethan bed inlaid with ebony, a door which has its curious cat-hole with a sliding panel, and a gorgeous drawing-room. In one of the windows are 60 shields, and among the treasures of the house are rare tapestries, a portrait of Edward VI, and a remarkable Italian table supported by cherubs. A huge stone fireplace has a sculptured panel showing a quaint Judgment of Solomon, two soldiers holding the living child, Solomon on a throne like a swing.

The house has original documents and books from the time the monks were at the abbey, gargoyles, and carved stones. There are panels with saints, and one with a rare treatment of the Annunciation, the angel kneeling by St Mary. There are coins found during excavation, old glass, fragments of an alabaster reredos, and one of the old earthen jars which were placed in the church to amplify sound, the first loudspeakers. We may see the deed conveying the estate to Sir Stephen Proctor, and, more precious still, the actual foundation charter of Fountains, a scrap of paper which may be described as the beginning of one of the loveliest sights that have come down to us from our wondrous past.

Fountains Abbey and the Studley Royal Estates were purchased by the West Riding County Council in 1966 and the Abbey is now in the care of the Ministry of Public Buildings and Works.

Frickley-with-Clayton. A surprising spot where the industrial world might be far away, it has a lonely church embowered in trees, standing in a field a mile from Clayton. The small tower with a stumpy spire may be 500 years old, and one of its gargoyles has two figures holding hands. The north aisle and arcade are chiefly 13th century, a chapel may be 15th, the west wall is old, and the fine Norman chancel arch has short shafts set high from the floor. The rest of this quaint and trim little place was made new in 1875. The arresting thing inside is the organ, overhanging the west wall and gleaming with blue and gold. It makes a fine vaulted frame for the doorway to the tower, and its pinnacled canopies almost reach the roof. The organ was a tribute from the lord of the manor (living at Frickley Hall in the fine park) to the memory of his father, who died in 1925. The father's portrait plaque is in the church. The font in the quaint baptistery may be 600 years old, and in the north chapel is an old altar stone.

Gargrave. Road and river and the long green are side by side in this big busy village of cotton mills, pleasantly set in Craven. The War Memorial cross is facing the bridge which takes us over the Aire to the church. It was made new in 1852 except for the tower, which is over 400 years old and rests on three stout arches. Remains of earlier days are in the north porch—a small coffin lid with a sword carved on the edge, and a fragment of a Saxon cross. Some of the glass is by Capronnier, the east window having an unusual Crucifixion scene with the thieves, the women, and St John. The reredos is a triptych with ten coloured saints, and fine modern carving is in the chancel screen and on the font cover. The pulpit was restored in memory of Charles Marsden, who was vicar for 57 years last century.

The road to Rylstone and a stream flowing to the Aire run through the great park of Eshton Hall, a stately house (rebuilt last century) with stone walls and a domed tower, looking from its lovely mantle of trees to the great mass of Flasby Fell, with Sharp Haw rising 1171 feet. Not far away is the site of a Roman villa.

Garsdale. Road and river are close companions in this steep mountain valley of the Clough, winding in and out. On the north side of the valley is the long mass of Baugh Fell, with lakes on its summit 2100 feet above the sea; on the other side the long ridge of Rise Hill climbs over 1800 feet at Aye Gill Pike. Near a fine waterfall, almost in the middle of the dale, two yews make an arch to the bellcot church.

The country round is a wild and lonely bit of England. Eastward is Mossdale Moor where rare plants and lichens are found. On the northern slope of Widdale Fell, the noble mountain ridge with Knoutberry Hill 2203 feet high, are Mossdale's beautiful waterfalls. Three miles north of Hawes Junction the rapid waters of the infant River Eden rush down Hell Gill (a deep narrow cleft in the limestone), forming the boundary between Yorkshire and Westmorland and crossed by an old packhorse road.

John Dawson, born at Raygill here in 1734, taught himself mathematics and went on to become a famous teacher of the subject.

Giggleswick. With its famous school and its famous well, the old church, houses piled one above another, and a bridge over the Ribble separating it from Settle, grey old Giggleswick is one of Craven's fascinating villages.

Its setting amid mountain scenery is superb. Ingleborough rises only eight miles away, and Pen-y-Ghent nearer still; and high above the road to Clapham (Buckham Brow) are the lofty limestone scars marking the line of the Craven Fault. At the top of the cliff is a cairn of stones built by the boys of Giggleswick School; there are caves in the cliff face, and at the foot (a mile from the village) is the curious Ebbing and Flowing Well, its picturesque stone trough by the wayside shaded by sycamores. Sometimes the water sinks and does not rise for an hour; sometimes it will sink and rise in less than ten minutes.

The clear stream by the well runs to the village in company with yews and sycamores and ferns. A road crosses it by the low bridge near the church, and a tiny footbridge of a single stone spans it by the gates of a fine house among the trees. The stocks, the splendid cross, and the tithe barn are still near the church, and there are delightful old houses, an inn where George Fox was a prisoner in 1665, and the home of Ann Bankes, who married Pepys's cousin Roger.

Tucked into the hillside are the fine modern buildings of Giggleswick School, one of the most famous in the North. It was founded as a grammar school in the time of Edward VI, but of the original school (founded earlier in the 16th century by Sir James Carr) there is still preserved the inscribed stone which was set above its doorway.

The fine library was built in memory of Old Boys who fell in the Great War.

From the great spur of rock on which it is built, the wonderful school chapel looks down on the rest of the school and the village, and has a magnificent panorama of the mountainous countryside. The gift of Walter Morrison, the millionaire of Malham Tarn, it is like a mosque with its great copper dome over the crossing, and is extremely rich within. The furniture is of cedar wood. There are bronze statues of Edward VI and Victoria, and mosaics of angels. In the windows are fine portraits of great men, including William Paley, an old boy of the school and author of the famous book on Evidences of Christianity. His father, headmaster here for 54 years, sleeps in the parish church.

Entered by a lychgate, the churchyard has the fragment of an old cross shaft, and a flagged path with a stone bearing an inscription to a wife of 13 years. The church is almost entirely 15th century, though the roofs are new, and has a west tower at the end of a continuous nave and chancel, separated from narrow aisles by tall arcades under tiny clerestory windows. We enter through an old studded door with rough planks and strap hinges. There are old altar rails, a splendid pulpit of 1680 with carved panels, an almsbox of 1684, and an extraordinarily big reading-desk (perhaps as old as the church) with carvings of the ensigns of the Twelve Sons of Jacob and a quaint inscription.

Other things to be seen are the mediaeval font, an old piscina, and old coffin lids, one having two crosses, shears, and a sword. Curious possessions are two painted drums and an old bass fiddle. There is a lovely silver altar cup made the year Elizabeth I was crowned, and a silver chalice of our time has for the stem a soldier with a lily and a sheaf of laurels. One of the scenes in the west window is of the martyrdom of Princess Alkelda, to whom the church is dedicated; she is believed to have been a Saxon saint who was strangled for her faith.

The battered knight in the north aisle is thought to be Sir Richard Tempest who fought at Towton and is said to have been buried here in 1488 with the head of his favourite horse beside him. The two headless figures of women by the tower are believed to be his wives. Dr George Birkbeck of 1841, founder of our Mechanics Institutes, has a memorial with his portrait plaque.

The eyes of the world were turned on Giggleswick for an hour in 1927 when it became the Mecca of thousands of pilgrims. To this small place came folk to see the eclipse of the sun, and to stand in the great shadow as it swept across the world.

There lies here the remarkable Richard Frankland, who was born at Rathmell near by in 1630. He was an energetic Nonconformist, the first man to be attacked for his Nonconformity after the Restoration, and the first man to arrange a Nonconformist ordination in Yorkshire.

Gisburn. A noble avenue of old beeches and limes leads to the great house in Gisburn's fine park of 150 acres, bounded on one side by the River Ribble and the Stock Beck, which here join forces. The tiny town has wide streets and cobbled ways, 17th century houses, an inn with 1635 over the porch, and a church with something left of Norman days. There are Norman windows and a Norman arch in the sturdy low tower, but its belfry windows and battlements are 14th century. On the east wall of the chancel is an original flat buttress, and at the east end of its north arcade is part of a Norman arch. The arcades of the nave and chancel are a striking array, an extraordinary feature being the two massive round pillars (which seem to be Norman) serving each as a support for four arches. The old porch shelters a mediaeval doorway. There are a few old pews, and restored screenwork of about 1500. In the glowing medley of old glass in the south chapel are three angels holding shields, and a St Andrew's cross; it is probably 15th century. In a window of the north aisle is a big figure of a weeping saint in a blue and gold robe, unusual and striking.

Glass Houghton. Mountainous slag-heaps of collieries and iron-works are about this place, whose name tells of the fame which came to it because of its sand and limestone, used in making glass. In the 20th century church is a font with a bowl like a Dutch cheese, brought from Castleford. It may be 12th century.

Golcar. It looks across the valley of the Colne and up to the great hills and moors. Some of its houses are in a deep hollow, some perched on the heights where stands the church of 1829. Below the tower is a stone hurled from the spire by a lightning flash in 1835.

Goldsborough. The River Nidd makes a winding loop between Knaresborough and this village, where trim stone houses and cottages and farms are clustered near the great house and the church. It is these we come to see.

One of the royal homes of England, the house has been here since Elizabethan days. We have charming peeps of it through archways to the courtyards, and may see it well from the churchyard. The high walls of mellowed brick, splashed with creeper, have many gables and oriels looking on to lawns and terraces. Inside are a handsome oak staircase, a richly panelled library, a room with a plaster frieze and a ceiling ornamented with birds and foliage, and a stone fireplace with panels showing Abraham and Isaac, Cain and Abel. The home of generations of Lascelles, it is now a school.

The church is Norman and mediaeval, and was restored last century. From Norman days come the masonry of the nave and the south doorway enriched with zigzag and beak-heads. The chancel shows the passing of the 13th century style, though the sedilia and double piscina are copies of the old ones. The south arcade, with leafy capitals, is 600 years old, and the leaning north arcade, with tall frail pillars, was made new 50 years later. The tower, with a vaulted roof and a stout arch, is over 500 years old, and one of its bells was made just before Agincourt, while another was about 200 years old when it was remade on the eve of the Spanish Armada. At the modern font under the tower were baptised two grandsons of George V, the King and Queen Mary looking on.

The north porch shelters an old stoup and a tiny coffin lid with a fleur-de-lis cross, and the 15th century east window of the south aisle has shields and crests in 17th century glass. Most striking are the black and white roofs of the nave and chancel with their mass of open timbering, the chancel having over 30 ribs. In a 14th century recess of the chancel lies a splendid stone knight in chain mail, with helmet, sword, and shield; he wears a surcoat, and his elaborate belt has lion heads. On an arcaded tomb lies another fine knight in armour, he too with a sword, a lion at his feet. Both knights have crossed legs, and may represent Robert de Goldsborough of 1308 and probably his son. Under a panelled arch of the nave is a tomb with names of six sons and seven daughters, thought to be that of Sir Richard Goldsborough. Robert Byerley's huge wall-monument, with medallion portraits of the family and figures of Faith and Charity, was the work of Joseph Wilton, sculptor to George III and an original member of the Royal Academy. Sleeping here is George Crackenthorpe whose 62 years as rector ended in 1534. Resting on steps in the churchyard is a big hollowed stone believed to be the base of an ancient cross.

Goldthorpe. Lord Halifax has given this mining village a big concrete church in Italian style, effective in the distance with its campanile crowned with a clock. Its treasure is a fine old pulpit carved with cherubs, foliage, and figures of the Four Evangelists.

Gomersal. It has a 19th century church with a tower rising among the woollen mills and the old houses which were here when Charlotte Brontë came to see Red House, still a charming place with low creepered walls and a rustic arch shading a gate, all much as it would be when Charlotte wrote of it in *Jane Eyre* as Briarmains and immortalised it as the home of Hiram Yorke.

Goole. It is part of a flat countryside where dykes and canals, windmills and willows, are everyday things; it stands where the Ouse is met by the Don, known on its journey between Snaith and Goole as the Dutch River, a cutting begun in Charles I's day for draining the marshes of Hatfield Chase, now 70,000 acres of fertile land. Though it makes paper and has engineering, chemical, and other works, Goole looks to the sea for most of its living.

In less than a century it has become a notable port. England's farthest port inland, 50 miles from sea. Its liveliest scenes are on the water front, where ships from far and near come up on the tide to enter the fine docks which were opened in 1826; funnels and masts, cranes and warehouses, making a ragged skyline, with the tall spire of the 19th century church rising by them.

Between the town and its neighbour Hook is a bridge carrying the railway over the Ouse. Said to weigh 670 tons, it is 830 feet long, and has a movable section of 250 feet which can be opened in less than a minute. Two miles from Goole the fine Boothferry Bridge takes the road traffic to and fro.

Goole's great Water Tower, the biggest in England, is 145 feet high and holds three-quarters of a million gallons. The War Memorial is a small copy of the Cenotaph in Whitehall, standing in green lawns among roses and orange blossom. Close by are fine schools in their own pretty gardens. In the cross-shaped church are memorials to heroes of land and sea. There is a tribute to those who went down with the *Calder* in 1931, and another to men of the *Colne* who sailed from Goole and sank in the North Sea in 1906 with the loss of twelve lives.

Grassington. Many people in search of health or lovely scenery have been to this small town 700 feet above the sea. North of the town are the ramparts of an ancient Celtic encampment; the road to Conistone skirts the charming Grass Wood; and near a great sycamore by the road to Hebden is a 16th century barn. Linton across the river has a beautiful waterfall, and a church which Grassington shares.

The old grey buildings are packed in narrow cobbled ways and round the small market square. Hiding behind the square is the old hall in a lovely garden, two windows in a gable end telling of its mediaeval origin, though much of it is Tudor. It is said to be the oldest inhabited house in Yorkshire.

Once famous for plays given in an attic, Grassington remembers that Edmund Kean acted here in 1807, and that the audience recognised his worth long before London flocked to hear him. His stage was dimly lighted with six halfpenny candles, and his audience was chiefly farmers and men from lead mines. The town had an important lead-mining centre until 1875; remains of the mines can be seen on the moors. The stage manager was a countryman who insisted on wearing his clogs when he played King Richard. Grass Woods nearby has been scheduled as a Nature Reserve.

Great Houghton. There are a few old houses among much that is new. It has a quaint, lowly church with scalloped battlements, standing as it stood when Sir Edward Rhodes built it about 1650, still furnished with the old altar rails, pews with bobbin ends, and a carved pulpit.

Great Mitton. Lancashire is on three sides of this delightful little place, the two counties bounded by the Hodder and the Ribble, which meet by Mitton Wood. The old church is perched on the hill, looking across to the white crag of Clitheroe. The old farmhouse west of the church was perhaps the old manor house, and the cottage post office is at the gate of the churchyard, which is like a garden, sheltering a 17th century sundial, the head of a mediaeval cross with four figures (dug up in 1802 and set on a pedestal), and the much worn figure of a 13th century rector, his head on a pillow.

More imposing outside than in, the church has a 500-year-old tower, a nave and chancel of the 13th century, with a 14th century low window. The Shireburne Chapel was built in 1594 on the foundations of a 15th century chantry, whose original roof is still here. There are steps down into the nave (which has a fine old roof), and more steps down into the chancel. The chancel screen has a 15th century base with an inscription, but its top is of wood, terracotta, and iron. There are two terracotta ends in the rich old stalls, and some old tiles in the chancel floor. The fine Norman font has a cover of 1593, the pulpit has Jacobean corners and Queen Anne panels, and in the Elizabethan screen of the chapel may be 15th century timbers.

Dazzlingly light in contrast with the nave and chancel, the chapel has a great display of monuments of the Shireburnes, a proud race whose old home across the Lancashire border is now the famous Roman Catholic School of Stonyhurst. The tablet to Sir Nicholas Shireburne of 1717 was set up by his daughter, the Duchess of Norfolk. His son Richard, the last male heir, had died before him as a boy of about 13, his monument showing a draped figure with cherubs and two mourners. Sir Richard of 1594, knighted on the battlefield, was the first to be buried in the chapel he had built, and lies with his wife on an imposing alabaster tomb, their three sons with swords, their three daughters in court dress. The figure of a knight lying in the chapel resembles this Sir Richard, and may have been placed on the tomb. Sir Richard's son was Governor of the Isle of Man. We see him kneeling with his wife in a charming wall-monument, two of the seven children below them asleep in a cradle. The next three generations are represented by three Richards sculptured in marble, one with his wife, all the fine work of William Stanton. The men with crossed legs are among the latest examples of this attitude to be found in England.

Great Ouseburn. A long placid village over a mile from the Ouse, it has many old creepered houses and an avenue of limes shading a wayside path. The elms sheltering the church are higher than the 12th century tower, which has belfry windows divided by shafts, a Norman slit in one wall, a 13th century lancet in another, and later battlements. The chancel arch and the slender arcades (with arches taller than their pillars) are 13th century. Remains of the old cross are built into the churchyard wall.

Greenfield. The hills hereabouts are 1800 feet high, and the famous Greenfield Rocks are near vast stretches of moorland where we may travel for miles with hardly a sign of life. There is rare charm in the valley, and Nut Bottom, a wooded glen, is a favourite spot in October, when the beeches are a fine spectacle.

There are two 19th century churches a mile apart. St Mary's has a window in memory of 39 men and a nurse who gave their lives in the Great War. Christ Church, at Friezland, has a slender tower with a broached spire, and much woodwork carved by Saddleworth craftsmen. The golden light of the chancel falls on the rich stalls, the rails, and the panelled walls; there is more carving in the panels and stairway of the pedestal pulpit, and fine tracery adorns the door through which we come and go. In the churchyard sleep a man and his wife and eight of their nine children, all killed by the fall of a factory chimney in 1864.

Green Hammerton. It is green by name and nature, for trees are all about it. The Hall is behind the trees at the end of the long green where the old houses gather, and many new houses have come to share the magnificent views of the great wooded plain and the Wolds. The red-roofed church has a bellcot in the middle of a cross.

In this pleasant spot lingers a queer story of Henry IV, who is said to have spent a night here after the execution of Archbishop Scrope in 1405. It is said that he cried out in the dark, and that when his servants came to him they found him smitten with a disease something like leprosy.

Greenhow. Lead mines were worked here before the time of the Romans. In a dip of the high moors between the Wharfe and the Nidd, its houses, the inn, and the 19th century church are about 1300 feet above the sea. We see the dark forbidding moors in the north and west, but dropping down the long steep hill to Pateley Bridge a great view of hills and dales unfolds. Greenhow's own magnificence hides from the light of day, and was unknown until 1860, when the remarkable series of limestone caverns by the road to Grassington were discovered. Known as the Stump Cross Caverns, the cavities are joined by narrow passages and amaze us with the splendour of their glittering stalagmites and stalactites, formed at the rate of little more than an inch every thousand years. The system extends for about two miles, and exploration continues.

Greetland. It has an old timbered house looking oddly out of place among much that is new, seeing from its tiny mullioned windows scores of mills and miles of hills. On the road above the house is the 19th century church, adorned inside with much carving.

Grewelthorpe. At one end of the pleasant straggling village is a big green with a duck pond; at the other end is a green bank near a row of nine fine trees—seven beeches and two sycamores which grow from the top of a wall and embower the road. Between the two greens is the modern church. Close by are Hackfall Woods, where the River Ure flows through a valley once more charming than it is today, but still beautiful with thickly-wooded dingles, water falling in cascades, scars of naked rock, and fine views.

Guiseley. It has a link with four immortals of two continents, but we come to it for its own sake, for, though it has the mills and machinery of a busy manufacturing town, there are still a few reminders of the days when Guiseley was a village linked by packhorse roads with the world beyond. It stands on the high ground between the Aire and the Wharfe, with the Chevin (rising 850 feet and crossed by the line of a Roman road) between the town and its neighbour, Otley.

The village cross and the old stocks are in the marketplace, and at a green corner are the church of St Oswald and the Elizabethan rectory. With its mullioned windows and gables, its three-storeyed porch, its old trees, and the lawns going down to the site of the old moat, the rectory is a charming picture. It has a sundial on the porch, and within are massive beams, handsome panelling, Tudor fireplaces, and a fine staircase.

A beautiful lychgate with a stone figure of St Oswald, soldier, king, and martyr, brings us to the spacious churchyard, with scores of 17th and 18th century gravestones, one saying, "Here lies an honest man". Near the porch are a few massive stone coffins.

The church the Normans began has become in our time part of a greater structure, but has not lost its own identity. We enter through a Norman doorway with shafts and simple capitals, and the south arcade which the Normans gave their nave still stands, its four round arches on clustered shafts with scalloped capitals. The east window of the old chancel, and the west tower with its projecting parapet, are 15th century. On the south side of the chancel is a 13th century chapel with three lancets in its east wall, a striking south window with plate tracery, and arches remarkable for their detached shafts. There are other arches between the old chancel and the new.

From the 17th century come the altar rails of the old chancel, and a screen, a chest, and a box-pew in the chapel. There is an old pulpit, and among the modern woodwork are bobbin-ended pews, screens, and stalls with linenfold panels and vine borders. On the roodbeam are coloured figures of Our Lord, St Mary, and St John, and at each side are scenes of the Annunciation and Christ meeting Mary in the garden, shining with gold and colour. Surmounting the oak panels of the reredos is a group of figures on the ledge of the window above, glittering with gold and showing the Wise Men, the Shepherds, and angels adoring.

The shields of Yorkshire families are in the modern windows of the north aisle.

Very charming is the window in memory of James Francis Howson who did so much for his church. Hanging in the nave is a white ensign, the old rector's gift of thankfulness that his son, Commander Howson, was rescued after being torpedoed at sea.

Among the names of rectors on a beautiful wooden panel is that of Robert Moore, who came in 1581 and finished in 1642; and there is a memorial to Alice Ingham who taught for 50 years. In the old chancel is a quaint old gravestone to Robert Markham's 21st daughter, and under the tower is a Norman stone with a carved edge, and the shaft of a Saxon cross with knotwork on its four sides. By this is a fragment of one of the arms, carved with a dragon on top of a man's head. It is probable that the Normans built where the Saxons had been before them.

So much we may see, but it is of things unseen, immortal chapters in the story of our literature, that we think as we stand in this church, remembering the Longfellow we gave to America and the Brontës who bequeathed us an immortal picture of English life. Generations of Longfellows came here to pray and to be married, and in the churchyard they sleep. It was from Guiseley that the grandfather of Henry Wadsworth Longfellow set out to try his fortune in the New World. Here he knelt for the last time in the church of his forefathers.

There was a simple service here one winter's day in 1812 when to these old altar rails came two young people, a curate and a frail Cornish girl; the curate was Patrick Brontë from Hartshead, and his bride was Maria Branwell from Penzance, and when the Reverend William Morgan had pronounced them man and wife he stepped down and stood in their place with Miss Branwell's cousin Jane Fennell by his side, while Patrick Brontë performed the same service for him. The bridegrooms married each other and the brides were bridesmaids to each other.

Halifax. From old Halifax, tucked away in the deep valley of the River Hebble, we look up to hills rising to the wind-swept moors, and from new Halifax, with its spacious streets and gardens, we look down on the gaunt chimneys of countless mills. It is one of the chief clothing towns of the Riding, and the chief carpet works are probably the biggest in the world, over 4000 people being employed at their mills. Engineering, chemicals, machine tools, and wire are among the other industrial concerns of Halifax.

There is a fine view of the town from Beacon Hill, rising steeply on the east side of the river, and a grand view over the moors and the valley from Wainhouse's Tower, a curious 19th century stone structure which was meant for a chimney but has always served as a tower; crowned with a lantern and a cupola, it is climbed by 400 steps and is 250 feet high; it is sometimes open to the public.

Down in the valley below the frowning hill is the grand old parish church of St John the Baptist, once in a fair setting but now companioned by the railway and the viaduct, huge pepper-pot condensers, and mills. It is one of over a score of churches and one of only a few really old buildings still left in the town. Near it is the old street with the curious and probably unique name of Woolshops. There are quaint old houses and inns, old halls which have come down in the world, and fine houses now belonging to the town, together with their parks and gardens. They are delightful, and help to give the people over 300 acres of green spaces.

Belle Vue, the old home of Sir Francis Crossley, one of Halifax's industrial princes, houses the public library and natural history museum, and the lovely gardens are open for all. Facing Belle Vue is the People's Park, with 12 charming acres laid out by Sir Joseph Paxton and given to the town by one of its generous sons, Sir Francis Crossley. From a fine terrace adorned with statues, and from its gay flowerbeds, we look to the hills, and in its colonnaded pavilion (by which fountains play) is a lifesize marble statue of Sir Francis set up by the town. The Crossley brothers were great benefactors of Halifax, where they found work for hundreds of men and women, their gifts including almshouses, an orphanage, and a school. The buildings are in the 73-acre Savile Park not far from the River Calder, near the fine block of the Royal Halifax Infirmary.

On the north of the town is a splendid house called Bankfield, reminding us of an Italian villa with its round-headed windows, broad eaves, and pillared front, standing in the ten acres of Ackroyd Park, and now the home of a museum and art gallery. The entrance hall has painted walls, a domed ceiling, and a marble staircase leading to spacious rooms with valuable art treasures, including pictures, pottery, and carvings. There are handsome marble mantelpieces, statues, and an amazing bust known as the Veiled Lady. She has a veil falling over her face and shoulders, her features shining through, and only when we come up to it do we see that it is all carved in marble. There are pictures of old Halifax, an old mayoral chair used till 1901, a pillory, a quaint coach, and a fine collection of weapons, tools, boats, and idols from the South Seas.

Other things to see at Bankfield include Thomas Ogden's 18th century clock, still keeping good time, and there are examples of old weaving tools and machinery, hand-looms, spinning wheels, spools, and shuttles, and a unique collection of what are known as the Crossley mosaics—really tapestries made by machinery. On a huge chart are shown 120 houses of the 17th century or earlier; a rich field for the local historian, although some of them, such as High Sunderland which had Brontë associations, no longer exist. The house also has a considerable collection of military items and uniforms, part of it being the official Regimental museum of the Duke of Wellington's Regiment.

Out of sight of the workaday chimneys is Shibden Hall, oldest and most gracious of the great houses now in the town's possession. Standing in 55 acres of lovely grounds going down to Shibden Dale, it is on the far side of Beacon Hill, and we come to it by a drive along a steep hillside and over a deep ravine clothed with rhododendrons and sycamore trees. The formal gardens are ablaze with colour, and daffodil banks, and by a lake in the hollow is a small timbered house which once stood in the town. An outside stairway in this house brings us to a room with an old fireplace and tiny windows.

The hall itself, now an Ancient Monument, is a charming medley of timber and stone, begun in the 15th century by the Otes family and enlarged about 1500 and in the 19th century. It was the home of the Listers for 300 years till the last of them died in 1933, and it is furnished mostly as in their early days. The reception hall is delightful with its huge fireplace, and black and white walls above a panelled dado. Here in a window with nine mullions are lovely old quarries showing shields, monkeys playing, a goose, a fox playing pipes, and many birds—one with a spade, one holding a fish, and one pushing her chick in a barrow; and at the end of the hall is a handsome staircase adorned with figures of a knight, two women, and a lion. Another room has a 16th century four-poster bed with inlaid panels and a mass of rich carving. With old documents in a case are two fine illuminated books of the 15th century, a Book of Prayers and a Book of Hours. A Folk Museum has recently been added where we see a 17th century barn, a collection of horse-drawn vehicles, many agricultural implements and we peep into the shops of a saddler, an apothecary, a nail-maker, and a clogger. The Shibden Valley in which the hall stands is for the most part delightful and contains the impressive 17th century Scout Hall.

Two old foundations which have benefited the town still carry on in modern buildings—Heath Grammar School founded in Elizabeth I's day and now a secondary school; and Bluecoat School and almshouses, maintained by Nathaniel Waterhouse's 17th century bequest, which has steadily grown in value. A less pleasing reminder of the old days is a grim witness to a curious local law which was relinquished in the middle of the 17th century, the Halifax Gibbet law, framed for the protection of the clothmakers by making the crime of cloth-stealing punishable by execution. The Halifax Gibbet was something like the guillotine, and is said to have had 50 victims between 1550 and 1650, when it cut off the head of a cloth-stealer for the last time. The base and steps of it remain in a garden off Gibbet Street, brought here when they were found at the time of the laying-out of People's Park last century, and now preserved as an

Ancient Monument. High on Lee Mount is Shroggs Park, with a lake in its 25 acres; from the terrace in West View Park (once a moorland waste) there is a view of woods and valleys and moorland ridges, with Stoodley Pike crowning a hill near Todmorden.

There are shopping arcades and ample markets. The fruit and vegetable market has been held since 1871 in the open space of about 10,000 square yards enclosed by the Old Piece Hall, another of the town's ancient monuments. Built of stone in 1779 as a place where the cloth for sale could be displayed on market days, the Piece Hall has 311 rooms in its four sides, which are of two and three storeys following the slope of the hill, and every storey has a colonnade in front.

The Town Hall is a Renaissance building designed by Sir Charles Barry, architect of the Houses of Parliament; its clock tower is enriched with sculpture, its spire (with a balcony near the top) rises 180 feet above the pavement. There is a bust of Cobden on the staircase, and at the top are three paintings of the Dedication of Alfred, Alfred founding the Navy (both by J. C. Horsley, RA), and Alfred playing his harp in the Danish camp, by Daniel Maclise. The council chamber is richly panelled, and in the library are books of value for their bindings by the Edwards of Halifax, booksellers famous in Yorkshire and London last century.

Below Bankfield (his old home) is the handsome church of All Souls which Edward Ackroyd built and Sir Gilbert Scott designed. Said to have cost £100,000, it is a striking cross-shaped building in 14th century style, its tower adorned with over a dozen statues, its spire rising to a height of 236 feet. There are buttresses with saints in niches, handsome windows, and an ornate south porch with a figure of St Wilfrid in the gable; over the west door is a figure of Our Lord. The interior has rich arches and an ornate display of carving on capitals and corbels; the clerestory has marble shafts, and fading away above the chancel arch is a painting of the Adoration of the Lamb. There are stalls with angels, an elaborate pulpit of French stone with Devon and Italian marble, and a great marble font in the vaulted baptistry. Figures of Colonel Edward Ackroyd and his wife stand above the south door, and outside is a bronze statue of the colonel.

Grimy with the smoke of industry is the stately old church of St John the Baptist. It is chiefly 15th century, but the north aisle has some 14th century windows and remains of Norman masonry, and the north and south chapels are 16th century, one founded by the bequest of William Rokeby, vicar of Halifax and Archbishop of Dublin, whose heart is buried here in a lead casket; the other built by Robert Holdsworth, a vicar murdered by thieves at the vicarage 400 years ago. The whole of the church was much restored last century.

In the impressive view of the south side of the church we see the noble tower rising 118 feet at the west end, the clerestory of the chancel with its embattled and pinnacled parapet, the chancel aisle enriched with gabled buttresses ending in leafy pinnacles above crested battlements, and the chapel remarkable for its buttresses, which have slender shafts supporting pinnacles and linked to the wall by huge gargoyles, among them winged monsters, a ram, and a man with bagpipes. There are lofty arcades in the spacious interior, but the nave is dim through having no clerestory. Two of the pillars are curious for having three capitals each, from which spring the chancel arch, the adjacent arches of the nave and chancel arcades, and the arches across the aisles. Another unusual feature is the evidence that a tower was to have been built at the west end of the south aisle, shown by the curious western pillar of the arcade, the arch across the aisle here, and a doorway to a winding stair.

There are old roofs with moulded beams and faded painting of heraldry, a fine array of Jacobean pews with bobbin ends, six old stalls with carved misericords showing little men among branches, a pelican, and angels, and three more old stalls serving as sedilia, with figures of a bishop reading and a monk praying, their misericords being carved with a mermaid, an angel, and a grotesque. More old carving is in the screenwork on the south side of the chancel, but the chancel screen and the rich oak pulpit are modern, the screen having a cornice with three rows of carving, the pulpit adorned with figures of the Four Evangelists. Standing by the old pillar almsbox is the lifesize wooden figure of an old man with a long beard, wearing a long coat and breeches; he is known as Old Tristram, and is said to be a portrait of a beggar familiar in Halifax streets in the 17th century. The south door is of that century. There are twisted altar rails 200 years old, and the cover of the font is partly 15th century, its shape like a spire enriched with tracery, buttresses, and pinnacles.

Kept in a case is a small 14th century stone head of a tonsured monk, and in the porch are four gravestones looking old enough to be Norman. On part of a gravestone above the south doorway are a man in armour and a shield of arms. Both doorways to the roodstairs remain, and in a crypt under the chancel (with old painting on the roof) are old books, some of the 15th and 16th centuries.

Under a tiny canopy is the painted bust of John Favour in his robes and ruff. Vicar in Elizabethan days, he was well known for his piety and his skill in medicine. He was the author of a curious work called *Antiquitie Triumphing over Noveltie*, written in defence of the Church and dedicated to Archbishop Tobie Mathew, to whom he was Chaplain.

A modern canopied monument adorned with angels is in memory of Robert Ferrar, a bishop, friend of Cranmer, a native of Halifax, and a man of high principles for which he was not afraid to suffer.

Hampole. A handful of farms and cottages below the highway, it is famous as the home six centuries ago of Richard Rolle, who is said to have been buried here in the church of a vanished nunnery. One of the celebrated hermits of his day, he became a powerful preacher, and was famous for his writings, among them a poem called the *Prick of Conscience*, illustrated in a 15th century window of All Saints Church in York.

Hampsthwaite. In a lovely setting in the wooded valley of the River Nidd, four miles from Harrogate, it was the home of six generations of the Thackerays. They sleep in the spacious church-yard on the river bank, and in the church porch is a 17th century stone with an inscription by one of them who had a fancy for rhyming, but was less gifted with his pen than the descendant who was to make the name immortal.

There are many other gravestones lining the walls of the porch, some very crude, coming from Norman and mediaeval days, relics of the old church which has been almost entirely rebuilt. Much of the tower is mediaeval and the lower masonry of the nave pillars is old. There are two coffin lids by the arcade, and the font may be Norman. From the 17th century come the low seats in the nave, panelling round the walls, and two richly carved chairs. There is an old carved pulpit, and a small brass has the portrait of a 14th century civilian with long flowing hair and a beard, a cape over his shoulders.

The captivating possession of the church is a tomb with angels watching over the lovely sleeping figure of a composer of our own day. She was Amy Woodforde-Finden, whose *Indian Love Lyrics* are known the world over.

She was one of a group of interesting people we found here. One was a vicar for 59 years who lived through Cromwell's time; another a little lady, Jane Ridsdale, whose quaint portrait is in the south aisle. She died last century, 59 years old but only 31 inches high.

Spofforth has its blind John Metcalfe, and Hampsthwaite has its blind Peter—Peter Barker, whom they laid here to rest in 1873. Sightless as a child of four, he taught himself all he needed to know and became the village joiner.

Harewood. The park is famed for the three buildings it en-shrines: Harewood House; the ruined 14th century castle of the Aldburghs, backed by woodland and looking on the river; and the church, sheltering a group of alabaster tombs unrivalled in York-shire. They are of the Redmans and the Rythers and the Gas-coignes.

For over two centuries Harewood has belonged to the Lascelles family, and in 1759 the first stone of Harewood House was laid. Said to have cost £100,000, it was designed by John Carr of York, who also built the model village of Harewood, but was much altered by Sir Charles Barry. A stately place in classical style, it is 250 feet long, has a noble flight of steps, a broad terrace, and a handsome portico with six tall pillars. The house is frequently open to the public and contains incomparable work by Adam, a great deal of furniture by Chippendale, china, and a wealth of pictures, including work by Turner and Girtin (who came here together in 1797), El Greco, Bellini, Titian, Tintoretto, and Veronese. "Capability" Brown worked for nine years on the park and it stood as a monument to his ability until, in the disastrous gales of 1962, 20,000 trees were destroyed: it will be many years before we see the full glory of Harewood Park again.

Sir William Aldburgh's mediaeval castle, though a ruin, is still a lordly pile with walls seven feet thick and towers 90 feet high. Above the main entrance (which keeps the grooves for the port-cullis) is a charming window of the 15th century, with the shields of Aldburgh and Baliol at each side, and above it the Aldburgh motto, *What shall be, shall.* The Great Hall occupied all the ground floor of the main part of the castle, and we can still see part of the hearth-stone of the open fireplace, and a lovely recess. A doorway in the hall leads to one of the towers, and another doorway opens on the steps to a cellar. High up in the entrance tower is a small chamber with a great show of heraldry; it was probably an oratory.

A charming drive shaded by trees brings us to the church, a fine building 130 feet long. Of the church William de Curci founded early in the 12th century there is nothing to see except the bowl of a font. Most of the old work in this place of dignified simplicity is 15th century, but it was much restored in the 18th and again by Sir Gilbert Scott. The tower stands between the aisles at the west end of the nave. There are splendid arcades without capitals, memorial windows to the Lascelles, and a monument with the bust of Sir Thomas Denison, an 18th century judge who died at Harewood.

Among the splendid figures on Harewood's lavishly carved tombs, all of which come from between 1400 and 1500, is one of another judge, Lord Chief Justice Sir William Gascoigne, born at Gawthorpe Hall in 1350 and buried here four years after Agincourt.

A knight with his head resting on a crested helmet of a bull's head is believed to be Sir John Neville of 1482, lying with his wife on a superb tomb with niches in which are figures of their children and a group of saints.

The loveliest of these six mediaeval tombs is that of Sir Richard Redman (1475), showing him in armour. Sir Richard was grandson of another Richard Redman who was Speaker of the House of Commons, and died in 1427. He lies on his tomb on the north side of the chancel, wearing plate armour; with him is his wife, who as Elizabeth Aldburgh, shared with her sister Sybil the Aldburgh estate. Sybil married Sir William Ryther, and it is said that the two families lived together at Harewood Castle. Sir William and Sybil are believed to be the figures on the tomb under an arch on the south side of the chancel.

Harrogate. It is halfway between the capitals of England and Scotland, set at the gateway of a wonderful countryside of moor and plain and hill and vale. It is fitting that it should give us one of the most superb views in this unrivalled county. From the top of the observatory tower on Harlow Hill (built in 1829 by John Thomson, and reaching to nearly 700 feet above the sea) can be seen the Tees and the Humber, York and Ripon, a score of towns, a dozen castles, 70 parks, 200 villages, and the sites of four battles: Stamford Bridge, the Standard, Towton, and Marston Moor. As if this were not enough, some of the loveliest scenery in the county lies within walking distance of the town.

Harrogate itself is full of flowers and trees. We find them in the busiest streets, and even at the station. There are leafy avenues, gardens in the squares, and over 350 acres of green spaces and parks, among them Harlow Moor with its stone cross rising finely against a background of pines, and the Valley Gardens which have been growing in beauty for half a century, leaving nothing to be desired with their lawns, riot of flowers in beds and borders, trees and shrubs, exquisite rockeries, and delightful vistas. At Harlow Carr nearby are the Northern Horticultural Gardens, trial gardens affording a permanent and varied display of plants, shrubs, and flowers. Most remarkable of all is the Stray, a magnificent common of 200 acres reaching into the heart of the town. Part of the old Forest of Knaresborough, and preserved for all time by Act of Parliament, it is like a spacious lawn, shaded by avenues of trees and criss-crossed by paths and roads. It is a perfect setting for the dignified buildings and palatial hotels, and contributes the chief impression of space which is the first thing that strikes the traveller passing through the town.

The fame of the town has come through its waters, and of its natural springs, numbering more than four score, over 30 are in what is known as the Bogs Field. The Old Sulphur Well, now the Pump Room, and used as a small museum, is an octagonal building of last century, crowned by a big dome. The Royal Baths are in a splendid building with a dome and a great hall with marble pillars. The discovery of the waters was made in Queen Elizabeth's day, but owing to its inaccessibility then Harrogate's popularity is little more than a hundred years old. Smollett described it as wild and bleak; Sydney Smith could not find a good word to say for it. But it grew into favour last century and was visited by Byron, Wordsworth, Southey, and Dickens. It was while sitting by the Stray one Sunday evening in 1876 that Bishop Bickersteth wrote the famous hymn, *Peace, perfect peace*.

There are fine houses and shops and public buildings. The great concert hall seats 2000 people. In Prospect Square is an imposing white obelisk to those who fell in the Great War, 75 feet high, with bronze panels by Gilbert Ledward on the massive base containing the names. With the public library goes the art gallery and museum, where we may see pictures of Old Harrogate and local scenes, and portraits of blind John Metcalfe of Knaresborough and of Jane Ridsdale who was 31 inches high; a collection of books and clay tablets from the East, a fragment of a stone coffin with a Viking inscription found a few miles away, Egyptian bricks and vases, Roman lamps and coins, an oak chest from a house immortalised in *Wuthering Heights*, a chained Bible of 1595, three Breeches Bibles, an Apron Bible, and wonderful carvings in pith of a Hindu temple and a bullock team and waggon.

The town has a fine group of churches and chapels. Christ Church, standing on the Stray, was built in 1831, and has rich glass at the east end showing the Revelation of St John, figures of Moses and Elijah, Peter and Paul, and the Crucifixion with John and the mourning women. There is an inscription to William Powell Frith, the artist who was born at Aldfield near by and once lived at Harrogate.

St Peter's, in the heart of the town, is a lofty cross-shaped church in mediaeval style, and has grown gradually from the building of the chancel in 1870 to the building of the fine tower in 1926. On the tower are stone figures of St Peter with a bunch of keys and a book, and St George with the dragon at his feet. Among other rich stone carving are the heads of Dr Bickersteth (Bishop of Ripon) and

above
Detail of a monument in the Shireburne Chapel, Great Mitton.

above right
Tomb of Richard Shireburne and his wife Isabel, Great Mitton.

Monument to Sir George Savile (died 1622) in Thornhill Church.

The doorway of Scout Hall, Halifax.

Houses in Harewood village.

Archbishop Thompson of York, at each side of the sanctuary; a panel over the west door with an angel appearing to Peter in prison; and a panel with Jesus blessing the children.

A wonderful church is that of St Wilfrid, a massive stone pile shaped like a cross, built in the first generation of our own century and given its loveliest corner (the lady chapel) in 1935. It has a clerestoried nave with aisles, a chancel with triforium and clerestory and chapels, and a low embattled tower with a pyramid roof over the crossing. Its style is largely 13th century, and its architect was Mr Temple Moore. By the great sculptured Crucifixion at the north door are the initials of Miss Elizabeth Trotter, whose generosity brought the church into being. A fine hall is linked with the church by an arcaded cloister, the whole group making a very charming picture in a setting of lawn, unseen from the road.

Very impressive are the nave arcades, with great pillars and arches, and the three-tiered chancel with two rows of windows in the east wall above an open arcade through which we enter the lady chapel, an exquisite little place seeming already to wear the charm of age. Lighted by tall lancets, it has a passage in the thickness of the wall, and a continuous arcade of eight bays with slender pillars supporting the vault. Four golden angels hold candles over the lovely altar, and on the wall above is Alfred Southwick's stone carving of the Crucifixion. Higher still is an oval window showing the Madonna and the Child, who is standing to bless all who come. A companion oval window at the west end of the church has God the Father holding an orb.

The striking south transept chapel has an apse with arcaded stone seats under five great lancets, between which are shafts meeting in the domed ceiling. On the massive roodbeam between the nave and chancel are Mary and John by the Cross (where Our Lord has the serpent under His feet), and two seraphim, all painted in mediaeval style. On the rail of the fine table in the north chapel is the carved mouse of Robert Thompson of Kilburn. The beautiful lectern of wrought metal is enriched with vine and oak, and has four arms holding candles. There are paintings of saints on the wooden pulpit.

The coloured windows have the virtue of not keeping out the light. One in the north porch, showing St Hugh of Lincoln, is in memory of Mr Temple Moore. The east windows are a blue mosaic of scenes concerning the story of Our Lord. The west window is interesting for being a memorial to Miss Trotter's sister, whose sudden death at Harrogate, while they were breaking a journey to Scotland, was the cause of Elizabeth coming to live here.

E   117

The series of reliefs on the walls, showing the Life of Christ from the Annunciation to the Ascension, were modelled and painted by Frances Darlington, once a member of the church, and the faces of some of the figures are portraits of folk who have worshipped here.

In the wall of the stone stairway to the organ is the oldest thing the church has to show, a cinquefoil opening of mediaeval days, which was brought from an old church at Kimberley in Norfolk.

On the north fringe of the town the church of Bilton is a handsome building designed by Sir Gilbert Scott, with a striking tower and beautiful doorways. The lovely capitals of overhanging foliage in the doorways of the porch are an introduction to much beautiful carving within and without, seen on the corbels and on wonderful capitals springing from the clustered pillars of the nave arcades. The visitor to Harrogate is well catered for. The great Yorkshire Show now takes place here annually on a permanent showground; one or two county cricket matches are held here; there is an annual Spring Flower Show, and French and Italian weeks show Harrogate's links with sister towns in Europe. The antique shops are justly famous.

Harthill. Collieries have not robbed it of charm. Among its fine trees are the cedars of the rectory, and the churchyard has far horizons. Near the church is an admirable thing—a swinging sign (made from timbers of the old belfry) telling briefly the story of the village, its people, and its church. We read that its street was part of the Harthill Walk in Ivanhoe, that the church was first built by the Conqueror's son-in-law, Earl de Warenne, and that a unique illustrated history of the place is kept in the school. The tower of the church is mainly 15th century, but the nave arcades were built when the Norman style was passing. The old font has a Jacobean cover, there is a fine old chest, and the modern woodwork is richly carved.

The famous Osbornes are sleeping here. They lived at Kiveton near by, and gave England several distinguished Dukes of Leeds, seven lying here with their wives. Lady Margaret (who "died comfortably" in 1642) kneels at a desk with one child behind her and another in swaddling clothes.

In a dark corner sleeps the most notorious of them all, Sir Thomas Osborne. He lies fittingly in the shadows, for his ways were dark, and his life was a scandal of two generations. He was born in the happy days of Charles I and lived to see the Stuarts toppling off the throne, and all his life he was corrupt. His love was scorned in his youth by his cousin Dorothy Osborne, and we may wonder what her life would have been like had she accepted him. Pepys thought him a comely gentleman when he first saw him at the court of Charles II, but he was a self-seeking politician, a trickster, and a traitor to the State, though he marched from dignity to dignity, baronet, baron, viscount, earl, marquis, duke.

Hartshead. A grey village far above the River Calder, it has old mills, old stocks, and a mounting stone facing the church, which looks far over the hills. Nearly half a mile beyond the church is Walton Cross, a fine block of stone just inside a field; it was carved a thousand years ago with strap ornament, two queer animals, and a tree with four birds among the branches. The churchyard has a fragment of another cross, a sundial of 1611, and the trunk of an immense yew that was here in mediaeval days.

The squat little church has a low tower rising above the nave's stone roof, and has been refashioned in 12th century style; but it still has its Norman doorway with an arch of zigzag on two shafts at each side, and a Norman chancel arch enriched with zigzag and lattice pattern. The font is a modern bowl on a Norman pillar.

The church (with two dormers in its roof) is charming inside with low black and white roofs, pews with bobbin ends, a pulpit with carved panels, and windows bright with Bible story. There are two carved chairs, a fine old chest, an old candelabra hanging in the nave, and an oak reredos said to have been made in Italy in the 16th century.

It was at Hartshead that an Irishman met a Cornish girl on holiday. He was Patrick Brontë, a curate (vicar here from 1810 to 1815), and the girl was Maria Branwell. They were married at Guiseley one grey December day in 1812, and their first child was born here. The parish registers record Maria Brontë's baptism on April 23, 1814.

Hartwith. It is on a windswept slope of the moor, with the River Nidd flowing in a great curve over a mile away. Close by is Winsley, its woods and parkland going down to the river, and two miles north are the fantastic Brimham Rocks, one of the natural wonders of Yorkshire. There is a magnificent view of Nidderdale and the distant moors from the church, which stands by a wayside lawn, the school and an old cottage keeping it company.

Hatfield. Hereabouts is the famous Hatfield Chase, its thousands of broad acres (extending into Lincolnshire and Notts) once a swampy fen where wild geese, herons, badgers, and otters abounded. The draining of the marshes was partly accomplished in Charles I's day by the Dutch engineer Cornelius Vermuyden, in spite of the fierce opposition of the fenmen, who destroyed his dykes and fired on his men.

The history of Hatfield goes back a thousand years before that, for it is believed to be the Haethfelth mentioned in Bede, where was fought the battle in which Edwin, first Christian King of Northumbria, was killed by Penda in 633. Edwin's head was laid in the small chapel which was to become York Minster. Thomas Hatfield, Bishop of Durham and keeper of the privy seal, is thought to have been born here, and we may still see the old manor house in which are said to have been born a son of Edward III in the 14th century and a son of Richard Duke of York in the 15th.

The Hatfield of today is a pleasant village with many old houses of mellowed brick and a lofty and stately church which can rightly claim to be one of the noblest in the Riding. It has grown from one built at the close of Norman days, and of that 12th century church there are still the tall arcades with pointed arches on round pillars, the west window of the north aisle, the west doorway through which we enter, and the south doorway with a hood, both these doorways being Norman. A striking feature of the mediaeval reconstruction of the church are the six arches spanning the north aisle, making it like a cloistered walk to the north transept. The rest of the church—the clerestory, the shallow transepts, the spacious chancel and chapels, and the great central tower—is 15th century. The tower rests on four great arches with lovely mouldings, and above them are four windows flooding the crossing with light.

There are beautiful old roofs with floral bosses, an ancient chancel screen with traceried vaulting supporting the floor of the vanished loft, and part of a simple old screen between the north chapel and the transept. In the other chapel are old pews, and the mediaeval south door has its old iron hinges. A fine mediaeval chest has scratch carving of circles and stars and rounded arcading, and another grand old chest is bound with iron and studded with a mass of great nails and has a slot for coins, and may have been used for Peter's Pence. The font is over 700 years old. There is a chained copy of Jewel's Apology. The south chapel has a 15th century altar tomb and fragments of old armour.

A man who knew this church well was Abraham de la Pryme, whose grandfather came from Holland with Vermuyden. A student of natural history and antiquities. Abraham kept a marvellous diary from his boyhood till a day or two before he died in 1704.

Hawksworth. The years have left it unspoiled, a lovely out-of-the-way village without a church, set on the high ridge between the

River Aire and the Wharfe. From the road winding over its moor there is a wonderful panorama of the industrial heart of Yorkshire. It has a charming picture of Elizabethan England in Hawksworth Hall, now a home for spastics, with its fine array of chimneys and gables, mullioned windows and round ones. Here the Hawksworths lived for many generations, and here James I is said to have slept. Fame came suddenly to this village, of which few people had heard till a writer of our own day made it the home of Mother Hubbard. She was not the Mother Hubbard of the nursery rhyme, but the charming old lady who comes into William Riley's story *Windyridge*. Here is her little stone cottage with only one storey, and tiny windows from which she looked down to Bradford where Riley was born, and up to his beloved moors.

Haworth. It is here that we must come if we would understand the Brontës. We must see this melancholy place that they have put for ever into literature. We must see these mills and houses and climb the steep and narrow street up which long ago came Patrick Brontë with his Cornish wife, their six children, and seven cartloads of furniture. His father was plain Prunty, a poor Irish farmer with ten children.

They arrived at the parsonage, and perhaps the children may have been thrilled by the sight of the moors about them. They have a touch of beauty when the heather is out, but for most of the year they are vast wastes scarred with black quarries, littered with rocks, brown with a coarse grass, and unspeakably lonely. Behind their home at the parsonage they would soon find the rough track they were to tread down so often when they would escape to the moors to forget the tragedy of life. In one of the glens is a waterfall known by their name today. Here is a massive stone, known as the Brontë Chair, at which they would rest and tell tales to one another long before they told them to the world. Farther on is Top Withens, a desolate house; and Ponden Hall which comes into *Wuthering Heights*; and the Ferndean Manor of *Jane Eyre*, at Wycoller. Other interesting walks are to Ponden Kirk and Soudens, home of William Grimshaw.

Between these lonely moors and the busy valley down below stands Haworth with the church, the parsonage, and the inn clustering about the churchyard in an unlovely mass at the top of the street. The church must disappoint us, for it is not the church they knew; only its tower is old, and as they saw it. It is a bitter thing that the old church should have gone, with all its loveliness and its human appeal. Here we have little to see except an alabaster pulpit, a 17th century Bible, a silver chalice of Shakespeare's day, a window of the Acts of Mercy put here by an American admirer of Charlotte, and an inscription with the names of the eight Brontës who came to Haworth in that spring of 1820; Maria the frail mother who pined for her Cornish home, little Maria and her sister Elizabeth, who slipped away as children; Branwell the drunken ne'er-do-well; delicate Anne who sleeps at Scarborough, Emily with her brilliant genius and dauntless courage; Charlotte the incomparable; and the strange melancholy father who outlived them all and would sit alone by the fire at the parsonage after his 41 years, thinking.

We come to the Brontë house up the stony little hill which is no more "a little and a lone green lane, that opened on a common wide", as Emily wrote; but it has hanging over the pavement a sign that draws us to it. It is a silhouette, such as were fashionable in the Brontë days, and is a fine piece of craftsmanship by Herbert Scarborough, the village blacksmith, designed by the then Curator of the Museum, Harold Mitchell. It shows Charlotte writing with a quill pen, and the table she writes on, the chair she sits in, the little desk on the table, the lamp and the inkwell, are all copied from the originals indoors. It is one of the best village signs in all England.

The parsonage overlooks the churchyard, a depressing spectacle enclosed with iron railings, with a few trees shading a wilderness of black gravestones (hundreds of them happily flat on the ground). A Haworth boy who lived to be a knight (Sir James Roberts) bought the house for the Brontë Society and a new wing has been added and some changes made indoors. But we see the rooms much as the sisters knew them. It is a simple stone house with a small garden at the front, cold stone floors, and six or seven rooms, a home of suffering and struggle, but a house of pilgrimage for all who cherish the thought of these sisters whose spirit could not be quenched but whose genius burned intensely like a fire and died down quickly.

A door on the right in the narrow hall brings us to Patrick Brontë's room, where he took his meals alone. It has an old-fashioned piano with little shelves for candles, and the couch on which Emily died. Also off the hall is the room in which the children spent half their days; in it is the table round which they marched hour after hour telling stories and reciting poems. Here is the kitchen in which the old Yorkshire servant Tabby spent most of her life, and upstairs is a tiny room (nine feet by five) which the girls used as their nursery, in which they would spend the few happy hours they knew.

For thousands of people there will not be any room in England more appealing than this. This little nursery has in it the cradle in which the three sisters were rocked to sleep, and on the walls are pictures painted by them, and their faint pencil scrawls. It was this room of which Charlotte wrote long afterwards:

Pen cannot portray the deep interest of the scenes I have witnessed in that little room with the low narrow bed and bare whitewashed walls. There have I sat on a bedstead, my eye fixed on the window, through which appeared no other landscape than a monotonous stretch of moorland, a great church tower rising from the churchyard so filled with graves that the rank weeds and coarse grass scarce had room to shoot between the monuments.

The rooms are full of intimate small things, many of them brought back to their old home from distant parts of the world. Here is the lamp which threw its light on the manuscript of *Jane Eyre* and *Wuthering Heights* as they were being secretly written in the long dark hours. Here is the temperance pledge that Branwell signed in a moment of high resolve which he could never sustain for long. Here is Emily's mug with her name on it in gold letters. There is a picture of her dog Keeper, and Keeper's collar. Emily's rosewood writing desk has in it the letters and newspaper cuttings as she left them, and here is the comb which fell from her hand when she died, a tea-cosy worked by Charlotte, and a sampler she embroidered, with the alphabet and a text. Charlotte's workbasket is as she left it, with the silks and reels as she arranged them, and there is a lock of her hair, her drawing of a squirrel, and a tea-caddy she made. A tiny magazine with 12 pages of microscopic writing has been preserved, one of their first literary enterprises, and there is a painting of Anne's dog Floss. It is all as if the Brontës had been here yesterday, so friendly seems the touch of these small things.

Sad as are the memories haunting us in this grim house, we like to think that perhaps there was some merriment in it in the spring of 1820, with little feet pattering over the cold stone floors, and children laughing. The first shadow came when the mother died, longing for the sunshine of the Cornwall she loved and killed by the winds and fogs from the moors. Aunt Elizabeth came up from Cornwall to look after the children, but they were shy with her, and she never understood them; never had they an understanding soul about them, for Tabby was too busy scrubbing and polishing to find time for stories, and brother Branwell was too surly, and the father was becoming daily more and more forbidding and melancholy, shutting himself up for hours and terrifying them at times by firing his pistol into space. The pistol is here for us to see.

So more and more the sisters were left to themselves, telling tales, writing stories, making books and magazines, and painting pictures of things they had not seen. Their notebooks and diaries, and their miniature volumes, are here in plenty in the Branwell Collection, now in a room to itself. An extension loggia is dominated by a bronze group of the three sisters, cast in 1951 by Jocelyn Horner.

It would be a mistake to assume that Haworth was a place remote from civilisation in the days of the Brontës. Keighley had a railway and was a growing industrial town, as was Haworth itself; an interesting exhibit in the museum is a proclamation of the Queen ordering the reading of the Riot Act against troublesome workers in the West Riding in the times when the family lived here.

The Brontës were gone and Mr Nicholls, Charlotte's husband, had gone to Ireland when the Worth Valley railway line from Keighley was begun in 1864. Its opening was written about by a local wag Bill o'th' Hoylus End in his work *Th' History o' Haworth Railway fro th' beginnin' to th' end, wi' an ackaant o' th' oppnin' suremuny.* The little line was taken over by the Midland Railway Company in 1881 and passenger services went on until 1961. Recently a Keighley and Worth Valley Railway Preservation Society has been formed with the object of reopening the line as a private concern. The Society has established a small railway museum, and here we may see, and climb aboard to inspect a collection of old steam locomotives and rolling stock.

Hazelwood Castle. It stands in a park of 200 acres, an embattled house with old yews among lovely trees, between Leeds and Tadcaster. For eight centuries it was the home of the Vavasours, whose shield is over the doorway, and it has remains of the 13th century. The builder of the castle, Sir William Vavasour, gave stone from his quarry for building York Minster, where we may see a statue of him with a lump of stone in his hand. Another Vavasour was knighted at Flodden Field, and Thomas equipped ships and men to sail against the Armada, a service for which Elizabeth gave him permission to worship as he pleased in the chapel here.

Nestling under the walls of the house, the small mediaeval chapel is notable chiefly for the Vavasour monuments, and it has a piscina, a font, and a stoup of the 14th century, an almsbox sunk in the wall probably in the 17th century, and a long stone panel with recessed figures of a bishop, the Madonna and Child, and a saint, with a figure above a tiny niche. The reredos, an oil painting of the Crucifixion with the Women and St John, is under a broken pediment supported by great pillars.

The first of the monuments on the south side of the chapel is a cross-legged knight in chain armour and surcoat, the Vavasour arms on his shield; he lies on a tomb enriched with quatrefoils, in a recess dotted with flowers and with a leafy hood. Next comes a big canopied tomb on which Sir Thomas Vavasour of 1632 and his wife are kneeling, seven of their children on the front of the tomb, and two babes. Looking as if they are posing for a photographer is the family group on the third monument, Sir Walter Vavasour of 1713 reclining, his wife kneeling, one of three children holding a cross and another lying on a cushion. Beyond this classical memorial is a lovely 14th century tomb recess with a traceried gable, sheltering a poor battered knight. There are three great floorstones down the middle of the chapel, a memorial to little Constance Vavasour of 1851 showing her in the arms of an angel, and the wax figure of a maid dressed in white. She lies under the altar, and on the glass front of the case which shelters her we read, Clara Puella.

We come and go through a 15th century door with beautiful tracery and an iron grille. In the little burial ground is a lovely 14th century cross with four headless figures at the foot.

Headingley. The new has gathered round the old, for here, in the heart of this suburb of Leeds, stood the famous Headingley Oak. Its great days have long been over, but its blackened trunk, leaning over the busy road, a single arm held aloft, remained after a thousand years of change, until 1941, when it collapsed; it is now commemorated by a plaque.

Close by is St Michael's church, one of the noblest churches hereabouts. Shaped like a cross, with a huge tower and spire rising between the aisles at the west end, it is a place of many arches. The tower has a vaulted roof, the alabaster pulpit has many figures and scenes illustrating the preaching of the Gospel, and angels and lions adorn the brass lectern. The striking east wall has two rows of lancet windows with rich arches and clustered shafts, and the reredos has 21 coloured figures of saints and bishops in canopied niches gleaming with gold.

An avenue of trees leads from the busy road to St Chad's, a 19th century church of which Headingley is justly proud. With a spire 186 feet high, it is dignified and beautiful and filled with light. There is a fine vista of arches along the nave and chancel (an avenue of nine bays), and the aisles have flying buttresses to the arcades. There are capitals with rich foliage, quaint carvings of lizards, and a handsome oak pulpit, its stair crowned with a figure of St Chad, its stem carved with a serpent, a dragon, an eagle, and a bat chained to a tree stump.

In the West Riding "Headingley" means to many thousands cricket and Rugby League, for here is the headquarters of the Yorkshire County Cricket Club, a ground which has seen many

Test matches: a double grandstand serves cricket one way and the Leeds Rugby League ground the other.

Headingley gave England a famous man of letters, for here in 1835 was born Alfred Austin who died a year before the Great War, and is remembered as a poet who loved gardens and quiet places, the first journalist to be Poet Laureate—only politicians know why.

Healaugh. Perched on a hill, and nestling among great trees, the little church looks over the rich Plain to the towers of York and the distant Wolds. Near it stood a castle of the Percys, and by it still stands the fine Old Hall with the shaft of an ancient cross in the garden. Over a mile away is the moated site of a 13th century Augustinian priory, of which slight remains are still to be seen in the house called Healaugh Manor Farm.

The church has much of its Norman work left. The top of the tower has been rebuilt, but the old base has its plain Norman arch to the nave, and a fine 12th century corbel table of heads of men and animals runs along the south side of the nave and chancel.

Facing the sun and rain without a sheltering porch, the Norman doorway is indeed a thing of beauty. In the rich carving of the capitals we see a man's head, a horse and dog in entwining scrolls, and two wild animals. The arch has a band of 28 beak-heads and a quaint medley including beak-heads with faces of men and animals, figures kneeling and sitting, two men kneeling upside down, a dove, and a man with a woman carrying a child. The studded door, still on its old hinges, may be 15th century, and it opens to a nave divided from the north aisle by an arcade of Norman arches.

The priest's doorway was built by the Normans, and their chancel arch is remarkable for its long and short shafts, all richly carved. The chancel itself is a great space divided from the north chapel by one of the most extraordinary arches we have seen in a church—its span about 30 feet, its depth so shallow that it is like the arch of a bridge. The sedilia and most of the windows are 15th century. A Norman window is in the aisle. There is a little old glass, and some old woodwork is in the pulpit. The brass lectern set with jewels is modern. The panelling of the sanctuary has a border of vine and grape, and over the altar is a canopy like a spire, with a king and a bishop each side.

On his imposing alabaster tomb in the chapel lie Sir Thomas Wharton and his two wives, he a knight in armour, they in elegant gowns, one having chains round her neck and on her bodice. Round the tomb are dainty figures of knights and ladies. One of the few distinguished men of his day who never lost the favour of Henry VIII, he was made a peer for defeating the Scots.

Heath. Time seems to have stood still in this place, its houses dotted about where the common becomes the village green. One house is the Hall, a stately stone mansion with pilasters supporting a heraldic pediment. The Old Hall, originally one of the finest Elizabethan houses in Yorkshire, standing above the River Calder and overlooking meadows once fairer than now, is fast falling into ruins.

Finely built of stone, the house was delightful with oriels, battlemented turrets, and a handsome parapet. There is still a small courtyard with the ruins of outer walls. The entrance, reached by broad steps, had over it the shield of John Kaye, who built the house about 1568. There were many fine windows, some with fragments of 16th century Flemish glass, one with Bible scenes, including the Last Supper, the Scourging, and the Way of the Cross.

Two centuries after John Kaye built this fine house it became a refuge for nuns escaped from France in the Revolution; here they ended their days in peace, being laid to rest in the churchyard at Kirkthorpe near by.

Hebden. Its glory is its setting by a deep wooded glen, where the Hebden Beck comes from a pretty waterfall on its way to the Wharfe. There are two bridges side by side, the big one carrying the moorland road. The old houses and the century-old church look up to the enfolding hills, and from the rocky crags across the stream is a wonderful panorama of fell scenery.

Hebden Bridge. A pleasant little manufacturing town with mills and foundries, it lies in a deep hollow of the moors, where the Hebden Water (crossed by an old bridge) joins the River Calder.

The 19th century church on the edge of the town has a reredos shining with colour and gold, showing the Crucifixion, the grief of the Madonna, and figures of four saints. The town has an interesting collection of Nonconformist churches—one of them now the offices of a local newspaper. But its claim to interest is its situation, sheltered by a hillside of rocky crags and trees, crowned by the fine church of Heptonstall.

Some of the waterfalls that are a feature of the scenery hereabouts are seen in the lovely Grimsworth valley, and three miles north-west of the town are the picturesque Hardcastle Crags, clothed in magnificent firs, in a wooded glen. There is a splendid view from this huge mass of rocks.

Two miles south-west of the town is Stoodley Pike, a great column crowning Stoodley Hill, which rises 1300 feet above the sea. It was set up in 1856 in place of an earlier Memorial of Waterloo.

Heckmondwike. It has been a town since the Romans came this way, and suffered much when the Conqueror destroyed the country round and when the Scots were burning and plundering the Spen Valley. It has little that is beautiful, but has a very old farm-house (Stubley Farm), with ancient beams and something left of the buildings in which the first Stubleys were weaving wool 800 years ago. The farm is on the hillside, with new houses gathered about it. Close to the market square is a garden with a War Memorial. The parish church is 19th century, with a chancel of the 20th; the Congregational Chapel in Dewsbury Road, with a handsome pediment on lofty columns, is one of the most striking Nonconformist churches in Yorkshire. The famous Heckmondwike Lecture is still delivered annually here. In its graveyard is a simple memorial to a youth who has been described as Yorkshire's Chatterton, Herbert Knowles.

There was born here in the year after Waterloo a man who taught millions of children to sing, for he gave us Tonic Sol-fa. He was John Curwen, a minister's son and a minister himself. At Norwich he met a clergyman's daughter who was teaching music by a simple method out of which developed the tonic sol-fa system. Here also lived for 20 years a man more famous than either of these, the immortal Joseph Priestley, also a Nonconformist minister. He lived at Old Hall with his aunt, coming when he was six. We may see the room he slept in, and the garden where he bottled spiders and made experiments which were the forerunners of his discovery of oxygen.

Hellifield. A meeting place of busy roads and rails, threading their way through the fells, it has a few old houses among much that is new. Sheltering under a little hill, and hiding in a great company of noble trees, is Hellifield Peel, a fine embattled house which has grown from the Peel castle of six centuries ago. Fine lawn and borders of flowers are a setting for the trim 20th century church, with a stone roof and a sturdy north tower.

Hemsworth. A venerable yew, old before the first pit was sunk in this big village, stands in the churchyard, high above the busy road. The yew lost most of its branches in a storm in 1884.

Rebuilding has left little of the old church except the 15th century nave arcades and the 14th century chancel and chapel, and these are restored. A worn old font is idle now, the modern one is much enriched with tracery, and two bells are said to be 15th century. It is dedicated to St Helen, seen in the east window, who is said to have visited the area.

The hall where the first Viscount Halifax was born in 1800 is now a school, set among lovely trees. The most famous man associated with the village was Robert Holgate, who is thought to have been born here in 1481. He became Archbishop of York, and founded three schools and a hospital still sheltering old folk in a fine new range of buildings a mile from the village.

Heptonstall. It is one of the most fascinating places in the West Riding. With desolate moors all round it is set high on a ridge between the narrow valleys of the Hebden Water and the Colden Clough which join the Calder at Hebden Bridge. It is a very steep climb up to this place with stone houses and streets crooked and so narrow that only one car can go at a time. It is said that Paulinus climbed this hill and preached here centuries ago, when he was persuading King Edwin to accept Christianity. Two churches share the churchyard; the old one comes chiefly from the 15th century, but it was dismantled in 1854, leaving a west tower and stone-ribbed porch, two naves side by side, and now roofless, and two chancels; a service is held once a year in the old church shell. The new church, raised when the old one was abandoned is in 15th century style, and takes one by surprise on entering, for one is amazed at the newness of the woodwork, which was indeed installed by a bequest as recently as 1964.

The village has also an exceedingly interesting octagonal Wesleyan Chapel, in Northgate, dating from 1764. Other interesting buildings include a grammar school of 1642, now used as an old people's club, in which are preserved the master's desk, a table for the scholars and a cupboard full of the old books they used for their studies; in Northgate is White Hall, with the date 1578 on its lintel; there are weavers' cottages in the main street, and in the cellars of the Co-operative Society branch some old dungeons have been found. On a doorhead of 1736 in Northgate a man and a woman clasp a tree. This is truly a delectable place for lovers of history and the atmosphere of old Yorkshire.

Hickleton. A small place embowered in trees, it is altogether charming, though the pits are not far away. The picture of the wayside group of embattled church, the stone Crucifix on a little green, and the imposing gateway to the hall, is delightful. The great house stands in a park with beautiful grounds and has a fine view across the Dearne Valley. The Crucifix is a monument to King Edward VII; the former home of Lord Halifax, now belongs to the Sue Ryder Forgotten Allies Trust.

The church comes chiefly from the close of the 15th century, but it has a Norman chancel arch, and a massive Norman font with flowers round the rim. Through a porch with a ribbed roof we come to an interior richly furnished with fine hanging candelabras, modern screens enclosing the chancel and chapels, and windows with a rich display of heraldry. Two shields in a west window may be 18th century. There is an old carved pulpit, and on an old gravestone are a cross, a chalice, and a book.

A treasured possession is the flag of the Dutch Admiral de Winter, captured at the battle of Camperdown in 1797. It was taken by a middy on Admiral Duncan's ship and given to Sir Francis Lindley Wood. The most striking monument is an altar tomb on which lie Sir Francis's son, the first Viscount Halifax, and his wife. There are busts of William Reginald Courtenay, eleventh Earl of Devon, and of George Frederick Bodley, who designed many churches and houses and was a friend of Burne-Jones, William Morris, Ford Madox Brown, and Rossetti.

The churchyard has a mediaeval cross with three grotesque figures on the top (seeming to be two pelicans and a boar), and a lychgate with three grim skulls behind a small barred window, as if to say that Death comes to us all.

High Hoyland. It is well named, for it stands on a tremendous hill with views so wide that the Derbyshire hills can be seen on clear days. Far above Denby Dale, the village has old yews by the road, old houses on the hill, and old stones in its church, which is like a long schoolroom.

The tower was refashioned by a carpenter in the 17th century, but much of the church is twice as old, and some windows are new. We counted nearly a score of fragments of old stones in the walls, among them mediaeval gravestones and Saxon crosses.

The stone of Ann Copley declares that she was born in 1600 and died in 1705, and the rectors' list shows that Christopher Bird was preaching here for sixty years.

High Melton. The church and the big house (now a College of Education) are companions in this pleasant place on the hillside, with spacious views of the Dearne Valley. The house has elephants carved in stone on the parapet; the church has a 15th century tower with curious gargoyles, including a little man in a hat with a horn. Two figures are on a buttress, one touching the other's chin. It is odd inside, with a chancel longer than the nave, the tower opening to both the nave and the aisle. The fine arcade of two bays is Norman, and in front of the Norman chancel arch is a fine modern screen with a vaulted loft, the rood figures reaching the roof. The 15th century chapel (with its old piscina) is enclosed by lovely old screenwork. The font may be 12th century, fragments of ancient crosses are in the porch walls, and old coffin lids serve as lintels to windows. In the rich remains of 14th century glass are many shields, three figures of Our Lord, saints, the Madonna, and a bishop.

Holmfirth. A small grey town busy with wool, it stands in a deep valley where the Holme and the Ribble meet, some of its houses perched on the steep hillsides which climb to wide moors dotted with reservoirs. A row of gabled almshouses with a little spire commemorates the bursting of the Bilberry reservoir in 1852, a catastrophe Holmfirth will for ever remember. On a pillar near the 18th century church we see recorded the extraordinary height the water rose when 90 million gallons came thundering down the valley one moonlight night. The pillar itself was set up in 1802 to mark the "short Peace of Amiens". High on the moors to the south towers the great mast of the Holme Moss Television Station, opened in 1951.

Hook. Two miles from Goole and as far from Howden, its long road is like a ribbon in a big loop of the River Ouse, whose banks are at times so high that we can see only the masts of the ships sailing up to Boothferry Bridge. Many old houses with red pantile roofs are among the fields and orchards, and the lowly bellcot church looks north to Hook Hall peeping from the trees. In a field by the church is a moat round hummocky mounds where a monastery is said to have stood; the water is still in the moat.

It is an old church restored last century, with black and white roofs looking down on cream walls and arches. The arcades are mediaeval, and the narrow 13th century doorway to the vestry has an old studded door and hinges. There are two old carved chairs. The glass showing four choristers is in memory of two of them. A window in a corner of the chancel has a scene which may be unique in a church—Queen Victoria near the close of her long life, visiting the wounded of the South African War.

Hooton Pagnell. It is one of the surprises which Yorkshire produces at unexpected moments. It is almost incredible that the coalfields are within a mile or two of the green fields and rich woodlands hereabouts. Perched on the hillside, it has stone houses growing quaintly out of the rock, and others on an island site encircled by roads. On the high road are the fine remains of an ancient market cross; and from here is a magnificent view to the west. At one end of the village is the little church with Norman remains, a companion for the old hall, occasionally open to the public, whose story is said to have begun with the Norman Ralph de Paganel. There are great beeches in the lovely grounds, and from the fine modern gateway with stone-capped towers we have a delightful peep of a wing of the house with a charming oriel, and a passage through which we see another oriel and the porch.

So high above the road is the church that a steep flight of 13 steps brings us to it. The tower has traces of herringbone masonry, and a massive Norman arch. Another massive arch of this time leads to the chancel, which was lengthened in the 13th century and has some of its lancets restored. An original Norman arch and a modern one open to the north chapel, and the two stone seats for priests may be 12th century. The nave arcade is over 700 years old, its pointed arches resting on fine pillars with capitals showing the beginning of leaf ornament. There is an ancient font, and an old coffin lid has a serpent twined round a rod. Fragments of others are with many carved stones in the porch, and the Norman doorway through which we come has a key and a dagger engraved on some of its stones. It frames a door perhaps as old as itself, still swinging on its original hinges. A few panels of a mediaeval screen are under the tower. The inlaid pulpit may be 18th century, and the beautiful glass with St Michael, St George, and St Raphael is a thankoffering for the men who came back from the war.

Hooton Roberts. This hillside village above the River Don has had a church since Norman days, and, though some of it is modern, there is old walling in the nave, a round Norman arch in the chancel, and a pointed one only a little younger leads to the chapel. The new chancel arch is in the old style. The tower is 15th century. A stone coffin has a lid with a cross and a chalice, and in a window with fine old glass are a tiny monk and a big bishop. Robert Burrowes was rector for 53 years of the 17th century, and Charles Eyre served 63, dying in 1860.

After the death of the first Earl of Strafford his widow lived in the house by the church till she was buried by torchlight in the chancel in 1688. It had always been thought that her husband was buried at Wentworth Woodhouse, where there is a memorial to him, but in 1895 workmen repairing this church of Hooton Roberts found three skeletons near the altar, one looking as if the head had been cut off, and it is thought possible that they may be the earl and his wife and daughter.

Horbury. Most of its old possessions have vanished. The Saxon fort on the hill and the ancient bridge over the Calder are gone, and the old church has given place to one built by Horbury's greatest son. He was John Carr, and this is the old church he designed in classic style, building it in 1794 and paying for it. Born here in 1723, he began by building small houses and went on to build town halls and to rebuild Wentworth Woodhouse and Farnley Hall. Two of his noblest achievements were Lytham Hall and Harewood House. Beginning life as a workman, he died in 1807 worth £150,000, and one of the last things he did was to give his own village the church in which he sleeps, a church looking as if it might have stepped out of Wren's London. Of John Carr of York as of Wren himself we may say, "If you seek his monument, look around."

The lofty tower of tapering stages is crowned with a spire, the nave has Corinthian columns between it and the narrow aisles, the ceiling has moulded panels. There is an imposing pulpit. A fine modern brass shows John Sharp kneeling in his robes, and in roundels below him we see this church, the old one it replaced, and the buildings in the town to which he was benefactor. The much loved hymn *Onward Christian Soldiers* was written by a curate of the town, and was first sung here.

Horsforth. A busy little town making woollen goods and quarrying stone, it looks down on Airedale, and on a deep glen well named Woodside. In the new part of the town is Stanhope Drive. It is an avenue of 212 trees, one for every man and the one woman who gave their lives in the Great War. There is a name on every tree, and on a massive boulder are the words, We lie in many lands that you may live here in peace. Thousands of daffodils make the avenue a golden way in spring. There is also a cenotaph at a corner of Horsforth Park where the gardens and playing fields are now the fine possession of the people. The 18th century house is used by the Council.

The church stands on the hill just above the park, looking over the river to the patchwork of fields, towns, villages, and innumerable mills of a vast countryside. Built in 1883, it has a tower added early this century on the south side of the chancel. There are over a score of arches, some spanning the aisles, four resting on one pillar in the north transept. The best window is in the north chapel (entered by fine iron gates), the lovely mosaic of colour showing the Crucifixion, Christ crowned, and a great company of saints and angels. Across the east wall is a stone reredos with the Resurrection, and saints.

In this village there was born in 1734 a boy who grew up to be the greatest walker of his day, Foster Powell. In 1773 he tramped 400 miles from London to York and back in 138 hours, and later won £10 by doing the same walk in three hours less.

Horton-in-Ribblesdale. It lies in a wild moorland valley cradled by the mountains, Ingleborough rising 2373 feet in the west, and Penyghent (only 100 feet less) to the east. Nowhere is there a better place from which to begin the climb up Penyghent, and from no place is there a more pleasing view of this shapely mountain mass. It is the limestone country of Craven, and hereabouts are some of the famous pot-holes such as Hull Pot and Hunt Pot on the slopes of Penyghent, which have made this village a centre for Northern pot-holers.

Horton has cottages of sombre grey, bridges over streams flowing to the Ribble, and remains of the old stocks in a lane near the charming little church to which we come by two quaint lychgates, each with a roof made of two great stones. Aisles running the length of the nave and chancel make the church an oblong, with a sturdy west tower coming from about 1400, when the Norman building was restored. Except for the pointed arch on each side of the chancel the arcades are Norman; so is the fine font carved with crude herringbone, and the 15th century porch shelters a Norman doorway enriched with zigzag and a hood of diamond pattern. The windows are chiefly 15th and 16th century, the west window of the tower having old glass showing the mitred head of a bishop.

Hubberholme. Sternly beautiful is the narrow cleft in which this village lies, far up the valley where the Wharfe comes through Langstrothdale from the wild country about Cam Fell. The fells are like huge walls on both sides of the village, with Buckden Pike 2302 feet up. On one side of the bridge is the George Inn, once the vicarage and owned by the Church until 1965; an old custom here is the annual land-letting on New Year's Eve—on the other side is the rugged church in a churchyard where time is forgotten.

The churchyard has an old cross and a sundial. Stones of all sizes and shapes are in the walls of the church, which was once flooded so deep that fish swam in the nave. Much of it has stood 700 years. The sturdy tower is without buttresses, and the nave arcades are roughhewn, one of the arches 22 feet wide. There are windows with massive mullions, an old seven-sided font with two queer faces and a cover like a crown, and an old door. On the floor is a bell of 1601, looking almost new.

The chief treasure of the old woodwork is in the remains of one of the few ancient roodlofts left in Yorkshire; there is also modern woodwork by Robert Thompson, the "Mouse Man".

Huddersfield. It is in the Conqueror's Domesday Book as Oderesfelt and there are traces of Roman life about, but Huddersfield is a modern town. No place makes finer cloth than the chief centre of the fancy woollen trade in the West Riding. Engineering, the manufacture of chemicals and dyestuffs, machinery and tools, are a few of its many industries, but its worldwide fame has come with its making of worsted and wool fabrics, silk and cotton goods, and their companion trades.

It was a "little town" when Richard Pococke came this way in the 18th century, but today, bristling with scores of mills and hundred of chimneys, it lies in the valley of the Colne, which gathers here the River Holme and falls into the Calder two or three miles away. The moors are within easy reach, and the rocky hills have furnished the stone for the well-built town, where spacious streets and imposing buildings have displaced much that was cramped and depressing.

The Town Hall is in the Italian style, relieved with pilasters and columns supporting a cornice and pediments. In striking contrast is its neighbour, the public library and art gallery, designed by E. H. Ashburner. A massive building, it reflects the spirit of the 20th century in its severe box-like lines with slightly projecting bays and overhanging cornice, and in the bold figures set at each side of the flight of entrance steps; sculptured by James Woodford, the figures represent the inspiration of Literature and Art. Between the windows here are two panels of sculpture in relief, symbolical of Navigation, Engineering, Song and Dance, History, Bird Life, Tragedy, Music, and Poetry. The Art Gallery has a good collection of oil paintings and water-colour drawings by well-known artists, 85 engravings by Turner, and the Henry Moore sculpture *Fallen Warrior*.

Facing the station (which has eight fluted columns adorning its

Grecian front) is the spacious St George's Square, where a statue of Sir Robert Peel stands, having on the pedestal a bronze panel showing a man giving bread to the poor, symbolical of his public benefaction by abolishing the tax on bread. Not far away is the church of St Peter in the heart of the town, an imposing 19th century building in 15th century style, standing where the de Lacy family are supposed to have founded a church in Norman times. Ten bells ring out from the tower. There are long arcades, and galleries over the aisles, the south gallery like a bridge, beyond which is another aisle. The fine black and white roofs have floral bosses (shining with gold in the nave and chancel) and spandrels with roses and leaves. On the great pillared canopy over the altar are angels, and in the golden rays of the canopy roof is a dove. There are two Jacobean chairs with carved backs, and an inscription telling of an astonishing record for a father and son, organists for over 90 years; Thomas Parratt played his first voluntary here in 1812, and Henry Lister Parratt, who followed in 1862, touched the keys for the last time in 1904. The town centre is in process of extensive rebuilding and already a Civic Centre and several blocks of flats have been constructed.

Greenhead Park, one of Huddersfield's open spaces houses an impressive War Memorial, and plans are afoot for the building of a form of theatre here.

High above the town and the railway viaduct, crossing the River Holme with 30 arches, is Beaumont Park, charming with its rocks and woodland. Grimscar Woods are delightful when the hillside is covered with bluebells. Norman Park at Birkby (in a hollow by a stream) has a soldier monument in memory of men who died for peace. Fixby Hall, on this side of the town, was long the home of Richard Oastler, the courageous Yorkshireman who rescued young children from slavery in the factories; now it is a golf house. Another house which the same fate has overtaken is Woodsome Hall, a charming Tudor house also the clubhouse of a golf club, beyond Almondbury, a suburb of the town which once looked up to it as its superior. Crowning Almondbury Castle Hill (which rises to 900 feet and is said to have been an ancient hill fort) is the Victoria Jubilee Tower, a landmark for miles; at the foot is Longley Park with its golf course.

In Ravensknowle Park, on the Wakefield Road at the suburb of Moldgreen, is a fine house of last century near the site of a mediaeval manor. It is now a museum of exceptional interest, and here, arranged to illustrate the origin and development of plant and animal life, are links with prehistoric times, admirably set out. We see a good model of the first known bird. There is a fine collection of fossils from the coal beds round about, and framed on a wall are skeleton leaves and flowers more delicate than the finest lace. Here we can study the origin and structure of the rocks, and the minerals of the neighbourhood. There are relics of Stone Age Men and of the Romans and Saxons who lived in Colne valley or on the hills around. There is a Roman altar found at Longwood, fine models of Danish crosses, examples of the old-fashioned machinery used in the mills which have brought wealth to the town, an old clogger's tools and bench, and a good collection of birds and their nests.

This museum, together with the park, was the gift of Mr Legh Tolson in memory of two nephews who gave their lives in the Great War. On the lawn near the house is a shelter, of which the pillars, the doorway, and the clock tower are from an old Cloth Hall which stood near the old market cross, which has recently been cleaned and repainted.

Huddersfield has no prettier wayside picture than the Cottage Homes of 1929, beyond Ravensknowle Park. They have hipped roofs with central chimneys, and porches with pilasters supporting pediments, and the groups of dwellings are linked by a pillared loggia. Rose beds adorn the terrace, and in front of it is a sunken garden with lawns and flagged paths, approached through dainty iron gates.

Outside the Methodist Mission in Queen Square is a tablet to a remarkable family: George Browne Macdonald was once minister here and had seven children—Alice became the mother of Rudyard Kipling, Frederick became President of the Wesleyan Methodist Church, and Louisa became mother of the Prime Minister Stanley, Earl Baldwin.

Huddersfield has drawn to itself a group of neighbouring villages: Almondbury, Bradley, Lindley, and Longwood. Almondbury, which keeps its village character among trees on a hill, is dealt with separately in this book.

At Bradley, which has a 19th century church, the River Colne joins the Calder near by. The old bridge, built by the monks of Fountains Abbey probably in the 14th century, has been widened. An odd thing remembered here is that in the 15th century the land belonged to the Pilkingtons in return for a pound of pepper to the monks of Fountains every Christmas day.

Lindley, on the heights behind Longwood Edge, has a fine clock tower facing a 19th century church, in which are two chairs with carved panels showing the stoning of Stephen and Christ calling the children. The tower, rising above the busy road, and wearing a pyramid copper cap with projecting eaves, was the gift of James Nield Sykes, and is enriched with gargoyles and angels, figures of Youth sowing, Age reaping, and Time with his scythe and hourglass. Here now is the modern Huddersfield General Infirmary.

Longwood has great woollen mills in the valley, and rocks rising above the houses on the steep hillside. Of its 18th century church only one pillar is left, near the 19th century church, to which a tower was added in our own time. In its War Memorial window are men and women of the war years, and figures of knights, priests, and kings. From the stone tower above the church (on Longwood Edge) we look for miles down the valley and away to Scapegoat Hill above Golcar. At Slack, a mile or two away, have been found many Roman remains, including tiles and coins and an altar.

Hunsingore. From its hilltop above the winding River Nidd, Hunsingore's 19th century church has a fine view over the plain, and its spire is a landmark long before we reach it. There is an old mill by the river, and a 17th century house by the church, which is encircled by splendid trees. The tower is at the west end of the aisle, and the chancel is an apse, with a floor of Italian marble. There are panels from the Goodricke pew in the old church and the Goodricke shield is in a window. A fine Bible box is Jacobean, and the altar table is of Queen Anne's reign. A beautiful mosaic of St George kneeling is in memory of one who fell on Hill 70 in the Great War. Tributes to Joseph Jonathan Dent, who served 52 years as curate and vicar, are a brass cross on the sanctuary floor and the striking stone lychgate with four massive arches and a vaulted roof.

Idle. Anything but idle is this busy manufacturing place linked with Bradford, its steep roads high above the River Aire. A lychgate with a carved bargeboard (a War Memorial) brings us to the modern church perched on the hillside, looking out on the wooded valley sprinkled with villages and mills. One of its three fonts is from an older building no longer used as a church. Another, elaborately adorned, has a still more intricately carved cover like a star-shaped tower with a spire and flying buttresses. There is a list of seat-holders of 1634, and gathered round Our Lord in one of the windows is a quaint group of Victorians in eastern dress.

Thackley, near by, looks up to Baildon Moor, and has ceaseless traffic pouring along its wide road. Here was born in 1855 one of the most remarkable men who lived into our own century. He was Joseph Wright, and he started work at six by driving a donkey cart between a quarry and a blacksmith's shop. At seven he went into a mill, doubling his wage of eighteenpence a week. His widowed mother struggled with poverty, and life was always hard for the four little Wrights, but by the time he was 14 Joseph was earning nine shillings a week, trudging to the mill early in the morning in his clogs, rough cap, and muffler. He taught himself as well as he could, and then, filled with pity for those who knew less than he, started a little night school, and the day came when he had saved £40. He went to Germany with it and took a degree at Heidelberg. He translated German books and wrote on German dialects, and soon this poor Yorkshire boy had built up a European reputation as a master of languages. He wrote grammar books, and set to work on one of the greatest achievements imaginable by preparing a dictionary of our English dialects. He copied out quotations from every known book with dialects in it, and his records were written on two million slips of paper. No publisher would publish so great a book, for there was little profit in it however great its learning; and Joseph Wright (then a professor at Oxford) published the book himself. It came out in parts and was acclaimed unique and incomparable. There is nothing else in the world like this triumph of a man poor in money but rich in scholarship, and the dictionary has ensured for him an everlasting niche in English literature.

Ilkley. It is a gateway to the Yorkshire dales, lying in an open stretch of the romantic valley at the foot of Rumbles Moor. This range of rocky hills on the south bank of the river rises to 1323 feet, and the moors on the northern side are higher still.

There is ancient history written in barrows and enclosures, and rocks remarkable for what is known as Cup and Ring Carving, a curious ornament probably linking British art of the Bronze Age with the Vikings. The strangest of the carvings here is one in the form of a curved swastika, symbol of fire known throughout Europe and the East long ago. The Ilkley example (believed to have been a thousand years old when the Romans came this way) is on a great rock on the ridge of the moor, not far from the top of Heber's Ghyll. This charming wooded ravine to the west of the town takes its name from the Hebers, whose beautiful old hall is below; their names are in the church of All Saints. Near the Ghyll is one of the town's reservoirs, and the Panorama Rocks with a fine view of the valley.

A favourite spot with all who love a climb are the Cow and Calf Rocks, and not far away is the stony ravine known as Rocky Valley, the Tarn with skating in winter, and the 18th century bath houses known as White Wells, their white walls on the moorside seen long before we reach Ilkley. Above their two round baths, hollowed out of the rock, is Ilkley's well-known spring of pure water.

The story of modern Ilkley, with its wide streets, enchanting gardens, avenues of trees, and imposing buildings (hotels, hydros, convalescent homes), began with the founding of a hydropathic establishment at Ben Rhydding. Ilkley was a village when Cromwell and Prince Rupert came riding through it during the Civil War. It belonged to William de Percy when Domesday Book was written; relics of days before the Norman Conquest are in All Saints churchyard, and in the church are stones from Roman England. Ilkley is believed to be the Roman station marked on Ptolemy's map as Olicana, and the church is actually within that area. Excavations in 1962 revealed important evidence about the walls and buildings. In the small museum are relics found on excavations of the site. There are beads, rings, lamps, pottery, coins, and a piece of oak from the lining of a Roman well; stone querns and millstones; fragments of Saxon carved stones; and spearheads. The musuem is now contained in the Manor House originally built in the 13th century and from which justice was administered for many years. The present façade was added in Tudor times.

Near the ford where the Roman road to Boroughbridge crossed the River Wharfe is a charming old stone bridge, but a modern bridge carries the traffic not far away. Standing finely on the moorside are the modern buildings of the grammar school founded in the days of James I.

The church was much restored last century. What is old is chiefly from the close of the 15th century, but the porch leads to a lovely 13th century doorway enriched with continuous mouldings, and the chancel has a piscina of the same time. A massive font looks ancient enough to have been in the Saxon church. There are old beams in the black and white roof of the nave; the altar table is Elizabethan; and from the 17th century come the font cover, a little panelling near the tower, and a beautiful pew with balustrades. The splendid figure in chain mail, lying under a modern arch, is believed to be a knight of the Middleton family; his legs are crossed and a lion is at his feet.

Curious are the small brass inscriptions in the chancel, most of them to the 17th century Hebers of Holling Hall. One to Captain Heber has a man's face in a corner and a woman's head above a crown at the top; another shows Reginald Heber (only two when he died) and two grim angels holding a crown several sizes too big for his small head. In a corner of the plate to Robert Hodgson of 1639 is his quaint portrait, and a brass with an inscription to

William Robinson of Queen Elizabeth's day has an earlier inscription on the other side, so that the brass is a palimpsest.

The chief treasures of All Saints are five remarkable stones, two in the church and three outside. The two indoors are believed to be Roman, one showing a skirted figure said to be the infant Hercules killing the serpent, the other having part of a man's figure with a kind of flask beside him—probably a vessel for sacrificial wine. The arresting group in the churchyard is of three crosses, all believed to be over 1000 years old and to have been carved in Saxon times. Two are only shafts, one with animals and human figures in its carving and the other with knotwork and animals entwined. The tallest and oldest of the three is complete with its head and carved on the edges with knotwork; on one side are figures of the Four Evangelists with their symbols for heads, and on the other side is supposed to be a representation of Our Lord, with curious creatures, symbolical of evil, below Him. This cross is thought to have stood since 750, and the others from the 9th century.

The church gates were made by a son of Washburndale who was apprenticed to an Ilkley blacksmith and grew up to be Dr Robert Collyer, a famous New York preacher.

A fine and spacious place is St Margaret's, a towerless church designed last century by Norman Shaw, and set magnificently on a hill with a superb view. Everything here is on a big scale—the arches, the east and west windows, the stone pulpit with angels in the border, and the font under a projecting canopy richly carved with tracery and vine, and crowned with four angels. Near it is a marble panel showing the Madonna and Child, in memory of "Tenny", aged two. The reredos is a triptych extending across the east wall, its mass of carving shining with gold.

Ingleton. It is a gateway to some of the grandest scenery in the north of England. Here are wooded glens with exquisite waterfalls, and far above towers the huge mass of Ingleborough. Rising 2373 feet above the sea, it is Yorkshire's third highest mountain. Whernside not far away is second with 2414 feet, and together with near by Penyghent the three comprise the famous Three Peaks Walk.

The great limestone plateau of which Ingleborough and Whernside are a part is famous not only for its heights but for caves, which run far into the sides of the hills, and for pot-holes which swallow the mountain streams. White Scar Cave (penetrating the base of Ingleborough on the western side) and Ingleborough Cave near Clapham (piercing its south-eastern flank) are famed for their glittering stalactites and stalagmites. The pot-holes known as Gaping Gill

Hole and Alum Pot are on the east side of the mountain mass. Skirwith Cave is only one mile from Ingleton and can now be visited.

With traces of ancient fortifications on its mile-round summit like a table-top, Ingleborough is the south-western spur of a mountain ridge of which the eastern spur is Simon Fell rising 2088 feet, and Park Fell the detached northern summit, 1836 feet up. On two of its sides Ingleborough has a precipitous drop of nearly a thousand feet. The best near view of it is from Chapel-le-Dale, and its easiest climb is from Ingleton, by way of Storrs Common and Crina Bottom; but however we come to it the view is its own reward. It is a glorious panorama of hundreds of miles over England and out to the Irish Sea; the Lakeland Fells, Penyghent, and Coniston Old Man (highest point of Lancashire and one of Ruskin's favourite views), are only a few of the mighty landmarks in this vast stretch of countryside.

The waterfalls which are Ingleton's chief charm are in the rich green valleys of the Kingsdale Beck and the River Greta, which meet in the village. We see them all in a 5-mile walk from Ingleton and back. Descending a great staircase we come to the lovely Swilla Glen where Kingsdale Beck rushes over the stony bed, and rocks rising sheer on each side are painted with lichen and moss and crowned with trees. Then come the cataracts known as Pecca Falls, and the splendid Thornton Force with its fall of over 40 feet into a deep pool. In the Greta valley are Beezley Falls, with their triple spout and wealth of old oaks; Black Hole Falls, with a pool 80 feet deep; Baxenghyll Gorge; Yew Tree Gorge with a living bridge of yew, and Snow Falls as white as their name.

Some of Ingleton's houses climb the hillside, others are with the church at the top. Far below roars the River Greta, dashing over boulders and spanned by a railway viaduct 800 feet long. The spacious church has been rebuilt except for its 15th century tower, but it keeps a wonderful Norman font with sculptured scenes such as Christ's Entry into Jerusalem and the Massacre of the Innocents. Unfortunately it still suffers from the threat of subsidence.

Keighley. It is a hundred years and more ago since Charlotte Brontë would walk four miles across the moors from the lonely parsonage at Haworth to this town full of shops and mills and factories. It was her great shopping place, the place where she found not only paper to write on but books to read. It was from Keighley station that she took the train to London to make her secret known; and it was from here that the dying Anne took a train to Scarborough, to die there in four days.

Even then Keighley (pronounced Keithley) was growing, with the little narrow windows giving way to great panes of glass; and Mrs Gaskell noticed that almost every house was given up to business, and that even the smallest had stone doorways and windows, all neatly kept. Today thousands of wheels are always turning here, and people are busy on worsted and woollens, machinery and tools. The town is nobly set near the meeting of the Aire and the Worth, and it has the grand moorland scenes of the Brontë country all about it. On Haworth Moor is a massive stone seat with an inscription to one who loved these open spaces, a beloved townsman of Keighley, Tom Stell. He must have known that other famous Keighley man, Timmy Feather, whom Patrick Brontë baptised in 1825.

Timmy's memory lives in the museum as the last weaver to work at a hand-loom in England. For 70 years he lived in a cottage and worked his loom at neighbouring Stanbury, and in Keighley Museum is his loom, with a piece of cloth half-finished on the roller. The loom is in one of the reconstructed workrooms at Cliffe Castle, Keighley's art gallery and museum. Given in 1950 to Keighley by Sir Bracewell Smith, it has housed since 1959 the contents of the former Victoria Park Museum in more extensive and modern surroundings. The Castle has rooms devoted to children's games and toys, geology, pre-history, natural history, and textiles. There is also a vast collection of local "bygones" of the Victorian era.

Tucked away in a corner, but not a stone's throw from the busiest street in Keighley, is the church of St Andrew, twice built last century on the site of the mediaeval church. It was first rebuilt in Trafalgar year, and again in the year of European revolutions, 1848; a sampler picture of the first 19th century church hangs on the wall. The fine tower rises at the west end of the clerestoried nave, and a few memorials from the ancient church have been preserved, including two worn gravestones from the 15th century and a crude cross with four circles forming the head; it is thought to be Saxon. The gravestone of the founder of Keighley Grammar School is near the lectern; he was John Drake, who founded the school in the 17th century, and his epitaph here was written by his friend the rector. This is it:

Here lies the body of John Drake
Who never did his friend forsake.
Houses and land he left to be
A free schoolmaster's salary.
He lived and died without a mate
And yielded to the laws of fate.

143

The font (1661) came back to the church after being in a black-smith's shop, in a garden, and finally in the museum. There is also a modern font, and the striking cover, like a spire with tracery and pinnacles and figures of saints, serves as a canopy for the pulpit. There is nothing more beautiful in the church than the oak reredos at the east end of the north aisle (now the War Memorial chapel), with figures of Our Lord, St Michael, and St George.

On the fringe of the town is a striking Roman Catholic church built in the Norman style. Shaped like a cross with a massive central tower, its walls are a motley of golden-tinted stone, and the light of day streams through over 100 windows. The nave has a clerestory and aisles, and above its fine west doorway is a wheel window. Above the sweeping arches at the crossing are the lantern windows of the tower. The chapels are impressive in their severe simplicity, one having a solitary statue of the Madonna, the other a figure of Our Lord on the altar.

In splendid contrast with the rest of the church is the rich chancel with its ambulatory, a triforium with 36 interlacing arches, and a clerestory above. The main arcading has arches enriched with zigzag, and short massive pillars carved in the Norman fashion, one with lattice ornament reminding us of Abbot Hugh's pillar in Selby Abbey. There are stone altar rails with metal gates, fine simple oak roofs, and a dainty baptistry with a font adorned with lattice pattern. The registers of St Andrew's have in them the name of Patrick Brontë, who frequently officiated at marriages in the church.

Keighley has in its keeping the library of a great Englishman who knew the town in his boyhood and loved to use its books, as Charlotte Brontë did. He was Philip Snowden, a member of the town council here in the early days of his public life, and in memory of those struggling days Lady Snowden has given the town her husband's library of 3000 volumes. He knew them all. He read them again and again. They were the tools and weapons with which he fought his way through poverty and obscurity to fame and power, and it is good to think that the books that made him what he was will have their chance, in the place he knew, to fashion other minds like his.

Kellington. Watching over the cornfields, away from the village, is the lonely church, an impressive grey pile from Norman days. The nave has original walling, a blocked Norman window seen in the wall outside, and a simple Norman doorway in the splendid stone-ribbed porch. Its 13th century arcade leads to an aisle made new. The old tower was altered in the 15th century, but it keeps its fine arch on imposts and an arched opening above it, both over 700 years old. A new arch leads to the spacious chancel with a mediaeval arcade between it and the old chapel, and among the windows filling the church with light are six 13th century lancets and a clerestory from the end of the 14th. The font is said to be older than the Restoration date it bears, old bosses adorn the roof of the nave, and one of the bells was ringing in Queen Elizabeth I's day.

A mediaeval coffin lid has an engraved cross and sword; another has worn sculpture of a floral cross, and an angel over what seems to be the figure of a woman in flowing robes, with an animal at her feet; on the other side is a dragon.

The churchyard has a gateway of 1698, and at Sherwood Hall, about a mile east of the village, is one of 1621.

Kettlewell. It has been a market town famous for its fairs and is now a village, but its lovely setting in Upper Wharfedale has not changed. Great Whernside and Old Cote Moor rise grandly on each side, and into the glorious view down the dale comes Kilnsey Crag. The charming road bringing us up the valley is like a maze threading between grey walls. Under a bridge in the village is a stream from the slopes of Whernside, and below its meeting with the Wharfe the river is crossed by a fine old bridge and stepping stones. In a churchyard like a garden, entered by an oak lychgate, lies Isaac Trueman, who is locally believed to have been 117 when he died in 1770. The church is rebuilt, but it shelters a fine tub font carved in the 12th century with simple leaves and an animal's head. Near here is the famous Dow Cave of interest to pot-holers. The modern building which attracts the eye a little farther down the dale is Scargill House, a Church Holiday Centre.

Kildwick. Green hills are about this unspoiled village in the valley of the Aire, which is crossed by a mediaeval stone bridge. Grey houses are grouped here and there, and high on the hill above the striking church is the gabled hall, built 300 years ago and refashioned in the 18th century.

Known as the Long Church of Craven, it is astonishing for its length, 170 feet with a width of only 50. The arcades are like a long stone avenue from east to west, with no chancel arch to break the vista of ten bays on each side. The four western bays of both arcades, and the corresponding portions of the aisles, are 14th century. The rest of the church, including the tower and the clerestory, is chiefly Tudor, of the time of Henry VIII. The old font is enriched with lettering and symbols of the Passion, and its huge cover, like a spire, has tracery and 24 grotesques. A fine old roof crowns the nave and chancel. There are some handsome 17th century pews with rich carving, an old chest, and chapels enclosed with screen-work old and new. The charming Children's Corner has a tiny altar and a Jacobean screen.

Among the old glass are shields of Bolton Priory, of the Cliffords and Plumptons, and of Marmaduke Huby who built the great tower of Fountains Abbey. Among many fragments of broken stones from the earlier church are parts of Saxon crosses, one carved with the figure of a little man. In a case are a key made 600 years ago, a big bassoon once played in this church, and a letter written at Scutari by Florence Nightingale thanking the people of Kildwick for their help. The stone posts of the stocks stand near the church, which has also part of the timbers.

Lying on a modern tomb is a stone knight, his face battered, his feet on a dog. Wearing chain mail, he has a sword about four feet long, and is believed to be Sir Robert Stiveton, who fought at Crecy.

In the churchyard is a remarkable gravestone surely unique in England, for it is carved like an organ. Below it lies John Laycock, an organ builder who died in 1889 at the age of 81, his tombstone being a copy of the first organ he built.

Kilnsey. Looking over the Wharfe to Conistone sheltering under its Beacon, and linked to it by a bridge with a string of arches, Kilnsey has a barn (with Tudor windows) built by the monks of Fountains Abbey. But its fame is in its Crag, a limestone cliff towering above the road, an impressive spectacle in this broad green stretch of the dale. It was "conquered" in 1957 in a tour de force of modern mechanical climbing methods. The Upper Wharfedale Agricultural Society has an annual show and sports near by, including a Crag Race.

Kippax. It is an unlovely place, but its church is in a green spot on the hill, and between the village and the River Aire is the handsome Elizabethan hall in a deer park of 250 acres. Traces of an ancient stronghold are on what is known as Manor Garth Hill.

The aisleless church has an imposing tower seen from afar. Its belfry windows are 15th century, but much of its walling is the herringbone work of the Normans. The font and its tall carved cover are 17th century, one of two piscinas has a double bowl, two loose old stones are carved with faces, and a fragment of a Saxon cross shows a man trampling on two snakes.

Kirk Bramwith. It has a green setting by the River Don and its canals, its one possession a simple 12th century church which has been much restored, crowned by a narrow tower which seems to be 15th century. The nave has original walling, and its beautiful Norman south doorway has an arch enriched with zigzag and 21 beak-heads, resting on shafts with scalloped capitals. In the Norman doorway now blocked in the north wall is a window with four panels of old glass, one of the portraits showing Archbishop Usher of Armagh, who died in 1656. There is zigzag in the Norman chancel arch, and the font is also Norman. One of the old coffin lids has an inscription to a 15th century rector, Nicholas Lynn.

Kirkburton. On the wooded slopes of the Pennines, five miles from Huddersfield, it has woollen mills and collieries, and a fine old church. Most of the church is over 700 years old, the time of the base of the tower and its beautiful west doorway, enriched with four-leaved flowers all round. The west window and the rest of the tower are nearly two centuries later. The striking nave has tall arcades of six bays, and a splendid old flat roof with bosses glowing in colour and gold on the dark moulded beams. In the modern stone screen behind the altar are two good stone doorways found in the vicarage garden. The old font has an extraordinarily tiny stem for its great bowl, and its unusual modern cover is a canopy sheltering Our Lord in golden robes, a child on His knee. There are many rough-hewn pews. A few with bobbin ends and a desk with two chained books are 17th century, a chest and old glass fragments being older still. A tall stone cross by the chancel arch is old and new, part of a Crucifixion and of interlacing work being perhaps the work of a Saxon mason. Near by on rough-hewn stone steps stands Highburton Cross.

Kirkby Malham. It is one of Airedale's lovely villages. We drop steeply down through a green tunnel of trees to a bridge over the Beck, where the inn hobnobs with the lychgate and old yews flourish by the old stocks in the churchyard. The 17th century vicarage has been restored. Above are the towering moors and fells, and travellers come this way to Malham with its remarkable Cove and Tarn.

The church is a spacious place, with great stones in its grey and amber walls. The fine porch shelters an old latticed door, and the west tower stands between the aisles resting on massive arches. The clerestories and the arcades of golden-tinted stone run the length of the church, with niches carved on some of the pillars. The old

147

roofs are only a part of the beautiful woodwork adding to the charm of the church. There are low box-pews, and high ones with balustrades make a delightful corner at the east end of an aisle. There are old altar rails, old chests, and two richly carved chairs with six legs.

One of several old coffin lids has a chalice and a book. There is an old piscina, and the font has a Norman bowl adorned with crude bands and scale-work, resting on a square stone with beak-heads at the corners. A little old German glass shows the shepherds at Bethlehem, and a saint with two children. Among the wall-memorials is one to the son of Cromwell's friend Honest John Lambert. In the parish register is a record of a marriage witnessed by Cromwell himself, who is said to have used the church as a garrison. The lovely panelling of the sanctuary, its deep pinnacled cornice enriched with 16 coloured shields, is a tribute to a million-aire who is at rest in this lonely place among the mountains he loved, Walter Morrison of Malham Tarn; he was 85 when they laid him in this church to which he gave so much beauty.

He was a rich man who spent over 60 years on the moors, and gave away immense sums of money in secret. He was a Liberal MP and sat in Parliament for 40 years, but he was not built for a party man and remained a lonely figure in politics. To Malham Tarn came Charles Darwin, John Stuart Mill, John Ruskin, and Charles Kingsley, and no one left without a great regard for this lonely man.

It was while staying with Walter Morrison, walking at Malham Cove, that Charles Kingsley conceived the idea of *Water Babies*, and Morrison was his Squire. It was the bells of Malham church that poor Tom heard ringing as he came down to the river. These bare mountains, the lovely valley of the Aire, and the old church of Kirkby Malham, all come into Kingsley's story. Walter Morrison was the model for Sir John Harthover, Malham Tarn the grand house where Tom was surprised to see himself in the mirror.

Kirkby Malzeard. Near the moors where the River Laver comes to life, it has charming stone houses with creepered walls and gay gardens, a modern cross on the site of a mediaeval one, majestic trees, and a fine church above a lovely little glen where a bridge crosses the Kex Beck as it flows to the lake in Azerley Park.

The Norman castle of the Mowbrays has been gone for many centuries, but fragments of the Norman church remain in this one, which was restored after fire swept through it in 1908. We enter through a lovely Norman doorway, its arch (with three rows of

Prospect Gardens, Harrogate.

The bridge at Kettlewell.

The railway bridge and river at Knaresborough.

bold zigzag) resting on stones carved with star pattern; the new door has good ironwork and the oak tympanum has a rich cross. The striking arcade of nave and chancel, with pointed arches on round pillars and bell capitals, was originally 13th century. One of the pillars is a support for four arches—two of the arcade, one between the aisle and chapel, and the chancel arch, which rests on the south side on a fragment of the Norman church. The chancel is chiefly 15th century, with restored sedilia and a battered piscina. In the massive east wall of the chapel are two fine lancets of about 1200, leaning in their great splays and now blocked. The 15th century tower is adorned with a band of quatrefoils and angels with shields, animals in a hunting scene, and two men with a chalice. Queer animals crouch on two buttresses.

A 16th century brass with portraits of William Mann and his wife has an inscription telling us that it had been lost for many years before it was found on the eve of the passing of the great lunar shadow of 1927. In a jumble of old glass are saints, the head of Our Lord, and shields with lions.

Beautiful woodwork is in the low poppyhead benches, in screens with lacelike tracery and in stalls, reading desk, pulpit, and all the roofs—hammerbeams in the nave and chancel. A piscina near the pulpit is hidden by new panelling in the nave, but can be seen if we open a little trapdoor.

In the churchyard are fragments of Norman stones, a 13th century gravestone, an old cross, and the stone of George Wharton who lived to be 112 and died in 1844.

Kirkby Overblow. Its glory is its place on the high ridge between the River Nidd and the Wharfe, the grey stone houses and the church set charmingly on the hillside, looking down on lovely miles of Wharfedale. Britons were sleeping here before the coming of the Romans. Over a mile from the village is Morcar Hill, where the Saxon Earls of Northumbria are said to have had a stronghold, and across the river Harewood's great park clothes the hillside. Buried in trees on the north side of the village is Low Hall, a charming Tudor house with an iron-studded door weighing nearly half a ton. One of Wharfedale's many wells dedicated to St Helen is near the church.

It is a mediaeval church much restored, its 15th century tower with an inscription telling of its rebuilding in 1781. The oldest fragment is a crude doorway now blocked in the north wall, its round arch cut from a single stone and resting on big stones each side; it takes the church's story back to early Norman or Saxon

F   149 times. The 14th century transept has a piscina, there are three fine old brass candelabra in the chancel and four golden angels holding candles over the altar, and an inscription tells of Sir William Codrington, an admiral's son who, finding himself commanding a brigade in the Crimea without any experience of war, boldly charged a fort at the Battle of the Alma and carried it.

Kirkby Wharfe. The river is near this tiny place with a few trim cottages, one or two big houses, a green, and a church, all at the edge of Grimston Park, where the great house stands in gardens with statues and vases and rare plants. Restored a hundred years ago, it is in classical style, with a noble portico; and in the park of 800 acres is the Emperor's Walk with busts of the Caesars and a temple with a bust of Napoleon. A company of huge sycamores must have been noble trees when Sir John Caradoc was living here after his adventures with Sir John Moore as a soldier.

The church where he has been sleeping since 1839 dates from the 12th century. The tower has a 12th century base with its original arch oddly askew on the imposts, and its battlements and pinnacles are 15th century. A studded door with panels of rich carving lends charm to the plain Norman doorway, its round arch on shafts with leaf capitals. From about 1200 come the nave arcades with pointed arches, the north massive and tilting, with traces of colour on some pillars. The pointed chancel arch rests on Norman stones, and the Normans shaped the tub font. There are older stones here than these, however; fragments of Saxon crosses with one cross almost complete, carved with interlacing work and two figures. There is a tiny stone coffin, and the brass portrait of a 15th century priest.

In old glass we see the Descent from the Cross, the Flight into Egypt, Abraham and Isaac, the Madonna, Jesus with the Doctors, the Agony, and symbols of Matthew and John, Martha and Mary and the Crucifixion are in glass by the famous Belgian craftsman Jean Capronnier.

Between the chancel and the chapel is finely restored old screenwork with mediaeval tracery and quaint old carving. Richly carved chairs furnish the chapel for the squire, and there is good modern carving in the pulpit.

Kirk Deighton. Near the great house with creepered walls, the lovely old church is perched high above the busy road from Wetherby to Knaresborough. Stately trees rise about it, and from the churchyard Spofforth's grey tower nestling in trees comes into the wonderful view.

The fine 15th century tower has a stone spire, a vaulted roof, big gargoyles, quaint faces by windows and doorway, and an animal crouching on a buttress. The striking feature inside is the north arcade built by the Normans, the stout round arches resting on clustered pillars. The south arcade is a little later, and the chancel is much restored, including its round arch. The nave, south aisle, and porch have roofs of old moulded beams; fragments of old screenwork are in the tower; the heavy door with wooden pegs and an immense lock is 15th century. An old gravestone has a cross and plain shields, and a curious painting in the vestry has the Ten Commandments between pictures with castles. Richard Burton, who has been sleeping in the chancel since 1656, has a monument showing him at prayer, a book before him. An inscription is to Ursula Walker, mother of the George Walker who courageously defended Londonderry in 1688.

In the park of Ingmanthorpe Hall, a mile east of the village, are lovely gardens.

Kirk Hammerton. Here in the byways, amid green pastures by the River Nidd, is one of Yorkshire's rarest fragments of Saxon England—a small church with chancel, nave, and tower, standing sturdy and strong after nearly a thousand years. It stands at a charming corner of the village. The Saxon fragment is now the southern part of a 19th century church much bigger than itself, with the old nave linked to the new one by a 14th century arcade which led to a vanished aisle; the ancient building reminds us of the simple models often held by saints in old glass windows. The walls of nave and chancel are surprisingly high, and are a fascinating medley outside of great and small stones in colours of rose, amber, and grey. One of the windows is Norman. The plain tower has a pyramid cap, a curious doorway, and a tall narrow arch to the nave. There are old altar rails, an ancient piscina, and a reredos with old carving showing over 50 figures in quaint scenes from Our Lord's life. Between the nave and chancel is a richly traceried oak screen.

Kirkheaton. Below the village and the mills, the church is tucked away in a peaceful hollow, with a little inn for company. It was much rebuilt last century, but the 15th century tower and the spacious chapel are still here, the chapel having bits of old glass and memorials of the Beaumonts, who were here seven centuries ago.

One of the family is represented with his wife in brass, he in jack boots with a child by him, she wearing a veil, a child in her arms and another at her side. Sir Richard Beaumont of 1631 (the famous "Black Dick") lies under a pillared canopy, and another monument has busts of a later Richard and his wife.

The wide north aisle is bigger than many churches. Two carved chairs are 1687 and the pulpit is Georgian. The brass lectern with a figure of St John is modern, and there is also a beautiful modern font, though it has a massive Norman font with seven sides to keep it company. There are fragments of coffin stones perhaps also Norman, stones carved with Saxon ornament, and a stone with a Runic inscription.

A sad thing in the churchyard is a stone pillar over the grave of 17 children who were trapped in a mill by fire and burned to death at their work, ten of them under 14.

The village has always had a fine cricket tradition, and two of the county's most famous players were born here: George Hirst and Wilfred Rhodes.

Kirklees. If Yorkshire has a claim to Robin Hood it is here; it is part of the old legend that here the merry outlaw died. We may think what we will about it. Here are the stones from the old priory in which he is said to have breathed his last. They are in Kirklees Hall, made new in Stuart times, and in a farmhouse close by the scanty ruins of the priory. There is also a buttress and a few stones of the priory church, all 500 years old. Near by are the graves of two of the prioresses, and a little way off, in the greenwood far above the River Calder, is a spot called Robin Hood's Grave, a lonely place among the rhododendrons on the hill. There is a modern stone and a poor epitaph.

Kirklees Hall is in a park of 170 acres, and has fine gardens with a lake and a stream and magnificent beeches.

Kirk Sandall. Cinderella may have had a glass slipper, but Kirk Sandall has a glass hotel. Its walls outside glitter with rose, blue, and black. There are rooms delicate in colour, as well as a gold room and a black room. Even the floors are glass, and a round pillar outside is a mirror. The glass-works for which the village is renowned (Pilkington's, the builders of the glass train many of us have seen) are near the canal and the River Don, running side by side. Here too is the church, tucked away by an old farm and cottages, and not far off is the big house called Sandall Grove, with a fine elm avenue leading to it.

The church is charmingly odd with its tiny tower growing from the south aisle roof, the nave and aisles wider than they are long, and a chapel bigger than the chancel. The tower is chiefly 19th century. Of the Norman church there remain the tall arcades, two fine windows in the south aisle, and the round font. There is a Norman doorway in the modern porch, and traces of herringbone in the west wall.

The chancel was made new in the 15th century, and the chapel was built as a memorial of William Rokeby, a 16th century rector who became Archbishop of Dublin and Lord Chancellor of Ireland. His canopied monument is on the panelled wall. Sir Thomas Rokeby, a judge who died in 1699, also has a monument here. The son of a Cromwellian officer who fell at Dunbar, he received his judgeship for using his influence on behalf of William and Mary in 1688. He was a wise judge and a pious man.

In a spacious medley of old fragments in a window are a bishop, a saint with a sword, St Margaret with a dragon, and two other women saints. Glass showing Our Lord risen, King Oswald, and St Hilda lends a touch of colour to the chancel. The south aisle has a piscina, and inside the church, by the vestry door, is a mass dial upside down.

The arresting things in this small place are two exquisite mediaeval oak screens across the arches of the chancel and the chapel, and the chapel's wonderful old roof. This has lovely floral bosses and a central pendant rose; all the beams are carved with tracery between their mouldings, that of the main beam being undercut. The screens are complete with gates, but most of the tiny figures adorning them are renewed. Leafy arches frame the rich tracery of the base panels, lovely canopies are in front of the tracery in the open bays, and the cornices are splendid with crested vine and grape. Statues of St Oswald and St Hilda stand at the gate of the chancel screen, which has its original iron handle.

Kirk Smeaton. Its pleasantest spot is where the church stands above a green hollow through which flows the little River Went, looking across to a decrepit post-windmill crowning the other hill. Though much restored, and wearing inside a dress of unlovely grey, the church has some treasures, its Norman story told by a beautiful font with interlaced arcading. From the close of the 12th century comes the leaning entrance to the chancel, the roll and zigzag mouldings of its great pointed arch resting on fine capitals. Of the same time is the pointed arch of the 15th century tower. The nave arcade and the aisle are perhaps as old as the lovely 14th century sedilia, which are striking and unusual with pinnacles, finials, and a mass of leaves adorning their trefoiled canopies. We come and go by a door swinging on its old strap hinges.

Kirkstall. It belongs to Leeds, but its place on the fringe of that great city is still a green setting for its noble possession, a Cistercian abbey ranking among the best preserved of all the ruined monasteries in our land, and surpassed in Yorkshire only by Fountains. Kirkstall's old walls rise from lovely grounds with lawns and trees, and a new Geological Garden, the River Aire flowing by. In a charming garden across the road stands the old gatehouse, now a museum, and farther along the road is an obelisk telling us that here we are midway between two capitals, just 200 miles from London and the same from Edinburgh.

Founded by Henry de Lacy, Lord of Pontefract, the monastery was established by a little colony from Fountains who settled at Barnoldswick in 1147, and came a few years later to this site, where a few hermits then lived. Much of the abbey still standing was the work of the monks of the 12th century. The church is almost complete except for the nave roof and the broken tower, and there are substantial remains of the domestic buildings.

An impressive sight towering above the road, the great church has the shape of a cross, with an aisled nave of eight bays, transepts with six eastern chapels, and a choir. The original central tower was raised another storey in the 15th century, but it has been a ruin since the 18th; the fragment remaining is one of the familiar landmarks round Leeds. Other 15th century work includes the corner turrets here and there, the great east window, the tracery in the older windows of the west front, and a small window in the gable.

Looking along the roofless nave we are impressed by the simple grandeur of the majestic arcades, with pointed arches on clustered shafts, harmonious yet exhibiting much variety. On one of the bases on the north side is 12th century carving of the interlacing ornament the Saxons used. The Norman windows of the clerestory are adorned with shafts outside, and the aisles are a fine sight with their vaulted roofs. The six transept chapels have vaulted roofs and Norman piscinas; the vaulted choir has a huge piscina and sedilia under a round arch with scalloped capitals.

The west doorway has a pediment enclosing a row of interlacing arches; it is one of several beautiful Norman doorways. One in the north aisle was reached by a Galilee of which the foundations remain, and in the south transept we see the doorway and part of the stairway by which the monks reached the church from the dormitory. A doorway in the south aisle leads to the east walk of the cloister.

Of the range used by the lay brothers there is still some of the walling with blocked arches, a few windows, and a doorway in which hangs a fine Jacobean door with rich carving. From this door we have the loveliest view of the abbey gathered round the cloister. On our left we see the church—the south aisle with its Norman doorways and the clerestory above it, the south transept with a recess where the monks kept their books, and the gaunt south wall of the tower soaring high. Facing us across the square is the chapter house, with its lovely double entrance and windows. The chapter house is a beautiful fragment, built in the 12th century, and refashioned eastward in the 13th. The floor is of two levels, and the different periods are seen in the fine vaulting rising from central pillars, one a solid cluster, one with detached shafts. At the east end are two arches, each framing a group of three Norman windows. Some stone coffins are built into the walls.

On the south side of the cloister are the blocked doorways which led to the warming-house, the refectory, and the kitchen, and here, too, are remains of the trefoiled arcading of the lavatorium. The refectory ran from north to south, and was divided in the 15th century into two floors. The abbot's house is a fine ruin of three storeys, keeping some of its fireplaces, and an oval window in the gable; it is not generally accessible to the public. There is a kneading trough by the kitchen, and two great arches to the west.

In the very interesting museum housed in the vaulted gatehouse is the trunk of a mulberry tree which may have been growing here in the abbey's great days. In a little oak panelled room is a 16th century four-poster bed lavishly carved, and a fine mantelpiece has a carved scene of the surrender of the monastery, with the abbot and the monks at the church door, the people beside them, and the king's men riding up. There are cannon balls and bullets from Marston Moor, an old printing press, samplers of the 18th and 19th centuries, a set of valentines, old watches, spice-mills, rush-holders, candle-snuffers; dolls, bonnets, parasols; old jet necklaces and bracelets, bridles for scolds, dental tools of the 17th century (grim-looking instruments), a man-trap, and one of the first type-writing machines. A modern feature is a reconstruction of Victorian scenes and a collection of "bygones".

In Kirkstall's 19th century church sleep Richard Oastler and his wife, and a window in their memory shows the Resurrection, the Good Samaritan, and Our Lord with the children. John Wesley held the little Richard in his arms and blessed him, and he grew up to be a blessing to thousands of children, for he helped to relieve their toil in factories, earning for himself the name of the Factory King. Having helped to abolish slavery in the West Indies, Oastler never rested till he had abolished it in Yorkshire factories.

In one of two windows with charming stained glass we see the Madonna and Child, and a picture of the abbey before the great tower fell, the smoking chimneys of Leeds shown in the background; the other window has a portrait of Francis of Assisi, and a picture of a shepherd with his dog and sheep by a hillside Calvary. A fine Jacobean chair has carvings of the Crucifixion, showing the soldiers throwing dice, and in the baptistry, panelled with linenfold and enclosed by screenwork, is an oak font set on a marble base.

Kirkthorpe. Life goes slowly by in this peaceful place, though Wakefield is only two miles away. There is a delightful almshouse for four old men, the old stone stocks with the original rests for a seat, and a 15th century church on the hillside. The church has a line of high and low arches running east to west, windows with a little old glass, and black and white roofs. The oak lectern is an angel holding a scroll. A group of stones east of the chancel marks the resting-place of nuns who fled from France in the Revolution.

Knaresborough. One of Yorkshire's most surprising towns, a small neighbour of Harrogate and a great rival of Richmond in its enchanting natural setting, it stands on the summit of a rocky hill and climbs down the steep bank of a gorge carved in the limestone by the River Nidd. In this gorge, clothed with deep woods on the other bank, lies Knaresborough's great charm.

The river scenery is magnificent. The dark stream flows from High Bridge to a railway viaduct with high arches and an embattled parapet, and swings round to Low Bridge at the southern end of the town. The picturesque jumble of houses and gardens rise tier on tier on rocky ledges, caves and crags and overhanging cliffs are draped with greenery, and flights of steps climb from the river to the stately church halfway up the hill. Reflected in the water, where pleasure boats flash in the sunshine, are the gaunt ruins of the castle crowning the rocky bluff, and from the castle itself is a superb view of the valley and the climbing town. The castle brings back memories of dark pages in our story; the caves are linked with the strange tales of Mother Shipton, Eugene Aram, and a mediaeval monk.

Knaresborough has many old and curious houses. Conyngham

Hall is in a splendid setting of trees in a loop of the river. It now houses a small zoo. Where the steps mount to the church is a lovely white cottage, and facing it stands the Old Manor House, where we may have tea, its walls painted like a draught-board, its garden with a 300-year-old mulberry tree and the river running past. Said to have been built originally round a living oak, this fine old place has huge beams and old panelling, a 17th century chimney-piece with quaint figures and rich ornament, a carved beam of Charles II's day, a bed in which Cromwell slept, and windows framing charming views of the river and the castle.

One of the most remarkable of these old houses is Fort Montague, an 18th century dwelling of three storeys halfway up the cliff, two rooms with stone stairs and one with a passage cut through the rock. Very odd it is· to see these floors and walls and ceilings of rough-hewn rock, to look out of windows cut in the cliff, and to go downstairs to the bedroom and upstairs to the kitchen.

Next door is St Robert's Chapel, believed to have been hollowed out of the solid rock 500 years ago. It is ten feet deep in the cliff, and its doorway is guarded by the figure of a knight drawing his sword. The roof is ribbed, and the simple altar has a niche behind it and a piscina at each side. There are four queer faces keeping watch, a stone bench, and a small window with fragments of old glass probably from Fountains.

The chapel is a memorial to a monk who came from Fountains in 1200, and lived here as a hermit. We remember that something of his story is told in a window of the village church of Morley in Derbyshire, where old and new glass shows St Robert shooting and penning the king's deer (which have been eating his corn), and the king granting him as much land as he could plough with the deer in a day.

Farther down the river is the cave St Robert lived in, much of it washed away but part of the boundary wall remaining, with steps cut in the stone, the doorway with a hinge of the door left for us to see, his stone bed (so small that he could never lie straight in it), and his stone pillow. We see the altar at which he knelt, and the shallow grave he is supposed to have made for himself.

It was in the home of this good man St Robert that there occurred in the 18th century a crime which thrilled all England and has never been forgotten, for it has a place in literature, both in poetry and prose. It was here that Eugene Aram wrote his name so grimly on the page of history. In this spot he buried the victim he had murdered. A poor man's son with a genius for scholarship, he became a schoolmaster, and his life was spoiled by an unhappy

157

marriage. Suspecting that his wife was in love with a man named Clark, he and a man named Houseman joined with Clark in announcing a supper and entertainment, for which they borrowed much valuable plate, and that night Aram and Houseman murdered Clark and sold the plate, expecting that Clark's disappearance would lead to his being blamed for the missing silver. The fact was that they had buried Clark in St Robert's Cave and covered the body with earth. It was as Aram thought—Clark was suspected, and Aram left Knaresborough and settled down in a school at King's Lynn. Fourteen years after the bones in the cave were brought to light, Houseman gave himself away, and the two men were arrested and hanged on a gibbet in this place.

By the Low Bridge, near what was once a ford, is a white-walled inn which attracts many travellers by its associations and possessions. Among these are a Jacobean chair, a carving of an old pedlar shaped from the root of a rose tree, a grandfather's clock which has kept good time for two centuries, the chest in which Sir Henry Slingsby kept his deeds at Scriven Hall, and a portrait painted 200 years ago of Mother Shipton, whose prophecies set all England talking. She is said to have lived in a cave near by, a hollow in the cliff at a romantic spot, in the days when people would believe anything. Facing this cheerless home, under rocks and trees, is the Dropping Well, a petrifying spring which is one of Knaresborough's natural curiosities. The water runs over an overhanging rock and falls like a silver curtain into the huge rock below, and the limestone with which it is highly charged covers whatever is thrown into it with a deposit like stone. In a queer museum is a collection of boots, hats, birds, animals, and scores of odd things looking as if they were being turned into solid stone.

Leaving all these strange sights we come to the parish church, lovely in itself and in its setting. It has come down from the 12th century, when Henry I gave it to Nostell Priory, and rebuilding at the close of that century made it a fine place with the plan of a cross. The transept is said to have disappeared when the present nave and aisles were built in the 15th century, but the line of its old roofs is still seen on the face of the central tower. The lower part of the tower, with fine arches on clustered columns, is part of the second church, and its top storey is two centuries later. The chancel has remains of the Norman church in its masonry (fragments of a stringcourse and traces of windows) but the beautiful east window is 14th century, and the south windows are 15th. The north and south chapels are chiefly 14th, and the clerestory above the high arcades of the nave is modern. A fine piece of the Norman stringcourse is seen in the vestry, into which we come by an old door showing the marks of the carpenter's adze.

A picture for an artist is the south side of the church, where the aisle buttresses are topped with handsome pinnacles, and the porch has a grille of fine ironwork in the head of the doorway. The tower has a short slender spire, and the west front has a doorway between niches. There are aumbries and a piscina with a shelf in the chancel, and two sedilia, a piscina, and a fine niche in the south chapel. A treasure found in the churchyard a few years ago is an ancient altar stone, now against the north wall of the chancel: it is probably 13th century, and on it are five crosses. The font is 15th century, and its elaborately carved cover, like a crown, is Jacobean. A quaint poor box of 1600, looking like a small grandfather's clock, has a lid fastened with three padlocks. The screen in the south chapel has some 14th century tracery, and two of the church windows are notable for Burne-Jones glass.

On the modern screen separating the Slingsby Chapel from the chancel are Jacobean figures brought from Red House, the family's old home near Marston Moor. The earliest of their monuments here is the tomb in the middle of the chapel, on which lies Francis Slingsby, who fought in three reigns of the Tudors and died just before Queen Elizabeth I; his wife, lying at his right side because of her high estate has the Percy arms on her dress. Their son Henry was knighted by Elizabeth for his services in repairing the castle, and his figure in a niche on the north wall shows him as a sad-looking man holding his shroud about him. Thomas, his elder brother, was drowned in the Nidd, and his younger brother Sir William, carver to James I's queen, is said to have discovered the mineral springs at Harrogate. A black gravestone has an inscription to Sir Henry Slingsby who fought at Marston Moor and Naseby for Charles I and lost his head as his reward.

The last of the direct line of the Slingsbys was Sir Charles, who was drowned in 1869 on returning from the hunting field and lies here in marble on his tomb, like

> *One who wraps the drapery of his couch*
> *About him, and lies down to pleasant dreams.*

Since its dismantling by the Parliament, after being held for the king during the Civil War, the castle has been a ruin, but today it is in a charming setting with lawns and trees, winding paths and gardens, ledges bright with flowers, a memorial to those who fell in the Great War, and a quaint Tudor court house which, though shorn of much of its charm, is fascinating still. One of the rooms has

159

white walls, two mullioned windows, a dock with steps down to the cells, roughly adzed seats like a square pew, a massive oak table, and a huge beam serving as a seat for the justice and his clerk.

Protected by natural ravines on three sides, the castle was defended towards the town by a moat, which is now a children's playground. Of the castle built by the Norman baron, Serlo de Burgh, the foundations are now revealed, but most of the remains are mediaeval. The Norman wall is gone, but there are fragments of the round towers built to strengthen it, and two of these have their portcullis grooves. An underground passage 70 feet long leads from one of the ravines to the inner courtyard, and towering above all is the massive rectangular keep, built in the 14th century and still over 50 feet high, though sadly broken. The builders intended the first floor or keep to serve as a gatehouse, leading to the two courts of the castle, with a raised approach on each side.

We are shown the banqueting room with its two fireplaces and a doorway 10 feet wide and 15 high. Two stone faces look down from a moulding, and a stair in the thickness of the wall is curious (and probably unique) for having a stone handrail. The fine chamber on the ground floor has two central pillars supporting the arches of the vaulted roof, and is used as a museum, where may be seen the old stocks, armour worn at Marston Moor, iron cannon balls from Civil War sieges, stone balls shot from catapults in mediaeval days, fragments of carving from the vanished priory, an early fire engine, and two chests—one with nine locks said to be 800 years old, and one thought to have been the record chest of Queen Philippa of Hainault, to whom Edward III gave the castle, the town, and the Forest of Knaresborough as part of her dowry.

In a small room at a corner of this chamber is a window with a fine view of the gorge, and on the other side is a cell once used as a debtor's prison. It has had its iron door wrenched from the hinges, but we see the ingenious arrangement for giving a prisoner food without allowing him to see the gaoler. We go down steps to the dungeon—a gruesome place 23 feet long and 20 feet wide, with the 12 arches of the vaulted roof springing from a central pillar 9 feet round. In the walls (which are 15 feet thick) are traces of iron staples to which prisoners were chained, and there is a shaft which throws a spot of light on the floor at the place where they were executed.

At times a prison and at other times a royal house, the castle has strange tales to tell. It was held for a time by Hugh de Morville, and here he and the other three murderers of Thomas Becket hid while all England cried shame on them. Edward I gave the castle to his beloved Queen Eleanor, and Piers Gaveston held it for Edward II. Here John of Gaunt's wife found refuge during Wat Tyler's rebellion. Chaucer's son was one of the castle's keepers. But of all who ever passed into the shadow of these walls the most wretched was surely King Richard II, the prisoner of his bitterest enemy. He was confined here on his way to Pontefract after his deposition by Bolingbroke and it was from this castle that he passed out to Pontefract Castle.

It was a skirmish at Knaresborough in the Civil War that brought one of his saddest hours to Oliver Cromwell, for in it he lost his son Oliver, whose fall in battle went as a dagger to the Protector's heart.

Knottingley. It is an old place which now has chemical and bottle works, shipbuilding yards and corn mills, standing by the River Aire, which is here both deep and wide. The church, set in a trim churchyard by a rocky ravine, has part of a Norman tower: the nave was rebuilt in the 18th century and the chancel in 1887.

Langcliffe. There are mills by the River Ribble, houses and cottages on and round the green, a church, a sycamore tree said to be 300 years old in front of the old vicarage, and a Tudor hall where Sir Isaac Newton would come as a guest of the Paleys, the family which gave us the great William Paley, moral philosopher and writer of the well-known *Evidences of Christianity*. It is a fine old L-shaped house, its gates open in friendly fashion by the wayside. Grandeur is all about us here. We look over the river to a lovely line of hills, and down the valley to where the heights give place to the rolling plain. On the hill behind the village is a striking range of cliffs with the Attermire Cave at one end, and at the other the famous Victoria Cave 1450 feet above the sea.

Langcliffe had a Naked Woman Inn of which only a stone with a figure and "1660 ISMS" remains. It has this in common with the 17th century "Naked Man" sign in Settle—neither figure is naked!

Laughton-en-le-Morthen. All who travel in this countryside see from afar this splendid old church with its superb 15th century tower and spire, a rare crown for a hilltop. It stands within a stone's throw of the site of a Norman castle, a church begun by the Saxons, refashioned by the last of the Normans, and made largely new in the 15th century. The tower and spire, soaring 185 feet, are perhaps the most beautiful of any village church in Yorkshire, resting on massive piers and arches at the west end of the nave and between the aisles.

Of the Saxon church there is still some masonry in the north aisle wall, with a Saxon doorway built up to allow for one of later time. Of the 12th century building there are still the pillars and capitals of the north arcade (supporting 15th century arches), and a window in the chancel, which has five Norman buttresses and part of the original stringcourse. Angels adorn both stately arcades, and on the aisles outside are sculptures of old men, a knight, a king, a queen, an angel, and a demon carrying off a woman. A Madonna in a niche is on the east wall of the tower, which has a fine vaulted roof.

A gabled piscina may be Saxon, and a simple stone seat 12th century. There are many Saxon and Norman fragments, an altar stone which may be mediaeval, a bell over 300 years old, and some doors older still. The low stone screen between the nave and chancel may be Norman, its border carved with battlements perhaps in the 15th century. High on a wall kneel a man and wife of Elizabeth I's day.

Lead. It has an inn, a farm, and a church, standing in the middle of a field with sheep grazing by its walls. The church is only a simple oblong with a bellcot, stone roof, and one doorway letting us in. There are 11 rough old benches, a quaint three-decker pulpit, and an old oak roof; the old altar stone is in the floor, and the font looks crude enough to be Norman. There are fragments of coffin lids, a complete one of the 13th century, and some gravestones of the Tyas family who lived in the vanished manor house to which this old church belonged. Another coffin lid is in the little garden where antiquaries digging a few years ago found some stone coffins and foundations of what was perhaps a chancel.

It is said that after the Battle of Towton, fought close by in 1461, scores of dead were buried near this lonely building and the near-by Cock beck ran red for 24 hours.

Leathley. It is an attractive old village in the valley of the River Washburn. There are lovely trees in Leathley Park, and round Farnley Hall, where Turner painted many of his pictures; beeches and sycamores are among those by Leathley's old water-mill. Above the old humped bridge is the green, round which are gathered the 18th century almshouses, the school, and the church on its knoll among clustering trees. The old stone stocks and mounting stone are at the churchyard gate.

The Normans built the church, and their two-storeyed tower and plain chancel arch still stand. The rest was refashioned in the 15th century, and is today a simple place with cream-washed walls, and arcades of golden-tinted stone dividing the wide nave from narrow aisles. Carved on the capitals are the crescent and fetterlock of the Percys, the Sacred Monogram, and other devices including a cross and a Tudor rose. The mediaeval piscina has a leafy gable and finial.

Sturdy and strong enough to suggest its use as a place of refuge during raids by the Scots, the tower has small Norman windows below the belfry, and a lofty west doorway. There is no tower arch, but three feet above the level of the nave floor is a plain Norman doorway in which after these 800 years still hangs the original oak door, covered with remarkable ironwork showing the quaint simplicity of style typical of the early smith. There are two hinges enriched with dainty scrolls, and a band of scrolls wrought in charmingly haphazard fashion.

Somewhere in the churchyard sleeps Mrs Elizabeth Watson who was 104 when she died in 1898. Tradition says her father lived to be 110 and her uncle 115. Jack Watson rang the church bells for 60 years of last century.

Ledsham. A pretty village in a wooded dip of the green hills, it lies between the Great North Road and a straight Roman road, with the River Aire two miles away. It has gay gardens, almshouses with sunny windows, and a vicarage among fine trees, but its great possession is the church on a knoll above the road, sheltered by chestnuts and sycamores. It was begun by the Saxons, and much of their work remains in the nave, the chancel arch, and the lower part of the narrow tower, to which the Normans gave the belfry stage, and the 15th century builders the parapet and stone spire. The small round-headed doorway on the south side of the tower has new imposts carved with interlacing work, and a new band of carving all round it, but there are original round-headed windows in the tower and the nave, though some of them are blocked up. The chancel has been refashioned. The chapel on its north side is 14th century, and the north aisle of the nave, with its arcade of three tall bays, is 15th. There is an ancient font no longer used, and in old glass is a panel with figures of a saint and a priest.

In her 17th century monument we see Lady Bolles in a winding sheet. Lady Elizabeth Hastings, daughter of the seventh Earl of Huntingdon, reclines as she reads her book in a monument which has also the figures of her two sisters on pedestals. She was called

Lady Betty and was a famous beauty, but never married, choosing to spend her days at Ledston Hall, where she was always busy with good works. Congreve extolled her charms, and it was of her that Steele wrote in *The Tatler*, "To love her is a liberal education." She endowed Sir John Lewis's almshouses here, founded scholarships at Oxford, and after her life of well-doing came to rest in this church in 1739.

Ledston. The old gabled stone hall stands on a hill, with spacious views of Airedale from the park (which has magnificent beeches) and looking down on the village, which seems almost untouched by time. The hall has kitchens built about the time Columbus sailed to the New World, a stone stair and an oak mantelpiece of Armada year, and a beautiful little chapel where a priest has been lying near the altar since the days of Magna Carta. In this great house lived Thomas Wentworth, Earl of Strafford; Sir John Lewis, a rich merchant who was a friend of the Shah of Persia; and the much-loved Lady Betty (Lady Elizabeth Hastings) who entertained bishops and gave to the poor. One of the most beautiful women of the 18th century, she sleeps in Ledsham church close by.

Leeds. It is now a huge place of over half a million people, which is for ever spreading outwards. Within the city boundaries prehistoric flints have been found, there is evidence of Roman occupation, there is a Saxon cross in the parish church and a mediaeval abbey at Kirkstall; it had its first charter granted in 1626 and it was made a city in 1883. There is very little now that is old in Leeds, however; demolition is going on so fast indeed that huge areas of the city are unrecognisable from 20 years ago.

No-one, especially if travelling in from the south, could forget that this is an industrial city, largely the creation of the 19th century. Its trade began in earnest with the weaving of woollen cloth (of which fact we are reminded by the statue of the Black Prince which dominates City Square) and expanded with the coming of steam power to take in engineering, concrete, ready-made clothing, leather, printing, and many other trades—some of which, such as flax and Leeds Pottery, have disappeared. The vast goods traffic of Leeds is, or has been carried by road, rail, canal, and river, and among the network of railways is the line of the oldest rail track in the world; laid down in 1758 from mines at Middleton to the River Aire, its trucks were drawn by horses until 1812, when the horses were replaced by a pair of steam locomotives using the Blenkinsop rack-rail system and designed by Matthew Murray, a Newcastle man who came to Leeds where he greatly developed his powers as an inventor. There is an obelisk to his memory at St Matthew's church, Holbeck, a wall plaque in the city and recently a modern comprehensive school has been named after him. Local enthusiasts in 1959 formed the Middleton Railway Trust, and the public are occasionally admitted to their premises to see their collection of old engines and to ride a little way along the oldest railway in the world.

The city has been the home of other pioneers too, for one of its bricklayers, Joseph Aspdin, discovered Portland Cement, and one of its citizens took what were some of the first moving pictures; he was Augustin le Prince, who took pictures showing moving traffic on Leeds Bridge, and had a workshop in Woodhouse Lane, where, near the present BBC studios, is a memorial to him. Joseph Aspdin is commemorated by a tablet in bronze at the entrance to the Town Hall.

Leeds is not merely associated with commerce and industry, however, for it is a University city too. Beginning as the Yorkshire College of Science in 1874, the University achieved independent status in 1904. An enormous scheme of reconstruction has made it one of the best equipped and largest of provincial universities; the expansion continues at a great rate and departments for long housed in old terrace houses now have or will soon have fine new, extensive premises. There are vast buildings to house the Engineering department, the Houldsworth School of Applied Science, the Chemistry, Mining, and Agriculture Departments; a showpiece is the famous circular Brotherton Library, named after its benefactor, which has among countless other books a magnificent collection of rare books and manuscripts. A prominent landmark standing out from most parts of Leeds is the white tower of the Parkinson building, also named after its donor. The University's 1914-18 War Memorial is by Eric Gill, and caused much controversy when it was first unveiled.

Near the University is the Leeds Grammar School, one of the city's two public schools. It was founded in 1552, but the present buildings date largely from the mid-19th century, with some very recent additions; famous old boys include Sir Thomas Denison, John Smeaton (builder of the Eddystone Lighthouse), Christopher Wilson (Bishop of Bristol), and Sir John Hawkshaw, who built the Manchester and Leeds railway, Charing Cross station, and who co-operated with De Lesseps on the planning of the Suez Canal. Opposite the grammar school is Woodhouse Moor, one of the city's many open parks, which now holds several statues of famous people, including Wellington and Queen Victoria.

The city's main public buildings are quite close together. Mention should be made first of the Town Hall, built in the mid-19th century by Cuthbert Brodrick, who was responsible for other fine buildings in Leeds too. It is 250 feet long and 200 feet wide with a tower, a local landmark 225 feet high and housing a clock with a face 13 feet in diameter and a bell weighing four tons. Broad steps guarded by four now distinctly worn lions lead to a lofty portice, and carved in stone above the main door are figures of Industry, Music, Art, and Commerce. The vestibule leads to the Victoria Hall (we remember that the building was opened by Queen Victoria herself in 1858) in which are held events ranging from wrestling bouts to concerts and the Triennial Music Festival; it also houses a fine organ.

Standing impressively behind the Town Hall is the Civic Hall, opened in 1933 by King George V. Its front has a portice with six columns and twin towers on which perch owls (a prominent feature of the city's coat of arms) some eight feet high. Inside are a fine reception hall, a banqueting hall wherein are remembered many Leeds worthies, including John Green, inventor of Leeds pottery, Aspdin, Congreve, Richard Oastler, and Phil May; a Council chamber wherein yet more famous men are remembered, including Ralph Thoresby, a local historian whose name has been taken by a well-known Leeds historical association; Matthew Murray, and Joseph Priestley, who was minister of the Mill Hill Unitarian chapel facing City Square, where there is a statue and a wall plaque to him; a Lord Mayor's room and many offices.

Behind the Town Hall again are the buildings of the Leeds General Infirmary and the Leeds Medical School, the former with an impressive block known as the Brotherton Wing, named again after the man who gave so much to the City. The Art Gallery and Central Library are next to the Town Hall, the former housing a fine collection of water colours and oil paintings, both old and modern, and a good selection of sculpture; the Gallery was indeed one of the first patrons of Henry Moore (trained at the Leeds School of Art) and Jacob Epstein. Among recent directors of the Gallery have been Sir Philip Hendy and Sir John Rothenstein. Within the same block of buildings are the Education Offices and the Police Headquarters.

Near by stood the Leeds Museum, which housed a collection based largely on natural history; but it was damaged by enemy bombing during the World War II and is now being rebuilt.

The Corn Exchange is one of Cuthbert Brodrick's buildings, with an elliptical dome 75 feet high; it dates from 1863. Near by are the old Assembly Rooms, now used as a warehouse, the former Royal

Exchange of 1873 and a remnant of the Old White Cloth Hall. Other features of interest among the buildings of central Leeds are the Leeds Library on Commercial Street, a private proprietary library, the oldest of its kind in England, and whose first secretary was Dr Joseph Priestley; the old Stock Exchange in Albion Place; the arcades, a famous feature of the shopping centre of Leeds—one arcade has a clock with revolving figures based on characters in Scott's *Ivanhoe*; rather farther out are two buildings of industrial interest—Benjamin Gott's woollen mill, known as Bean Ing, dating from 1793 and now used as a warehouse, and the exceedingly curious Marshall Mill on Marshall Street, which was built about 1840 on the model of an Egyptian temple, and it is even said that the owner had a roof garden with sheep grazing on it, presumably in an attempt to introduce a rural note into the fast-growing industrial scene.

The old parish church of St Peter was rebuilt in 1841. Successor to at least three other churches on the site, it is 180 feet long and 86 feet wide, and its great tower has walls enriched with traceried panelling, fine belfry windows, and a handsome crown of crested arcading and tall pinnacles. The interior is dim and rather overwhelming with its display of woodwork. The galleries have an elaborate show of tracery and pinnacles; the organ case looks like part of the church with its buttresses, tracery, and pinnacles; and the high pedestal pulpit is one mass of carving. There are screens near the north door, above which stands an oak figure of St Peter with two keys. The massive 15th century font has a big cover.

Over the high altar is an alabaster reredos of Our Lord crowned, against a background of mosaics of the Apostles. The altar and reredos in the north chapel are of carved and painted wood. Looking from the west window is the face of Dean Hook in stone; his marble figure lies on a richly arcaded tomb in the chancel. He came as vicar to this church in the first year of the Victorian era, finding the church empty and crowding it by his eloquence.

Among many old brass inscriptions on the walls is one with tiny portraits of seven people, the biggest only about three inches high. There is a brass portrait of an unknown woman wearing a quaint headdress of the style of 400 years ago; and engraved in brass are portraits of a knight and his lady of the 15th century. A brass with a chalice is a memorial to Thomas Clarell, vicar for 40 years in the 15th century. Fading away in a recessed tomb of the 16th century are portraits of Thomas Hardwick and his wife, with Death shaking his spear at them. On the head of a bronze processional cross fashioned some 400 years ago is the Crucifixion scene. A splendid

Saxon cross is made up of fragments found when the old church was pulled down in the 19th century; one figure at the foot of the cross has been thought to be Wayland the Smith, of Viking legend. There is a tablet to that very gallant gentleman Captain Oates who was a member of Scott's ill-fated Antarctic Expedition of 1912 and who lived at Meanwood, a suburb of Leeds (his house, Meanwood-side, has recently been demolished) and a tablet to Ralph Thoresby who died in 1725 and was a notable historian. A Flaxman sculpture is in memory of two soldiers who fell at Talavera, and on a pedestal is a statue of Michael Sadler, a Leeds merchant who strove to abolish the factory system in the days of factory slaves.

It was John Harrison who gave his native town its most interesting church, that of St John in New Briggate. It was consecrated in 1634, a time when church building was not common and St John's is one of the few surviving specimens of early Stuart craftsmanship in churches. It is divided into two naves and two chancels by an arcade of seven bays, with a tower at the west end of the north nave and in the south nave is a doorway sheltered by a porch with the same enrichment as the rest of the building. The gabled roofs have plaster panels adorned with flowers and birds, the moulded beams have golden bosses hanging, and the beams themselves rest on quaint painted angels with golden wings. The walls are panelled below the windows. There are scores of box-pews with ornate carving; the modern font is set within old rails and has a quaint old cover; there are two pillar almsboxes, two chests (one handsomely inlaid) and a pulpit richly panelled with strapwork. Animals and a man's head are on the ledge of the pulpit, and its huge canopy, lavishly adorned, rests on fluted pillars. A superb chancel screen extends across the church, massive enough to last a thousand years; above it are two huge wooden structures like bridges, serving as chancel arches.

Here is John Harrison, in a portrait by an unknown artist, and here in the chancel, under a simple monument, lies the man who owned immense estates in the Leeds of his day, and devoted much of his wealth to the welfare of others. We see him in an east window, standing in the cloth market where he made his fortune, talking to a man he is bringing to the door of his almshouses (which stood until 1967 near the church; they have recently been demolished to make way for a car park). Another scene in the window shows a room of the old Red Hall, a Roundhead guarding the door while John Harrison offers Charles I a tankard.

Trinity Church in Boar Lane is built in Christopher Wren's style and dates from the 1720s; inside it has interesting mural monuments, fine pews with key and scroll pattern and a richly carved pulpit. It has recently been threatened with extinction, and at the time of writing its future is by no means certain. Mill Hill, near by in City Square, dates from 1848 when it was built to replace a simple chapel of 1672. Originally a Presbyterian foundation it became Unitarian in the 18th century; Dr Joseph Priestley was associated with it. Other churches of note in the centre of Leeds are the Roman Catholic St Ann's Cathedral, which replaces a church erected on the spot in 1837–8; a reredos by Pugin remains from this building in the present church: Brunswick Methodist Church is a severe Georgian building containing a very fine organ: St Matthew's in Holbeck is the work of R. D. Chantrell, architect of the Leeds Parish Church—some woodwork in the church is by Thompson of Kilburn and the churchyard has a monument of Matthew Murray; another of Chantrell's churches is Christ Church in Meadow Lane, one of the first "Million" places of worship in Leeds: Salem Congregational Church in Hunslet dates from 1791.

Churches in the suburbs of Leeds include St Matthew's at Chapel Allerton, in a setting of lawn and trees. It is a late 19th century church with a long roof, a detached tower, a great reredos and a font with a bowl 300 years old. St Wilfred's at Halton was designed by Randall Wells and built in 1937–9; it is in the form of a huge cross and contrasting with its stone is the dark timber of the spire. White from floor to ceiling it is full of light from gable-headed windows. An interesting church is St Aidan's in Roundhay Road: built from brick, with turrets and an apse at the east and west ends, it has little to suggest the attraction within. This is a series of mosaics by Sir Frank Brangwyn, unveiled in 1916. At the west end is a lofty dais with a very large font, supported on sixteen green marble pillars.

The city of Leeds has always been at pains to provide its people with amenities of various kinds. The Quarry Hill Estate of flats, designed in 1935, was the largest municipal housing development in England of its time: it occupies some 28 acres and provides homes for over 3000 people. There are other housing estates in Leeds and none bigger than the recent development of Seacroft and adjacent villages into something which closely approximates to a new town, complete with its own industrial estate. New and very large blocks of flats have been built and are in process of being built at many points in the city, both near the centre and on the outskirts.

The recreation of the people is also taken care of in the provision, for instance, of several parks—amounting to some 5000 acres in area; there is a Soccer club, several Rugby League clubs, golf courses, including two which have been used for international competition, and provision for various other sports to be played or watched. Of the parks two deserve more than passing mention. Roundhay Park, where John of Gaunt used to hunt, was bought at a cost of £139,000 in 1872—and was regarded by many as a "White Elephant". Here are acres of parkland and woodland, two lakes where we may boat, a large arena where the annual Leeds Children's Day is held, a mansion house, now used as a café, and attractive flower gardens known as the Canal Gardens.

Temple Newsam is one of Yorkshire's great show-places, a magnificent house set in a large park which contains two golf courses. It is the house itself which we come to see. It came into the hands of Leeds Corporation in 1921–2 from the Earl of Halifax in whose family it had been since Jacobean times. Originally the house was built for Thomas, Lord Darcy and in it it is said Darnley the husband of Mary Queen of Scots was born. We see it much as it was left by Sir Arthur Ingram who bought it in 1622 and enlarged the old house; the stables were added about the middle of the 18th century as were the barn and lodges—the avenue of trees leading to the house and the general layout of the park date from the same time. It is now used as part of the city's art gallery, and special exhibitions and events are held here periodically.

It is built round three sides of a vast court; in front of the court is a crescent lawn with fine flowerbeds. Viewed from here we have perhaps the best view of the house, and its inscription in bronze letters:

All glory and praise be given to God the Father, the Son, and Holy Ghost on high; peace on earth, goodwill towards men; honour and true allegiance to our gracious king; loving affection amongst his subjects; health and plenty be within this house.

The house is full of treasures of art. The great oak staircase is Victorian, with massive posts covered in figures and beasts; among the pictures on the walls is a portrait of Queen Elizabeth I and there are portraits and works by Kneller, Guardi, Gainsborough, Stubbs, Crome, and Reynolds. There is a wealth of oak panelling, a series of superb plaster ceilings and friezes, a splendour of tapestry and fine collections of pottery, porcelain and other objects, including furniture by Chippendale.

The standard tour is made by proceeding from the Great Hall to the New Library which has 18th century furnishing; thence to the Blue Drawing Room, notable for its Chinese wallpaper. The Great Hall follows again and then the Terrace Room, which houses a fine collection of snuff-boxes; the West Lobby is followed by the

Staircase Hall which has a sedan chair. The Blue Damask room follows shortly after, with Georgian furnishings, damask wall-covering and paintings; the Green Damask room houses old furniture and paintings too. Paintings by Constable and de Wint are in the Boudoir and soon after we come to a fine series of portraits in the Long Gallery. After some smaller rooms, including a chapel, we come to the famous Darnley Room, in which Lord Darnley is said to have been born. Remaining rooms have a variety of objects including Queen Anne furniture, a portrait of Cromwell, and pottery of Leeds and Staffordshire.

Two Leeds eccentrics deserve mention: first T. S. Kennedy, a famous Victorian traveller who made the first ascent of the Dent Blanche—he lived near Meanwood in an extraordinary house built by E. W. Pugin and known as The Towers from its array of chimneys in the form of organ pipes: Kennedy also had a vast Schulze organ (which is now in Armley parish church) installed in his house. Robert Arthington was the son of a Quaker brewer who closed down his brewery because his conscience forbade him to sell drink. His son Robert, a millionaire by his father's will, lived in one room of his great house in Headingley, virtually a hermit, eating little, spending hardly any money and seeing very few people. When he died in 1900 he left close on £1,000,000 to the Baptist Missionary Society and the London Missionary Society.

Letwell. It is charming with its few grey houses in a green world, and a pretty church made new except for the 15th century tower looking over hill and dale. The nave and chancel are under one roof, and the bowl of the font has a wreath of blackberries.

Lightcliffe. There are factories round, but no village near Halifax is more spacious or pleasing than this, with its fine trees and fine views. Like Harrogate, it has its own Stray, 11 acres of lawns and trees. Its 18th century chapel is now derelict; the 19th century church of St Matthew is attractive outside with its great tower, a turret climbing above the battlements. There are saints in the clerestory windows, the font has a tall cover with angels at the foot of pinnacles, and tracery enriches the pulpit of white stone. Near by are the scanty remains of Crow Nest House, where Sir Titus Salt lived and which was later occupied by a famous local personality, Richard Kershaw, better known as "Dicky Pop".

Linton. It was the home of a Yorkshireman who has given us charming tales of the moors. He was Halliwell Sutcliffe who wrote stories in his beautiful garden at the 17th century White Abbey House, where he took his last walk in 1932. We do not wonder that he loved this old village, where a mountain stream flowing by the green is crossed by an old footway, a modern bridge carrying the road, a packhorse bridge, and clapper bridge. There is a maypole on the green, and at one end are the imposing almshouses founded in 1721 and enlarged in the 19th century, looking like a little town hall with their domed tower. Framed in trees near the other end of the green is the charming Linton House. Right away from the village the church stands in a lovely spot by the River Wharfe, near the cataract known as Linton Falls. A quaint low building with a curious overhanging bell turret, its old work is chiefly 14th century (when the Norman church was made new). The font and two rounded-headed bays of the north arcade are Norman, and the pointed chancel arch is only a little later. There is part of a Saxon cross, and on one of the pillars hangs a small brass crucifix found in a garden, and centuries old. On the green is a sundial won by the village in 1949 in a competition for the prettiest village in the North.

Little Ouseburn. Away from the red-roofed cottages by the grass-lined road, the small church stands where an old bridge crosses the stream. It is the Ouse Gill Beck, which comes through green meadows, makes pools for the swans, and flows through the big park of Kirby Hall to join the Ouse bounding its eastern side.

The church is chiefly Norman, with later aisles, and is as charming within as without. Its walls are splashed with ivy, the steep roofs are of stone, the fine unbuttressed Norman tower has belfry windows with shafts. Through the Norman windows in the north wall of the spacious chancel we see the distant Wolds; the double lancets on the other side frame pictures of sycamores and the dainty bridge. Three carved bench-ends are 16th century, the chest is Jacobean, and the piscina is mediaeval.

Like a little temple in the trim churchyard is the round mausoleum of Henry Thompson of Kirby Hall, its pilastered walls supporting a cornice and a lead-roofed dome. It is most striking.

A Roman road ran by the village, and Moat Hall, by the church, is said to be on the foundations of a Roman house. Many of its beams are 800 years old, and some of its stones are Roman.

Two miles away is Thorpe Underwood Hall, ending a vista along a short avenue of limes from its gates. Here four years of a precious life were unhappily spent. It was at Thorpe Underwood that Anne, the loveliest of the amazing Brontë sisters, with violet eyes and brown ringlets, was a governess. These four years were years of torture which became more intolerable when her brother Branwell joined her as tutor, for he grew so brutish that he was soon dismissed, and Anne, broken-hearted by the cruel treatment she received, sat down on August 28, 1841, and wrote:

> *Oh, I am very weary,*
>   *Though tears no longer flow;*
> *My eyes are tired with weeping,*
>   *My heart is sick of woe.*
>
> *My life is very lonely,*
>   *My days pass heavily,*
> *I'm weary of repining;*
>   *Wilt thou not come to me?*

Liversedge. It is busy manufacturing woollen goods for the world. Here, at Rawfolds Mill in 1812, was the scene of one of the Luddite riots, the weavers attacking Edmund Cartwright who was then developing his new power loom.

Withdrawn from the streets, the church stands finely on a high mound, looking over the valley to Healds Hall on the other hillside. It was built about the time of Waterloo, and has a fine alabaster font, a screen with fan-vaulting, a rich vine cornice, and panels with 12 relief figures of saints, kings, queens, and bishops.

Healds Hall was the home of Hammond Roberson whom Charlotte Brontë portrayed in *Shirley* as the Reverend Matthewman Helstone.

Long Marston. Its name stirs with the memory of one of the most important battles of the Civil War, and its old church, standing by the road to Hutton Hall, brings to mind the Conqueror of Quebec, for in it the father and mother of General Wolfe were married.

The grey tower of the church is at the end of a nave whose walls are attractive patchwork of boulders and rough-hewn stone. The tower and the north chapel are 16th century, and the vestry at the east end of the chapel is 15th. The chancel, the nave, and the aisle represent the church the Normans left, and here are still the fine Norman arcade with massive pillars and arches reaching the roof, a lovely round south doorway, and two Norman windows. The font is mediaeval.

Marston Moor, lying north of the road to Tockwith, was the scene of one of the decisive battles of English history, fought on the evening of July 2, 1644. Prince Rupert came over the hills from Lancashire with nearly 20,000 men to relieve the Marquis of Newcastle, who was besieged in York seven miles away. Learning of his approach, Cromwell and the Earl of Manchester raised the siege and brought their forces to Marston Moor, where the two armies met with a ditch between them. They faced each other in silence for over an hour, until Newcastle, thinking there would be no fighting, returned to his carriage and went to sleep. There came a rude awakening for him, for the battle began at seven and went on till ten, fortune swaying on both sides.

It was Cromwell who turned the tide, and the Cromwell Association has set up on this field a great obelisk paying tribute to his victory.

Long Preston. A spick and span village four miles from Settle, it looks down from the highway on the green valley of the River Ribble, where the Romans had a camp. A chapel with a tower and spire stands by the green, and tucked away in a corner is the old church, a fine lychgate leading to its great churchyard. Across a stream coming from the summit of Kirkby Fell are the almshouses and little chapel founded by James Knowles in 1613.

A noble silver birch and a sundial of 1667 are by the long, low church which has weathered six centuries except for the new chancel. The tower breaks into the stone roof by one of two dormer windows, and opens to the nave with one of the tiniest of doorways, five feet high and 21 inches wide. The unusual and pleasing interior has walls of crazy stonework, leaning arcades, a black and white roof covering the nave and aisles, and some of Capronnier's brilliant glass in ten windows telling Bible story. There are three shields and a head in old glass, thought to be pre-Reformation, and through the north aisle windows is a charming view of the fells. Under the double chancel arch hangs a lovely candelabra. The crude six-sided Norman font has a cover of 1726 like a tower; the splendid pulpit, a fine settle, and two chairs are all 17th century, and are carved. There is an old chest, and in the chancel is a big stone of 1445 with an inscription to Laurence Hamerton which has long been a puzzle to antiquarians, for almost every word is cut short so that it is extremely difficult to interpret. There is a Saxon tomb-stone and a very fine altar table.

Lothersdale. Its place in a deep valley in the heart of the moors gave the Quakers safe refuge in the time of Charles II, and Friends from afar still visit the quaint little Meeting House, with a gallery which has hatches for folk to look through. From the Raygill quarries near by came the bones of a mammoth.

The grey houses are clustered about the mills by the stream, but the 100-year-old church is high on the hillside, with a magnificent view of the moors rising about it in grand array.

Above the church is Stonegappe, hidden in trees, a house which charmed Charlotte Brontë, who called it Gateshead in *Jane Eyre*.

Lotherton. Charmingly grouped are the great house with a pillared portico, and the small Norman church at its doorstep. The house has iron gates made by John Addy, Yorkshire's fine blacksmith. Colonel Trench Gascoigne, who lived at the hall, saved the church from neglect in 1916, and in it is a fine St George to his memory. Sir Alvany Gascoigne, former British Ambassador to Russia, has recently given the hall to Leeds Corporation.

The nave and chancel are divided by a square 18th century arch with an oak lintel. There are two Norman doorways, and round the Norman east window is ancient painting of brickwork dotted with flowers. The pillar piscina may also be Norman. The canopied pulpit and several chairs are Jacobean, the old reading desk is a two-decker, and the altar, with fine carvings of Adam and Eve, Abraham and Isaac, the Annunciation, Nativity, and Resurrection, is an old German chest. There is an ancient Bible box, and there are two Florentine candlesticks. Over the entrance to the chancel is a fine Crucifixion, with Mary and John standing on dragons; it is a memorial to forty men who died when the hall was a hospital during the Great War. Two flags which flew over it then are here, and a tablet tells of a flying officer whose body rested in the church after his plane fell in the park.

Loversall. The new road passes by, but the old brings us to the few houses near the hall among stately trees, and the church tucked away behind farm buildings and screened by an avenue. Its tower is 14th and 15th century, the nave and aisle are partly modern, with a mediaeval arcade between. In the Tudor chapel is a tomb thought to be that of the founder, John Wyrall. The knight without armour, though girt with sword and shield, may be a Middleton of the 13th century. Two of four old stalls have carved misericords, an old bench has a man's head and a pelican, there is an old helmet, the font may be Norman, and William Dixon's bust shows him wearing what looks like a nightcap. A 14th century tomb with a cross and a sword is in the churchyard, where the coffin stone of a child shows parts of a figure as if under a lid.

Low Bentham. A mile from High Bentham, it is among green fields and little hills, the River Wenning dividing it from Lancashire. At one end of the village the church and the lovely rectory are charmingly grouped. The rectory was built when the church was refashioned last century. The tower is 15th century, other old remains being the arch to the chancel, those to the chapels, and the unusual arch at the east end of the north aisle, which is really one arch set into another. One of two carved stones (which are probably Saxon) has a face in the middle of a cross, and the other has a quaint and crude Crucifixion. The massive alabaster font has a remarkable canopied cover, carved with wild roses and honeysuckle and adorned with 12 pinnacles, which are crowned with golden pomegranates.

It is unique, we think, to find in the porch a tremendous old bell hanging only just above our heads. It once rang out from the tower; now it tolls for the dead. The metal of other old bells is in the six now in the tower.

There are inscriptions to Thomas Lupton of 1720, rector for 56 years; Christopher Featherstone, of whom we read that his soul like a feather flew aloft in 1653; and a woman of 1683 who became a Husband on her wedding day. She was Anna Husband. An old sundial is on the south aisle wall, and one of the gravestones in the beautiful churchyard, like a broken tree with a spade by it, is to Robert Poole, who was sexton for 30 years.

Luddenden. There can be few villages with more sharp corners, narrow streets, and steep hills than Luddenden. Lying in a deep glen, hemmed in by great hills, it is a remarkable place to find, with Sowerby Bridge two miles away and Halifax only as far again. Some of the houses are perched far above the church, which is charmingly tucked away by the stream, with old stone dwellings and a 17th century inn which has a library used by Branwell Brontë when he worked here, clustering by it in a maze of cobbled ways. It was built last century, and in it loaves are given every Sunday to the poor. William Grimshaw, perpetual curate of Haworth for 21 years, and friend of John Wesley, is buried here.

On the hills above have been found traces of Roman camps, and Holmes Falls and Wade Wood are much-loved beauty spots.

Malham. An oasis in a wilderness of limestone, it has only a few white cottages and trees, nestling round a quaint little humped bridge over a stream where trout play among the stones. But the stream is the River Aire, and all round is some of the wildest moor and fell scenery in the country. Kilnsey, Malham, and Winterburn

Moors rise in the east; in the west Kirkby Fell climbs to 1788 feet, and Fountains Fell to the north has a cairn 2150 feet above the sea. The huge ramparts known as Malham Lings are above the quiet village.

Malham Cove, a magnificent curving wall of solid limestone rock, stands nearly 300 feet high; it is a stupendous work of Nature, and is one of the amazing sights of Yorkshire. A wild dry valley extends from the top of the Cove to Malham Tarn. Covering 150 acres about 1200 feet up, the Tarn is one of our biggest mountain lakes. Here Great Close Scar rises 300 feet higher still, and plantations come down to the water's edge. At the head of the Tarn is the house where Walter Morrison, Yorkshire's strange millionaire, lived for 64 years. He has been sleeping at Kirkby Malham since 1921, but he will long be remembered here. To his lonely house came John Ruskin and Charles Darwin, and there Kingsley began writing *Water Babies*. His estate is now National Trust property and the House is leased to the Society for the Promotion of Field Studies.

On its way from the green moors to join the River Aire below Malham, the Gordale Beck continues its spectacular journey through the remarkable Gordale Scar, cascading over fantastic rocks and rough-hewn steps, shut in by precipitous cliffs 300 feet high. It inspired James Ward to paint his huge canvas which now hangs in the Tate Gallery. This was early in the 19th century; the 20th century artist John Piper also has a fine study of the Scar. Wordsworth was greatly impressed by Malham Cove and Gordale Chasm and wrote a sonnet on each.

Maltby. The old village in the green valley is being swallowed by the new, which creeps down from the crags. The church perches charmingly on a bank by the stream, and above it is an old cross at the meeting of the ways. A lychgate brings us to the church, re-built except for its tower, with a short spire. There is herringbone masonry in its Norman stages, and the rest is mediaeval.

Markington. At one end the 19th century church stands on a bank; at the other end, with the stream in the hollow, are cottages among trees, and the Tudor hall with its stone walls in a gracious setting of flowers.

A mile and a half away as the crow flies, but twice as far by the rough road over the fields, is Markenfield Hall, a fine manor house which the Markenfields were allowed to fortify 600 years ago, though some of the buildings are later. It was from this stronghold

177

that Sir Ninian Markenfield rode off in his armour to Flodden Field. Now it is a farmhouse, occasionally open to the public.

It looks its best as we come from the fields, the whole range of buildings round four sides of a rough grassy court, and surrounded by a broad moat where ducks and geese swim and children row their boats. A bridge crosses to the Tudor gatehouse on the south side. East and west are cottages and stables, and rising above them is the embattled manor house itself, with a stair turret climbing to the parapet and crowned with a little spire. On the first floor are the chapel and banqueting hall, the chapel 30 feet long, with a beautiful 14th century east window, an aumbry, and a piscina with the Markenfield arms. Fine 14th century windows light the hall, which is 40 feet long and has still some of its old roof beams.

In the village is the ancestral home of William Wilberforce, famed for his part in the emancipation of slaves.

Marr. Its cottages and farms are on the highway. At the old hall (now a farmhouse) lived John Lewis of 1589, whose brass portrait is with those of his wife and six children in the church. On the pulpit are initials of another Tudor gentleman, Christopher Barker, printer to Queen Elizabeth.

Born at the vicarage here, he was one of the first printers of the Bible, and the first man to use Roman type in printing; nearly 40 editions of the Bible or parts of it are known to have borne his name. He lies at Datchet, near Windsor, where he died at the end of 1599.

In the small mediaeval church is herringbone masonry of an earlier time. The curious tower with short spire is 13th and 14th century, its smaller top resting on arches which form recesses in the base. The aisle, the stone-ribbed porch, and the font may be 15th century. A little old painting is on an arch, and there are two panels of the old screen.

Marsden. It looks up to the wild heights of Standedge, crossed by a road which rises 1300 feet above the sea and pierced by tunnels for a railway and a canal entering the rock at Diggle (three miles away) and coming out at Marsden. The village lies in a deep valley, where a stream comes down from the wastes of Wessenden Moor, filling some of Huddersfield's reservoirs on its way. There are many lovely glens about the infant river, and spanning one of its feeders is a fine packhorse bridge below an old mill near the church. Near-by remains of a Middle Stone Age settlement have been found.

The old church on another site was pulled down in 1896; its stately successor has a 20th century tower with one of a group of soaring arches, and in a fine gallery of glass we see Noah and Solomon, saints (including Paulinus and the Madonna), and New Testament scenes. The chancel screen is exceedingly high, and magnificent with vaulting on both sides, a cornice with five rows of carving, traceried bays and panels, and vine carving round the entrance. St Bartholomew is on the west side, and facing the chancel are the Madonna and eight angels. Handsomely framed in the rich panelling of the east wall is a sculpture of the Last Supper, under a canopy of trailing foliage. Three chairs are Jacobean, and we were told that a carved bench in the chancel was made from an old mill-wheel.

From this village came the mother of the Conqueror of Quebec. She was Henrietta Thompson, who married Colonel Wolfe of Westerham. Her home was at the big red house at the bottom of Westerham's street, but it was on a stormy night when she was staying at the little white vicarage that James Wolfe was born.

In the days of the Luddite rioters against machinery a mill owner of Marsden was killed for daring to adopt mechanical improvements. In his mill in later days worked Samuel Laycock, the Lancashire Rhymer who was born at Marsden in 1826. He wrote homely songs of factory life and stories in dialect, and long before he thought of putting his verses into a book he sold forty thousand sheets.

Marton. Between the Great North Road and the Roman road its farms and cottages are clustered on a ridge of little hills, with Grafton's red-roofed patch of houses nestling on another slope. Standing apart on a green lawn is the church of 1875, preserving fragments of the older one. The works of the clock can be seen in the church, and in a small bellcot hangs one of the oldest inscribed bells in the county. The Norman doorway through which we enter has a sunken tympanum filled with cobble-stones and a crude cross, and leading from the chancel to the vestry is another lovely Norman doorway cleverly restored, its arch enriched with zigzag and cable moulding, and resting on rich capitals.

The vestry is like a small museum, eloquent with the story of the vanished church, for in addition to a pile of fragments the walls are almost entirely of old work, including a Saxon window with a stout pillar and projecting shaft between its two lights, other Saxon pillars and part of another early window, a superb fragment of Late Anglo Saxon cross, two tiny niches which may be Saxon, coffin lids, and two almsdishes about 300 years old.

The church was built while John Robert Lunn was vicar here. His little brass portrait on the sanctuary wall shows him in his robes, holding a chalice and wafer. On the scroll at his feet is the name Paulinus, and on two leaves of the canopy over his head are charming engravings of the church and the gabled vicarage. The vicarage is indeed the house that Jack built, as an inscription on its wall tells all who read, for it was designed by a man called Jack, and the builder and all his men were Jacks.

Marton-in-Craven. It is East and West Marton, charmingly set in the wooded hills. West Marton has the great house called Gladstone, rebuilt from designs by Sir Edwin Lutyens, the trees of its 150-acre park a rare sight in spring.

The small church at East Marton is tucked away from the road, looking over billowy green hills to the moors. Remains of the Norman church are the plain font, and the base of the tower with its tiny windows and arch to the nave. The aisle was added late in mediaeval days, and a sundial of 1714 is on the tower. Oldest of all is a fragment of a Saxon cross with an unusual pattern and an odd figure, perhaps Thor with his hammer.

Meltham. Man has been living in this exposed hilly place for many centuries now, for recently two Iron-Age settlements have been found nearby. The church dates from 1651, but of the original building little remains except a date-stone, a tablet on the pulpit, and some windows in a nearby cottage; it was extensively rebuilt in 1782–6 and the west tower was added in 1835.

Menston. Here we found an interesting venture in bringing things of beauty to the West Riding. The Goosewell Art Gallery has been built from part of a house and holds art exhibitions—we found pictures of a local artist being show. Looking over a lovely part of Wharfedale from the slope of Ilkley Moor, this growing village has come into Ilkley's care. There is so much new, including the 19th century church, that the old may be missed, but it is worth the finding. Behind a high wall and trees stands the Old Hall in a pleasant garden, with two charming bays among its mullioned windows, and old oak panelling within. Known as Fairfax Hall from its association with that family, it was built mostly in the 17th century. Here lived Charles Fairfax, the antiquarian who was far more interested in ancient pedigrees than in the quarrels of the king and Parliament, but was for all that linked with the fighting.

Near Old Hall is the beautiful 17th century Menston Grange, with stringcourses on its weathered walls, a two-storeyed porch, and

he original building.

LEEDS UNIVERSITY

The Parkinson building.

The courtyard.

MARKENFIELD HALL, MARKINGTON

A vaulted undercrof

old timber within. The village also has High Royd, one of the largest mental hospitals in the North of England.

Methley. It stands between the Aire and the Calder (meeting at Castleford not far away).

Crowned by a 15th century tower, the church has a 14th century nave and a chancel made almost new but keeping its mediaeval arch and a south chapel built with the bequest of Robert Waterton about 1424. The nave has a grand old roof, the 14th century font has a Jacobean cover, and there is a door still with its old ironwork. Robert Thompson of Kilburn, a craftsman of our day, made the tower screen, signing it with his little mouse. The pulpit is 18th century.

The striking possession of the church is its group of fine monuments, most of them in the south chapel, where sleep the Watertons, the Saviles, and the Earls of Mexborough. Its old roof has gilded suns and shields and green angels with yellow wings, and here are tattered banners, tabards, and three helmets with the owl of the Saviles. In the beautiful old glass filling the east window are the four Latin Doctors and portraits of St Margaret, St Christopher, St John, and John the Baptist.

Under the founder's arch Robert Waterton lies with his wife, their alabaster figures on a tomb enriched with shields and a representation of God holding a Crucifix. Robert wears armour, headdress like a jewelled turban with a rose over the forehead, a rich collar, and rings on his fingers; his beard is curled in French style, a lion is at his feet and a dagger at his side. His wife has a long gown, ornate headdress, a handsome collar, two rings on her fingers, dogs at her feet, and angels at her head. On an alabaster tomb with angels holding painted shields is a knight thought to be Lionel, Lord Welles, who fell at Towton in 1461. He has a long sword and an ornamented belt, and with him is his first wife, Robert Waterton's heiress, who wears horned headdress and has angels by her cushion and two dogs at her feet, both with bells on their collars.

On an unusually high tomb are the figures of Sir John Savile of 1606, his son Sir Henry, and Henry's wife. Sir John, who is shown as a knight in armour, was Baron of the Exchequer, and his brother was Provost of Eton. Sir John's son Henry is in cap and gown and furred mantle. In the height of fashion of the day is the lady in a gown with puffed and slashed sleeves and a beautiful collar. At her feet kneels her son in court dress with a mantle and ruff and a skull in his hand; and below, as if forgotten, lie two babes.

There are marble figures of Charles Savile of 1741 and his wife,

G   181 and one of Sir John Savile, first Earl of Mexborough, who died in 1778 and is here with his coronet, wearing an ermine gown in many folds and sleeves with lace cuffs.

The oldest monuments are the stone figures of a priest and a civilian lying in recesses in the nave. Near the chancel arch is a mediaeval stone carving of a seated figure wearing a crown and holding a sceptre; he is believed to be St Oswald. The sculptor Henry Moore has said how impressed he was, as a boy, with the carvings in Methley Church.

Mexborough. Below the humdrum streets of this small mining town stands the church where the canal and the River Don run side by side. The tower and its short spire may be 15th century, the chancel has some 13th century lancets, and a 12th century arcade with slender pillars leads to a 15th century aisle. Mediaeval relics are the font (recovered after being buried), fragments of coffin lids, and what may be part of a Saxon cross.

Middlesmoor. In a region of wild moors, streams, and caverns, Middlesmoor stands a thousand feet above the sea, on a wind-battered height round which the How Stean Beck and the River Nidd are drawing to their meeting. The Beck comes from a deep limestone gorge with waterfalls and a cave to explore, the river from the slopes of the Whernsides filling the great reservoirs for Bradford in the early part of its journey. After turning south the Nidd is sometimes swallowed out of sight at Manchester Holes; and in time of moderate flood it will enter Goyden Pot (a remarkable cavern which can be explored) and be lost to sight for two miles till it emerges by Middlesmoor's old vicarage.

Huddled together as if better to withstand the elements, the cottages, the inn, and the church are reached by a very steep road, which goes on as a rough track towards the Bradford reservoirs. The stiff climb has the reward of magnificent scenery. Of rare beauty is the view from the church down Nidderdale, with the fine Gouthwaite reservoir gleaming in the sun.

The church has been rebuilt on the old foundations, but some of the old windows are in the aisle, and the font is Norman, with later carving. There is a small coffin lid, and a tiny carved stone is said to have been in some ancient church. But older than all this is a Saxon cross, having the unusual design of a head with four arms, and an inscription said to be to St Chad, who is believed to have erected it.

Eugene Aram, who was born at Ramsgill down the valley, must

have come this way, for the church register tells of his marriage here in 1731, and of the baptism and burial of his daughter a year later.

Middleton. High on the hillside, it looks to Ilkley and the great Moor across the River Wharfe, where the old packhorse bridge, narrow and hump-backed, has a new companion for taking the traffic. There are many fine houses in lovely gardens, and above them is Middleton Lodge standing superb far above the river.

Looking out on a magnificent view of dale and moor, this Elizabethan house is now a retreat of the Passionist Fathers. The spacious grounds have a great show of rhododendrons, and a sunken garden with rockeries and flowers, serving as an open-air sanctuary, has a canopied Madonna looking down. At one end of the shaded path leading to the sanctuary is a magnificent company of trees, a charming and inspiring retreat from the busy world.

Middleton. An unlovely spot near Cowling, with a few cottages, it has round about it steep and narrow ways seeming to lead to nowhere as they wander over the hills.

The village has come into the story of our land as the birthplace of Philip Snowden, who would see from this early home a world of rocky crags and hills, bounded by far horizons.

The school where young Philip learned his lessons is now a Sunday school; the school where he was a pupil teacher is at Cowling, the neighbouring village where his father and mother lie. It was from Ickornshaw close by that he took the title of his peerage, and on the moor above, at Pad Cote, a cain of moorland stone has been raised to his memory, on the spot where his ashes were scattered. On the cottage where he first saw the light is a bronze plaque saying:

In this cottage was born, on July 16, 1864, the Right Honourable Philip Snowden, PC, First Viscount of Ickornshaw, three times Chancellor of the Exchequer of Great Britain.

Midhopestones. The great moors are above this tiny place, set between two of Sheffield's reservoirs in the valley of the Little Don. Quaint simplicity is the keynote of its tiny 17th century chapel, with a Jacobean pulpit, old box-pews, and a gallery.

Mirfield. Fine wooded hills rise above this market town standing on the River Calder on the road from Dewsbury to Huddersfield.

We read its oldest story a mile north-east of the town, where the church of St Mary is attractively grouped with the tower of a vanished church in a setting of trees, the old stone stocks, and the tree-clad mound on which a Norman fortress stood. On the opposite side of the town is a group of gabled houses and an inn with a porch and a painted sign of the Three Nuns. It has some fine stained glass windows and reminds us of Kirkham Priory which was near by. In the middle of the road, not far away, is a stone cross known as the Dumb Steeple where the Luddites met, and from here it is only half a mile to the spot where Robin Hood is said to have died.

The beautiful house called Roe Head was once a school where three immortal sisters worked hard. They were the Brontës. Emily, who wrote three poems here, pined for the moors round Haworth, but Charlotte made good use of her time. Anne came back to Mirfield as a governess at Blake Hall, where she thought out much of her story of *Agnes Grey*.

The two-storeyed tower of the old church is 12th and 15th century, and one of its steps is an ancient coffin lid. The church of 1871 has a noble tower rising about 140 feet, its roof vaulted, its lofty arch opening to the nave, which has high arcades. In the panelling of the chancel walls, carved with linenfold and tracery is an imposing canopied seat. Relics of the old church in the new are a pillar half hidden, a gravestone carved in Saxon days, a stone block (perhaps part of a Saxon cross) with sculpture of knotwork, a quaint figure under an arch, a dragon, and an animal's head. There is also an old chained book.

Mirfield is one of the homes of the Community of the Resurrection, who have here an impressive group of buildings with a domed church. The Community has trained hundreds of priests here since it foundation with the help of Dr Gore, the famous Bishop of Oxford.

Monk Bretton. An industrial place on a hill, it looks over the smoky valley to Barnsley. It has the steps and base of an old cross where the ways meet, and one of the oldest Quaker burial grounds in England. The high altar in the 19th century church has painted panels showing St George, a miner, and angels, and a reredos of the Last Supper carved in oak. The singular green and gold altar and reredos in the lady chapel is surmounted by a slender figure of Our Lord.

In the hamlet of Burton Grange a mile away, in the once peaceful valley of the River Dearne, are remains of the old priory, founded about 1154, and important today as the only surviving example in Yorkshire of a house of the Cluniac Order of monks.

For long the ruins above ground have been farm-buildings, but the Ministry of Public Building and Works is bringing back something of the spirit of the past in this ancient place. The whole plan of the church and monastic buildings is now revealed, and carpets of green lawn are spread.

The fine 15th century gatehouse, with three arches, has lost the floor between the storeys, so that we see it from ground to roof, lit by windows still in the walls. We can walk into the porter's room and see his fireplace, and can climb the stairs to the top of the tower. To the east of the gatehouse stands the gabled Guest House.

South of the gatehouse was the cross-shaped church, the long wall of its south aisle forming the northern boundary of the cloister round which the rest of the buildings gathered. There is still a round arch in this aisle wall, which, like much of the church walling (rising five and six feet here and there), comes from late Norman days. The west wall was 14th century, the chancel and its chapel 15th.

In the range of buildings east of the cloister were the chapter house, the parlour, and the sleeping quarters, all from between 1210 and 1230, and now only low walling. There are two coffin lids in the chapter house, and part of a stout pillar in the dorter. The warming-house and refectory on the south side of the cloister are about 1280, the refectory still an impressive fragment of high walling, windows with fine tracery, west doorway, and serving hatch from the yard which led to the kitchen. West of the cloister were the cellarium and the prior's lodging, both 14th century. The cellarium has high and low walls with windows and doorways, a well, a stone tank, the base of a pillar, and part of a fine arch to the prior's lodging, which is the most imposing of the domestic buildings. It is of three storeys, with windows and doorways and fireplaces. An oak pillar still supports part of the first floor, and there are parts of a spiral stairway. We can see where the infirmary lay south-east of all the rest, and can trace the drain which ran to the river.

Monk Fryston. It lies on the Leeds and Selby road, attractive with an old church on the hill, many old houses, and Fryston Hall, now a hostel, hiding in the trees, though its gates come to the small village square. It is a stately Tudor house with remains of a much older building, set in a park with copper beeches, noble pines, old yews, charming gardens, and terraces running down to a lake. On a rise a mile along the Leeds road is Monk Fryston Lodge, a charming old house with a wide view, looking to the towers of York Minster 18 miles away.

Fryston found the other half of its name when an Archbishop of York gave it to the monks of Selby Abbey. Part of the Saxon church believed to have been here at that time survives in the tower, of which the three lower storeys were here when the Normans came.

185

The four original belfry windows have recessed shafts between two lights. About 1400 the tower received its top storey, its buttresses, the west window, and the arch to the nave. Part of the 11th century walling is seen at the ends of the 13th century nave arcades, these opening to aisles which were widened in the 14th century. The 13th and 14th century chancel has windows of both these times, and its 700-year-old entrance arch has new piers and corbel brackets. The clerestory and the peephole on each side of the arch are 15th century. The roofs and much of the rich woodwork are from the end of last century, when two mediaeval windows were set in the new walls. The wallplates in the chancel have carving of vine. The 20th century oak reredos has Our Lord enthroned, on a background of fine carving of trailing roses and grapes, but its beauty is lost in the dim chancel. From the 17th century come the altar rails, several chairs, and the finial crowning the modern cover of the font, whose bowl is said to be 13th century on an older base. There is a 700-year-old piscina, windows with fragments of old glass, and one or two mediaeval coffin lids. The south aisle has a scratch dial, and an old sundial on the modern porch says Now or Never.

In a garden by the church is Prebendal House, which has been much changed since the time of its 15th century doorway. Some of its old oak was used in the vestry.

Moor Monkton. At the end of a long straight lane we enter the village between two old gateposts which join on to a cottage at each side. Here the river nears the end of its journey as the Nidd, and a mile away, in the lovely meadows by the Ouse, is the Red House where lived one of Charles I's best friends, Sir Henry Slingsby.

With beeches and chestnuts for company in its loneliness, the 12th century aisleless church has a modern tower and a fine doorway built by the Normans, its round arch on shafts with water-leaf capitals. Built into the porch is a stone with a headless figure; and in the opposite wall is a tiny coffin lid showing parts of a figure, the head with curly locks and the hands in a deep quatrefoil, the tiny feet peeping from a trefoil at the foot of the stone.

Simple but charming is the interior. A massive Norman arch divides the nave and chancel. By a fine Norman window in the nave is a modern window of Hubert with a stag which has a cross between its antlers; and there is surely a touch of irony in the window to a hunting parson, which has the kindly St Francis and his birds! The chancel has a tiny Norman window, two of the 13th century, and a charming group of three new ones in Norman style in the east wall, framed in arcading. The font with a fluted bowl may be Norman, the altar rails are Jacobean, and the fine black and white roof of the nave, with queen-posts, is 17th century.

Dorothy Slingsby, who was two years old when she died at the Red House in 1667, has a brass with an inscription and a hand with a finger pointing to a skull and cross-bones. Very quaint is a wall-monument under the tower, where a child lies sleeping peacefully in its bed within a curtained recess.

Morley. It boasts that, like Rome, it is built on seven hills. With its skyline of roofs and chimneys bearing witness to its business with woollens and manufactories, mining and quarries, it is dominated by the fine Town Hall in Queen Street, opened in 1895 by a towns-man Morley will never forget. He was Herbert Henry Asquith, whose bust is in the stately vestibule. The handsome tower is crowned with a dome, and the colonnaded front (approached by a broad flight of steps) has a pediment adorned with figures repre-senting arts and crafts.

One of a group of modern churches and chapels is St Mary's Congregational chapel, interesting for what may be a unique history. Rebuilt last century on the site of what was once known as the church of St Mary's-in-the-Wood, it was originally the parish church, and was let in 1650 by the Earl of Sussex to the noncon-formists on a 500-years' lease. It is said to be the only example of a church surviving a change of this sort after the Reformation. In its graveyard is the mausoleum of the Scatcherds, one of the most im-portant families of old Morley. Their name lives on in Scatcherd Park, where the town's War Memorial has Britannia holding a winged figure. Norrison Cavendish Scatcherd, born at Morley House in 1780, was a well-known antiquary.

Others remembered here are James Smith, a missionary born in 1817, and Sir Titus Salt, founder of Saltaire. A pioneer manu-facturer of the 19th century, not only making riches for himself but seeing to the welfare of his workpeople, Sir Titus was born in 1803 in a house opposite the Town Hall, its place now taken by shops.

But it is the Earl of Oxford, the famous Mr Asquith, who is re-membered as Morley's greatest son. On Dawson's Hill is the 19th century Rehoboth Congregational chapel (founded in 1650) where he would hear his first sermons.

The oak cradle in which he and generations of Asquiths have been rocked is now in the little museum housed at the town's library, where there are collections of fossils, shells, and birds.

It is also a famous place for cyclists: one of its mayors was a well-known rider and its cycling club has had several record holders, and a world champion, Mrs Beryl Burton, who held one of the national men's competition records.

Nether Poppleton. Tranquil by the River Ouse; it is old-fashioned and friendly with its cottages, the inn, and the hall standing by the green-verged road. The hall has cream and red brick walls, and its great stable is about 20 yards long. Where the road greets the river, on its pleasant way to Upper Poppleton, is the unusual War Memorial, a rocky cairn strewn with flowers.

The quaint little church is tucked away near a farm in the meadows, looking to the towers of York Minster four miles off. Much of it is Norman. The chancel has a stout Norman arch dividing it from the galleried nave, and on each side of the chancel is a Norman arch which led to a chapel in olden days. A low window has a trefoiled head, and the east window, 500 years old, has fine old red, blue, and golden glass showing four saints. Old glass in a 15th century nave window has fine little figures of Our Lord and St Mary, and two quarries with birds. An old coffin lid has a cross and a chalice.

There is a captivating group of 17th century wall-monuments of the Huttons. Sir Thomas kneels in armour on a cushion. Anne, a widow for 30 years, wears a black dress with white cuffs; she is a natural figure, with long tapering hands, and an anxious expression on her tinted face. Richard Hutton has top boots and a lace collar. One of his wives has a child at her feet; the other is nursing the baby she only knew for an hour.

Newmillerdam. Three miles from Wakefield we come to this pleasant spot in a valley, the road skirting a lake which mirrors the trees. There are leafy lanes and old houses veiled in foliage, and in a beautiful park stands Chevet Hall, with an inscription telling of its building in 1529. Here in 1788 was born John Lonsdale, who grew up to be one of the best bishops Lichfield has known.

Better known to most of us is the granddaughter of the dramatist Sheridan, Caroline Norton, who lived in the Georgian Kettlethorpe Hall here. She was one of the first advocates of "women's rights". Her lyrical verses were very popular, and she wrote that almost immortal poem *The Arab's Farewell to his Steed*.

The dam and adjacent woodlands were purchased by Wakefield Corporation in 1954 and are now open to the public.

Newton. It is a pleasant village in Bowland, with a Friends' Meeting House of 1767. Near by is a famous house—Browsholme

188

Hall, which is often open to the public. Dating from 1507, the house was given its present red sandstone frontage in 1604; it contains many treasures from Tudor times, portraits by Romney and Lely, relics of Bonny Prince Charlie and a variety of elegant furniture by Hepplewhite, Chippendale, and Grinling Gibbons as well as tapestries and other objects of historical interest. The Parkers, who still own the Hall, have always been patrons of the arts and entertained here, among others, Turner who came on a painting expedition from Farnley.

Newton Kyme. It has a lovely park with the River Wharfe running along one side of it, and a quaint little church, with its mediaeval tower, standing by the lawns of the colonnaded Newton Hall, home of the Fairfaxes. Here in 1666 was born Admiral Robert Fairfax, who restored the old house and planted the noble avenue of limes running from it to the highroad, with no gates to bar the way (it is said they were removed by royal decree at the Restoration as a punishment for the part the Fairfaxes had taken in the Civil War). The road through the park is another avenue of limes, the two avenues being almost side by side.

The admiral has been sleeping in the church since 1725, and on his marble monument is a carving of a ship. All his life he loved the sea, sailing with Captain Bushell of Whitby when he was only 15.

The walls of the nave are Norman, and only a little younger is the arcade of two round arches, with the north aisle to which it leads. The south doorway with flowers dotted in its mouldings, and the sheltering porch adorned with curious carvings, are 14th century. Engraved and in low relief, they show St Andrew on his cross, a boar's head, a stag looking rather like a bull, and a Madonna. The chancel was new about the end of the 12th century and has round arches on the sedilia. In the north chapel is a peephole to the altar.

The font is Norman; a little old glass has shields and fleur-de-lis; and the altar plate includes a chalice said to have belonged to Owen Oglethorpe, the old Bishop of Carlisle who was born here, and grew up to crown Queen Elizabeth I.

In the churchyard are some old gravestones, the base of an old cross, and a stone arch, a memorial to Ruth Bethell. In the hall grounds is a fragment of walling which belonged to some old hall or castle; and there are fragments of a tithe barn on the way to the station, by which runs a Roman road.

Nidd. Half a mile from the river whose name it bears are the bright red almshouses of 1900, and a stone monument with a sculpture of Our Lord on the way to Calvary; it is the War Memorial. A narrow walled lane crossing the 150-acre park brings us to the church at its other side, a companion for the fine stone hall, both nestling in trees. Made new on an old site last century and enlarged in ours, the church has a round Norman font and a modern altar carved with vines and pomegranates. In the churchyard is the shaft of a cross about 600 years old, but it is said that the story of the village goes back twice as far, and that here a great church council met over 1000 years ago.

Normanton. The River Calder flows between Wakefield and this mining town, which has part of its old village cross, a park of 16 acres with a moat round a hill where the Romans had a camp, and a big church with a 15th century tower and an old stone-ribbed porch. The chancel is mainly 14th century, and its chapel comes from the end of the 15th. The south arcade is about 100 years younger, and the north arcade is 13th century, both of them leaning. The 500-year-old font has fine panels of varied tracery, and a piscina with a projecting bowl is at the end of the north arcade. There is an old altar stone, and a chalice of 1674 with leaf pattern and a rich shield. An extraordinary pillared tomb is 17th century, and under one of Queen Elizabeth I's day sleeps John Freeston who gave Normanton its grammar school, the scholars being now in new buildings.

Here too sleeps James Torre, who finished a life of patient service in 1699. His father had fought for Charles I, but James loved the pen more than the sword. Even as a young man he spent all his time studying church registers, and early in life began copying and arranging their entries with marvellous care. His volumes of minute and laborious copies are vast stores of information for historians.

North Stainley. Stainley Hall and the cottages are strung in pleasant fashion along the road from Ripon, which bounds one side of Sleningford Park on its way to West Tanfield; we see Sleningford Hall, mantled in creeper, from its park gates, all in a winding loop of the River Ure. The 19th century church has a striking doorway carved with flowers, faces, animals, and fruit. Rich mosaics show trumpeting angels on each side of the chancel arch, and the Annunciation in the reredos.

By the road to Ripon are traces of the ancient moated encampment known as Castle Dikes. Here have been brought to light foundations of a great house of Roman times, thought to have been one of the most luxurious of its kind in the North.

Norton. Set like a green oasis between Sheffield's steel and Derbyshire's coal, it is fitting that it should be so, for here was born and here lies one who, beginning life as a donkey boy, died with his name on our roll of fame.

In the heart of the village, on the green between the rectory and the church, is a granite obelisk with the name of Chantrey. The cottage where he was born (near Jordanthorpe Hall) has been made new, but his little school still stands where the lane goes to Hazelbarrow, though it is a school no more. Here he learned to love the beauty of our countryside; from here he would tramp with his donkey taking milk to Sheffield every day, and it is said that he would loiter by the way to shape figures in clay and to draw on a grinder's wall. It was the Sheffield poet Ebenezer Elliott who wrote of him:

> *Calmly seated on his panniered ass,*
> *Where travellers hear the steel hiss as they pass,*
> *A milkboy, sheltering from the transient storm,*
> *Chalked on the grinder's wall an infant form.*

All the world knows what happened to this donkey boy, who, after about half a century with his brush and chisel, left a fortune of £150,000 as the Chantrey Bequest for buying pictures for the nation, and came home to sleep in this place which Derbyshire has recently lost and Sheffield has gained.

He lies in this serene churchyard next to his father and mother and his father's father, their graves covered with simple granite stones. His monument is in the church, where he sits sculptured in marble, with a tablet and a medallion portrait on the wall. A coffin stone near his statue is perhaps the oldest possession of the church, which has little left of its Norman days—perhaps the round arch with a quaint stone head at the east end of the south arcade, and a few round pillars. The fine font is 13th century, the bowl carved with heads and foliage and a strange figure like a bird with the tail of a reptile. The chancel arch is also about 13th century, its capitals being carved with foliage.

In the timbered house still standing at Norton Lees, where the family had lived for generations, were born two 15th century bishops, Geoffrey and John Blythe. Geoffrey built the Blythe chapel in Norton church as a chantry to his parents, who lie on a fine alabaster tomb with angels under canopies, battered by time. William Blythe is in a long robe with full sleeves, with a bag or scrip under his arm and his feet on a dog, and his wife has a close-fitting gown and a headdress with lappets. Two engraved stones in the chapel have

13 figures, one thought to show William with his wife and nine children, the two bishops among them. The arms of the family are on a buttress and among the bosses of the chapel's 400-year-old roof.

The bells that ring today in the 15th century tower are modern, but near the door is the clapper of the old tenor bell which rang for centuries and will ring no more, saying now to all who come:

> *I rang for the living, I tolled for the dead,*
> *I gave the first greetings to those who were wed;*
> *And still in God's house I stand by the door,*
> *To open the portals to rich and to poor.*

A fine oak pulpit has eight apostles, and the east window has prophets and saints and Christ as the Good Shepherd, all the figures by modern craftsmen.

Nun Monkton. The long lane ends at this lovely piece of Old England, where the River Nidd falls into the Ouse after flowing for 35 miles. On the great green, fringed by houses of mellowed brick, are two ponds, the base of an old cross, and a maypole 65 feet high, made from a tree grown in Russia.

A charming picture at the end of an avenue bordered with laurels is the rare old church (a fragment of a nunnery) with the Priory, a beautiful house believed to stand on the nunnery site, and to have been built about 1690 by Nathaniel Paylor, whose memorial we find in the church. Though partly reconstructed in our time, the house is much as it was in the time of William and Mary, with tall chimneys, dormer windows, and a carved staircase climbing to the top. Its garden is a paradise of flowers in summer, and has lead statues by the Dutch sculptor Andrew Karne. Fragments of two 13th century pillars have been found in a corner of the garden.

The village came into the Conqueror's Domesday Book and was given to one of his knights, and about the middle of the 12th century William de Arches founded the nunnery. After its suppression Nun Monkton was granted to John Neville, the Lord Latimer whose widow, Catherine Parr, lived long enough to be the lucky widow of Henry VIII. It is thought that the ferry over the river dates from his time. Through the marriage of Lord Latimer's grand-daughter the estate came to Henry Percy, Earl of Northumberland.

Under a noble beech like a green cascade we come to the church, one of Yorkshire's gems. It is the aisleless nave of the nun's chapel, begun at the close of Norman days and completed in the 13th century, except for the modern east end. The two styles in the old work are plainly seen in the strikingly beautiful west front, where the red-capped tower grows from the gable after rising within the nave. The west doorway has a Norman arch enriched with zigzag and resting on shafts, and in the gable framing it is a trefoiled niche. At each side of the doorway are two niches, a statue in one of the four. Very lovely is the second storey, with its three slender lancets, their pointed arches on banded shafts.

The tower has an extraordinary appearance within the church, where its north and south walls rest on pointed arches springing from brackets, and its eastern arch grows from piers without capitals and soars like a huge lancet to the roof. The interior arrangement of the old walls of the nave is exceedingly rich. The windows are high up, and in front of them is an arcaded gallery of wide and narrow bays; and above the narrow bays are trefoil-headed niches probably meant for statues. The bowl of the font is 700 years old, and in its modern base is an old stone with a cup-like hollow. In the floor beneath the altar lies the original altar stone with five crosses, and there are still to be seen old coffin lids, old pewter dishes, a flagon in a wall recess, and three old bells in the tower. The sedilia and piscina are part of the modern east end, where the three lancets have William Morris's glowing glass showing angels with red and gold wings, the Madonna and Child, and Annunciation and Nativity scenes.

Oakworth. High in the hills, above the little River Worth flowing on to Keighley, it has trim stone houses and a 19th century church. There is fine panelling in the sanctuary, and the reredos has the Crucifixion with Mary and John and four saints, the figures coloured. The marble font with mosaic inlay is under a striking oak canopy three yards square, crowned with a figure of Our Lord; its traceried arches are supported by corner pillars.

The village has a delightful wayside garden, made from what was once the garden of a great house and preserved as a memorial of Sir Isaac Holden, whose bust is here for us to see. Here lived this extraordinary man whose span of life covered 90 years of last century. He began life as a poor boy in a cotton mill, but gave himself enough education to become a mathematical teacher. Then, when he was 22, the idea of the lucifer match occurred to him, and he appears to have given it to the world. About the same time he thought of entering the ministry, for he was a good Methodist, but chance turned him in another direction, and he passed into the counting-house of a mill, then into the mill itself, and finally became associated with a mind as inventive as his own, Samuel Cunliffe-Lister, who became the first Lord Masham. He made a great fortune, went to Parliament as a Liberal, and was made a baronet by Mr Gladstone.

It was his grandson, Francis Illingworth, who laid out this garden in his memory when the great house was pulled down. The noble classical porch was left standing, but on the site of the house a lovely bowling green has been laid out. The unusual feature of the garden is the rock work enclosing most of it, high and sheer outside but rising like crags within, riddled with caverns and passages through which we may walk.

Another thing to see at Oakworth is what is still known as the Old Gentleman's Grave. The old gentleman was James Mitchell, who seems to have been an oddity. Shortly before he died, about 100 years ago, he ordered a servant to set a big stone rolling down the hill from his home at Oldfield Hall, still standing outside the village, and it was his wish that he should be buried wherever the stone came to rest. There he sleeps.

Ossett. A manufacturing town with a great trade in rag and wool, it has an imposing Town Hall and a War Memorial with a soldier looking down on the marketplace. Holy Trinity Church, rebuilt last century, is a lofty pile looking its best outside, its great central tower crowned with a spire.

Benjamin Ingham, the Ossett boy who began life in 1712, became an enthusiastic member of the Oxford group known as Methodists, and was a lifelong friend of John Wesley. He was with Wesley in Georgia, but when he came back he joined the Moravian settlement near Leeds, and afterwards formed a strange religious order of his own known as Inghamites.

Otley. Above its grey houses and narrow streets rises Otley Chevin, the great hill ridge with a glorious panorama of the country round. For a thousand years the dalesmen have come to sell their wool in this little town, and it has its own link with industrial Yorkshire (on the edge of which it lies), for it makes worsted and leather and printing machines. It still has its maypole, old houses and many old inns, a court house of 1875, and an ancient bridge of seven arches. Prince Henry's Grammar School here was so named by James 1 who granted its charter.

It was one of the manors given by Athelstan to Archbishop Wulstan as a thankoffering for the victory at Brunanburgh which made him first King of All England a thousand years ago; and the Archbishops of York remained its overlords until our time. It is said that Paulinus came to Otley when visiting Edwin's court at York, and that he built here a church which the Norsemen destroyed. Eleven centuries after Paulinus came John Wesley, preaching sometimes from the foot of the Chevin and sometimes in the church. His name is in the register for 1788, when he officiated at a wedding.

The church we see was begun in Norman days, but treasured within are fine fragments of crosses set up long before the Conqueror came, and found in the walls last century. Four of them, including one carved with the busts of three Evangelists, are believed to have been part of a great cross of the 8th century. Much of the church is 15th century, but the chancel has a Norman window on each side, and the Normans built the plain north doorway. The tower is 13th and 14th century, and the clerestory comes from the middle of last century; the capitals of the 15th century nave arcades were cut away in 1750 and have been restored. The altar rails and the pulpit are Georgian, and among the modern woodwork is the reredos, elaborate with vine cornice, angels in niches, and the Madonna and the boy Jesus in a rustic shelter.

One of two crude 17th century monuments in the chancel is John Dyneley's tomb, with a shield and crest; the other is a wall-monument with a man in a shroud, to William Vavasour of Stead Hall. In the north transept (where is an old piscina) is a curious brass of 1593, reminding us of a Jesse window. At the foot is Francis Palmes, the last of his family, lying on a mattress, and from him grows a tree representing the pedigrees of the Lindleys and Palmes as far back as the 13th century.

One of the 18th century monuments to the Fawkes of Farnley Hall is a plain tomb in an elaborately carved recess. Under the tower is an old coffin lid, the gravestone of one of the Longfellow ancestors of the poet, and the stone of Henry Fairfax, a member of a famous family remembered in the church. On an imposing tomb lies Thomas, first Lord Fairfax, with his wife, he wearing armour, with a helmet for his pillow and a lion at his feet. Four of his seven sons died fighting, and an archbishop said of three of them that one had wit without grace, one grace without wit, and one neither wit nor grace. One of the sons was Ferdinando, second Lord Fairfax, and his son Thomas, the third lord, was the famous Parliamentary commander in the Civil War.

Another monument is to the youngest of the seven sons of the first lord, Colonel Charles Fairfax, who brought up his 14 children at Menston Hall, and was visited there by Cromwell and Sir Thomas Fairfax when they made plans which ended in the Battle of Marston Moor.

Curious but striking is the monument in the churchyard, set up in memory of more than 30 men who were killed when the Bramhope Tunnel beneath the Chevin was being made. It is a stone model of the tunnel, and has been rebuilt because the Caen stone decayed.

One of Otley's most famous sons was Thomas Chippendale. He was baptised here in 1718 and the building that is now on the site of his birthplace has a memorial plaque on its wall. Recently a Chippendale Society was founded in the town. Otley Agricultural Show, held in May, is the oldest of its kind in the north.

Oughtershaw. Set far up Langstrothdale it is a tiny, lonely hamlet with a hall built by the Woodd family of London, and a small school built by John Ruskin. At nearby Yockenthwaite is an excellent Bronze Age stone circle and even farther up the dale is the lonely outpost of Cam Houses, often completely cut off in winter.

Oulton. Its hall, now a hospital, is among the trees, but the most charming of its old houses is one with black and white walls, quaint gables, tiny windows, and great beams of 1611. The church of 1827 (designed in the 13th century lancet style by Thomas Rickman, author of a celebrated work on Gothic architecture) is imposing, its tower and spire rising above fine beeches and old yews in the church-yard. The interior is striking with vaulted roofs and a great array of rich arches on slender pillars clustered with shafts. The windows have a mosaic of Bible scenes, and the quaint font has an arcaded stem.

It was at this pleasant place midway between Leeds and Wake-field that Richard Bentley, one of England's greatest scholars, was born in 1662. A famous student and critic, he tells us it was here he learned his first lessons, not from a tutor, but at his mother's knee.

Owston. It has in its church the brass portrait of a man from the days of Agincourt, but never from Agincourt till now has this place or any place seen a more remarkable man than the son of two old folk who sleep in this churchyard. The fine 200-acre park, with its old hall and its noble company of cedars, birches, copper beeches, and yews, shelters these old folk, for the church is in the park. The handsome tower (of about 1190) has herringbone in its walls, two original windows over the doorway to the nave, and later battle-ments. The three western bays of the north arcade are 13th century, and its eastern bay comes from the 15th, when this end of the north aisle was made into St Mary's chapel. The two aisles and the chancel are mainly 14th century, and the clerestory has two windows of that time, with others a century younger. The chancel has a stone bench for the priests, a double piscina, a mediaeval altar stone, and a big recess which may have been an Easter Sepulchre, with a "watcher's seat". The south aisle has a piscina. There is a figure of

The west front of Ripon Cathedral.

Ripon Cathedral: the crossing and north transept.

Above left
The hand at the west end of the choir.

Above
A bench end in the choir stalls.

RIPON CATHEDRAL

One of the bosses in the choir.

Rotherham Church.

a priest in old glass, a 15th century chancel screen, and a quaint old almsbox. Two beautiful marble monuments by Chantrey are of Bryan Cooke and his wife, he sitting with his face on his hand, she kneeling on a pedestal, her head bowed, her arms crossed. In the floor, under an arch in the nave, are two brass portraits of the early 15th century, showing Robert Hatfield and his wife holding hands, both wearing the SS collar. Robert founded a chantry here.

It is in a humble grave in this churchyard that there lie an old couple unknown to the world. Little did they think of fame or dream that their name would be known among men; but their boy is among the strange heroic figures of the British Empire, and in all our tour of England we have come upon no more romantic tale than his. He was Walter Greenway, street arab of Sheffield.

Pannal. It lies in a green hollow near Harrogate, with a bridge over the Crimple Beck flowing to the Nidd. Restoration has taken much that was old from the church, but the embattled and buttressed tower is chiefly 15th century, and the chancel is 14th, with a modern arch between it and the nave. The oak altar is interesting for its quaint carvings. There are floorstones to the Wilsons of Pannal Hall, of inlaid coloured marble, with mosaics of flowers round some of them.

Greatly treasured here is a fire shield in old glass in the quatrefoil of a chancel window, showing a gateway between two trees and a red and blue cross below it. The gateway represents the Friary of Knaresborough to which this church was given. We see the shield again in a beautiful picture, in which it is being presented by a kneeling angel to St Robert in his monk's white robe.

In the churchyard is a flat stone said to weigh a ton, used in days gone by to prevent the snatching of bodies from their graves. Near by, at Follifoot, set in superb gardens, is the Regency house Rudding Park, frequently open to the public. The house contains Chippendale furniture and a fine collection of tapestries, china, pictures, and books. In the church attached to the house is a crucifix which belonged to Pius X.

Pateley Bridge. A small town made a market town by Royal Charter in the 14th century in one of the loveliest of the Yorkshire dales. It is a fine centre for exploring the dale and the high moors. Half a mile below the bridge the river is joined by the stream from Ravensgill, a deep wooded glen above which towers the lofty Guise Cliff.

From the town building in the valley the narrow crooked street climbs the steep slope rising to Pateley Moor, the stone-walled fields creeping down to meet it. There are old houses and odd turns, vistas of hills and crags, and high above the rest is the old church, a trim ruin with a charming porch, a nave and chancel with windows in the roofless walls, and an odd little tower with a small window through which is a charming peep of Nidderdale. The wonderful views from this old churchyard are a rich reward for the hard climb we have to reach it. Two miles up the valley the river fills the Gouthwaite reservoir, a lovely lake two miles long; and closing the distant view is the ridge of Great Whernside, where the Nidd comes to life. We see the road across the valley climbing the great hill to Greenhow, 1300 feet above the sea, famous for the remarkable Stump Cross Caverns which extend for over a thousand yards, glittering with stalactites.

Far below the old church, but still high above the river, is the 19th century church with one possession which must stir our thoughts, for on the floor of the nave, for ever silent now, is a bell which may have rung for the monks of Fountains Abbey. There is a processional cross carried before Dr Edward White Benson when he was Archbishop of Canterbury, and a brass inscription with the names of a host of Bensons from 1496 to the 19th century, ending with the archbishop to whom death came in Mr Gladstone's pew at Hawarden. The richly coloured glass of the east window, is the work of Capronnier. The Nidderdale Agricultural Society holds its annual show here in September.

Penistone. Few towns in England have climbed so high. Built on a hill with great moors round, it is far above the valley of the Don. In the churchyard sleep many Wordsworths, descendants of a family which lived here as far back as Edward III's day, and lived on to give us our poet. Here are the gravestones which a blind boy used as his books, teaching himself to read by running his fingers over the inscriptions. He was Nicholas Saunderson, who became a noted professor of mathematics at Cambridge in the 18th century, and was described as one who taught others to see though he saw nothing himself.

The old church crowning the hill has an imposing tower of the 15th century and a chancel of the 14th. The glory within is the nave, with long and leaning arcades built when the Norman style was passing, a 15th century clerestory, and a lovely old roof with magnificent bosses and a gallery of faces on the ends of the beams. The font is 13th century. At near-by Gunthwaite Hall is a magnificent early 16th century barn.

Plompton. Here lived the Plumptons, fighting men of six centuries ago. Their lands are peaceful enough today, and the famous park is a wonderful mass of woodland paths winding among huge rocks. Thousands of people come every year to see the old oaks and beeches, the giant firs and yews, the ash woods, and the amazing rocks carved by centuries of wind and rain into the strangest imaginable shapes. There are many beeches among the lovely bower of trees where we turn from the highway. Trees cling to some of the fantastic rocks rising from the steep wooded banks by the lake; other rocks have gnarled fir trees on their peaks. An overhanging mass with a peephole through the middle of it is known as the Needle's Eye.

We may walk through the Tunnel Rock, wish at the Wishing Steps, sit in the Old Chair, or leap (if we will) from the majestic Lover's Leap. One rock is 100 feet round. It has been thought that the Devil's Arrows at Boroughbridge may have been quarried here.

Pontefract. It is in Shakespeare and in every history book, for it has been the scene of great events for 20 centuries. Its little black Pontefract cakes, every one with the castle stamped on them, have been carried round the world. The making of these sweets and their more colourful descendants keeps many people busy in this town, although no liquorice is now grown here.

Much that was old has gone from this ancient town on a hill, a few miles from the meeting of the Calder with the Aire, and collieries have come to its door. But there are old houses and inns, almshouses, an Edward VI school now in modern buildings, a park of 360 acres, a quaint marketplace with the old pump Queen Elizabeth I gave the town when she stayed at the castle, and the Butter Cross of 1734—an arcaded stone shelter.

The Town Hall, at one end of the marketplace, is a stone building from the close of the 18th century, standing where stood the Moot Hall, destroyed during the Civil War; it has pilasters supporting a cornice and a pediment, and a clock turret with a pillared canopy. Just below the marketplace the hospital stands on a steep rocky bank, looking over a deep hollow to the crooked Waterloo column. Under the hospital are a cell and an oratory, known as the Pontefract Hermitage and founded in 1368, fashioned out of the rock by Adam de Laythorpe, a mediaeval monk who cut out a flight of over 50 steps and a shorter flight leading down to two chambers.

In the marketplace of this garrison town stands the church of St Giles, refashioned in the 17th century, with a chancel made new in the 19th. It keeps a 14th century arcade of five bays, and the windows have tracery in the style of that time. The square tower, with vases for pinnacles and an octagon lantern, comes from 1795, and the altar plate includes an Elizabethan chalice and paten. We found here a memorial to Thomas Blanco who lived to be 90, served through the Peninsular War, and was at Corunna when they buried Sir John Moore. The colours of the King's Own Light Infantry, to which he belonged, hang in St Giles's, which has been the parish church since All Saints was destroyed in the Civil War, when it was used as a base for an attack on the castle.

Standing in a ring of trees by the wayside, with the top of its tower almost level with the castle grounds, All Saints today is a curious combination of church and ruin. The 15th century nave and aisles, and the 14th century chancel and chapel, are roofless and forlorn, their old windows almost without tracery, their old walls enclosing graves and tombs and shrubs and trees. The mediaeval arcades still stand; the south porch has a little of its old grace, and the old north porch has a fine doorway leading to a room above. In 1832 the ruined crossing was restored for use, the transepts forming the body of the church, the chancel occupying the space under the central tower, with a three-sided bay added for a sanctuary, and a western bay in which is a doorway and a fine niche. Stone heads of men and women and angels are set in the walls. But the tower is the arresting feature of this strange place; it has richly moulded arches and a vaulted roof, and from within its own parapet rises an embattled and pinnacled lantern with eight sides. It is recalled that Edward Lee, Archbishop of York, was dragged from his pulpit here during the Pilgrimage of Grace, when the castle was taken. We found considerable restoration going on here to make the old church live again.

Near All Saints was a litter of stones and fragments of walling, all that is left of the Priory of St John founded here about 1090. The ruins have recently been demolished. Over the hill is New Hall, a splendid pile in Elizabethan days, built from the priory ruins but now itself forlorn, with mullioned windows in roofless walls, broken bays and turrets, all ruinous, but dwarfing the farmhouse beside it. It was in the priory that they laid the bodies of the Duke of York, who fell in the Battle of Wakefield, and his young son the Earl of Rutland, who was pursued into the streets of Wakefield by Lord Clifford.

Near New Hall, where the road cuts through the rock, is what is known as Nevison's Leap, a great gap across which a highwayman is said to have leapt on horseback. It is a romantic tale, but an impossible leap. Farther along this old Ferrybridge road is the Stump

Cross, a square block of stone hollowed out at the top and carved on the sides with Norman arcading. It reminds us of a font, but the hollow seems too shallow to have served that purpose, yet too deep to have been the socket for a cross. Tradition says that the fallen Wolsey, when on his way to his home at Cawood, paused at this Stump Cross and confirmed 200 children from the country round; it must have been the last service the old churchman rendered the Church.

The glory of Pontefract Castle is no more, but here is still its site magnificent, crowning a bold and rocky hill, and the lovely gardens that have grown about the old stones make it a quiet retreat high above the housetops. Covering about seven acres, it was surrounded by a ditch and a wall, defended by towers and a barbican with a drawbridge. There was probably a Saxon stronghold here, but these remains are of a Norman fortress which grew in splendour till it was one of the noblest of all the Plantagenet castles in the North. It was begun by one of the Conqueror's captains, Ilbert de Lacy, added to by his son Robert, and by his grandson, to whom Kirkstall owes its abbey. The castle remained with the de Lacys for six generations, and then came to the Earl of Lincoln for four generations, being at length brought by Alicia of Lincoln to Thomas, Earl of Lancaster, for whom it became a prison from which he went out to die. From the end of the Wars of the Roses it has been with the Crown.

Crossing the site of the old drawbridge we come to an antique shop with an old shield of one of the Earls of Lancaster over the doorway. The building has old brickwork at the back, and stands on part of the wall which enclosed the inner ward in the shape of a rough oval. Beyond the modern entrance to the grounds are remains of the main gateway of 1138, showing portcullis grooves in low fragments at each side, and a crude pinnacle of masonry of the porter's lodge.

The chief remnant of the castle is the Round Tower, as it is called in spite of its curious plan; and the most impressive view of it is from the entrance to the grounds, where the grim and battered walls rise above a rock garden ablaze with colour. The tower stands only to the ground floor, and much of what we see is the casing of the rocky spur from which it rose. But we can climb through this solid rock from the postern at the foot, passing on our way the steps leading to a dungeon, and then climbing to the top with a view over the town and country round. Here among the broken walls is a sunken room.

Of the rest of the castle there is little more than foundations and fragments to tell of its lost glory. Walking round the west side we see the postern at the foot of the vanished Piper Tower (its site now a yawning chasm), the base of the Gascoigne Tower, and a few traces of King Richard's Chamber, the stables, the kitchens, the bakehouse with two fine ovens, and the Treasurer's Tower. The Queen's Tower and the King's Tower on the north side of the garth (both said to have been built by John of Gaunt), and the Constable Tower on the east side, complete the ring of towers.

Side by side within the garth are remains of two chapels. In a hollow ringed with trees in front of the King's Tower is the low walling of a Norman chapel, still keeping the three steps which led to the altar, and the broken priest's doorway. Of the 14th century St Clement's Chapel, refashioned by Queen Elizabeth I, there are low walls left. Soldiers who fought in the Civil War were buried in St Clement's nave, but now there are flowerbeds here, and a great cross of daffodils, blooming when we called. Here, too, is a stone coffin with its lid, and near by is a tiny chapel with a window at each side of the doorway, which has in it Norman stones.

In a room of the porter's lodge is a small museum with pictures of the castle, Roman pottery, coins lost during sieges, panels with a medley of 15th century English glass, foreign roundels, the old bell from the Moot Hall, and fragments of tiles, carved stones, and earthenware from the priory ruins.

It is a moving thing to walk among these ruins and think of the captives who lost all hope here. It was here that the last scene in the life of Thomas, Earl of Lancaster, cousin of the king, was played out. After the Battle of Boroughbridge in 1322, he was brought back in chains to his own castle, to be imprisoned in the Swillington Tower he himself had built as an outpost, now mere fragments on the north side. A rebel against Edward II, he was found guilty of treason and dragged from his castle to die on St Thomas's Hill. The mob threw mud at him, and the king laughed to see him riding a wretched horse (his head to the tail) till he came to a field of green barley, where his head was struck off. The prior and monks of St John's begged his body, and laid him by the altar of their church.

Here lived John of Gaunt, Shakespeare's time-honoured Lancaster. It is believed that he heard Wycliffe preach within these walls, and that here he entertained Chaucer, who speaks of Pontefract's white-walled castle. Archbishop Scrope and Lord Mowbray were dragged to Pontefract, where Henry IV ordered Judge Gascoigne to try them for treason. The bold judge refused, but the old archbishop and his young companion were condemned to death at Bishopthorpe. To Pontefract came Edward IV on the eve of the Battle of Towton, where the Red and White Roses fought in the snow; in these dungeons Lord Richard Grey and Sir Thomas

Vaughan spent their last hours. They were with the young Prince Edward at Ludlow at the time of the death of Edward IV, and on their way to London were met by Richard Crookback, marching through blood to the throne, and hurried off to execution.

With them at Ludlow was a still more famous man whom Richard of Gloucester sent to his doom in this castle. He was Anthony Woodville, Earl Rivers, famous for all time because one of his books was the first book ever printed in English, a translation of the Latin Sayings of the Philosophers. He translated it for Caxton, whose friend he was. The British Museum has a picture of Rivers presenting the book and its printer to the king. Rivers was a zealous reader of religious books and went on a pilgrimage to the shrine of St James at Compostella. It was on this journey that he read the book, which a friend had lent to him. It was nothing to Richard of Gloucester that a man should love noble things, and Rivers was executed with the rest of those who stood in his way.

But the most tragic event in all the history of Pontefract is that which gives us one of the bitterest pages in Shakespeare, the death of Richard II. His kingship taken from him, he had longed for a little grave, or some small space to lie in in the king's highway; but never did he dream that the head that wore the crown would be battered and beaten, and his body hacked to death in this ominous Castle of Pomfret. It is not certain how he died, but an examination of the skull in 1871 is said to have proved that it was not through a blow on the head; yet it is certain that the life he was weary of ebbed out in this place, and a fragment of a dungeon always known as his is still shown.

Pool-in-Wharfedale. It is on the Chevin side of the River Wharfe, here crossed by a handsome stone bridge of seven arches. Otley is three miles away, and from their pleasant gardens the Pool folk look over the river to Leathley with its old church, and Farnley where Turner painted many of his pictures. Flowers grow round the cenotaph to those who died for peace, and by it stands the small modern church with a tiny tower and spire, and a window with a fine St George.

Near by is Almscliff Crag, famous as a training ground for rock-climbers since 1890.

Pudsey. Its factories make boots and shoes, its mills worsted and woollens, but to thousands it is the place that makes cricketers, for here were born two of the Yorkshire Immortals, Herbert Sutcliffe and Len Hutton. On the edge of the town, at Fulneck, is the

Moravian settlement where the poet James Montgomery was ten years at school. The Moravians settled here in 1744, naming the place Fulneck after a German town, and for years there existed a great friendship between Fulneck and Moravia, students coming from the continent to be trained as ministers. The German village has long lost its characteristic features, and today a long flagged walk below the road runs in front of an irregular array of houses, all in a row, with a small Moravian church in the middle, looking on the other side over a deep green valley. Fulneck school here has fine views from its very long imposing frontage—Richard Oastler studied here.

Pudsey's imposing 19th century church is a lofty place in which 2000 people can find room. It has a massive tower, a clerestoried nave, great windows and galleries, and a big array of buttresses. The unusual arch to the sanctuary is really two in one (one over the other), the space between them filled with traceried panelling and a vaulted roodloft. One of the Methodist chapels in the town is a striking structure, with a domed clock tower and classical columns supporting a pediment.

Queensbury. Industrial Yorkshire has perhaps no better view of miles of hills and valleys than can be seen from Queensbury, a manufacturing village over 1100 feet above the level of the sea. Its own great mills were founded by the Fosters, and hereabouts stone is quarried and coal is mined.

Built in 1843, the church has a tower with an unusual double archway leading to the nave; crowning the pillar between the two openings is an angel holding a shield, and tracery is carved in the head. There is nothing lovelier here than the embroidery, which is the handiwork of Mrs Foster. The red and gold panels below the organ, enriched with jewels, have angels playing and singing.

Ramsgill. It gave the world a scholar and a murderer, for here in 1704, in a house now gone, was born Eugene Aram. It is strange that he so narrowly missed fame as a student of grammar by a crime which has given him an everlasting place in literature. Ramsgill is a surprising place to come upon in this lonely stretch of Nidderdale between high moors, standing at the head of the beautiful Gouthwaite reservoir which is a favourite place for bird-watching hereabouts. Round a little green are gathered the old houses, and the church, which dates from 1842, looking down the lovely valley beyond the shining lake. Near the church are a few stones and the gabled end of a chapel built by the monks of Byland. The ivy-covered Yorke Arms was formerly a shooting lodge of the Yorke family.

Rastrick. High above the River Calder is this busy town of quarries and mills. Its 18th century church has a lofty pulpit on a pedestal, reached by a spiral stair. In the churchyard is Rastrick's oldest possession, a fragment of a cross with a carved design like clover leaves, the work of a Saxon mason.

A mile or so away stands Fixby Hall, once the home of Richard Oastler, the children's friend of the 19th century, known as the Factory King. It is now the clubhouse of a golf club.

Rathmell. Its grey houses and its high stone walls are on a green hillside above the River Ribble, with a small church of 1842. Two of its windows have Capronnier's glass, and under the tiniest of towers (about seven feet square inside) stands the font with a slender stem and a domed cover. Below the church are three 17th century cottages under one roof, known as College Fold, and it was here that the first Nonconformist College in England was founded by Richard Frankland, who was born in the village in 1630. To this lonely spot came pupils from near and far, and from this seat of learning went out good men to preach. Frankland was one of the first Nonconformists to be persecuted after the Restoration, but he was a man of great courage and persisted in his faith. Frankland inspired the first Nonconformist ordination service in Yorkshire, and though his pupils were imprisoned he himself remained free, dying with his scholars around him. He lies at Giggleswick.

As we come from the neighbouring village of Wigglesworth we see a magnificent vista of the fells, ending in the massive form of Penyghent.

Rawcliffe. Part of a flat countryside, with Lincolnshire only six miles away, it stands on the River Aire. The busy road from Goole bounds Rawcliffe's fine park before passing through the heart of the village, where many old houses and a modern church are gathered round a spacious green shaded by trees.

It was the home of one of Yorkshire's oddities, Jimmy Hurst, who lived here in George III's day and sleeps in the churchyard. He wore yellow boots, a rainbow waistcoat, and a hat nine feet round, and lived in a house near the river. He made a pair of wings and tried to fly, but his most remarkable invention was a coach like a China-man's hat on wheels.

Rawmarsh. A neighbour of Rotherham, it has a church of 1839 dominating the hill above the Don. In the smoke-grimed doorway of the tower are fragments of a Norman arch, and the shaft of the churchyard cross may be Norman too. There is an old font, and in a 17th century brass John Darley and his wife are kneeling at a desk, he in ruff and elaborate gown, she in rich headdress. With them are six children and two babes in cradles.

Ribston. The fine wooded park on the banks of the River Nidd was the first English home of the Ribston Pippin, grown from a sapling nearly 250 years ago. It is said that of three seeds brought from Normandy two died and one grew up here to become a forest of apple trees. The original tree was blown down years ago, leaving a dead stump.

There is more to see in the 300 acres of park with its beeches and Spanish chestnuts, its oaks and alders, and the river flowing under elms and willows. There are 20 acres of garden famous for rare and beautiful shrubs, and over 70 kinds of firs, larches, and pines. Nowhere in Yorkshire shall we find nobler cedars or finer yews; and a superb Oriental plane over 100 feet high is among the biggest in England.

Ribston Hall was the home of the Goodrickes in days gone by, and is said to have been a meeting-place of Sir Henry Goodricke and Lord Danby in those momentous days when a plot was laid to drive James II from his throne. Sir Henry, who was among the first to welcome William of Orange and was made a General soon after, sleeps in the simple chapel at one end of the house. Believed to have been built about the end of the 13th century, the chapel is much restored. In the little graveyard is a very old mulberry tree, and by the blocked mediaeval doorway is the head and part of the shaft of a Saxon cross. The interior is notable for the lavish floral carving of the old panelling in the sanctuary, and for the fine collection of old chairs on the raised platform at the west end, where the family used to sit. The benches have poppyheads, and two mediaeval stones once held brasses. A lovely fragment of alabaster sculpture in the sanctuary shows three figures, and in a panel of the oak pulpit is a dainty and quaint little Nativity in alabaster.

Riddlesden. It is a mile from Keighley, and has much that is new with a little that is old. Some of the houses are on a steep hill above the road to Bingley, and with them is a 19th century church where we look down on an old house interesting enough to be in the care of the National Trust. It is East Riddlesden Hall, sheltered by splendid beeches and reflected in a great pond where swans glide. On the other side the River Aire flows deep down in what is here a green valley, though industry is creeping near and gas-works have taken possession of one bank. Grey with the smoke from Keighley, the hall has high and low gables crowned with balls and clustered chimneys, and two embattled and pinnacled porches, each with a round window. Heavily studded doors lead to a passage linking the porches, and there are huge rafters, fine old fireplaces, and plaster ceilings. The Hall houses a fine collection of 17th century furniture and portraits. The fine barn, 120 feet long and 40 wide has two round-arched entrances, and stout timbering supporting the high roof: it now houses a collection of carts and coaches. The house and the barn were built on the eve of the Civil War, and here in stone are the faces of Charles I and Henrietta Maria, with the motto, "Vive le Roy".

Ripley. Its long broad street has wayside lawns shaded by trees, and the houses and cottages have creepered stone walls, gay window-boxes, and garden borders. In the charming cobbled square are the stocks and the old village cross on four steps. Looking on to the square, the church stands in a churchyard of tragic memories, and close by is Ripley Castle where generations of Ingilbys have lived and were living when we called. It is frequently open to the public. At the other end of the village is a stone building in 15th century style, with turrets and battlements, and traceried windows like those of a church. It is the 19th century village hall, with Hotel de Ville on the front, reminding us that the village was remodelled in 1827 by Sir William Ingilby, on the plan of a typical French village of Alsace Lorraine.

The heavy door of the castle gateway opens on a fair courtyard, spacious and beautiful with green lawns, a sundial, ancient yews, and an air of tranquillity. It is all guarded by embattled walls, and has the gatehouse with the little windows from which the guard looked out five centuries ago. In a park with lovely grounds, and lakes filled by the Thornton Beck on its way to the River Nidd below the village, the castle has indeed a perfect setting.

The castle, made largely new about 1780, is stored with precious pictures, books, and furniture. The tower of Mary Tudor's day is a museum of old and beautiful things. Here is the library, a spacious room with hundreds of rare books, portraits of Cromwell, Philip and Mary, Elizabeth, and James. In it is the original foundation charter of Mount Grace Priory, richly illuminated; and there is a piece of lead found on Hayshaw Moor 17 centuries after a Roman overseer had stamped it. It is the Knight's Chamber which fascinates us most of all, its wagon roof finely preserved, its walls handsomely panelled, its collection of carved oak inscriptions by a craftsman of Edward VI's day; one of them has a prayer for the souls of Sir William Ingilby and his wife, and the words:

> *Better is poverty with mirth and gladness*
> *Than riches with sorrow and sadness.*

Among the treasures in this chamber are pieces of armour, a leather jerkin of Cromwell's day, a chest with one of the most complicated locks we have seen, and a travelling chest which belonged to Eugene Aram. A Priest's Hole, which must have been installed about 1555, was discovered in this room in 1964.

The oriel window of the Knight's Chamber is a gem of masonry, exquisite seen from without. From within, it frames a lovely view of the village, with the trees close to the castle, houses beyond, and the grey tower of Nidd church across the fields. Looking from this window into the courtyard below, we remember that King James was welcomed here as he rode in at the gateway one spring day in 1603. In the Civil War his son brought on England the gallant Jane Ingilby rode off to fight at Marston Moor. They brought her home sorely wounded, but the Ripley banner was in her hand. Tradition says she was closely followed by Cromwell, and that Oliver spent a night at the castle, but if so it must have been an unpleasant one; the story goes Lady Ingilby kept a watch on him all night with a loaded pistol.

We are reminded of the battle when we come to the church, for in the east wall are many hollows in the stones which, if story be true, speak of the most desperate hour Ripley has known. They are said to have been made by the bullets of Cromwell's troopers who came riding here from Marston Moor with a handful of prisoners, Ripley men, who were lined up against the east wall of the church and shot. Some of the bullet holes are high up, as if the firing squad had missed their aim.

An attractive picture outside, the church is believed to have been built on this site by Thomas Ingilby about 1400, replacing the church which had become ruinous owing to its nearness to the Nidd. Some of the stone of the older church (known as the Sinking Chapel) may have been used in the new one. The clerestory is Elizabethan.

There is an old north door, and the very old south door (with fine simple hinges) is curious for its unplaned boards, strongly riveted in primitive fashion. The remnant of a mediaeval screen across the south aisle is thought to have come from the Sinking Chapel. The south aisle has a piscina, the vestry a peephole to the chancel, and there is a coffin lid engraved with a chalice.

In the north chapel are a helmet and a black banner probably used at Ingilby funerals. The tomb of Sir William Ingilby, who died in Cromwell's youth, has his figure in armour, and above it a rhyming inscription. It is said that Cromwell stabled his horses in the church after Marston Moor, and ordered the carving of the words on Sir William's tomb, "No pomp nor pride; let God be honoured." The oldest Ingilby monument is the 14th century tomb of Sir Thomas and his wife, brought from the old church. Sir Thomas was a judge, and grandfather of the namesake who built the new church. He lies in his armour, head on crest, a lion at his feet, his wife in draped headdress with a dog at her feet. Round the tomb are figures of their children, most of them headless. There is also a window to Admiral Sir Robert Barrie, who in his youth sailed round the world with Captain Vancouver. By the south wall outside are old tombstones and a stone coffin brought from the Sinking Chapel, one of the stones crudely carved with a flagon. On the other side of the churchyard is a round pedestal, its upper stone having a socket as if for the shaft of a cross, and the lower stone having eight curious recesses round it big enough for a child to kneel in. Probably 700 years old, it may have been a kneeling cross, or a weeping cross used by penitents.

Ripon. It is one of the smallest of our cities, an old-world place in the shadow of cathedral towers, yet it has a pump room and baths which bring it up-to-date as a 20th century health resort. Its attractive gardens, green spaces, and river banks are delightful. Ripon slopes down to the River Ure, which comes from a many-arched old bridge, and gathers the waters of the River Skell and the River Laver, which join forces on the west of the town. On one hand lies the wide Plain of York, on the other the lovely land of moors and dales, and a mile or two away is one of the incomparable splendours of our incomparable land, Fountains Abbey.

Ripon, proud of its past, does not let its ancient customs die. It was already old when Athelstan, First King of All England, gave it the privilege of sanctuary. It had a bishop for a few years in the 7th century, and was made the seat of a bishopric again last century, when the fine old church became the cathedral. It is not one of our most impressive shrines, but it has a wonder that few of our cathedrals can boast, a Saxon crypt going back for 1300 years.

The cathedral is linked with St Wilfrid, Ripon's patron saint, and once a year, at the opening of the Pleasure Fair, the saint rides on a white horse in grand procession through these old streets, the citizen who plays his part wearing a mitre and carrying a crozier.

The blowing of the Wakeman's Horn (the horn in the city arms) is another of Ripon's old customs, coming down from Saxon times. Till the end of Queen Elizabeth I's reign the town was governed by a Wakeman and a number of aldermen, and as insurance against robbery every householder paid a small fee to the wakeman, who made himself responsible for the safety of the town from the hour the horn was blown till sunrise. He made it his business to set a watch, and if a robber broke into a house he made good the loss. The last wakeman, Hugh Ripley, became Ripon's first mayor. At nine o'clock every evening, when the bell rings out from the cathedral, the hornblower in his three-cornered hat sounds his horn at the mayor's house and the market cross.

This fine cross, a mighty obelisk rising 90 feet above the market-place, is from the end of the 18th century and is surmounted by ornamental ironwork and a gilded horn as a weathervane. Near the cross is the Town Hall designed by James Wyatt, with the pediment of its front supported by four columns and a cornice on which in letters of gold are the words, "Except the Lord keep the city the Wakeman waketh in vain", a motto which has been copied by the Ripon in Wisconsin.

The horn used today is only a century old, but the ancient horn is still preserved in the Town Hall. The crescent-shaped horn of an ox, it is 30 inches from end to end, covered with purple velvet and enriched with five decorated silver bands of different dates. The horn hangs from a broad shoulder belt of purple velvet lined with silk, which is thrown over the shoulder of the sergeant-at-mace on special occasions. On the belt are more than 40 badges and shields of wakemen and mayors and town clerks from early in the 16th century —five shaped like a cardinal's hat believed to be of wakemen elected while Wolsey was Archbishop of York and lord of the manor of Ripon. On the velvet band attaching the ends of the horn to the belt are badges and emblems of wakemen and trading guilds, among them a pair of scissors, a Tau cross, a stag, an axe, a horseshoe, a barrel, and a helmet; and with the silver chain attaching the belt to the middle of the horn hang a silver crossbow and a silver spur which has a rowel of Ripon steel. The town was long famous for its spurs; Ben Jonson mentions them, and a man could have no higher praise than the words of the Ripon motto, "as true steel as Ripon rowels".

Another old custom still living on here is the Seeking of the Mayor, the procession of the City Fathers to his residence after his installation, and the hanging of the mayor's lamp outside his doorway.

The first mayor of Ripon lived in the gabled house in the marketplace, still known as the Wakeman's House, and dating back to the 13th century. It has a quaint stairway to a minstrel gallery, so small that two musicians could have had little elbow room, and there is a dark place known as the bolt-hole, with peepholes ingeniously hidden under the stairs. There are old beams, and the original stone slabs covering the roof are kept in place by bone pins. In one of the rooms at the back of the house is a Folk Museum with relics of Old Ripon—pictures of the town in painted panels, a chair in which bad-tempered women were punished, a 600-year-old chest in which pikes were kept and a town chest half as old, an 18th century Bible chair on rockers and an old Bible in a little drawer at the side. A small cross was made from one of the yews which sheltered the first monks at Fountains, and there is a jug with the shield of the last of their abbots, and some fragments of glass and lead from the east window of the abbey. Here too is a painting of Charles I, whose eyes seem to follow us about, and a portrait of Old Boots, a Ripon character "who could hold a coin between his nose and his chin".

From some of the river bridges are charming views of houses clustering round the cathedral. The 17th century deanery is almost hidden by a stone wall in which is a fragment of a mediaeval doorway. St Agnes Lodge is an old house with a long roof and round windows, and in the garden of the house where the canons live is a circular mound known as Ailcy Hill said to be the burial place of men killed in battle with the Danes. The bishop's palace, on rising ground about a mile from the city, is a century-old house in a 70-acre park. The grammar school founded by Edward VI has been removed from the centre of the city to fine buildings in Bishopton Close.

For the city's museum we must go to Thorpe Prebend House, St Agnesgate; we see it best from the stone bridge close by, its old walls sheltering a small garden where the stocks have come to stay. Thorpe was one of the seven prebends believed to have been founded out of the great parish of Ripon by Archbishop Ealdred about the time the Conqueror came, and this old house, though transformed in the 17th and later centuries, has its roots in the ancient building. It is possible that Mary Queen of Scots spent a night here when passing through Ripon on her way from one prison to another, and it is thought that James I was entertained here for a night in 1617. Of his time is the handsome chimneypiece upstairs and some panelling on both floors. The fine staircase, and the white panelling in the big room upstairs, are 18th century. In 1913 the house was given to the city, and it has now fine collections of birds, butterflies, shells, fossils, and minerals, exhibits of the Stone and Bronze Age, relics of the Roman occupation, and a rare sword of the Iron Age from Clotherholme. There are remains of Roman pottery, two bronze saucepans used in the Roman Army, part of a Roman pavement, Roman grindstones and Roman tiles—some with the footprints of a dog and one with the mark of a man's sandal. There is part of an alabaster carving of the Entombment, a collection of spurs, a trinket box which belonged to Mrs Siddons, and a grim thing which is said to be the skull of Eugene Aram, who lived in Bondgate.

Of Ripon's three mediaeval hospitals two still have their old chapels, but the chapel of St John's in Bondgate has been rebuilt. In High St Agnesgate are the broken walls of the little chapel of St Anne's Hospital; keeping watch over the modern almshouses, it has an old arch under a gable, and an east window above the old stone altar where tradition says the ransom of a Scottish king was paid. The old piscina remains, but the font has become a flower vase. The Hospital of St Mary Magdalene, in Stammergate, was founded for lepers eight centuries ago. Its almshouses are rebuilt, and a new chapel has been set up, but the Norman chapel, altered in mediaeval days, still stands across the road, its nave and chancel under one roof. The windows are mostly mediaeval, as is the south doorway, but above it is the original Norman hood, and near it is a Norman capital. There are old roof beams, a 15th century screen, a piscina, and the old altar stone on its old altar, in front of which is an ancient tessellated pavement. There is a curious wooden bell which once hung in the gable.

Both the cathedral and the Roman Catholic Church are dedicated to the city's patron Saint Wilfrid. The Roman Catholic Church (on Coltsgate Hill) is 19th century and has an ornate reredos and altar designed by the younger Pugin—the reredos having scenes showing St Wilfrid preaching, the dedication of the monastery at his crypt at Ripon, and his last hours; and the altar showing the Gathering of Manna, Christ the Consoler, and other scenes.

The story of the cathedral takes us back to the first mention of Ripon in history, when, about the year 660, land was given for the foundation of a monastery for the monks of Melrose. When Wilfrid became head of the monastery the Scottish monks gave place to Benedictines and Wilfrid rebuilt the abbey on another site, with the church on a more splendid scale. His crypt remains to this day. Except for the crypt, the abbey and town were devastated when

King Edred laid waste the north country in the middle of the 10th century; the monks were scattered, and the Conqueror's half-brother Odo, Archbishop of Canterbury, is said to have removed Wilfrid's body to Canterbury.

Except for the Saxon crypt, the beautiful cathedral was mostly built between 1154 and 1530, and restored by Sir Gilbert Scott. It is one of the smallest of our cathedrals, 270 feet long and remarkable for the width of its nave and aisles, 87 feet. There are aisles to the choir and eastern aisles to the transepts; the three towers (two at the west end and one central) are all about 110 feet high and were crowned with spires till the 17th century. The minster's plan of a simple cross is broken only by a structure on the south side of the choir—consisting of the vestry, the chapter house, a crypt below, and the library above. The Saxon crypt is under the central tower.

It was Archbishop Roger who began the great rebuilding, and much of his Norman and English work remains. We see it in the east and west bays of the nave and in the transepts, in three western bays on the north of the choir, and in the north and west sides of the central tower, which was partly rebuilt after falling in the 15th century. The 15th century men did not complete their scheme for making new the whole of this tower, and the result is a conspicuous blot on the beauty of the interior, for the two 12th century arches which they left standing with the old sides of the tower are cut into by clustered shafts.

Roger's aisleless nave had wide and narrow bays divided into three storeys—plain walling, an ornamented stage serving as a blind triforium, and a clerestory which had the only windows in the nave. With the addition of the aisles nearly four centuries later came the transformation of the nave walls into soaring arcades, and the clerestory with its great array of windows.

The imposing west front with its flanking towers was the work of a great builder, Walter Gray, Archbishop of York from Magna Carta year. He used the west bay of Roger's nave for the inner walls of his towers, throwing them open with two lovely 13th century arches. His west front is almost as wide as it is high, the towers only just topping the gabled end of the nave, which is a fine sight with its group of three doorways enriched with columns, and its tiers of windows with banded shafts.

The transepts have a triforium of blind and open arcading, and clerestory windows behind triple arches, and they are largely of Roger's time, though some of his windows have in them 14th century tracery, and each transept has a 16th century arch opening to the aisles of the nave. The rich arches leading to the south transept aisle are 15th century. The three western bays of the south side of the beautiful choir were made new at the same time. The corresponding bays on the north are 12th century, and the rest of the choir was refashioned in the 14th. Features of this 14th century work are the great gabled buttresses, the flying buttresses to the clerestory, and the seven-light east window, 51 feet high and half as wide. There is a lovely window in the gable above it.

A rare feature of the choir is the glazed triforium; in no other cathedral do we see this. The choir has an oak vault with splendid old bosses. The choir aisles are vaulted in stone, and each has at the east end a stone bench. The piscina and sedilia in the choir itself are charming with rich canopies and a wealth of carving. Master sculptors of the 15th century fashioned the stone screen at the entrance to the choir. Nearly 20 feet high, it has an entrance between niches where statues once stood on pedestals (some are enriched with heraldry), and a row of 24 small niches under an elaborate cornice. Over the entrance is a carving of God the Father among angels, and there are modern statues of St Mary and St John.

The chapter house is most probably of Roger's time, though there are authorities who believe it may have been built in earlier Norman days. It has a stone roof resting on two pillars (each of a single stone), round windows, and long stone benches. The mediaeval crypt below it has an apse end and was once a bone house; now it shelters a stone coffin and many mediaeval gravestones, some with elaborate crosses, and one or two remarkably small. Built over the chapter house in mediaeval days, the lady chapel has been the library for a hundred years. A fine room reached by stairs from the south transept, it has a collection of 6000 books, of which 300 are rare including a Prayer Book of Edward VI's day, an illuminated York Psalter which was new about the time of Agincourt, a 1501 Book of Rules, and books printed by Caxton's assistant Wynkyn de Worde. There is a Chronicle of England printed at Antwerp by Gerard de Leewe in 1494, and three copies of books printed by Caxton, one his Traveller's Book, for which £20,000 has been refused. Two treasures older still are an illuminated Bible of about 1250, and a page from a Gospel written 1000 years ago. There are fragments of old woodcarving, and a charter granted by James I, whose statue showing him wearing a hat and holding a sceptre is under an arch of the central tower. In a show case in the library are fragments of painted alabaster from an old reredos, one showing a dramatic Resurrection scene, another the Coronation of the Madonna, and one a charming figure of St Wilfrid. The most curious of the alabasters shows Herodias with the head of John the Baptist.

There is a Saxon spur, and a rosary brought home from the Crusades by a Norman knight.

Among old treasures in stone are what is probably the base of a Saxon pillar, a fragment of a Saxon cross, the battered bowl of a Norman font, and a 15th century font in a fine setting. Still standing where it stood five centuries ago is a stone pulpit enriched with tracery; the metal pulpit used today (on nine pillars of coloured marble) has its fine beaten copper embellished with shields, vine, cherubs, and saints. Among the old treasures in wood are carved chairs, a chest, a door with ancient ironwork, a magnificent Flemish cupboard, and mediaeval cupboards with hinges like fish bones. A splendid array of over 30 stalls has misericords, rich canopies, and tabernacle work; they were all made in the 15th century, but half of the canopies are modern. Among the fascinating misericords are monsters, birds, foliage, flowers, two little men long known here as Mr Somebody and Mr Nobody, Caleb and Joshua, Samson walking off with the gates of Gaza, and a quaint scene showing Jonah being thrown overboard, a whale waiting to catch him. In another carving we see him coming out of the whale's mouth. A lion is fighting a griffin, a pig is playing bagpipes with little pigs dancing, and there is a mermaid with her glass and a fox preaching from the pulpit, with a goose listening. Other seats have a dragon chasing a rabbit, a lion trying to catch a monkey, a man bringing down acorns with his club, and a man wheeling another man in a barrow with three wheels, the one in the barrow holding a bag of money. On the bishop's throne is an elephant on a turtle, a castle on his back, nine little men defending it, one peeping from a window, another with a stone raised above his head, and the elephant holding one of the attackers in his trunk.

There are shields and roundels of old glass, and of our own time is the reredos, Ripon's memorial to those who gave their lives in the Great War. It is of oak and alabaster, brilliant with colour and enriched with many statues of saints and famous men; chief among these is Our Lord holding the Resurrection banner, shown as a young man radiant and beautiful, while others are: Peter, Wilfrid, Michael, George, Paulinus, Aidan, Hilda, the Madonna, Augustine, Columba, Ethelburga, Cuthbert, Bede, John of Beverley, Caedmon, and Alcuin.

Carved in stone on massive tombs in the north transept are armoured knights of the Markenfield family, whose moated house still stands two or three miles away. The tombs, adorned with shields, are battered. Sir Thomas of Henry VII's day lies with his wife, who has fragments of angels at her head, and on the floor by their tomb is a worn gravestone carved with a cross. Another Markenfield, who may have fought at Agincourt, lies here, though only a fragment of his wife's figure remains; he has a long decorated sword, a curious collar like a fence with spiked palings, and a pendant with a medallion of a stag. The collar is thought to be the only one of its kind.

It is believed that Sir Christopher Wren designed the ornate monument to Sir Edward Blackett, showing him in his curly wig, lying on a mattress, with two of his three wives standing by. Round about are shreds of a funeral banner, gauntlets, and a sword. In the south transept is a bust by Nollekens of William Weddell, and other monuments include one with a bust of Hugh Ripley, last wakeman and first mayor; one with the figure of his contemporary Moses Fowler, first Dean of Ripon; and a tomb covered with a stone on which we see a man in a forest of trees, and a lion. Tradition says that the stone once rested over a Crusader. There is an inscription to William Finney, who was 103 when he died in 1813, and a marble monument has portraits of Admiral Oxley, his wife, and seven children shown as a group of cherubs. In memory of Ripon heroes who died abroad are tablets to Francis Waddilove, who has been sleeping since 1849 in India, the land where he suffered terribly in a march of 250 miles; Robert Waddilove, who was buried in the Pacific Ocean; John Elliott, who went round the world with Captain Cook; and Neville Elliott-Cooper, a Ripon VC.

It is in the Saxon crypt below the central tower that we feel the thrill of Ripon. While the great church above has been devastated by invading hordes and raised again, this small stone cell has survived the centuries. Built by St Wilfrid, who built also the wonderful crypt at Hexham, it is about 11 feet long and 8 feet wide, with a barrel roof 9 feet high, and is surrounded by passages on all sides except the east, where is a great niche in the wall. The passage on the south side extends beyond the west passage and is divided from it by a solid wall, and at the east end of the north passage are traces of a stairway which was the original entrance from the church. The present entrance was made in mediaeval days, and has a coffin lid for one of its roof stones. There are niches for lamps in the walls of the crypt, and a long narrow opening known as St Wilfrid's Needle was once believed to bring forgiveness to all who could scramble through it.

Standing in this rare little crypt, a piece of England little changed since Wilfrid's day, we may well think of the mighty changes that have taken place in the world outside while nothing has happened here. These walls were 200 years old when Alfred was king, and about 400 when the Conqueror came. Processions of pilgrims were coming here 12 centuries ago, and still they come to this old city, where the Wakeman's Horn is heard night after night, and some things have not changed from age to age.

Ripponden. There are still some old buildings near the river in this town near the Lancashire border, where in 1722 there was a disastrous flood which so damaged the church that it had to be moved. In the churchyard are several tombstones cut by John Collier, who, under the pseudonym of Tim Bobbin created the famous work *The Lancashire Dialect*.

Roche Abbey. We have only to follow a little road among rocks and trees (dropping down from the highway between Maltby and Blyth) to be in another world. The deep valley is famous for its oaks and firs and sycamores, for King's Wood with its old yews, and for the ruins of an abbey which probably took its name from this rocky site.

The abbey was founded in 1147 by Richard de Busli and Richard Fitzturgis, who gave land on opposite sides of the stream. The monks raised their monastery on both banks, some of the buildings bridging the water; they built with the splendid local stone still being quarried. When the abbey was surrendered under Henry VIII they made a bonfire of the stalls to melt the lead from the roofs.

Four centuries later, in grounds sheltered by the limestone cliffs and glorious with daffodils in spring, high and low walling marks the ground plan of the abbey, now carpeted with smooth lawn.

We come first to the beautiful arched and vaulted gatehouse under the steep cliff, now with only the ground floor made new in the 14th century. The chief remains of the 12th century church are the eastern chapels of the two transepts, the vaulting on the north side only half complete. The lovely arcading which divided these four chapels from their transepts has pointed arches on clustered shafts. Over them are the pointed arches of the triforium, and higher still the round windows of the clerestory. There are fragments of the pillars of the nave and the choir, and some walling of the west front. Traces of the sedilia, a piscina, and an Easter Sepulchre are part of 14th century alteration to the presbytery. Steps from the south aisle lead down to the walks of the cloister, which has only the plinth left of its outer walls. South of the cloister was the refectory extending over the stream, with the warming-house on one side and the kitchen on the other. In the eastern range of buildings can be traced the chapter house and the parlour, and the common room of the monks which had their dormitory over it; this also extended over the stream. The passage between the chapter house and the south transept was divided into sacristy and library.

Abbots and monks and other folk are sleeping in this green world of peace. One floorstone has a sacred monogram carved 600 years ago; another has a cross and a sword; a third has an inscription to Peryn of Doncaster and Ysbel his wife; and a fourth shows the wife of John Braithwaite, her hands at prayer.

Roecliffe. A small neighbour of Boroughbridge, with the River Ure dividing it from the North Riding, it has a great duck-pond on the green, which is bordered with fine trees. At one end is the little brick school, with stone windows like those of a church, and a slender octagonal tower with a clock, its delicate spire rising from an open belfry.

A path shaded by yews leads to the church, which was built in Norman style last century. Crowned with a bellcot, it is quaint and charming within; the middle of the nave filled with open benches, and raised pews looking like a low gallery round three sides. Rich linenfold panelling, old carved altar rails, and two old carved chairs are in the sanctuary, which is up five marble steps. There is rich carving in the fine two-decker pulpit, and carving in three 17th century panels of a box-pew shows interiors of rooms. The old cover of the font has a crown at the top. Entered by a 15th century door enriched with tracery, and still with its ring, the vestry has an old chair, and old panelling with carving of cherubs and seven Bible scenes, among them the Nativity, the Magi, and the Flight into Egypt.

Rossington. The new village has the coal mines, the old has the church and fine trees, and over a mile away is the hall among the woods. It is a church made new except for the 15th century tower, a Norman doorway arch enriched with beak-heads, and a lofty chancel arch which is a splendid Norman legacy. The arch itself is richly carved and rests on short pillars set high from the floor, their capitals carved with interlacing. A great possession is the 15th century oak pulpit, with traceried panels and an inscription asking our prayers for Richard Stansall and his wife.

Somewhere in the churchyard sleeps a king of the gipsies, Charles Bosville. After his death in 1708 it was a custom of the gipsies to visit his grave once a year, pouring over it a flagon of ale.

Rotherham. It is busy with collieries, a huge electric station, and great iron, steel and brass foundries; but it is not too busy to care for one of our noble 15th century churches, and to have built a fine new bridge over the River Don. Part of the old bridge still stands, with its 15th century chantry chapel restored for use, one of only two or three bridge chapels left to us.

In the charming Clifton Park of 56 acres is the cenotaph, and here also is an admirably arranged museum and art gallery. Amid beautiful flowers outside stand pillars and stones from the Roman town of Templeborough; inside is much Roman glass and pottery, with a collection of trade weights used 19 centuries ago, and two Roman tombstones with sculpture of a soldier and a funeral banquet. There are examples of pottery, fossils from neighbouring mines, and prehistoric tools and bones.

Rising superbly in the heart of the town, though begrimed with the smoke of its industry, is the splendid church, with a story old enough for its thousandth anniversary to have been celebrated in 1937. It stands almost as the 15th century builders left it, much of it the work of Thomas Scot, for this Chancellor of England and Archbishop of York never forgot his native town. He made the church a college in 1483, and a doorway from the college, which was destroyed by Henry VIII, is now high above the town in Boston Park, where there are a few stones of a castle, and great rocks overlooking the valley. Scot (also known as Rotherham) was a benefactor of Oxford and Cambridge, greatly enriching colleges in both universities. He was Chancellor during the terrible days when Richard of Gloucester was marching through blood to the throne, and one of his most dramatic experiences was to find Elizabeth Woodville sitting in the middle of the night among her trunks and household goods bemoaning the peril in which the boy King Edward and his brother the Duke of York stood. Scot assured the unhappy queen of his loyalty and put the great seal into her hands as proof of it—an act for which Richard threw him into the Tower. He was released after the coronation of Richard, and lived to see the Tudor dynasty safely launched. He lies in York Minster.

Rising from the middle of the church, the great array of pinnacled buttresses and battlements of the clerestoried nave and chancel, the transepts and aisles, and the rich porch, is the tower and spire, as handsome as the rest and with eight pinnacles rising above the battlements, others encircling the spire. There is older work than the archbishop's time in the lower part of the tower, and its fan-vaulting is a lovely part of the cathedral-like interior, where old roofs look down on soaring arches.

The south chapel has a splendid old vaulted screen with a vine cornice, and similar screenwork is in front of the organ. Fine old stalls have poppyheads of kneeling figures, and remains of old seats have traceried ends. The Jacobean pulpit is striking, with two carved pillars supporting a canopy adorned with cherubs and a dove. A carved door perhaps 500 years old opens to a charming vestry with old beams. There is a battered font, and a modern one with a cover like a spire. Under the canopy of their tomb are the brass portraits of Robert Swift of 1561 and his wife. An inscription tells of 50 young men drowned during the launching of a boat at Masborough in 1841.

Rothwell. The collieries have made it drab, and its old cross with a new head serves as a lamp-post in the middle of the road. The embattled church stands by an old pit-head. Here too is a fragment of walling of the fortified house of the Lacys, from which John of Gaunt is said to have hunted. In a case in the church is a tattered coat said to have been his.

The church was made almost new in 1873, but the tower is 15th century, the porch may be 17th century, and we enter by a massive door in a mediaeval doorway. The nave has its fine old roof with heavy beams and floral bosses, and the font is Jacobean. In the west wall is a Saxon stone carved with arcading, knotwork, and an animal. Among a pile of loose stones are some with Norman carving and one with two horseshoes. A striking feature is the array of over 130 poppyheads, most of them richly carved, few of them alike.

John Hopkinson, a 17th century antiquary, has an inscription here, and in the churchyard lies John Blenkinsop, one of the pioneers of railways. Not so famous as Stephenson, this clever Leeds man built remarkably fine locomotives, and had one running over Hunslet Moor years before Waterloo. He developed some of Trevithick's ideas, and his first engine ran to the top of Hunslet Moor with eight wagons of coal behind it, fifty spectators crowding on to the wagons before it ended its journey. The Blenkinsop engine was one of the sights of Leeds, and much interested the Tsar of Russia, who saw it the year after Waterloo. George Stephenson built up his engine on the same lines, but enormously improved it by getting rid of the cogwheels, so making it the ancestor of the railway as we know it. Blenkinsop died at only 48, and was laid to rest here in 1831.

Royston. It is plain and matter-of-fact, but the church at the foot of the hill is a stately place. Built originally by the monks of Monk Bretton Priory, it is chiefly 14th and 15th century, with a splendid tower of the later time remarkable for its west window, a charming oriel adorned with shields and crowned with a pointed roof. The tower arch nearly reaches the grand old roof of the clerestoried nave, whose moulded beams are enriched with great bosses carved with faces, shields, oak leaves, a pelican, a lion, a swan, an eagle, a lamb, and a king. There is old work in the roofs of the aisles, with more bosses. Three bays of each nave arcade are unusual for so early a date as the 14th century, their flattened arches rising from slender oval pillars without capitals. The pointed arch on each side is 15th century, when the nave was lengthened. There are simple 15th century screens between the aisles and chapels, a 15th century font and an old piscina, a few fragments of mediaeval glass, an old door in the sanctuary with iron handle and hinges, and an ironbound poor box on an oak pedestal. Over the chancel arch are faded wall-paintings of knights in armour.

Rufforth. At a bend of the winding road from York stands the attractive re-roofed church, with tall beeches for company. Built by the Middlewoods of Rufforth Hall, it has a massive squat tower and a stumpy spire at the east end of the aisle, and a fine porch at the west end, a canopied niche over its lovely doorway. Among the fragments from the old church which stood near by are two Norman doorways—one in the tower, the other in the porch, framing a modern door with a squirrel in a band of ironwork. A wolf and a rabbit are in the ironwork of a door which breaks into a mediaeval window with a shield of old glass. The old altar stone is in the aisle, a carved Jacobean chair has a lion's head at the top, and the oak lectern has on it the Four Evangelists in white wood. An oak barrel roof runs the length of the church.

Rylstone. It was the home of the Nortons, about whom Wordsworth wrote *The White Doe of Rylstone*, but only a few stones of their house are left in the buildings by the church. Hereabouts are mounds which may have been the butts where old Richard Norton watched his sons practising archery, and the great moors and fells rise between the village and the River Wharfe as it flows by Bolton Abbey, where the White Doe was often seen by moonlight. On the slope of the double-humped Rylstone Fell is the ruined hunting lodge of the Nortons.

It is said that Richard Norton, his brother Thomas, and some of his sons threw in their lot with the Roman Catholics who rebelled against Elizabeth in 1569, but the rising was soon put down and Richard escaped to the Continent.

It is a village of great charm in a glorious setting. The busy highway dips suddenly down to its leafy hollow, where swans glide on a wayside pool reflecting noble trees. For one of the most magnificent views in Yorkshire we must come to the church on the hillside. Above is the rampart of Rylstone Fell, crowned with a cross which commemorates the Paris Treaty of 1813.

The church was rebuilt in 1852. There are mediaeval gravestones with crosses in the churchyard, a stone in the vestry wall is carved with cable and rings, and old fragments in the porch include part of a Saxon cross, Norman capitals and shafts, and window tracery. Scale House near by has associations with the Society of Friends and is also the site of a Bronze Age burial.

Ryther. Here the River Wharfe is quietly nearing the end of its 60-mile journey, meeting the Ouse before Cawood is reached. Having only a cottage for company amid the meadows and cornfields, stands the finely restored little church, with an ancient story to tell and much for us to see. Though much is new, the church has Saxon and Norman stones in its walls. The shingled bell turret and the spire are modern, but in the new porch are Norman beakheads and a fragment of an old cross. The south doorway and the nave walls are 13th century, and the lofty arcade and the walls of the aisle and chancel are 14th. The chancel arch, massive and crude, with great stones and imposts, is believed to be part of the Saxon church; the huge stones of the priest's doorway are perhaps as old, but the arch has been renewed. There is a big peephole by the chancel arch, and the font and two piscinas are mediaeval.

A very rare possession for a village church is a group of five old altar stones, one now used. In the sanctuary is part of the gravestone of a 14th century prioress of Nun Appleton, across the river. The east window of the aisle has old quarries and shields of arms; the west window of the aisle is filled with original glass with a groundwork of formal pattern, shields, a saint under a canopy, and a border of squirrels and birds.

The imposing row of monuments in the aisle probably belongs to the Ryther family. One quaint couple are a knight and his lady; he, with crossed legs, wears chain mail, a surcoat, and a sword belt enriched with quartrefoils, and has a shield with the arms of Ryther slung from his shoulder. The strap of his lady's mantle is threaded through her praying hands, and her tiny face is delightful in a wimple and draped headdress. Lying alone is a woman in a richly embroidered gown, a heart in her hands, a broken angel at her head, and a dog at her feet.

A handsome 15th century tomb adorned with tracery has a dainty border of vine and grape, and another of quatrefoils. Most of the quartrefoils have roses in them, but six are frames for a little gallery of portraits of mediaeval folk. On a beautiful alabaster tomb lies the battered figure of a knight in armour, his collar of suns and roses having a pendant with a lion. A man's head (like a mask) and a dog are at his feet, and on the leafy panels are seven knights in armour and seven ladies in mitred headdress, with flowing veils.

Saddleworth. It is the head of a scattered group of villages and hamlets of the moors and valleys. High among the Pennines, with Lancashire only two miles away, it is among some of the most desolate scenery of the borderland. Only a narrow strip of Cheshire lies between it and the boundary of Derbyshire's High Peak. A mile south the Pots and Pans Stone rises 1300 feet above the sea, and less than two miles beyond is Alphin Pike, 1544 feet. South-east are Howels Head, Long Ridge Moss, and Black Chew Head, all climbing over 1700 feet. On the hills are the ancient graves of a forgotten people whose tools and weapons have been brought to light in our own time.

Under Broadstone Hill is the 19th century church, with a beautiful window by Capronnier showing the three kings in rich robes, offering their gifts. The font cover, like a tall spire with tracery and pinnacles, was made by Saddleworth men, and shown at the Great Exhibition in 1851. The pulpit and stalls are also their work.

Fragments of the old church are now in an odd little building in a public garden at Uppermill, a tiny park with a stream flowing under trees. There are 15th century windows, a Norman doorway carved with angels and dragons in roundels, and an ancient door with part of its old hinges. A stone by the doorway, carved with a Crucifixion and two angels under arches, may be 13th century. Here too is the War Memorial, a column crowned with an angel.

The house by the garden has been refashioned since it was built in 1560, but it has a curious doorway with dragons carved on pillars, and a fine door with tracery and linenfold. There are windows with old glass fragments, a room with old panelling, and a hall with fine 16th century woodwork, the splendid staircase guarded by grotesques, the ornate overmantel enriched with wooden figures. The town also has a small but interesting museum.

Saltaire. It was founded and built by a man of vision in the early years of the Victorian Era. Unique among our towns and not a century old, it is known the world over, the first town of its kind in England, a neighbour of Bradford, and a memorial to one of the dreamers of the 19th century.

To this valley where the River Aire flows at the foot of great hills came Sir Titus Salt who had been mayor of Bradford, and here about 1850 he began a new industry. A turn in Fortune's Wheel set him venturing on his great enterprise, determined not only to make a new material known as alpaca for the millions, but to prove to manufacturers everywhere that they could afford to make the welfare of the workers the first charge on the profits of an industrial undertaking. He built a factory with three miles of shafting and opened it amid great public rejoicing. They were the biggest mills in Yorkshire, and he went on to build 800 model houses, and added a public dining-hall, schools of which no educationalist need be ashamed today, baths, almshouses, a library, and a club, and he would allow neither pawnshops nor public houses to be built. He went into Parliament, but, Nonconformist and Liberal as he was, he preferred working to talking, and left the House after 18 months. Year by year Saltaire grew up between the river and the hills, a complete manufacturing town, the happiest and healthiest working community then in the world.

The smoke from the chimneys round about drifts up the valley today, for Saltaire is now linked with Shipley and Bradford, but the colony Sir Titus founded is distinct and easy to find. In these days of spacious housing estates the hundreds of stolid little stone houses do not strike us as notable, forming a great block, criss-crossed by streets, and going down to the mills by the river, the canal, and the railway. But we see how well it was all planned, and it is plain that nothing was left undone which would improve the lot of the people. A bridge over the river brings us to the spacious park given to the people by the Roberts family who bought the mills from the Salts. Here are hundreds of evergreen hollies by paths and lawns, and a bronze statue of Sir Titus Salt with a piece of fabric in his hands. On the pedestal are angora and alpaca goats, the animals whose coats he brought into the service of mankind.

The chapel he built facing the mills has an impressive west front, a flight of steps climbing to a porch with a circular colonnade. Above is a round tower crowned by a dome, its pillars having between them rich ornamental ironwork. Within are green marble pilasters, a roof with a great show of gilding, two ornate candelabra, oak pews with carved ends, and a fine pulpit and organ. In the porch is a bust of Sir Titus (by T. Milnes), given by his workpeople in his own lifetime, and showing him with a smiling gentle face. Since 1876 the great philanthropist has been sleeping in the mausoleum, which is richly carved outside and has a huge vase on a pedestal festooned with flowers. Over him stands an angel with spreading wings and a trumpet, all in a marble frame adorned with English flowers, a butterfly on one of them.

Sandal Magna. Wakefield has come out to meet it, but years ago it was a small place with a church in green pastures and a castle on a hill.

Impressive inside with its splendid array of arches, the spacious church has grown from one of Norman days, part of which remains in the central tower, the rest of it being 14th century. The Waterton chapel (with an arcade of four bays leading from the chancel) is 15th century, the arches of the nave were made new probably in the 16th, and the church was lengthened westward in the 19th.

The twilight of coloured glass fills the interior, a few old fragments showing oak leaves and acorns and a shield of the builders of the castle. The chancel is unusual for having three 14th century east windows—two of them moved from its south wall when the chapel was built. Enclosing the two eastern bays of the Waterton chapel are fine old screens carved with linenfold, tracery, and vine borders; a simpler old screen is between the north aisle and the transept (which is the Pilkington chapel). There is an old chest, two bench-ends have inscriptions and shields of the Percys (who worshipped here about 400 years ago), and two carved Jacobean chairs, in one of which a highwayman was captured asleep at an inn in 1684. The font is 1662, and fragments of ancient coffin lids are in the porch.

It is uphill all the way from the church to the site of the castle of the Warrens, who had a wooden fortress on this hill in the Conqueror's day and a stone one in the 13th century. The castle had a great keep and many round towers, and was one of the favourite homes of Richard III. It was besieged in the Civil War, and in the end the castle was destroyed, and there is little to see but two forlorn fragments of walling, deep moats which are now green valleys, and a grassy mound which has a good view of the neighbourhood. Excavation proceeds on a massive scale, and has included recently work on the outer wall, the bailey, the undercrofts of the lodging chamber, a large domestic building and the undercroft of the buttery, pantry and cellar, and finally the barbican. This work has revealed the earthworks, long obscured by growths of thorn, to be some of the best in the north of England.

Sawley. It lies under the hills by a lovely wooded reach of the Ribble, with the ruins of an abbey in the green fields near the river, here crossed by a fine old bridge below the weir. There are a few houses, and a long line of stone buildings which was a mill for the monks long before Sir Robert Peel's father put new machinery in it and began spinning cotton. No work is carried on in the mill today, and part of it is a chapel.

Across the road are the remains of the abbey founded by William de Percy in 1147. There is high and low walling of the church (which looks as if it should be turned east to west, owing to its curious plan), but of the monastic buildings there is little more than foundations showing among grass and trees. The melancholy little that is left is typical of the story of Yorkshire's unluckiest monastery. Cold winters and rainy harvests followed Scottish raids; then came quarrels with the monks of Whalley in Lancashire, and the last abbot was hanged for his share in the Pilgrimage of Grace.

The abbey church was almost in the shape of a perfect cross, but the total length from east to west (113 feet) was 12 feet less than the length of the transept, each arm of which had three eastern chapels. In the 14th century the monks built a chapel north of the nave, and early in the 16th they built a splendid choir with aisles, 118 feet long and over 60 wide. It is this choir, massive in proportion with the tiny nave, which gives the church the appearance of being planned the wrong way round.

Two of the fine old arches of the abbey are set up across the road near by, so that we drive through them. One of them has bands of carving, and on the side of the other are a niche and a shield.

Sawley folk go to the 19th century church at Grindleton, reached by a shady lane across the bridge. Trim and bright, it has black and white roofs and a wooden arcade, a modern screen with some old tracery, and a window with an unusual Nativity scene with the Wise Men, the Star shining over a band of cherubs. The font is a big tapering pillar with roses on its six sides.

From the lane to the church we have a charming picture of Sawley nestling under the hills, and the great mass of Pendle Hill across the Lancashire border.

Saxton. It hides from the world, and on the encircling hills are ancient British graves, Roman entrenchments, and quarries where stone for Yorkshire churches was hewn. At one side of the village is Lead Hall, a great place centuries ago; at the other side, at Scarthingwell, is a stately hall in a lovely park of 150 acres with a lake. At the near-by village of Barkston is a tree said to be the centre of Yorkshire. At the crossroads outside the park is the spot where Butcher Clifford is supposed to have fallen with an arrow in his throat, at the beginning of the Battle of Towton in the Wars of the Roses. The site of the battle lies north of Saxton, and many who fell in the struggle lie in this churchyard. In the churchyard is the tomb of Lord Dacre, a famous Lancastrian leader of whom tradition says that he was shot by a boy in a tree. He was one of the victims of the Wars of the Roses, slain with 30,000 other men at the Battle of Towton in 1461, and it is unusual to find an altar tomb of such great age in a churchyard, or the tomb of such a distinguished man out of doors at all.

Dominating the village, the church has something to show of Saxon and Norman days, and of the three mediaeval centuries. The striking 15th century tower has a great overhanging parapet of battlements and pinnacles, and the simple charm of the interior is helped by the crazy stonework of the walls. From the wide nave an arcade of two bays leads to a big 14th century chapel, and the Norman chancel arch frames a 13th century triple lancet shining with bright modern glass. By the arch is a great peephole. There are two Norman windows, an ancient doorway now blocked, mediaeval gravestones, a group of 17th century stones, and part of the head of a Saxon cross.

Scotton. Two of its old houses have known greater days. The grey walls of the pantiled house next to the 19th century church are said to be part of a home of the Percys, three of their coloured shields being on a ceiling within. Across a field is the Old Hall, attractively grouped with its buildings, the creepered walls crowned with stone roofs. It is thought that Guy Fawkes spent part of his boyhood in this rambling Tudor house. If it is true he must have climbed among these old rafters, hidden in these old cupboards, and romped in this great attic in the happy days before his head was filled with gunpowder, treason, and plot.

Sedbergh. Roads and valleys threading their way through a glorious countryside come to this remote little market town in the north-west of the county, the home of a famous school. Far above its streets rise the wild and mighty fells of Yorkshire and Westmorland, here the River Lune and the River Rawthey are nearing their meeting, after having encircled the greater part of the Howgill Fells under which the town lies. There are beautiful bridges over the streams, and magnificent views from the heights.

Rising steeply for 1100 feet above the town (and 1550 feet above the sea), Winder is the southern spur of the pear-shaped mass of Howgill Fells, Yorkshire's only slate mountains, which extend north into Westmorland. Their summits often shaped like domes, at their highest point on the border, 2220 feet up, we can see the Irish Sea, the Lakeland mountains, Swarth Fell (2235 feet), and Wild Boar Fell (2324 feet) to the east, and over the Rawthey to the Dee and the Clough (winding in narrow clefts between Middleton Fell) the mountain ridge of Rise Hill and the massive Baugh Fell. Still farther south are seen Dent Crag, where three counties meet, and Whernside and Ingleborough, Yorkshire's second and third highest mountains. Crags are rare in the slate hills, but near the highest point (the Calf) are the cliffs of Cautley Crag, and the charming glen where a stream flowing to the Rawthey falls hundreds of feet in a series of cascades known as Cautley Spout.

Set with this grandeur all about it, the little town has a narrow main street (which is part of the old turnpike road from Kendal to Kirkby Stephen), some old houses and fine halls, an ancient church, a famous school with beautiful grounds and playing fields, Queen's Gardens with a tall elegant cross commemorating the Victorian Era, and a 17th century Quaker Meeting House as delightful as could be. It is at Brigflatts, a hamlet by the Rawthey, with a cluster of old grey cottages, oaks and chestnuts, the Meeting House sharing a stone roof with a cottage, its walls gleaming white. Through the tiny porch and a fine old door with over 100 oak pegs we step into a room of days gone by, very quaint with its few plain benches, walls with simple panelling, and a gated stairway to the gallery. With Winder and Home Fell towering above it on two sides, the little garden is shaded by cypress, oak, and a spreading yew. At the Meeting House is treasured a fragment of a yew tree under which George Fox is said to have preached when he came to Sedbergh. He had a congregation of a thousand people over the border at Firbank, two or three miles away, and there we see the rock he used for a pulpit.

Sedbergh's church is a spacious place with a 15th century tower at the west end. The nave and chancel are continuous, and the arcades, running from the east to the west walls, are of eight bays on one side and six on the other, all the arches round-headed except the pointed one at each east end. The north arcade comes chiefly from the close of Norman days, and the south arcade is a little later. The doorway within the ancient north porch, and two buttresses at the west end, are 12th century; traces of two windows of that time are in the wall near the tower arch, which looks older than the tower itself. From the 14th century come the doorways of the south porch, and the west window of the south aisle; the rest of the windows are 15th century and Tudor. Some of the pews are 17th century, and an

The west front of Selby Abbey.

The nave of Selby Abbey, seen from the south aisle.

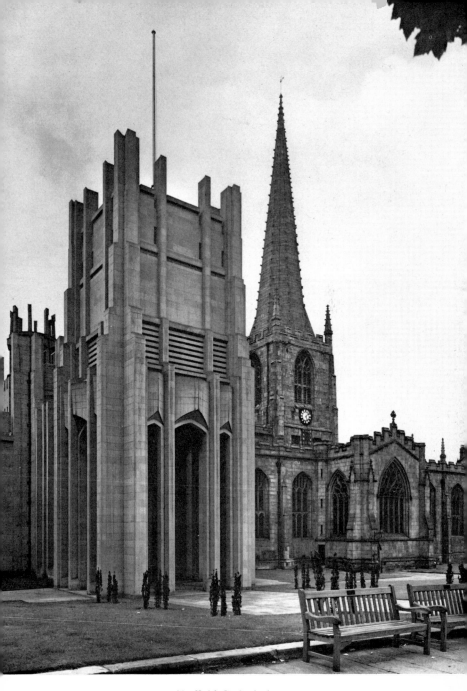

Sheffield Cathedral.

The west end of the nave of Sheffield Cathedral, seen from the new porch.

almsbox is 1633. Beautiful modern woodwork is seen in the north door, adorned with strips of roses and leaves, and in the splendid pulpit with carved panels, though its inlaid canopy is Jacobean.

The sundial on the south porch was given by Braithwaite Otway, who died in 1744 and has a memorial in the church. Remembered for his resistance to the enclosure of commons, he was one of many Otways to live at Ingmire Hall, which was partly destroyed by fire in 1928. Another of the memorials is to Sir John Otway of 1693, a Royalist who is said to have helped to bring about the Restoration of Charles II.

Flaxman's beautiful bust of John Dawson shows this great mathematician with a kindly face, his lips almost breaking into a smile. Born in Garsdale, he tended his father's sheep, learned a little about medicine, saved a hundred pounds by doctoring and teaching mathematics, and walked to Edinburgh with the money stitched into his waistcoat. There he studied medicine again, came back to Sedbergh until he had saved three hundred pounds, and then set off to walk to London, where he took his diploma. He won fame as a surgeon on returning to Sedbergh, but is best remembered as a mathematician. He taught at Sedbergh School, and a number of his pupils there became Senior Wranglers.

There are some four hundred scholars here today, for Sedbergh has become one of the famous schools of England. Founded about 1525 as a chantry school by Roger Lupton (a Howgill boy who became Provost of Eton), and refounded as a grammar school in the 16th century, it has a great tradition and a wonderful record of achievement. Nothing is left for us to see of Roger Lupton's time, but the charming building of 1716 still stands, having housed the library and museum since the fine new buildings rose last century. The chapel (1897) is of red stone, with chancel and transepts, and a nave with low arcades under a fine clerestory. In the rich glass filling nearly all the windows are scenes of the Annunciation, the Visitation, the Nativity, and a dramatic Crucifixion; and other windows have a fine gallery of portraits of famous men with scenes from their lives.

In memory of Sedbergh's Old Boys who fell in the Great War a beautiful arcaded cloister has been set up, its stone hewn from the slope of March Hill. Its entrances are in projecting wings, and on the central block are the arms of Roger Lupton and Edward VI, founder and patron of the school.

The school roll of honour includes the names of over 70 distinguished men. It stirs us to think of the scholarship which has been sent out from this hollow in the hills. Here were educated John

Otway, whom we meet in the church; Adam Sedgwick the geologist; Lowther Gerard, who was Sheriff of Cumberland in Queen Elizabeth I's day; John Barwick, one of Charles I's best friends and Dean of St Paul's; and Brian Mellbanke, who gathered proverbs and verses. Edward Eyre, the famous Governor of Jamaica and heroic explorer of Australia, was a scholar here, and others were John Hymers, who left £200,000 for a college at Hull; John Inman, whose nautical tables of a century ago are still used; and Anthony Fothergill, doctor and great philanthropist. Also on the roll of honour is the name of Robert William Sterling, a soldier-poet who fell on the first St George's day of the Great War, the day Rupert Brooke died.

Selby. The old town of Selby lies in the Vale of York, at that point where the River Ouse is crossed by a wooden bridge where people come twice a year to watch high tide rolling grandly up the river. The town goes back to the Conqueror, and it is believed that his youngest son, his only English-born son, was born at Selby. He was Henry I, the king who was known as Beauclerc in honour of his good learning. Certainly he was wise for the age he lived in. He ruled firmly, and though he was cruel after the manner of kings of his time he sought to be just in his administration and restored the laws of Edward the Confessor. We may believe, therefore, that Selby is one of the few provincial towns that have given a king to England, and it has another distinction in having the only monastic church in Yorkshire which has been used almost continuously for worship and has survived almost completely. Its abbey was the first great monastery established in the North after the Conquest, and after all these years we may still see part of its old tithe barn.

The people of Selby are busy with many things, building trawlers for Hull, dressing flax, making mustard, malting, manufacturing rope and bricks, and carrying on huge flour and oil-cake mills which dominate the picture of the town as we come down from the north; they compete with the towers of Selby's great possession, the wonderful abbey rising superbly above the marketplace, looking down on the 18th century cross still standing there.

Selby is fortunate in having had among its sons one who won great distinction in the worldwide realm of medicine and left his mark in a visible way on his native town. He was Sir Jonathan Hutchinson, who was born here long before the Victorian Era began and lived until the eve of the Great War. In his 85 years he made himself an acknowledged authority on various aspects of disease, so that there were wise men everywhere who waited to hear "what Jonathan had to say". Apart from all this, Sir Jonathan linked himself with Haslemere and Selby in an interesting way. He came to study natural history and geology with much enthusiasm, and his study led him to form the well-known museum at Haslemere, building it up on an educational basis which he hoped would be a model for other places. He afterwards did the same for Selby, and his museum here owes its great value largely to the lines on which Sir Jonathan laid it down. It has much more to see than the specimens he started with, including a fine model of a Hindu temple and a model of the old trestle bridge over the Ouse. The bridge was built in 1791, and this model is interesting because it was taken up to Westminster for Parliament to see when Selby needed authority to erect the bridge.

Every three hours a carillon plays hymn tunes which can be heard all over the town, and a fine peal of 10 bells rings out to draw the people to their famous abbey. It is one of the noblest of our cathedrals, which, in the early years of our century was threatened with destruction by fire. Danger has befallen it more than once. It was partly ruined by fire which swept through it 600 years ago. It fell into disuse for a time after the Dissolution, but became the parish church in the time of James I. It suffered damage in the Commonwealth, and lost its south transept when the central tower collapsed in 1690. For years during the 18th century the choir was the only part used for worship, and after the 19th century restoration came the fire of 1906, which gutted the interior and left the fabric so badly damaged that the restoration cost £40,000. It was money well spent, and since then the building has been ennobled by the building of the south transept on the old site and the raising of the three towers. Today it stands a noble cross-shaped pile, 310 feet from east to west, its stonework handsomely enriched without and within, especially in the west front, the north porch, and the choir. It is a magnificent spectacle, the great nave from the Norman and early English builders, the choir from the 14th century.

Its story begins with the 11th century monk Benedict who set up a cross on a bank of the Ouse and built a cell on what is now Church Hill. It happened that Hugh, Sheriff of Yorkshire, came sailing along the river and saw the cross, and on hearing Benedict's story he brought the monk before the king, who gave him authority to establish a monastery. So Benedict became the first of a line of over thirty abbots, and the abbey grew rich and famous. It was Benedict's successor, the rich Hugh de Lacy, who planned the church on a grand scale, building the lower part of the central tower, the transepts, a choir of two bays with aisles, and part of the grand aisled nave. This earliest work in the nave consisted of the two

231

eastern bays and their triforium, and most of the aisle walls. At the close of Norman days came the lower storey of the four western bays of the nave, the six western bays of the triforium on the north side, the completion of the north aisle with a splendid porch and a glorious doorway, and part of the west front, flanked by dwarf towers. The front was completed soon after by the first English builders, and at the same time the nave was given the six western bays of the triforium on the south side, and the whole of the clerestory on both sides.

We see the nave and the west front much as they were when completed about 1220, except that the dwarf towers have been raised in our time. The aisles are vaulted, and the early Norman vault still remains in two bays of the south aisle. The oak roof of the nave, renewed after the fire, has fine bosses with flowers and angels.

At each side of the 15th century west window is a panel pierced with trefoils, and in the gable over the window is arcading with the middle bay pierced, and between the window and the doorway is a row of dainty trefoiled arches. In the buttress niches in line with this arcading are modern statues of King George and Queen Mary. The great west doorway is one of the loveliest in the land, its five recessed orders enriched with zigzag, diamond pattern, and other ornament.

It is all 12th century, and of the same time are the charming north doorway and its porch. The doorway has four orders, and the mediaeval door has its old handle and is riddled with shot. The porch is a splendid tribute to the 12th century builders; its entrance is round, but there are pointed arches and trefoiled niches at each side, showing the passing from the Norman to the English style. The porch walls are arcaded inside, and the vaulted roof supports an upper room without windows.

Hugh de Lacy's central tower, with round arches on massive piers, was raised another storey in the 14th century, but the mediaeval storey fell in 1690, and its handsome 20th century successor, erected after the fire, is in the style of the original belfry, enriched with fine pinnacles and an open parapet with stone figures.

Standing under the tower we have a grand view of the three-tiered nave, with a hundred years of building in its charming variety of style. Near us are Hugh de Lacy's bays, all curiously out of shape (owing, it is said, to faulty foundations), and as the eye travels along the avenue of stone we see how the ornament of the early work disappears and the new styles come in. One of the striking features is the first round pillar on the south; known as Abbot Hugh's Pillar, it is carved with spirals, and has cushion capitals with carving not completed. Also unusual is the fact that some of the roof shafts are detached as they spring from the base of the triforium and rise in the middle of the bays, and rarer still are what seem to be two huge round tables on which two of the arches of the north triforium rest; each table is carved with leaves underneath, and is supported by a central pillar and a cluster of slender shafts, one having a cluster of eight, the other 16 shafts in two rings.

The north transept has some remains of Hugh de Lacy's time, including its deeply-splayed west window, but his eastern apse has been lost in the Lathom chapel, which was the last portion of the church to be built about 1463. A lovely arcade of two bays leads to it, and between the rich arches (resting on clustered pillars with foliage capitals) is a fine canopy above a bracket carved with a face. There are traceried clerestory windows with a band of flowing tracery in front of them, and in the north wall is a splendid 15th century window of seven lights. The elegant south transept is a fine tribute to our own century, which raised it on the site of Hugh's transept, keeping old fragments in the north pier of the vanished apse, a Norman arch leading to an aisle, and traces of the old triforium. The oak vault has lovely floral bosses, and there is a traceried gallery in front of the clerestory windows.

The new transept is in harmony with the old eastern limb of the church, the aisled choir of seven bays and the two-storeyed sacristy on the south, which took the place of the short Norman choir in the 14th century. It would be hard to find better work of its time than this, showing the development of the 14th century style particularly in the windows, ending with the flowing tracery in the clerestory and in the magnificent east window of seven lights (38 feet high and 18 wide); it is one of the loveliest existing examples of this tracery. Above it (but seen outside) is another fine window lighting a room over the choir and big enough to hold 1000 people. Adding to the charm of this eastern end of the church outside are gabled buttresses with gargoyles, openwork parapets, leafy pinnacles, and lovely lantern turrets with spires.

The choir arcades are delightful, the arches deeply moulded and resting on clustered piers with exquisite capitals like wreaths of natural foliage. The lovely canopies between the arches have finials supporting slender shafts of the vault, which has bosses three feet across, carved with figures, heads, and flowers. Under the canopies supporting the shafts are modern statues of St Mary, St Germanus, St Hilda, St Helena, St Columba, and St Aidan. One of the brackets on which they stand has a remarkable carving of the devil gnashing his teeth as he looks towards the altar.

There is no triforium in the choir, but in front of the clerestory passage we see again the bands of wavy tracery on which figures were once perched; of the few remaining, one is a bearded man in robes, one a long-haired man astride a lion. The reredos, carved by a peasant of Oberammergau and showing the Last Supper and the Last Days in Jerusalem, has at each side of it a 15th century stone screen ten feet high, enriched with tracery, diaper, and a lovely cornice. Also 15th century were the four sedilia with their soaring canopies and pinnacles, but they have been restored and the pinnacles are new. The five aumbries are modern copies of mediaeval ones destroyed in the fire, and near them is the cupboard in which the abbot's crozier was kept.

There is beautiful stone panelling behind the altar and on the sides of the sanctuary facing the aisles. The walls of these choir aisles, and of the lady chapel behind the altar (originally part of the Processional Way) are adorned with lovely arcading above stone seats, the trefoiled arches resting on shafts with exquisite capitals old and new. Some of them are perfectly hollow, like chalices of leaves; in some are cows, a cock and hen, a pig eating acorns, a stag, a fish, a hare, and a rabbit; and in one is a tiny bust of George V. Some of the capitals of this arcading, as well as the bosses under the east window, were carved by Thomas Strudwick, whom we found working here while World War II was going on, his spirit as tranquil as the spirit of this ancient shrine.

We come into the north choir aisle through a 15th century screen, and find a remarkable hole in the wall at a corner of the Lathom Chapel. It is over nine feet long, and through it the high altar could be seen from outside before the chapel was built. Above it we may note where the builders apparently made a mistake in their calculation for the vaulting.

Entered by double doorways below a modern statue of the Good Shepherd, the sacristy has its old stone vault springing from clusters of shafts resting on the stone bench round the walls. Under one of the south windows are three small recesses, and close by is the old lavatorium, a stone basin under a pointed niche. The three-light east window is notable for its old heraldic glass, one fragment showing two monkeys killing a pig. At the sides of the window are a piscina and an aumbry. A winding stair brings us to the room over the sacristy, the Scriptorium, used in the 18th and 19th centuries as a school for Selby's Bluecoat Boys.

The old shields in the sacristy are only a few of many in the windows of the church; one in the clerestory (in the window above the sedilia) has the Washington arms, with the two bars and three mullets which gave America its stars and stripes. It is not known what connection the shield has with Selby. In another window is a medley of old fragments, all that is left of the mediaeval glass which once filled the big window in the north transept.

The east window, famous for its tracery, is famous also for its old glass. In the tracery is the Doom, with men and women starting from their graves, St Michael weighing souls, angels carrying off the righteous to Paradise (represented by a church), and demons hurling the lost into the mouth of a great fish. In the first and last of the seven lights are Bible and historic figures; the glass in the five central lights makes this one of the finest of our Jesse windows, showing Jesse lying at the foot, and the tree rising from him and embracing his descendants (prophets, kings, and saints) till it reaches the Madonna and Child. In the borders are lions, squirrels, golden crowns, castles, and chalices.

The big six-light window of the south transept has figures of St Germanus, the Madonna and Child, the Conqueror, Abbot Benedict, Queen Matilda, and Abbot Hugh. Above these are scenes from the life of Germanus, and below are pictures of Benedict setting up his Cross by the Ouse, his consecration, the Conqueror granting the abbey charter, Hugh and his monks building, Queen Matilda and her ladies making the Bayeux Tapestry (with her little son Henry I in his cradle), and the dedication of this transept in 1912. There are also portraits of William Liversidge and his wife, who gave the glass.

In the 800-year-old window at the west end of the north aisle has been set a portrait of Abbot Benedict in a mitre. If we would learn more of the story of Germanus we must come to the 15th century window of the north transept, now rich with interesting modern glass. Here the story of the saint is told in 46 scenes, from his birth at Auxerre about 378 to his death. We see the French monastery he founded, the seaside village of Marske where he preached, and Winestead where he built an oratory under a tree. There are portraits of his mother wearing a curious lace headdress fastened with a brooch, his father in a queer black and white cap, and of young Germanus hunting. In beautiful pictures we see his marriage and his ordination (his wife standing by weeping), and his life as a hermit when he refused to eat and encouraged doves to drink from his cup. He is shown threshing barley (a boy stealing a few ears when Germanus was not looking), and again leading the British against the Picts and Scots, scattering them with his shout of Hallelujah. We see St Genevieve dedicating herself to God, and Germanus blessing corn, riding in state to Ravenna (where he died),

235

the people flocking to see him as he approaches the castle. His last hour and his burial are shown in this modern glass telling the church's oldest story.

The Norman font is plain, but has a splendid cover made by craftsmen of the 15th century. There is an ancient stoup, a collection of finely carved stones in the lady chapel, a beam with remains of a mediaeval inscription, a very old almschest roughly hewn out of the trunk of an oak, and a copy of a book on plants written by a Selby man, Thomas Johnson, our most distinguished botanist of the 17th century. He fought on the king's side in the Civil War, and took part in the heroic defence of Basing House, being there with a remarkable group of men—Inigo Jones (who had buried his money in Lambeth Marsh), old Thomas Fuller, William Faithorne the engraver, and Wenceslaus Hollar, whose engravings of London are famous. As the first botanist of his day Johnson revived the Herbal of John Gerard, the first garden book, written by a man who picked flowers on the banks of the Fleet. Johnson added to it over 800 new species and 700 figures. He was a member of the Apothecaries Company, and his account of one of their excursions is the first local catalogue of plants ever published in England.

Another precious possession of Selby Abbey is the Seal of Abbot William de Aslakeby who used it for the last time in 1293. Its story is a fisherman's tale which there is no denying. One day in 1914 two Yarmouth fishermen brought up with their catch what looked like a stone, but on it was the figure of a man and an inscription. The vicar of Gorleston recognised the word Selbiensis, and here was no other than the long-lost seal of the abbey come back home to be safely cared for after being under the waves about 600 years. It is in the vicarage safe, but we may all see an impression made from it, showing the abbot seated, wearing his robes, and holding his crozier.

The pulpit is part of the modern woodwork of the abbey, and is richly carved with tracery and figures of Our Lord, the Madonna, Elijah with the raven, John the Baptist, Abbot Hugh holding a model of his Norman church, and St Germanus with snakes chained, representing the ancient heresy. Under the pulpit canopy is a carving of the Crucifixion scene.

The abbey is not notable for its monuments, but the oldest is the 13th century coped grave cover of Abbot Alexander, whose rule ended in 1221. It is under the east window of the south choir aisle, and on the floor below are three gravestones with portraits of mitred abbots—John de Shireburn of 1407, Laurence Selby of 1504, and John Barwic of 1526. There are many stones which have been used for memorials a second or third time. A knight and a lady of the Hammerton family (about 1300) lie in the nave, she wearing a long tunic on which are the Hammerton arms, and holding shields not her own; he wears chain mail, has crossed legs, a sword from his belt, and a shield on which are six hammers. On an alabaster tomb in the north aisle of the nave is a fragment of the figure of Lord D'Arcy of 1411; his head and limbs are gone, but his shield and part of his SS collar are still here. Two 18th century characters are remembered in the nave, with doggerel epitaphs, and remembered also is John Edmonds, a Selby mariner brought safe home to port in 1767; we read his epitaph in the lady chapel:

> *And in this silent bay I lie with many of our fleet,*
> *Until the day that I set sail my Admiral Christ to meet.*

Settle. Over the Ribble from Giggleswick, this bright old-world town is a fascinating place to find among the fells. Sheltering it on the east is the precipitous limestone rock Castlebergh, the tree-clad path to the top well worth climbing for the wonderful view of hills and valleys round Ingleborough and Penyghent. Behind Castlebergh rise the limestone scars with caves where men and animals lived in the morning of time, and by the old moorland road from Settle to Airton, linking the valleys of the Ribble and the Aire, is the site of a Roman camp.

Seen from near and far, as the sun catches the mirrors with which it is panelled, is a great cross by Settle's Roman Catholic church perched on the hill. The parish church of 1837–8, is in the lower part of the town, in a churchyard carpeted with crocuses in early spring. It has an inscription to workmen who were killed while building the wonderful railway enbankment and the bridge which crosses the river here, and there is a Book of Remembrance to those who fell in the Great War.

Some of the quaint old buildings left in Settle are round the marketplace, where an old cross stands. One of the houses has the figure of a man holding a label with 1663 on it, and over the old arcade of the Shambles is a row of cottages. The 19th century town hall has gables and turrets and oriel windows. In High Street is the delightful 17th century house known as the Folly because Thomas Preston who began building it was too poor to finish it; it has many mullioned windows in its gabled stone walls, and one of its curious doorways is set between oddly-shaped pillars. There are old-world corners up Constitution Hill, a green where the gallows stood till about a century ago, a charming Friends Meeting House of the 17th century, and, in Upper Settle, tiny courtyards behind strong stone arches thought to have been for protection against the Scots in Border raids.

In the Pig Yard Club museum are many interesting things found in the caves hereabouts, including Victoria Cave 1450 feet above the level of the sea, reached on foot from Langcliffe. There are bones of man from before the Ice Age, a man's skull from the Stone Age, the skull of a brown bear, and bones of the reindeer, horse, badger, ox, lynx, and wolf. Among the relics are spindles and combs for weaving, pottery, and weapons, one of the weapons the finest example in England of a harpoon spear-head. From Roman times there are coins, ornaments, combs, bracelets, and brooches, one an enamelled brooch still bright in colour. There are many interesting things of everyday use in our great-grandfathers' time, and a sad note is struck by a stout piece of leather and the hand tools belonging to the town's last leather-worker.

Three men of Settle have won national fame: Thomas Proctor, the artist; Benjamin Waugh, the great friend of children; and George Birbeck, philanthropist and pioneer of education for mechanics.

Sharlston. With an old dovecot near the church, old Sharlston has its green, and the old hall where lived Nicholas Fleming, six times Lord Mayor of York. Built in 1574, it is now a farmhouse, keeping its old porch with the inscription: "In three things God and man is well pleased, brethren in unity, husband and wife in one consent, and neighbours that agree."

Sharow. The River Ure flows between Ripon and this secluded little place with houses big and small, cottages in gay gardens, a 19th century church with an embattled tower, many noble trees, and a National Trust fragment of the only remaining one of the eight sanctuary crosses erected round Ripon centuries ago. It stands where the ways meet between the village and the river.

The church's striking feature is the great panelled roof, a flat expanse over 40 feet wide. A monument with a panel of a broken bridge over a rushing stream is in memory of George Knowles, the civil engineer who designed the church; and an inscription tells of Walter Pick who was chorister, bellringer, and sexton for 65 years.

It is a pyramid in the churchyard which stirs the mind, for in it lies our pyramid man, Charles Piazzi Smyth, who measured the Great Pyramid of Gizeh and made a name for himself in studying the stars. His curious monument is of stone (crowned with a cross), a miniature of the pyramid he explored.

Sheffield. It has few ancient links with history, but it has given itself an abiding place in the modern world. It is the pivot of the Steel Age. If it has grown to be the biggest city in England's biggest county, with over half a million people, it is steel that has made it so. It has grown up anyhow, but it has made the best of a bad beginning, and today it is far from deserving Horace Walpole's stinging rebuke that it was one of the foulest towns in England in the most charming situation. We may not like its smoke, but we need go only a very little way across its 50-mile-long boundary line to find ourselves enchanted, for no city in the land is better placed than Sheffield. The city has recently done vast rebuilding of former slum areas at Park Hill and Hyde Park. Both close to the city centre, they now have some 2300 dwellings in blocks of flats ranging from four to fourteen storeys. The scheme incorporates an unusual architectural feature—street decks. Sheffield is justifiably very proud of its fine achievement here.

It stands on the River Don where it meets the little River Sheaf, and its smoke does not reach the hills and moors that gather about it and give it so grand and romantic a setting. The traveller who takes his car from the heart of the city will find himself in an hour in scenes he will never forget. Sheffield itself can never forget the Lincolnshire Quaker who set it on the road to fame 200 years ago. He was Benjamin Huntsman, the son of German parents living in this country in the 17th century. Benjamin was born soon after Queen Anne began to reign and he lived through most of the 18th century. He was a clever mechanic who was interested in clocks, and began experimenting with steel for springs and pendulums. He wanted something better, and he found it; the thing he found has made Sheffield what it is.

His was the old, old story of the pioneer who has all the world against him, for when he succeeded the cutlers of Sheffield would not use his steel and he had to send it abroad. It was in the Handsworth district of Sheffield that Huntsman perfected his process, and the business he founded is still being carried on at Attercliffe, where he has been sleeping since 1776.

Sheffield specialises in high grade steels of all kinds and it is this finely-tempered metal which is used for tools and knives and razors, and since the days when one of Chaucer's Pilgrims carried a Sheffield thwitel in his hose there has been no finer quality of craftsmanship than that demanded by the Master Cutlers who guard the good

239

name of this famous city. No man is allowed to injure its good name if Sheffield can help it; it will not allow its name to be used on anything that lets it down or falls below its standard.

The city makes scores of kinds of steel, among them one so hard that not even the incredible revolutions of the aeroplane engine can wear it down. It makes the biggest propeller shafts and the smallest watch-springs, and steel graded for a thousand uses. It was the centre of British armament production in the Great War, and it was in those dark days that there was discovered here the secret of stainless steel, now found in all our shopping streets. From Sheffield come the surgeon's scalpel and the schoolboy's pocket knife, and it is Sheffield that adorns the rich man's table with its shining plate.

It is wonderful to think of the things we may find in every quarter of the globe that come from these great foundries, to think of what lies behind these unnumbered chimneys, these mighty factories, the foundries in which the clang of steel is going on day and night, the workshops of the cutlers, the toolmakers, and the silversmiths, the engineering sheds in which the men handle girders and boilers and great masses almost beyond belief. All this has come from Benjamin Huntsman's small beginnings. But Sheffield owes much to Sir John Fowler, the engineer who built the Forth Bridge, to Thomas Boulsever, the inventor of silver plating, and to Mark Firth, one of the city's benefactors and founder of the celebrated Norfolk Works. It owes much also to John Newton Mappin, and to that remarkable John Brown who began the battle of life with a sovereign in his pocket, opened a foundry in 1844, invented a new railway spring, made rails and steel plates for our ships, and built up a mighty industry. He sleeps at Ecclesall within the city's bounds.

At Attercliffe is a small Works Museum where some of the machinery of the past is preserved: the area round about has been associated with lead smelting and cutlery since the reign of Elizabeth I.

Sheffield's birthday as a city was in 1893; and since then it has swallowed up Totley, Beauchief, and Chantrey's village of Norton, which have preserved enough character to deserve their separate places in this book. The university came twelve years later, and its bishopric dates from the year of the Great War. Those who would give it an ancient pedigree will tell us that Sheffield was old long before it was famous, reminding us that at Dore, on the city's moorland edge, King Egbert received the submission of the Northumbrians (so making all England for the first time a united people), and that long before that the Romans made a road on Stranage

Moor; while on Wincobank, on the other side of Sheffield, was a fortress of the Ancient Britons. All that is so, but Sheffield's is no ancient tale; it is one of the most modern cities of the world, and even Wincobank is now the site of a gas-holder fed from 13 collieries in Yorkshire coalfields.

A blacksmith stands guard over the heart of this city of thousands of smiths, for a seven-foot bronze statue of Vulcan crowns its civic dome. It is the dome of the handsome Town Hall tower rising 210 feet above the pavement. This imposing pile, enriched with turrets and gables, balustraded parapets, and fine sculpture by F. W. Pomeroy, stands on an island site joining on to the older building which has grown out-of-date since 1890; the extension was designed by the city architect and completed in 1923.

In the rich array of sculpture on the chief front are figures of Vulcan and Thor, with a statue of Queen Victoria to represent the era in which Sheffield rose to fame; and there are two figures symbolical of Electricity and Steam, holding the scroll of fame with the names of Watt, Stephenson, Wheatstone, Davy, Faraday, and Swan.

Through beautiful iron gates we come to the vestibule, with six panels of allegorical sculpture in frames of foliage. Very rich is the hall with its display of alabaster and marble, its big dome above the noble staircase with an alabaster balustrade, and a splendid bronze electrolier representing the globe, watched over by four angels with lamps and enriched by a band with signs of the Zodiac. Round the walls of the hall are carvings of trades, arts, crafts, and music, and over an archway is the story of the Dragon of Wantley told in stone—the children caught in a thicket and the knight killing the dragon with his sword.

Leading from a marble corridor 50 yards long (at the head of the staircase) is a fine series of reception rooms with oak-panelled walls, the lord mayor's parlour having a handsome chimney-piece with an alabaster panel showing two figures holding the Shield of Faith and the Sword of the Spirit. Above the fireplace itself is a carved panel showing wings spread over the city walls, and a watchman with his lamp. In this room is Onslow Ford's bust of Queen Victoria. The banqueting hall and the council chamber have rich ceilings. The whole building has 118,000 square feet of floorspace, 482 windows, 1000 yards of corridor, and 676 stone steps, 223 of them climbing to the top of the tower. With the fine collection of plate is a silver casket (made at the College of Arts and Crafts) with four enamel panels representing smelting, forging, grinding, and buffing, four galleons at the corners, and a figure of Vulcan on the lid. Among many portraits of mayors, aldermen, and other worthies are those of Lord Brougham and four poets: Ebenezer Elliott, James Montgomery, John Holland, and Samuel Bailey.

The site of the old St Paul's church has been made into a garden of lawn and gay flowerbeds by the Town Hall, and from it we have a fine and unexpected view of what is unpleasantly known as the Cholera Monument, ending a long vista between the city buildings; set in beautiful gardens in Norfolk Road, it is a reminder of the havoc wrought by cholera in Sheffield a century and more ago.

Splendid companions for the Town Hall are the City Hall of 1932 and the Central Library and Art Gallery of 1934. Designed by Mr Vincent Harris, and costing nearly half a million pounds, the City Hall is a dignified stone building in a modern interpretation of the classical style. Standing on an island site facing Barker's Pool, it is rectangular in plan, with projecting bays on three sides and a rounded apse at the back; and within its main colonnade are beautiful iron gates leading to an interior rich with heraldry and glass, and sumptuously furnished. One of its six halls, is a memorial to Sheffield men who fell in the Great War; another is the wonderful Oval Hall, 130 feet long and 105 wide, with a remarkable organ which cost £12,000 and has 3500 pipes. The City Hall is an ideal setting for the musical festivals for which the town has long been famous. In front of it is the striking and unusual tribute to those who gave their lives on service in the Great War; designed by Carus Wilson, a steel mast rises 90 feet high, covered with bronze, and four bronze soldiers with bowed heads and reversed arms stand round the base.

The story of Sheffield's Central Library began with two small rooms in the Mechanics Institute; today it shares with the Graves Art Gallery a building so well equipped that it leaves nothing to be desired from the point of view of the lender, the borrower, or the student. Designed by the city architect (Mr W. G. Davies), with the chief librarian (Mr J. P. Lamb) as practical adviser, the library covers an area of 3238 square yards, its brick walls faced outside with stone, and its furnishing of oak. The dignified front is divided into bays by pilasters rising to a cornice below the unwindowed wall of the art gallery; on the entrance are carved medallions representing Literature, Music, Drama, Architecture, Sculpture, Painting, Mathematics, Chemistry, and Astronomy. Above the cornice is a fine group of sculpture symbolising Knowledge, shown as a figure sitting upon the world, with the waters below and a severn-arched canopy above for the heavens; at each side is a figure holding a flaming torch, and for background there is the fruitful tree.

The library is capable of handling a million books a year. There are libraries of Science and Technology and Commerce, reading rooms, meeting rooms, research rooms, and a lecture hall. The Sheffield Room has a rich store of books and manuscripts relating to the city and its neighbourhood. Treasured possessions are the Jackson Collection of deeds and charters, and the Fairbank Collection of thousands of plans and hundreds of field and surveying books dating from 1739 to 1850, the pioneer work of the Fairbanks which was begun by William, the Quaker schoolmaster of the 18th century. The manuscript collection includes the Wentworth Woodhouse Muniments and the Arundel Castle Manuscripts.

Most attractive is the library for the children, with its fascinating painted frieze sketching the story of civilisation.

The Art Gallery which keeps the library company bears the name of its benefactor, Alderman John Graves, who christened it with nearly 400 pictures from his private collection, and added more later. It has eight galleries full of fine paintings, and a prized possession is the Grice Ivories.

Between the Town Hall and the cathedral is the Cutlers Hall, built of stone last century. In the oak-panelled entrance is a stone with the shield of the Company of Cutlers, founded in 1624 and now of national repute. There is a spacious banqueting hall (100 feet long) with marble walls, a great dome, fine portraits (among them the Duke of Wellington), and brass tablets with the names of 300 Master Cutlers. To this Company of Cutlers, whose yearly feast is held with much pomp and ceremony, Sheffield owes much of its greatness, for it has made the name of Sheffield (the trade mark which the company alone is allowed to use) a guarantee of high quality and fine craftsmanship. Sheffield University, given a Royal Charter in 1905, has its main buildings less than a mile from the city centre. Among its eight Faculties and sixty-five departments, the application of science has a prominent place. It is still in the process of expanding in accordance with a huge development plan which costs over a million pounds a year; already in existence are massive new blocks for several science departments; an Arts Tower, nineteen storeys high and a Library, opened in 1959 by T. S. Eliot, capable of holding a million volumes. The University, it is hoped, will cater for over five thousand students by 1968.

Sheffield cannot throw off its industrial garb, but there can be few places doing the world's work with more parks, gardens, recreation grounds, green spaces, and woodlands to their credit. Miles of moorland come within the boundary of the city, and

243

some of the parks have wonderful views of hills and dales. The south-western boundary extends to Millstone Edge above Hathersage, a spot famous for its incomparable Surprise View of Peakland heights and entrancing valleys.

The biggest of all the parks, covering over 200 acres near the southern boundary, was the gift of Alderman Graves, and from it we have a splendid view over the city. Weston Park of 12 acres (by the University) is nearest the City Centre, and is one of several of the parks sheltering museums and art galleries. There has been a museum in Weston Park since 1875, but in 1937 a new building rose on the old site, adjoining the Mappin Art Gallery of 1887, which was John Newton Mappin's gift with 153 paintings. The gallery has a front with a long colonnade, and a series of palatial rooms in which a permanent collection of about 500 works of art is housed—some of them the gift of the founder's nephew, Sir Frederick Thorpe Mappin, and many of them representative of the British School of the 19th century. It was re-opened after reconstruction in 1965.

The new home of the museum (another benefaction of Alderman Graves) is a fine block in classical style, with two columns supporting a pediment over the entrance. Over the doorway is a carved panel showing an altar with a book and a lamp, and figures at each side represent art and crafts. Above a window on another side of the building is a panel showing the steel worker. Many of the objects in the fine array of British antiquities ranging from the Stone Age to Roman and Saxon times belong to the Bateman Collection, the result of many years of digging last century in Yorkshire, Derbyshire, and Staffordshire by Thomas Bateman and his father. There are Stone Age hammers and axes; Bronze Age vases, cups, and tools; Roman tiles and pottery and vases; pottery from Cyprus, Greece, and Egypt; Egyptian ornaments and mummies; glass vessels of the first to the fourth centuries; a beautiful collection of stone and crystals, some polished and of exquisite colours; and vases of the lovely Blue John. There are fossil forms in geological periods, from the Cambrian to the last Ice Age and the Rise of Man—covering 500 million years; a fine show of birds and animals; and coins from 700 BC to Roman times, and brought up to date by our threepenny-bit with its picture of thrift and our farthing with little Jenny Wren. Other things to see are many examples of old Sheffield plate, beautiful cutlery made by European craftsmen, iron and steel work from foreign countries, and a splendid lot of medals. A very curious thing is the preserved head of a Maori chief.

Spofforth Castle.

Stockeld Park, Spofforth.

Studley Royal Church.

Lees Court, Thornhill Lees.

One of three memorials in Weston Park is a stone pillar by the art gallery, enriched with trailing foliage and bands of carving illustrating childhood, youth, and age; it was the work of Godfrey Sykes, a Sheffield man who was master of the School of Art, and it is now his memorial, set on a pedestal with his portrait. The terracotta gateposts at the entrance to the park were from his models. The second monument (a tall pillar with a bronze figure of Victory at the top and two soldiers at the foot) is in memory of the 8814 men of the Yorkshire and Lancashire Regiment who fell in the Great War. The third is the bronze statue of Ebenezer Elliott sitting on a rock; he never wearied in fighting against injustice, he helped to improve the lot of the workpeople, and he is famous, of course, for his Corn Law Rhymes. He sleeps at Darfield, but 20 years of his life were spent in Sheffield, where many of his poems were written, and where he was long the friend of James Montgomery, who lies in the general cemetery with a bronze statue over his grave.

Among other monuments in Sheffield is one at the Moor Head in memory of soldiers and sailors of the Crimean War. Alfred Drury's statue of Edward VII is in Fitzalan Square, and Queen Victoria is again in Endcliffe Woods. A bust of Sir Frederick Mappin is in the Camelia house of the Botanical Gardens.

In High Hazels Park (a windblown hilltop in the Darnall district) is a museum with pictures of the neighbourhood as it was years ago, and here we may look on the record of Sheffield's most terrible scene of desolation, wrought by the appalling catastrophe of 1864. Owing to the giving way of a new embankment, millions of gallons of water from Bradfield Reservoir (95 feet deep and covering 78 acres) came roaring down the valley, sweeping 250 souls to death and leaving 20,000 homeless. It is all here in pictures. In Whiteley Woods is the only known example in working order of a water-powered grinding wheel: it has been restored and the public may see it, thanks to Sheffield Corporation.

No wise traveller misses the Ruskin Museum, housed in the Hall of Meersbrook Park, nearly two miles south of the City Centre. It was removed here in 1890 from Walkley, where it had been since its foundation in 1875 by John Ruskin. Linked with his Guild of St George, it is a splendid attempt to teach us how to understand all that is best in art, sculpture, and craftsmanship. It was because Ruskin believed that nowhere in the land were there finer craftsmen that he chose Sheffield as the home of countless things of beauty, all precious, all perfect of their kind. He believed that his museum

I

would help us to appreciate true beauty. On the walls we read
such words of good counsel as these:

Pleasant wonder is no loss of time.
Every noble life leaves the fibre of it interwoven for ever in the work of the
  world.
All great art is praise.
Noble art is nothing less than the expression of a great soul.
There are so many things we never see.

We wander at will among these treasures, masterpieces of carving, casts of great sculptures, a library of famous books (many in exquisite bindings), and examples of superb craftsmanship in leather,
wool, lace, and needlework. A collection of casts of the great seals
of England is from the time of King Stephen to Victoria. There are
rock crystals and precious stones, rubies and sapphires, beryls and
emeralds, fine examples of lapis-lazuli, and what is said to be the
biggest topaz crystal in the world, a prism nearly eight inches long.
A fine crystal broken by a girl as she took it from a shop window is
here because Ruskin bought it to save her from getting into trouble.

Here are pictures by English artists, among them a charming
view of Sheffield by Turner. There are Ruskin's own drawings and
sketches in *The Stones of Venice* and *The Seven Lamps of Architecture.*
One of the loveliest of his paintings is a single peacock feather, and
there is an exquisite sketch of St Mary of the Thorn, made at Pisa.
Here are hundreds of water-colours of birds and insects and a
magnificent series of copies of the works of Old Masters, all chosen
for their perfection of style. The most famous picture is Verrocchio's
own painting of the Madonna and Child, of which Ruskin said:
"This picture teaches all I want my pupils to learn of art, and is
one of the most precious pictures in the country."

Two of the most pathetic things here are the miniature of Rose le
Touche, the Irish girl John Ruskin loved, painted on ivory three
years before she died; and what is said to be the last letter Ruskin
wrote, he having signed it and said of the hand that did so, "It will
never hold a pen again." There are precious illuminated manuscripts of the 13th and 14th centuries, the greatest of all being a
book known as the Missal Album of Lady Diana de Croy, a French
illuminated manuscript of the 16th century. It has a score of
miniatures all astonishingly beautiful with their blue and gold and
crimson and green, the details so perfect that we need a magnifying
glass to see how wonderful they are. It is not only for its 187 leaves
of vellum that this book is prized, but also for the signatures. When
Jean Foucquet of Tours had finished months of work on this rare

gem, Lady Diana, an aristocrat of France, set a new fashion in Europe by handing it round the Court, asking her friends to write a line or two for her, so that it became probably the first autograph album, with signatures of great people at the French court.

Mary Queen of Scots was one of two tragic figures linked with the city, both brought in their dark hours to the home of the Shrewsburys here. Sheffield Castle, the Shrewsbury fortress at the meeting of the River Sheaf and the River Don, was destroyed at the end of the Civil War, four years after it had been besieged and captured by Parliament. Its site is a marketplace, and only a fragment of its walling is now to be seen, but its name is kept green in the names of streets, and in what is called the Wicker, the site of the castle yard. Founded probably by William de Lovetot and rebuilt by the Furnivals, the castle is said to have covered four acres and to have had 14 acres of pleasure grounds. It was improved as a residence by the fourth earl, but about 1516 he built himself a more comfortable house on a hilltop, known as Sheffield Manor, and now a ruin. It was in the old castle and the manor house that Mary Queen of Scots spent 14 years of her long imprisonment in the care of George Talbot, sixth Earl of Shrewsbury.

A few gaunt walls with fireplaces, chimney-stacks, and cellars, remind us of the manor, once a fine place with banqueting hall and spacious apartments; but the small stone building, detached from the rest and known as the Turret House, still stands, its walls embattled, its spiral stair bringing us to a domed turret with a door to the leaded roof, where it is said the queen was allowed to take the air. The view is striking even now, and must have been sublime in Tudor days, before Industry had begun to spoil the countryside. Here still is the room the earl prepared for the queen, though most of the time she languished at Sheffield was spent at the castle. The handsome plaster ceiling is enriched with the Shrewsbury hound, the Scottish thistle, and the English rose. The heavy old door she must have hated is still on its hinges, and there remains a fireplace with herringbone work and a stone mantelpiece, and (in a case) fragments of pottery found at the manor, a holy water stoup, and what is believed to have been the queen's jewel case.

Of the many churches and chapels in Sheffield only one can claim an ancient story, the parish church of St Peter and St Paul, now raised to cathedral dignity. It stands in the heart of the city, and the transformation of the old church into a splendid pile worthy of its new honour is now going on under the plans of Sir Charles Nicholson, and more recently of G. G. Pace, as architects. The changes involve the setting of the church north to south instead of

247

east to west, and some idea of the work involved can be realised when we know that it is to cost about £180,000. The Chapel of St George and the chapter house, connected by a processional corridor leading also to vestries and rooms for the clergy, are already built, and extend from the north side of the eastern portion of the old building. The beauty of the new work is the promise of what we may expect when the cathedral is complete with a new nave and choir and all their chapels, and a second tower. Stones of the Norman church survive in the walls of the chancel, but much of what we see is 15th century, with a 14th century tower and spire rising between the nave and chancel. The clerestoried nave and the aisles, divided by tall arcades with embattled capitals, were rebuilt early last century; the chancel arcades are 15th century. But the finest arches of the old building are those of the tower, richly moulded and without capitals.

The three striking windows of the east front have unusual flowing tracery with rich cusping; four golden angels guard the high altar, and the reredos, shining with gold and colour, has figures of Our Lord and the Disciples. The reredos in the north chapel has a scene of the Upper Room at Emmaus, also in colour and gold; in this chapel is an old oak canopied seat, and in the south chapel is an old oak screen with simple tracery. Among the modern woodwork are handsome stalls with misericords, and a rich screen at the west end of St Catherine's Chapel; painted blue and gold, and enriched with angels and shields in the cornice, the screen is a memorial to Gertrude Elizabeth Western, a deaconess here for 14 years, and the chapel itself has been restored in memory of the wife of Sheffield's first bishop, Leonard Hedley Burrows. There is a fine figure of the bishop himself holding a model of this church; it is on one end of the beautiful throne at the crossing. On the other end is Paulinus, and adorning the fine pinnacled canopy are figures of Our Lord, St Peter, and St Paul. More figures (of Our Lord, Moses, and Apostles) are on the rich pulpit, and at the foot of its stairway are the two patron saints.

The lovely font has a grey bowl encircled with bronze bands, resting on a marble stem and four bronze niches sheltering figures of three saints and Our Lord with a child in his arms. Fine bronze statues of Abraham and Isaac on a pedestal are in memory of men who gave their lives in the Great War.

One of an array of busts in the chancel is a treasure of great price; it is of James Wilkinson, vicar here for half a century, but its interest lies in the fact that it was the first commission Chantrey received for a marble bust. Other 19th century memorials are a window to Samuel Earnshaw, notable in his day as a scholar, preacher, and mathematician; an alabaster portrait of John Kirk, a parish clerk for 60 years; and a monument with a medallion portrait of Sir William Sterndale Bennett, with two bars of the music he set to the words, *God is a Spirit*. He was born at Sheffield in the year after Waterloo, and has been sleeping in Westminster Abbey since 1875.

The Shrewsbury monuments are in the south chapel. Under a Tudor arch enriched with panelling, a pendant boss, and a cornice with cherubs and foliage, lie the fine alabaster figures of the fourth earl and his two wives. The gentle lord whose kindly welcome warmed the heart of the fallen Wolsey wears a cloak over his armour, the Garter below his knee, a collar of roses, and a medallion pendant with a rose and St George. He has a hound at his feet, and on his fingers are four rings. One of the wives has five rings, the other three, and both are beautifully attired in the fashionable dress of their day, with angels at their feet.

Reaching nearly to the roof against the south wall is the Renaissance monument of the sixth earl, who died in 1590. Guardian of Mary Queen of Scots, he was the best known of all the Shrewsburys, and was one of the four husbands of Bess of Hardwick. He lies in armour, with ruffs at his neck and on his wrists, his helmet laid aside behind him, a hound at his feet, and his cushion richly embroidered. The long inscription is said to have been written by John Foxe, author of the *Book of Martyrs*, some years before Shrewsbury died. A massive tomb with a great display of heraldry in the south transept is thought to be that of the sixth earl's son buried here in 1582.

In striking contrast to the smoke-grimed walls of the old church is the new clean stone in the cathedral. The Chapel of St George has a panelled ceiling gaily painted with red and white roses and the shield of St George, and in niches at each side of the sanctuary arch are statues of St Oswald and St Martin—St Martin cutting his cloak for the beggar, St Oswald wearing his crown; the raven on his arm has a ring in its beak. The altar is of Hoptonwood stone, and its silver ornaments and its rails are the Yorkshire and Lancashire Regiment's memorial to its colonel, Lord Plumer. The altar cloth is red and gold, and the black velvet frontal has red and white roses. On the wall behind the altar are three niches sheltering figures of St Michael, St George, and Our Lord in red and gold, holding a sphere and raising one hand in blessing. The Book of Remembrance is on an oak desk said to have been used by John Wesley when he preached in the town, and on the north wall is the foundation stone laid by the Princess Royal in 1937.

249

Very fine is the double entrance to the chapter house. At each side are statues of St Peter and St Paul, and on the enclosing arch are 12 carved scenes and figures representing festivals and saint days from the Church calendar—Epiphany (the Star and the Wise Men), the Presentation of Jesus, the Annunciation, St George, the Finding of the Cross by St Helena, St John the Baptist, St Mary Magdalene, King Oswald with cross and sceptre, St Michael weighing souls, Paulinus, St Catherine with her wheel, and the Nativity, with the ox and the ass in the stall. Equally rich is this entrance on the inner side, showing a lily, a rose, and the wise old owl in an oak. The owl comes again in one of the finials, the other having a serpent and a dove, and below them are four angel-heads which are a lesson in stone, teaching us to see, think, speak, and hear no evil.

Christopher Webb's lovely glass for the new chapel and the chapter house is exquisite in colour and wonderful in its conception, telling in portrait and picture something of the story of Sheffield in days gone by. The first of six portraits in three windows of the chapel (they are in memory of two soldiers, Bernard Alexander Firth and his son) shows Earl Waltheof, son of Siward and lord of Hallamshire, of which Sheffield has been the capital since Saxon times. Waltheof resisted the Norman invasion, married the Conqueror's niece after his submission, and was executed at Winchester in 1075 after being accused of treachery. The only man condemned to death by the Conqueror, he was regarded as a martyr by the English. Then comes William de Lovetot, the Norman baron who founded here the Norman church, a mill, a hospital, and probably the castle; he was also the founder of Worksop Priory. We see Gerard de Furnival, who married the Lovetot heiress and died in Jerusalem when on a crusade in 1219; and Sir Thomas Nevil, who, through marrying Joan Furnival, became lord of Sheffield and Hallamshire. He sided with Henry Bolingbroke against the king, and died not long after being made Lord Treasurer of England. Next comes that great hero John Talbot, first Earl of Shrewsbury, who married Maud Nevil; a daring soldier, whose brilliant exploits in France included the capture of Harfleur, he fell in battle in 1453, and lies at Whitchurch. Last in this brave company is Colonel Sir John Bright, who was baptised at Sheffield, raised companies for Parliament in the Civil War, fought at Selby, was Governor of Sheffield Castle and of York, and served under Cromwell in Scotland. He joined the Royalist party before the Restoration, and lived on till William and Mary came to the throne.

The chapter house and its glass were the gift of Miss Fanny

Tozer in memory of her parents, Edward Tozer having been Master Cutler and Mayor of Sheffield. The windows are captivating. They show the building of the Norman church, monks smelting iron at Kimberworth, and Thomas de Furnival giving a charter to his free tenants; the Archbishop of York dedicating the 13th century church, Cardinal Wolsey at Sheffield Manor, Sir Thomas Chaworth granting the canons of Beauchief Abbey the right to mine coal, and Mary Queen of Scots sitting in her room at the Manor with her faithful secretary Pierre Rollet; Mary Tudor giving her charter to the burgesses for the restoration of what the Commissioners had confiscated under Edward VI, the ejection of James Fisher under the Act of Uniformity, and Benjamin Huntsman with his crucible steel; William Elles receiving the first private mark known to have been granted to a cutler (in 1554), John Wesley preaching in Paradise Square, Bishop Burrows in his 80th year placing the cross on the Chapel of St George in 1938, and Robert Sanderson, born at Sheffield in 1587, chaplain to Charles I, and Bishop of Lincoln under Charles II; we see him at Rotherham Grammar School and presiding at the Savoy Conference. In a small window high in the east wall is a picture of the shaft of a Saxon cross which, after being in a Sheffield garden, has been given to the British Museum. It is believed to have been set up on this site early in the 9th century, and it seems a pity that it cannot come back home.

But the best of the chapter house glass is yet to be described. It is at the west end, one of the few great Chaucer windows we have found in our journey through England; there is one at Holt in Norfolk. Here in Sheffield the Reeve is telling his Canterbury Tale, and the motley band of pilgrims is winding down the hill to the cathedral, seen in the distance as it was in the 14th century. All are on horseback, and all in the dress of their day, led by the jolly host (who smiles as he looks back on the company), the Doctor, the Miller, the clerk of Oxford studying his book as he rides beside the sturdy friar, followed by the Reeve, near whom are the Wife of Bath, the Pardoner with a Crucifix, the Serjeant-at-law, the Franklin, and the Shipman sitting awkwardly on his horse. Next comes Chaucer, splendid on his prancing steed, in company with the Merchant, the Monk, the Knight, and the charming Prioress. The Poor Parson is with the Ploughman, followed by the handsome Squire with his Yeoman and Steward, the Nun and her Priest, the Summoner, the Cook, the Tapster, the Dyer, the Haberdasher, the Weaver, and the Goldsmith. It is a lively picture which Chaucer would have loved. In the tracery is the Miller of Trumpington, wearing the Sheffield thwitel, and here too are pictures of the forging and grinding of the knife known by this odd name. Chaucer wrote of him, "A Sheffield thwitel bear he in his hose", so giving the city's oldest industry a lasting place in literature.

Two things show us what the cathedral will be like when it is completed—a fine model in one of the rooms and Christopher Webb's picture of it in a window of the new entrance from Campo Lane, the window being a gift of the vergers of the diocese.

A fine spire, soaring from a pinnacled tower to nearly 200 feet above the road, calls us to the 19th century Roman Catholic church of St Marie, near the Town Hall. One of the most striking of the churches away from the heart of the city is St John's at Ranmoor, set finely among the trees on a bank of lawn, high above the smoke, with a view of the houses creeping out of the valley and over the hills. The ivied walls are of clean light stone, and the tower (with a lofty spire) serves as a porch. The nave has a fine floor, arcades with stiff leaf carving on the capitals, and three arches at the west end. A triforium runs round the three sides, and above it is a rose window in the west wall. The oak chancel screen has trefoiled arches, vine and grape cresting, and six angels keeping watch.

Not far from St John's is St Augustine's church at Endcliffe, on a hillside which has the Botanical Gardens at the top and End-cliffe Woods at the foot. Built in 13th century style, its unusual feature is the wall-painting at the west end, showing in soft rich colours the consecration of St Augustine, and the saint in white and gold preaching to King Ethelbert of Kent.

From here it is a mile to All Saints at Ecclesall, a charming tree-bowered part of Sheffield on the way to the moors and Hathersage, with the lovely Ecclesall Woods stretching to Abbeydale. The nave and west tower of the church are part of the building which re-placed a mediaeval chapel in the 18th century, but the tower was given its top storey last century and two rows of windows in the nave were made into the tall lancets we see. The clerestoried chancel and the transepts are a striking addition of 1908, showing an impressive array of lancet windows and fine arcades. Many of the windows glow with rich glass, some of it telling the story of old Ecclesall. In one is Sir Ralph de Ecclesall who built the 13th century chapel. Two windows have portraits of Robert FitzRanulph, who founded the abbey, and Thomas Becket to whom it was dedicated. Among the score of saints and famous figures in the five tall lancets in the south wall of the transept are Chad, Aidan, Benedict, King Oswald, Queen Ethelburga, Caedmon, Bishop Wilfrid, Elfleda and Hilda of Whitby, Paulinus, and Cuthbert. The handsome marble font is a sculpture of a kneeling angel holding a shell. Interesting for its association is an inscription to William Shore and his wife, for their son William (who assumed the name of Nightingale) was father of the Lady of the Lamp. The names of 124 men who gave their lives in the Great War are on the chapel wall; the cross to their memory, standing 18 feet high near an entrance to the churchyard, was designed by Mr Temple Moore, architect of the eastern part of the church.

The green bank on which All Saints stands was once called Carter Knoll, and the name lives on in that of the road along which we go to St Peter's church, Abbeydale. This (like All Saints) has the shape of a cross, and being built on to a steep hillside has a two-storeyed chancel towering above the road. Ending the vista along its nave arcades is a scene of the Ascension glowing richly in the east window. St Aidan's church on City Road, only a few years old, is a bright attractive building with a central tower, many arches, and high and low roofs; from its high place on Sky Edge it looks over the veil of smoke to the encircling hills.

Also now a part of Sheffield is Handsworth, so high that it looks far over Yorkshire and Derbyshire. Its church, built at the close of the 12th century, is made almost new, except for the lower part of the tower with its original arch, the chancel walling, the sedilia and piscina, the striking north arcade with pillars so high that the arches reach the roof, and the 14th century chapel with a peephole in the back of a piscina. The peal of bells is one of the best in Sheffield.

Our own generation has known two famous men of Sheffield who have made noble contributions to our fame in the world. One is Sir Henry Coward, the world's greatest chorus master; the other is Charles Jagger, the young genius who in his very short life enriched our sculpture with noble monuments.

Sherburn-in-Elmet. Famed for its plum orchards, the village spreads along the busy road from Pontefract to Tadcaster, but its splendid church, begun in Norman times, stands in solitary splendour at the top of a hill, its grey stone gleaming among the trees. Grey cottages with red roofs make a patchwork of colour near by, and share in the wide view of hills and plain.

Sherburn was old when the Normans came, having been, it is thought, the chief place in the little kingdom of Elmet which survived for a time after the Romans left. It is believed that a Saxon church crowned the hill, and that King Athelstan gave the manor to York as a thankoffering for his success in driving out the Danes. In a field north of the church are the mounds where

Athelstan had a manor house, and here and in the church itself Thomas, Earl of Lancaster, met with his supporters to plan a rebellion against Edward II. A round-headed cross, probably Saxon of the 11th century, stands on a 17th century base in the churchyard.

The Normans built well when they set up their church in the first twenty years of the 12th century, giving it a fine nave with wide aisles, each having an apse. The apses disappeared when they were extended to form chapels, the north chapel now opening to the chancel with a 15th century arch, and the south chapel with an arch of the 13th century.

The low Norman aisle still remains on the north, but its walls were raised and given new windows in the 15th century; there are traces of a Norman window, and the original doorway is blocked in the wall. The south aisle was widened and given its windows 500 years ago, but it has a little original masonry at the east end, and keeps the only piscina left in the church. The Norman chancel was enlarged in the 13th century and refashioned in the 15th, but 19th century restoration has made it almost new on two sides. The chancel arch is much restored. The porch is 19th century, but in its fine entrance arch are carved stones which may have belonged to the Norman doorway, which it shelters. A doorway in the east wall of the porch leads to a chapel thought to have been built three centuries ago, and lighted by a queer window in the south aisle.

The lower part of the sturdy tower comes from the end of Norman days, and the rest from the 15th century, when two great buttresses were added for strength at the west end. The original buttresses remain where the tower meets the nave, and in one corner is an astonishing gargoyle, a grotesque crouching ready for a spring. Standing half in and half out of the nave, the tower has a simple vaulted roof and opens to the aisles and the nave with its three original arches, round and striking. Above the eastern arch, which is tall and narrow and tilting, is a fine Norman window.

The glory of the church is the nave with its Norman arcades standing magnificently, their tall pillars massive and leaning, their arches moulded. Light streams through the clerestory above them, built in the 15th century and probably refashioned 300 years ago. Under the eastern arch of the tower is the gravestone of a 14th century priest, showing a cross, a chalice, and a book; and with the old glass in the curious west window are nine shields.

Preserved as a rare treasure are the two sides of the head of a Janus cross of the 15th century, now on the walls of the south aisle. Both these stones are enriched with quatrefoils under a leafy gable, and with tracery between carved figures of Our Lord on the Cross, St Mary, and St John. This exquisite fragment was whole when it was found among the ruins of a detached chapel which stood in the churchyard, and was sawn vertically in two apparently because a vicar and a churchwarden both claimed what belonged to neither. Near the church is a 17th century grammar school, now used for young children.

Shipley. It is linked with Bradford and Saltaire. What was once a village in a green valley of the Pennines has become a centre of the worsted trade, with factories and iron foundries. Below the Town Hall are still a few of the old houses, one with fine gables, stone roofs, and 1593 over the doorway. The modern church (in 15th century style) looks from its high place over the River Aire to the moors. Below is Shipley Glen, a paradise of trees and flowers sheltered by huge rocks, the Japanese gardens a rare sight in summer. There are playing-fields in Northcliff Woods, another of Shipley's green spaces.

The church walls are embattled, and the nave roof is so high that the beauty of the bosses is lost. The pulpit is unusual and striking, its oak richly traceried, its stone base and stairway growing out of the low stone chancel screen; the base is seven feet high, and in its canopied niches stand the Four Evangelists. The town is proud of its completely reconstructed town centre, with a prominent clock tower in the centre.

Silkstone. There is beauty in this mining village west of Barnsley, where the houses and the church stand above a glen with oaks and silver birches, watered by a stream on its way to the River Dearne. It is a beautiful church without and within. In the churchyard we read that this Minster of the Moors was founded before 1060, but most of what we see is 15th century, the time of the fine tower. The nave arcades are a little older, and the chancel has a round Norman arch in its north wall. The sides of its mediaeval entrance arch are also Norman, but the east end beyond the chapels is modern. The striking feature outside is the array of short buttresses ending in long pinnacles which are joined to the wall by flying buttresses and great gargoyles of weird animals. The nave, aisles, and south chapel have splendid old oak roofs with floral bosses on moulded beams. The old box-pews are charming, and across the chancel arch and the chapels are lovely mediaeval screens, adorned with elaborate tracery and delicate canopies. There is another old screen between the chancel and the south chapel.

Many of the Wentworths of Bretton Hall sleep in this chapel, where there is some old glass. The most imposing monument is of Sir Thomas, a Cavalier who died in 1675. He lies in armour, a helmet over his long hair, and with him is his wife holding a book: eagles are at their feet.

There is an inscription to Joseph Bramah, inventor of the hydraulic press, a famous lock, and many other devices. He was born at Stainborough and died in 1814 at Pimlico, where he sleeps in an unknown grave.

A sad thing in the churchyard is a stone monument with the names of 26 children drowned in the dark one summer's day in 1838. A thunderstorm broke over the valley, and a sudden rain flooded one of the pits where they were toiling. Of the 26 victims caught like rats in a trap, seven boys were under ten, and among the girls was a mite of eight. Those were England's bad old days.

Silsden. The canal passes through it, and a bridge over the River Aire takes the road to Steeton. It is a workaday place with worsted mills and nail factories, looking up to the Pennines, and was the birthplace of Augustus Spencer, Principal of the Royal College of Art for the first 20 years of this century. His memorial in the 18th and 19th century church is a striking window with a brilliant medley of colour, showing the Good Shepherd and the Good Samaritan. A window of the Adoration of the Shepherds is in quieter colours. The slender tower with a tiny spire has a flight of steps to its door.

Skelbrooke. In this out-of-the-way spot, where only the distant hum of traffic on the Great North Road is heard, the church and a cluster of cottages look down on the 18th century hall amid the fine trees of its 100-acre park. Of the old church (made almost new last century) there remains little more than the 12th century tower with new belfry and west windows, the rood stairs, and a few fragments. An angel holds a shield of arms on the porch, an exquisite niche in the nave has a canopy like a pinnacle, two of the bells are said to be mediaeval, and in a tiny window of the rood stairs are two heads in old glass.

Skelton. It is near Boroughbridge, and its cottages and farms are on the lane running by the lovely Newby Park which is bounded on the other side by the River Ure. The property belonged to the St Nubie family in the 13th century, but the main block was built in 1705, in the style of Wren, for Sir Edward Blackett. It was extended in the mid 18th century by William Weddell who engaged Adam to redesign the house to form a suitable setting for his antique sculpture, tapestries, and pictures. The house, which is frequently open to the public, has extensive grounds and contains the famous Gobelins Tapestries, sculpture, paintings and work by Adam, Chippendale, Zucchi and Angelica Kauffman.

A path between trimmed yews 20 feet high, made into a green tunnel by fine overhanging trees, ends in the park, where the wonderful church stands in a garden of clipped hollies and tiny yew bushes. It is a charming setting for this striking building, perhaps the most ornate village shrine in Yorkshire, lavish in adornment outside and almost bewilderingly so within.

Built by Lady Mary Vyner as a memorial to her son, killed by brigands in Greece last century, it has a tower with pinnacles like pyramids and a tall spire with gabled lights; a vaulted porch with rich doorways and sculptures of the Good Shepherd and figures representing Purity and Sin; pinnacled buttresses and windows finely carved. The nave arcades have flowers in the mouldings, and the banded shafts in front of their pillars rise to the corbels supporting the roof. The walls of the clerestory and of the aisles are richly arcaded. The chancel and glass are alike, magnificent.

Skipton. The stone-built capital of Craven, busy with spinning mills and the making of cotton and woollen goods, the bustle and stir of its modern life goes on in the shadow of a majestic castle and an ancient church, both rich in memories of names on the page of history. Here comes the Eller Beck on its way to the Aire; here is the canal from whose banks we have a charming view of the town. Its old courtyards and houses are delightful. There is the old-time Sheep Street, and in front of the church of Holy Trinity, looking down the spacious High Street, is Skipton's imposing memorial to those who fell in the Great War, a winged figure of Victory in bronze. Another bronze statue in the High Street is of Sir Matthew Wilson, MP for Skipton last century; he stands in front of the library, which is also the museum. In it are swords, pottery, and a sickle of the Iron Age; flints and spear-heads; Roman lamps, coins, plates, dishes, and a fine glass vase; a good collection of minerals, cinerary urns of the 9th century, a curious whistle made from the tooth of an Arctic bear and a folk-life room. William Ermysted's Tudor grammar school, founded in 1548, still exists.

The memory of the Cliffords clings to the church which shelters their tombs, and to the castle which was their home for more than 300 years till the death of Lady Anne Clifford, Countess of Pembroke. The proudest member of a family whose name was long a household word, Lady Anne was a great builder, and left her mark on both church and castle, part of which is still a stately home. The first of the Cliffords of Skipton was Robert, who entertained Edward I, and is said to have chosen to live here so that he might never miss an opportunity of fighting the Scots. He fought them all his life, and died fighting them at Bannockburn.

Imposing with four round and embattled towers, the castle gateway is mostly of his time, but its upper part is Lady Anne's restoration after the Civil War, during which Skipton Castle held out three years for the king, though food was scarce and men were dying. On the gateway is a quotation from Horace in honour of her father George Clifford, third Earl of Cumberland, and one of our great Elizabethans. In the open parapet is the Clifford motto in stone letters: *Desormais*. In a room of one of the gateway towers are thousands of shells lining the walls; it is like a mother-of-pearl grotto, and it is said that the shells were brought home by the famous Sailor Earl.

Through the gateway we come to the beautiful lawns, an impressive picture with the round towers creepered here and there and joined by a long Tudor range ending in a charming octagon. The oldest part of the castle has walls from nine to twelve feet thick, and is for the most part the 14th century work of Robert Clifford as we see it outside, though here too there is evidence of Lady Anne's restoration. She added the entrance with its flight of steps under an oriel, bringing us to a fragment of the Norman castle, a round doorway opening to the delightful courtyard, where a stately old yew shades a cobbled square set in the flags. In the shade of the yew is the old font from the chapel of St John still standing in the grounds.

As we come through the Norman doorway we seem to leave the austerity of the mediaeval castle for the grace and tranquillity of a Tudor house, for the walls facing the court were refashioned by Henry Clifford on the accession of Henry VII. He was the son of Butcher Clifford, who fell at Ferrybridge on the eve of the Battle of Towton, and Wordsworth has sung his story as the Shepherd Lord, who spent many years in hiding among the fells, and even when he came into his own preferred to live at Barden Tower and to have the friendship of the canons of Bolton Abbey near by. The most peaceful of the fighting Cliffords, he answered the call when it came, and led the men of Craven to victory on Flodden Field.

We think of him gratefully as we stand in the small courtyard so cut off from all the world, for his rebuilding of the castle made it one of Yorkshire's rarest spots. The enclosing walls are delightful with many bow windows and eight doorways. A flight of steps climbs to the great hall and the kitchen, where the fireplace is big enough to roast an ox. There is a long room once hung with gorgeous tapestry, and one bedroom has a guard chamber outside it. We can climb one of the towers (partly demolished in the Civil War) for a grand view of the country round, with the hill to the north-west from which the Parliament men fired; and we can go down to the dungeon, its floor below the level of the wet moat still seen on one side of the castle, so that escape by tunnelling was impossible. It is a tiny chamber devoid of light, the only air coming through a grille in the door. The inhabited part is the lovely Tudor range with its octagon, the Great Gallery built by the Shepherd Lord's son Henry, first Earl of Cumberland, for the coming of his son's bride. She was Eleanor Brandon, who, together with other ladies of the earl's family and their children, is said to have been staying at Bolton Abbey when Skipton Castle was besieged in the Pilgrimage of Grace. Word was sent to the earl that they would be held as hostages for his submission, and in the dead of night Lord Clifford and one or two others crept out of the castle, made their way through the camp unseen by the insurgents, rode over the moors to Bolton, and returned to the castle in safety with the women.

In a glorious setting by the castle, the church has walls patched with greenery and bordered with flowerbeds and roses. Long and lofty, it has a fine west tower, and a nave and chancel divided from their aisles by arcades running east to west. The three western bays may be 14th century, but the rest of the church, including the continuous clerestory, is chiefly 15th, restored by Lady Anne after its devastation in the Civil War. The beautiful 14th century sedilia in the south aisle may have been in the original chancel. The panelled roof has rich old bosses, and the lovely chancel screen, over 400 years old, is enriched with tracery, and has angels on its carved posts. Some of the windows have Anne's initials and the date 1655, and some shine with the lovely colours of Capronnier's glass; in the west window are figures of Our Lord and saints, among them Joan of Arc. The 12th century font has a fine Jacobean cover like a rich tower and spire; there are spears used about four centuries ago, two quaintly carved chairs, and a memorial with the names of 360 men who gave their lives in the Great War.

Many of the Cliffords sleep in the vault below the sanctuary, and their monuments are a notable feature of the church. On a great tomb enriched with tracery and shields is the modern brass of Henry Clifford and his wife; son of the Shepherd Lord, and builder of the castle's Tudor range, he died in 1542. His lady, Margaret Percy, lies at his right hand wearing kennel headdress, a dog at her feet.

At one end of his father's tomb is a marble block with the brasses of Henry Clifford the second earl, his wife and children, figures of the Four Evangelists, and a representation of the Trinity. The knights are in tabards and the ladies have heraldic mantles, and all these brasses are renewed except that of one of the sons and the rare engraving of the Trinity, which shows God the Father wearing three crowns and Our Lord with the dove on His shoulder.

Lady Anne's brother Francis, the little Lord Clifford who died in 1589 when he was five, has a small tomb with new brass shields, and an inscription believed to have been renewed by Lady Anne after the Civil War. The huge tomb of their father, the Sailor Earl, is famous for an astonishing display of carved and painted heraldry.

There are many other reminders of the past in the town: a Friends' Meeting House of 1693; a building, in Kendall's yard, which was Skipton's theatre where Edmund Kean played; in Sheep Street the old toll-booth and stocks; and plaques where Wesley preached and where the Pillory stood.

Slaidburn. It is a lovely ride to Slaidburn if we come over the moors, seeing wonderful views of the great fells; and charming is the village itself, the amber-tinted stone mingling with the green trees and the Croasdale Brook chattering under the bridge on its way to join the River Hodder.

The picturesque grammar school was founded in 1717. The 15th century church is a spacious place more attractive within than without. The tower has immense buttresses and two niches, and the south doorway is barred with a huge beam. The long arcades continuing into the chancel are richly hued with amber, and at one of the south pillars is the striking three-decker pulpit with a tall canopy. There is a grand old roof, but the great possession is the splendid Jacobean chancel screen, which has carved pillars, a pierced border under the cornice, and the squire's box-pews on its eastern side. The simple screens north and south of the chancel are 15th century. Other 17th century woodwork are two carved chairs, a fine chest, the cover of the Norman font, the plain screen between the south aisle and chapel, and some benches. The "Hark to Bounty" Inn has an old panelled Court Room.

Slaithwaite. Nature made it a quiet and secluded little place, but the industrial 19th century put it on the map and the scientific 20th century has added to its importance. On the high hills, rising far above the mills, are the huge masts of the Moorside Edge Broadcasting Station. The village is in a deep valley where the hum of industry is for ever heard. Here the railway, river, and canal are side by side, and there are two viaducts. There has been a church here since 1590, but the present one dates from 1790. Britannia Mills, near the bridge over the Colne, was once the manorial mill of the Kaye family and contains some old machinery.

Snaith. A tiny old-fashioned market town with narrow winding streets, it stands by the River Aire. A lane runs by the foundations of an old hall, and not far from the church is Nicholas Waller's grammar school, a little grey building supposed to have been built in 1628, and restored last century. There are fine chestnuts and beeches near the marshes.

The clerestoried church is a great possession, a splendid place 170 feet long, with battlements and pinnacles adorning walls of light grey stone, and a squat massive tower rising at the west end between the aisles. Except for its pinnacled crown, the tower is from the end of the 12th century, and it is about 30 feet square. Some of the transept walls and parts of the arches are Norman; the chancel arch, the two chapels, the aisles of the nave and the greater part of the arcades are 14th century. The clerestory is over 400 years old, the west door has 15th century woodwork, and an old chest is hewn from one block of wood. In the 19th century the porch was altered, and the striking east window was erected. Its lovely glass is arresting, showing St Laurence with the flaming grid-iron. In the Guild Chapel of the Holy Trinity is a fragment of a statue, thought to be of St Ethelreda, referred to in an Indulgence of the Bishop of Ely in 1491.

In the floor of the chancel is a stone on which one of the biggest brass portraits in England once lay; it was a mitred figure with a staff, perhaps an abbot of Selby, to which this church was given in early Norman days. In the Dawnay chapel is the tomb of Sir John Dawnay of 1493, adorned with painted shields. Here hang a helmet and shield, a sword and gauntlet, relics of a 17th century Dawnay, and here is Chantrey's marble statue of Viscount Downe, wearing a mantle with a fur collar. Among old glass fragments is the Dawnay shield with three rings, a link with Sir William Dawnay to whom Richard Lionheart is said to have given a ring. In the north chapel is the bust of Lady Elizabeth Stapleton of 1683. The church now has a carpet and stool used at the Coronation of Queen Elizabeth II.

South Kirkby. A gabled house which has lost much of its glory reminds us of the old days of what is now a mining village. Facing it is the old church, the churchyard wall and that by the house

261

curiously weathered. The 15th century porch has a vaulted roof, and heads of mediaeval people by doorway and windows. A bear with a staff and a man in short-skirted dress are among the many worn gargoyles, and at the end of the south aisle are striking buttresses ending in pinnacles which are attached to the wall by great grotesques. The windows and the top of the tower are 15th century, the tower arch reaching the roof. The interior is spacious with a chancel almost as long as the nave, whose arcades, coming from the beginning of the 13th century, are extraordinarily high and wide. The low arcade to the north chapel of the chancel is also 13th century, and the high bays to the other chapel are 15th century. There are fine old moulded beams in the roofs, some having on the ends angels and minstrels, and bosses with an eagle and a griffin in the low roof of the north chapel.

In an old niche we found a lump of coal and a safety lamp, tokens of those who dig treasure in darkness and danger.

South Milford. It is an ordinary place, but the Mill Dike flows under a low bridge among woods and meadows and by old houses.

The church is modern, but Steeton Hall is old, though it has a new wing and is a farmhouse now. A road shaded by elms and chestnuts brings us to its noble gateway, now scheduled as an Ancient Monument, with a fine corbel table of heads and shields, looking old enough to have come from the close of the 12th century, with high battlements and a small doorway (at the top of the steps leading to the upper room) of a later time. Carved in stone is a man weeping, and a bird pecking out a man's eye.

The hall has gables and mullioned windows, a room with a stone roof, and a chapel with a piscina. It was from this house and under this gateway that Sir William Fairfax rode off to Nun Appleton Priory to carry off one of the nuns and make her his bride. She was Isabel Thwaites, a rich heiress, and they were married at Bolton Percy. Their great-grandson was Ferdinando, and his son was the famous Thomas Fairfax of Cromwellian days. It is one of the little ironies of history that when the nunnery was closed by Henry VIII it was to Isabel's son that the abbess had to give up the keys.

Southowram. It is worth the long climb out of Halifax for the wonderful view of hills and vales, mills and towns. Hereabouts are old quarries and old houses. The church is 19th century, and what is left of an older one is now a stable. At the nearby "twin" village of Northowram is a church named after Oliver Heywood who preached a good deal in these parts.

Sowerby. It has magnificent views from its high place between the valleys of the Calder and the Ryburn, and the low road bringing us from Ripponden is charming. Bentley Royd, and Wood Lane Hall with a beautiful plaster ceiling, are two of the many old houses.

The parish church is 18th century, in classical style, its walls pilastered outside and its galleries breaking into great columns supporting the roof. The chancel has a colonnaded east window, big panels with coloured relief figures of Our Lord and Moses, and rich plasterwork in medallions and a coat-of-arms. A marble statue of John Tillotson keeps in mind a Yorkshire boy who rose to be Archbishop of Canterbury in the 17th century. Born at Haugh End near by, he was a great student, a powerful preacher, and a liberal-minded man with a spirit of tolerance in an age of intolerance. He married one of Cromwell's nieces, gave generously to the poor, and died penniless but beloved.

This church of St Peter tells the time in the ancient and modern way, for the face of the clock on the tower serves also as a sundial, with a gnomon fixed on to it.

Sowerby Bridge. This busy little town in the narrow valley of the Calder has a church of last century. Its walls are blackened by the smoke from mills and manufacturing works, and its galleries give it the look of a chapel, but it has rich carving of stone in the pulpit, and of oak in the traceried screen, and its roof (built after a fire in 1894) is striking for its great span.

There was born hereabouts in 1770 a farmer's son who became a preacher and essayist, John Foster. There are a number of 17th century houses near by.

Spofforth. Stockeld Park with its fine great house is a mile from this village by the little River Crimple, attractive with its houses and church both old and new, and its impressive remains of an old home of the Percys. Said to have been an earlier castle refashioned in the 14th century, the old fortified manor house built into the solid rock from which the stone was hewn was dismantled after the defeat of the Lancastrians and the death of Sir Henry Percy at Towton; and, though probably restored in Queen Elizabeth I's day, it has long been a roofless ruin.

The oldest part of the remains, coming from the close of the 12th century, is the basement, with broken pillars which supported the roof of the Great Hall, and two brackets projecting from the rocky wall. We look down on the basement from a doorway on the ground level, and come to it down a flight of rocky steps. The hall itself is chiefly 14th century, with original windows and a beautiful moulded doorway with carved capitals. West of the hall is a small compartment with a south window of lovely tracery. At the south-west corner is a turret with an old door at the foot of its spiral stair.

A handsome 15th century tower crowns the church, which rebuilding has made an exceedingly spacious and lofty place. Of the original 12th century church there remain the clustered pillars of the north arcade, and the round pillars on the south, their capitals carved with scallop and simple leaves; their only original arches are two on the north, carved with zigzag. Mounting in steps to the altar, the chancel has a pointed arch on clustered shafts, built when the Norman style was passing. A little earlier is the south doorway, with beak-heads in its fine arch. In a niche is the battered stone figure of Sir Robert Plumpton who fought in Wales and Scotland 600 years ago. There are four Jacobean carved chairs, two bells that were ringing in Shakespeare's day, and one said to come from Fountains Abbey. A fragment of a Saxon cross is on a windowsill, and by some walling of the old church outside are three stone coffins. One of the rectors was Richard Kay who preached for 53 years out of the 18th century into the 19th, and saw one of Yorkshire's most astonishing men buried here in 1810. He was John Metcalfe, known as Blind Jack, whose grave in the churchyard has the pathetic lines:

> *Here lies John Metcalfe, one whose infant sight*
> *Felt the dark pressure of an endless night.*

Blind Jack was born at Knaresborough in 1717 and became blind at six through an attack of smallpox. He grew up to be a roadmaker and bridge-builder, and his fame spread so that he had 400 men under him at one time and in all he laid down about 180 miles of roads.

Sprotborough. It is said that Sir Walter Scott lived here for some time, to gather local colour for his novel *Ivanhoe*. Three miles from Doncaster, it has a pretty setting on a hillside above the River Don. It is charming by the river, flowing between wooded banks, with two bridges and a fine weir. By the village are remains of a mediaeval cross which once bore an inscription inviting travellers to ask hospitality. It has one of several crosses which are sometimes said to have marked the sanctuary bounds of the church. In the church is a curious stone chair, carved probably in the 14th century, with a man standing at one side, and the head and shoulders of another with a forked beard.

The oldest fragments of the church are half a pillar behind the pulpit, coming from Norman days, and a relic of the 11th century in the shape of a carved stone in a chancel buttress. The 13th century north arcade was partly altered in the 15th when the west bay was added. The lower part of the tower, and the chancel with its arch, sedilia, and piscina, belong to the end of the 13th century; the rest of the tower, the font, the south arcade, and the clerestory are 15th. The nave has its 15th century roof. The mediaeval chancel screen has seven stalls with three misericords, their carving showing Adam and Eve driven from Eden, and Satan and his angels from heaven. On an arm-rest is a striking head of Paulinus, who played so great a part in bringing Christianity to Yorkshire. Carved on a panel of the Tudor pulpit are a pack of cards, a jug, and the dice-box, representing the world, the flesh, and the devil. The pews are as old, the carvings on the ends of two illustrating marriage "before and after", with two heads kissing and two turned away from each other as if in a huff. Others have shears and a ram's head (for the woollen industry), a snake with its tail in its mouth (for eternity), and a head with many faces (perhaps for hypocrisy). There are two Jacobean chairs, fragments of old glass, pieces of armour said to have been worn in the Wars of the Roses, and two flags carried before Charles I. A very long chest with three locks is over 400 years old.

Engraved in alabaster on the top of a tomb in the chancel are damaged portraits of Sir Philip Copley of 1577 and his wife, he in armour, she in mantle and kirtle and veil-headdress; some of their children kneel below them. Sir Godfrey Copley, who has been sleeping here since 1709, left money for the Royal Society's annual Copley medal to encourage research. He was a friend of Sir Hans Sloane and made a valuable collection of prints and scientific apparatus.

A floorstone showing a priest and a chalice may be to Thomas Fitzwilliam, a 15th century rector. William Fitzwilliam of 1474 and his wife are here in brass, he in armour with an unusual helmet, she with a mantle over her high-waisted dress. One of two fine figures in the chapel is a knight in chain armour and surcoat, perhaps Sir William Fitzwilliam, who was hanged in 1322 for joining in a rebellion. The other (a lady wearing the pleated wimple of a widow, holding a heart and having two praying figures at her feet) may be his mother. A tomb near the pulpit has an inscription to Sir William and Elizabeth Levytt of 1576, married for 59 years.

Stainborough. The mines are round about, but there are wooded dells and fair prospects below Wentworth Castle. The old house was the home of the Everinghams and Cutlers; the house we see is a lordly place built by Thomas Wentworth and his son in the 18th century. Described by Horace Walpole as one of the noblest homes in England, it is imposing with its open parapet, a great show of windows, and shields. There are rooms with elaborate ceilings and panels, a magnificent gallery 180 feet long and 30 high, many statues and pictures, and beautiful gardens. The park has a lake, a temple, and a mock castle with great towers rising above the fine house; the small modern church is close by.

A mile or two from the sham castle are fragments of Rockley Abbey, now chiefly a farm and an ivied tower rising by a stream.

It was at Stainborough that there was born in 1748 that remarkable man Joseph Bramah, one of the five children of a small farmer. He was the inventor of the hydraulic press and many other appliances.

Stainburn. Its cluster of farms and cottages look down into Wharfedale from a slope of the moor, the fine little church standing aloof, like a sentinel. Much of it is Norman, a simple aisleless place with a restored old bellcot rising between the nave and chancel. The stout walls are a rough motley of tinted stones outside, pierced by Norman windows and some of Tudor days. A mediaeval porch with old roof beams shelters a plain Norman doorway, the chancel has a Norman arch of golden-tinted stone, and the Norman font has four tiny faces in the spandrels of interlaced arcading. Its crude cover may be 17th century, the time of a carved chair. There are stout old oak benches and roof beams, and part of a coffin lid.

Stainforth. It is by the River Ribble, its haphazard array of houses looking up to the encircling hills. Through the heart of the grey village, where the embattled walls of the small modern church rise from a wreath of green and flowers, the Cowside Beck comes over the rocks and under the little humped bridge. It has come from Catrigg Force, a lovely waterfall closed in by rugged cliffs, and joins the Ribble below Stainforth Force where the river roars down limestone steps. Above this charming cataract are stepping-stones and a beautiful old one-arched packhorse bridge which we cross to Little Stainton.

Stainland. High up in the world, looking out to the great green hills, this big grey village gathers round a long narrow street, the mills almost at its doors. An old cross on three steps, with three St Andrew's crosses in its head, faces the church which began life as a chapel in the 18th century, and keeps its original tower with a cupola. The rest was much rebuilt half a century ago, the panelled ceiling of the modern chancel resting on tall columns.

Far below is Bradley Hall, where was born one of the most learned Englishmen of his day, Sir Henry Savile, who knew these lonely hills as a boy, taught Queen Elizabeth I Greek, translated part of the New Testament for the Authorised Version, and founded two professorships at Oxford. He died at Eton in 1622 and was buried by torchlight. His house, much altered since his day, is of stone from quarries near by, though part of it is timber.

Stainton. The Romans had a camp near by, and the Normans built a church which was made partly new in the 14th century, the time of the piscina and some windows. The Norman chancel arch remains, the font is 15th century, and there are fragments of old glass.

Stanley. It is half a dozen hamlets, with a church in a ring of trees crowning the hilltop at Lake Lock. Built last century and made new in our own after a fire, it is unusual with two octagonal lantern towers, many-gabled aisles with big windows, and soaring arcades. Some of the arches have gaping cracks and are supported by timber frames.

At Stanley Ferry, over the Calder, a Bronze Age canoe now in York Museum was dug from the river.

Two of the oldest houses are Stanley Hall (seen from the road), and Hatfield House where William Pilkington, a noted 18th century architect, was born. He built the Council House at Salisbury and the Naval Hospital at Yarmouth. At Stanley Ferry a bridge carries the canal over the River Calder.

Starbotton. It has a tragic memory of a day in 1686 when a cloudburst sent the River Wharfe roaring down the valley, drowning people and carrying away their homes; but all the grandeur of hills and fells is still about this peaceful spot, with cottages about a twisting bit of the road which runs between steep slopes. It has a Quaker burial-ground and a hall where Lady Anne Clifford stayed.

Staveley. It has an old well, a mill by a stream, and an ancient treasure in a church rebuilt last century. The tower has a spire of dark stone. The east window has Capronnier's brilliant glass showing the Crucifixion, with John and the two Marys. Two big old chairs have a mass of carving. There is a crude pillar stoup under the tower, but the church's treasure is the shaft and part of the head

267

of a Saxon cross, probably of the 11th century, carved with interlacing bands and scrolls.

Steeton. In a bower of fine trees by a stream flowing to the River Aire stands the graceful War Memorial cross, and just behind are hiding the 19th century church, two or three cottages, and the gabled High Hall, a delightful group undisturbed by the rush of the highway. One of Yorkshire's charming old houses, the hall was the home of one of the old family of Keighley when we called. There were Keighleys in the neighbourhood in Edward I's day, and Sir Richard comes into Shakespeare. Some of the splendid beeches shading this surprisingly secluded spot are in the hall garden, and its glorious yew was flourishing when the men of Steeton drew their bows at Flodden Field.

Hereabouts is Hawkcliffe Wood, one of the beauty spots of the Craven district, and on Hawkcliffe Crag, far above the valley, is a Jubilee Tower 60 feet high.

Studley Royal. It is famous for its magnificent park, and an amazing church. The house was built in the 18th century and altered in the 19th; it was destroyed by fire in 1945.

We all may come to the park with its herds of deer, its glorious avenues of limes and beeches, and the pleasure grounds in the valley, where the River Skell, flowing through some of the most beautiful gardens in Yorkshire, falls into lakes by which are statues and temples of rare beauty. There are rustic bridges, paths between walls of living green, tunnels of yew, magnificent hedges of laurel and yew, and splendid lawns in these grounds, which have been growing more and more charming since they were made by an 18th century gardener.

Said to have cost £50,000, the church was built last century in early 14th century style, and is lavishly adorned. The tower has a spire rising to 152 feet; the splendid west doorway has 21 birds in the quatrefoils of its arch, and there are birds in the ironwork of the great door. The handsome porch, with sculptures of the Madonna, an angel, and a dove, shelters a door with lovely ironwork; and over the east window are rich panels. All the windows have brilliant and arresting glass illustrating Bible story and Milton's Paradise. Between the nave and aisles are fine arcades with white pillars and shafts of dark marble, faces peeping from the foliage of the capitals. The massive marble font has figures representing infancy, youth, manhood, and old age; and a striking brass door has the Madonna with the Child on her knee.

There is an astonishing display of colour and ornament in the chancel, with walls of Egyptian alabaster and golden mosaic, a mosaic floor, steps of coloured marble, and a richly painted roof illustrating the *Te Deum*, the angels being in the arcaded dome of the sanctuary. Shafts of coloured marble support the arches and the traceried frames of the windows; on the tracery in the sanctuary are trumpeting angels, and one of the shafts rests on a crouching lion. Charming little birds are in the golden foliage of the cornice, and in the paving of the floor we see some of the chief buildings in Jerusalem.

A tall screen of marble and alabaster encloses the lovely chapel where sleep the first Marquis of Ripon (who died in 1909) and his wife. Their marble figures are on a magnificent tomb, the marquis wearing a rich cloak and buckled shoes, and the marchioness an ermine mantle over her lovely gown, with an exquisite lace collar. There is a plaque of the second marquis and his wife.

Swillington. Old enough to have had a church in Domesday Book (though little is known of it), Swillington is a mile from the River Aire, which is crossed by an old bridge.

The tower of the church looks as if it might have come out of one of the coal mines here, so black is its dress against the golden-tinted stone of the rest. The contrast is startling, and is all the more curious because the attractive walls of the nave, aisles, and chancel are as they were built of local stone nearly six centuries ago. It was in 1884 that the top storey of the 15th century tower was rebuilt, and the rest of it refaced. The capitals of its old arch are carved with four-leaved flowers. The walls inside are of rough grey stone, pierced with windows which are mainly 14th century, with some tracery renewed. The clerestory, and the porch with its old gable cross, are Tudor. Near the porch is an old scratch dial. The lofty arcades have moulded capitals, the nave roof has old timbers, and the old font bowl has a cover which may be Jacobean. The piscina has a projecting bowl, and the cinquefoiled arches of the sedilia are 500 years old. Under the feathered arch of a mediaeval recess in the south wall, with worn carving of flowers, is a glass case with the remains of an oak figure, the hands at prayer, its identity unknown. Two relics of the 13th century are the head of an engraved cross which has been given a new shaft, and a coped tomb cover lying outside the church, carved with a sword and a shield.

Swinefleet. There are many old brick houses with pantiled roofs, in this old waterside village, where the Ouse is broad and deep as it flows to the Humber, carrying ships to the sea. There are dykes with high banks, and from Swinefleet we look across the fields and woods in a big loop of the river to the tall spire of Goole's church and the cranes of its docks. Swinefleet's church is modern.

Swinton. Its church was built in 1887 in 13th century style, with a fine vista of arches in its arcades. In the shadow of the new are remains of a Norman church with the old chancel arch and the old doorway. Less than a mile from the church are the ruins of a kiln which is all that remains of the pottery which produced the famous Rockingham china.

Tadcaster. A busy little market town today, with a sprinkling of old houses and a big array of brewery chimneys, Tadcaster was important as the Calcaria of the Romans, an outpost to their military station nine miles away at York. There are still traces of the camp where coins and pottery and horseshoes were found, and Roman roads are about the town. The many-arched bridge over the Wharfe is said to have in it stone from an ancient castle which stood on the tree-decked mound above the river, and the neighbouring limestone quarries have provided stone for the repair of York Minster and the city walls. It was a leading coaching town, and brewing dates back here at least as far as the 18th century.

Among the trees above the river is the fine church which was moved here last century out of the reach of floods. Built of local white stone, it is chiefly 15th century, with some fragments of Norman days and nave arcades of the 14th century. The handsome tower is embattled, the nave and chancel are clerestoried, and the walls are enriched with a fine show of buttresses, pinnacles, and gargoyles. The east window of the south aisle is under a Norman arch carved with zigzag, and the wall here is dotted with fragments of Norman stones. Under the window is a coffin lid, another lid is in the other aisle, and a child's stone coffin is under the tower. In old glass we see St Catherine, a bishop, and a fine fragment of the figure of a woman. A piscina is cut into a pillar in the nave.

A fascinating place is the little Ark museum near the church. Built in the 15th century, it was in the 17th century known as "Morley Hall" and was licensed as a Dissenters' preaching place. It now contains many objects of local interest and a small library.

Tankersley. A green oasis among the coal-pits, it has in its park a tower where we see miles of woods and streams and the spot where a battle was fought in the Civil War. Cannon balls and a bullet found in a tree are now in the church, into which we come by a fine iron gate designed by Sir Edwin Lutyens.

In the park is a fragment of the old hall of the Saviles, which became for a time the home of Sir Richard Fanshawe, the Royalist poet imprisoned in the Tower but afterwards allowed to live here on condition that he never went more than five miles away. He lived through the most exciting years of the 17th century, strongly supporting the king in the Civil War, becoming Treasurer of the Navy, and attending Charles II in his exile on the Continent. At the Restoration he was Ambassador to Spain, and died in Madrid.

The nave and chancel of the church are mainly 14th century, the aisle was rebuilt in the 19th, and the tower is over 400 years old. The font, and a coffin stone carved with a cross, chalice, and book, are mediaeval, two bench-ends are 15th century, and many fragments of Norman coffin lids are built into the porch. Five of the Miracles are pictured in Christopher Webb's beautiful glass.

A quaint custom still kept up here is known as Embracing the Church. Once a year the young folk join hands and make a ring round it, buglers on the roof playing a tune, the people singing.

Temple Hirst. In this small place of the byways is a farm, near one of many loops of the River Aire, interesting for its remains of a religious house of the Knights Templars. The small mediaeval tower (with new brick battlements) still stands, and the porch has a Norman doorway with shafts and capitals. It frames the old studded door, and the old court is now the fold yard.

Thorne. Dutchmen made it what it is. Hereabouts were thousands of acres of marshes till Cornelius Vermuyden began to drain Hatfield Chase in Charles I's day, beginning a great task which others finished. What is known as Dutch River is still here, and everywhere there are canals and dykes. Near by is the River Don, and any day we come here we may see barges with brown sails moving slowly amid the green fields or passing the old houses of this busy little market town. There are willows by the canal, and in a garden near by is a War Memorial on an island shaded by trees. There is a grammar school founded in 1705, and what is said to be one of the four deepest coal mines in England, the shaft 3000 feet.

The old clerestoried church dominating the town has a chancel with traces of Norman windows, nave arcades with pointed arches and round pillars from the 12th century, and an arcade in the chancel perhaps of the same time. The south chapel and the top of the tower are 15th century; the rest of the tower is chiefly 13th with belfry windows of about 1300. The clerestory and the font are mediaeval.

Thorner. Set among the hills, it has a long street of grey houses, some having quaint steps to their doors. The church at a bend of the road was much rebuilt last century, but its splendid 15th century tower still stands, the battlements resting on corbels with worn faces. The arcades of the nave and chancel have embattled capitals, and the richly traceried font has a cover crowned with a dove. Here sleeps a very old man, John Philips, an inscription telling that he was born in 1625, and that when he died in 1742, in his 118th year, he was buried in the chancel. A stone in the churchyard has a cross and an inscription to William Nettleton of 1503.

Thornhill. On the southern fringe of Dewsbury, looking down on the River Calder and having a wide view of the valley from the height under which it lies, Thornhill has great possessions and proud memories.

Its fine church is in a charming setting, facing the rectory in its small park with oaks, elms, beeches, and willows. Below the house are the scant ruins of a 15th century mansion, still with its moat and all embowered in trees. Here lived the Saviles till the house was destroyed by the Roundheads in the Civil War, after a courageous defence by Lady Anne. The Saviles gave England notable men and came here in the 14th century through marriage with the Thornhills, the first of whom, Jordan Thornhill, has his portrait in a 13th century window in Canterbury Cathedral. Sir Henry Savile was loyal to the king in the Pilgrimage of Grace; Sir William fought for Charles I; and Sir George, Marquis of Halifax, opposed the execution of Strafford, defended the Seven Bishops, and presented the crown to William of Orange. Tolerant in an intolerant age, he stood for the liberties of the people, and sleeps in Westminster Abbey.

The rectory, built of stones from the great house, was the home of John Michell who was laid in his church in 1793. An astronomer and man of science, he is remembered for his experiments in electricity and magnetism. One of his friends was Herschel, who grew so interested in Michell's telescope that he took up the study of the stars and won fame as the greatest astronomer of his day. It is now a home for old people.

The nave of the church was made new last century, and the rest of the church (including the fine tower) is chiefly 15th. The beautiful modern porch has a vaulted roof, figures of Our Lord and angels on the gable, and fine doorways without and within, their arches dotted with flowers, the dainty capitals of leaves and berries on clustered pillars. Twelve angels hold up the rich roof of the chancel. There are two old chairs, and the modern font has a cover like a crown. The north chapel, where the Thornhills and the Saviles sleep, has an iron screen with splendid gates.

The church has a great array of monuments, and a display of old glass unsurpassed in the county except at York. It fills half a dozen windows and creeps into others, and is chiefly 15th century. The huge east window has a Jesse Tree in a rich medley of colour, the work of French craftsmen and considerably restored. It has an inscription to Robert Frost who was rector in Henry VII's day. Of the four windows in the Savile Chapel, the east has a Doom scene, red and blue contrasting with much faded colour; we see the battlements of heaven and angels with trumpets, open graves, Michael weighing souls, Peter with his key, and a host of men and women climbing a golden stair. A second window has scenes from the life of the Madonna and figures of three bishops. In the next are two saints with children, battered figures said to be Thomas Savile and his wife, and what looks like St Anne with the Madonna and Child. The fourth window has a background of trailing flowers, with a Crucifixion and Mary and John; it may be older than the rest of the glass. A host of small heads are in a medley in a south chapel window, and in the west window of the tower are four dull panels.

The oldest of the monuments is a stone knight in chain armour, his legs crossed, his face new, his sword by his side. He is perhaps Sir Brian de Thornhill of Edward III's day. On a beautiful alabaster tomb with 18 figures under leafy arches lies Thomas Savile of 1449 in a fine collar, with his wife in a gown from whose folds two dogs are peeping. On a handsome monument with an elaborate canopy lies George Savile of 1622 in armour. Even more magnificent is the monument of his son George, who died in 1614 before his father; we see him with his second wife (a sister of Strafford) and two sons. The rarest monument is an oak tomb with three oak figures, all splendidly preserved. Its knight in armour is Sir John Savile of 1529. His two wives have flowing robes and mantles with clasps, and draped headdress with garlands of flowers.

Thornton. It is now part of Bradford, but it was for long a little village in a setting of great hills. Many changes have come to it in the last hundred years, but it keeps much that is quaint, and has several halls which have stood 300 years and more, among them Leventhorpe Hall with old carved timbers in its barn. From Thornton Heights, a thousand feet up, there are fine views of the moors and of Bradford lying in the hollow.

Facing the new church with its tower and spire is all that is left of the old one—part of a wall with a 15th century window, and the lantern top of the old tower, now set up on the ground after lying in bits in the churchyard. Known as the Old Bell Chapel, its bell is now in the new church, which has a lovely window with three saints, Cuthbert, Columba, and Aidan, and good glass showing King Oswald, Bede, and St Wilfrid. Here are three fonts, one of last century, one dug up in the old churchyard, and one with an inscription of 1687. This last font is Thornton's great possession, for it is thought that the three most astonishing sisters of all time were baptised at it, their father being the parson here.

They were Charlotte, Emily, and Anne Brontë. Number 74 Market Street, the house where they first saw the light between 1816 and 1819, is still here, the street narrow, the small house having a tiny garden projecting on to the pavement, and five steps climbing to the front door over which is 1802. A tablet tells us that here were born the three sisters and their brother Branwell, children who were to bring all the world to Haworth, the village a few miles away where most of their lives were spent.

Thornton-in-Craven. As charming as its setting on the hillside above the Earby Beck, with a fine avenue by the stream, it has lovely views of the valley, almshouses of Waterloo year, a green with the old stocks, and a lowly little church with a cottage for company, reached by a shaded lane. Made new five centuries ago, the church has aisles as long as the nave and chancel, which have no dividing arch and are sheltered by one stone roof. The sturdy tower, fifty years younger than the rest, projects at the west end, a curious feature being two small chambers in its base, entered by massive arches. A third opens to the nave. Bobbin-ended pews carved with tracery give the nave a Jacobean air, and remains of old work are in the screens on each side of the chancel. In the churchyard sleeps a faithful servant for 70 years, Alice Cherich.

It was at Thornton that Honest John Lambert found his bride and married her. Born at Catton, he fought for Parliament at Marston Moor. A soldier of independent spirit and great courage, he parted from Cromwell on the question of kingship, but Cromwell gave him a pension. He remained true to Oliver's memory after the Restoration and died in captivity.

Thornton-in-Lonsdale. If we come from the west Ingleborough makes a noble background for the cluster of dwellings here, with the 17th century inn, and the church spire rising above the quaint jumble of roofs. Here are the old stocks, a stream flowing to the Greta, the old house called Halsteads at the end of a fine brake of trees, and Masongill House a mile away in 26 acres of woodland.

Not far away is Thornton Force, a splendid cascade made by the Kingsdale Beck before it tumbles in the delightful series of cataracts known as Pecca Falls. Three miles farther up Kingsdale is Yordas Cave on the slope of Gragareth, one of Yorkshire's most impressive caverns, where a waterfall is for ever plunging through the darkness. It has a huge hall like a cathedral, and one known as the chapter house, its domed roof resting on slender pillars; we see what is known as the giant's throne, his flitch of bacon, his water bowl, and the great oven. West of the cave are the Three Men of Gragareth, huge stones on a mountain from which we look over limestone hills.

The church keeps its 15th century tower, and is charming inside where walls and arcades are of grey and rose-coloured stones. The north arcade is chiefly in Norman style, with square pillars, and the fine south arcade has pointed arches on clustered pillars. One of several richly carved old gravestones has a cross with a branching stem, and another has a cross, a sword, and a knife.

Thorp Arch. On the hillside above the Wharfe the houses are gathered round a small tree-shaded green; on the hilltop gleams the 15th century tower of the restored church, looking out on a lovely countryside. The river, here broad and deep, flows majestically under the old stone bridge which links the village with Boston Spa. There is an old mill, and the imposing hall is in a park. Leeds has built a home for crippled children among these woods and meadows, which are famous for wild flowers.

Not far away is the Roman road called Rudgate. We meet the Saxons in the church, for among the old stones in the porch is one with their interlacing. Another stone has the draughtboard pattern of the Normans; in a niche is a quaint headless figure with a hand on the breast, and a stone on a bracket is carved with two faces. The doorway into the church has a Norman arch with beak-heads, and a Norman font is in the churchyard, where there are two stone coffins and a fragment of an old cross. A sundial on the tower has a worn inscription.

The chancel has a low iron screen, stalls with fine poppyheads, an

oak altar with a recessed carving of the Last Supper, and an alabaster reredos with carved and coloured scenes of the Annunciation,
the Crucifixion, and Our Lord appearing to Mary in the garden.

Two striking features of this charming interior are the woodwork
of Mr Thompson of Kilburn, and the delightful Children's Corner
given by the parents of little Charles Walker who died as a result of
an accident at play. In a niche in the sanctuary wall is the fine little
mediaeval gravestone of John Belew; and an inscription tells of one
who died in an aerial fight in the Great War.

An extensive new Trading Estate has been built near here of
recent years.

Thorpe. Backed by grassy moors which rise to 1661 feet at
Thorpe Fell Top, it hides from the world on a little stream flowing
to the Wharfe. It is reached by narrow high-walled lanes which
drop down to the sudden sight of the roofs and chimneys in a deep
green hollow. Above the village is Elbolton Hill 1100 feet high,
with a cave, Navvy Noddle Hole, where extinct animals once
sheltered, and where the bones of 12 men sitting in a ring were
found 20 centuries after they had died.

Thorpe Salvin. For charm and interest we know few Yorkshire
villages to surpass this small place near the meeting of three counties.
By a house with a lovely garden rise the impressive Elizabethan
ruins of the old home of the Sandfords—the south front complete
with corner towers, projecting bays, and tall chimneys. Near by is
the church amid chestnuts, sycamores, and old yews, its black
and white porch having a massive timber arch and sheltering a
magnificent Norman doorway enriched with zigzag. With the
old sundial adorned with four smiling faces, it is a delightful
picture.

Much of the church has stood since the last days of the Normans;
the nave arcade and the chancel arch are of this time, but the rich
arch of the tower is from the dawn of the 13th century. The nave has
a Norman window, the time of the east window, the handsome
sedilia and piscina, and the north chapel. The nave roof and the
way through which we come are centuries old. There are traces of
mediaeval wall-painting, an old coffin lid, and a chained Bible as old
as the Civil War.

One of many Sandfords sleeping here is Katherine of 1461, whose
portrait engraved in alabaster shows her in horned headdress and a
flowing robe, in the folds of which her many children are quaintly
grouped. Hearsie Sandford kneels with his wife and daughters on an

The town hall and court house at Wakefield.

Wakefield: St Mary's Chapel and the bridge.

Elizabethan wall-monument, and the man and woman kneeling on another may be Roger Portington and his wife Mary Sandford.

The remarkable possession here is a magnificent font from Norman days. In the arcading under rich moulding are scenes representing baptism and the four seasons—a man sowing in spring, a horseman riding through the fields (summer), a man reaping, and another warming his feet at a fire.

Threshfield. Its pretty cluster of grey stone houses are round a tree-shaded green 600 feet above the sea. The stocks are on the green, and an old stone bridge crosses a stream going to the Wharfe. Threshfield School was founded in the 17th century and was used as a grammar school until 1876: it is now a primary school.

It is believed that the famous topographer Thomas Whitaker went to school here, though he was born in Norfolk. One of his local histories contains 32 plates of Yorkshire scenes by Turner, and some of Turner's earliest drawings were in Whitaker's first book.

Throapham. Only half a mile from Laughton-en-le-Morthern's rare old church is that of this tiny hamlet, its Norman story told by the doorway with a shaft on each side. The nave arcades are 13th century, the tower and the clerestory 15th. The font is about 1400, an old screen is under the tower, and the shining brass portrait of a knight in armour is of John Mallevorer who died three centuries ago. The great possession here is a coped coffin lid of mediaeval days, carved in relief with a mass of trailing foliage about a cross. Fragments of stones built into the ancient porch show a cross and shears, and a battered head in a quatrefoil.

Thrybergh. Here, on a hill not far from Rotherham, lived the Reresbys, but their park is now a golf course. The name is familiar in literature for the memoirs of Sir John Reresby, a great friend of Charles I's widow, whom he visited in France. Sir John was born here in 1634, and met Henrietta Maria while still a young man travelling on the Continent. Reresby's *Memoirs*, published 40 years after his death, are valuable to historians as sidelights on the dramatic times through which he lived. He had five sons and four daughters, and his eldest son brought the house to its doom, gambling away his fortune and dying in Fleet Prison, a starving good for nothing.

Rising above the trees is the tower and spire of the 14th and 15th century church, its chancel restored with a new arch and windows. A great possession is a window full of old glass partly restored,

K   277 showing a seated figure of Our Lord, angels, and a man and a woman kneeling at desks. There are battered figures of two mediaeval priests, and engraved in stone is the portrait of Radulphus Reresby of 1526, fine in his armour, a dagger at his side. Lionel Reresby's 16th century wall-monument has a delightful family group of the father in gold-edged armour, mother and eight daughters in farthingales and ruffs, and six sons in cloaks, their swords with gold hilts. Eight mourning children are on a monument of 1818 to the wife of John Fullerton.

Thrybergh has the remains of two old crosses, both probably 13th century. The shaft in a field near the church is adorned with foliage, and on the carved cross in the cemetery is a man with a book.

Thurnscoe. It has become a colliery village in our time, and its neat church was made almost new in 1888; but the old masonry is seen inside, and under the 18th century tower stands a dainty wooden font in the classical style of that time, its cover carved with acanthus leaves.

Tickhill. The old church of St Mary claims to be the finest parish church in the south of Yorkshire and is certainly the glory of this little town, which has not lost its pleasant air in spite of collieries near by.

A mile from the Notts. border, it has spacious streets, and a marketplace with a curious cross set up in 1766, its dome resting on eight pillars rising from steps. Near the church are the almshouses known as Maison Dieu, said to have been founded by John of Gaunt, and in Northgate is a reminder of another old foundation, St Leonard's Hospital, with the timbering of its lower storey looking like a vaulted screen supporting the upper floor; it is now the parish room. The house known as the Friary, on the Sheffield Road, is on the site of Friary of the 13th century.

In the Conqueror's day Tickhill became part of the vast estates of Roger de Busli, and something of the castle he built is to be seen at a charming green corner of the town, where the wayside stream flows to an old mill. In place of the grim buildings of the castle is a stately house amid lawns and trees and flowers, but there is still much of the wet moat, and of the curtain wall with Norman masonry. There is also the roofless gatehouse with two original doorways in its Norman base, though the archway with portcullis grooves is 14th century; the upper storey was refashioned in Tudor days, and has a canopied fireplace of that time. The castle was visited by Henry I and Henry II, Prince John had charge of it while

Richard Lionheart was in the Holy Land, and it was garrisoned for Charles I but surrendered to Parliament, which destroyed it.

The splendid tower of the church, with its lovely crown of open arcading and pinnacles 120 feet up, is a tribute to more than one period, for its base is about 1200, and it was not completed till the 15th century, the time of its west window. Two of the old statues in niches round the tower are of Edward III and his queen; another is of Our Lord in Glory. The three 13th century arches by which the tower opens to the nave and aisles are a charming part of the stately interior, all having hoods of nail-head ornament and resting on clustered shafts. Remains of lancets in the chancel tell of its 13th century origin; the nave, with beautiful arcades, was refashioned in the 15th century, when it was given the splendid clerestory of eight windows at each side, and the chancel arch with the fine window above it.

The two chapels are chiefly 14th century, and each has an old screen, that of the south chapel having dainty tracery. Other old woodwork is in the pulpit, the reading desks, and a worn chest with iron bands. There are angels and saints in old glass, a font 500 years old, two piscinas, old gravestones with engraved crosses, and two stone coffins, one with a lid on which is carved a cross in relief. There is a brass inscription to William Estfield of 1386, and on a tomb enriched with shields lies William FitzWilliam with his wife Elizabeth Clarel, he a battered knight in armour, she wearing a long robe with slashed sleeves. Their monument, brought here from the friary, is said to be one of the earliest Renaissance monuments of its kind in England. Nearer our own day is the lovely alabaster of a woman asleep, a child at her side, a broken lily by her pillow. She was Louisa Blanche Foljambe, who died in 1871.

Tockwith. A mile from the River Nidd, whose journey through this flat countryside is curiously winding, it has a cross-shaped church with a bell turret and spire and two old carved chairs, and a prettily thatched house with a porch. Its interest lies in the small timbered house at one end of the village, said to have been the house to which Cromwell came at the Battle of Marston Moor after a bullet from the accidental firing of a pistol had grazed his neck.

Todmorden. It stands at the meeting of three valleys through which the roads set off to Halifax, Burnley, and Rochdale, the moorland hills rising grandly round. A busy industrial place, it has often been called Honest John's town. He was John Fielden, MP, who sleeps in the Unitarian graveyard, not far from the square where he stands, his bronze statue being by John Henry Foley. Born here in 1784, he worked in his father's cotton mill, became immensely rich, and spent his life thinking and planning and pleading for the welfare of factory workers. Much admired by Lord Shaftesbury, he helped to bring in the Ten Hours Bill, and was so upright that he was known as Honest John.

The Fieldens have left their mark on Todmorden. Dobroyd Castle on the hillside, now a school, was their home, though Fieldens lived at the beautiful house in Centre Vale Park till it became a museum. Here is an array of prehistoric weapons and tools from the hills above the town, one of the most treasured possessions being a book with 400 pages of illuminated script, the work of two monks of the 14th century.

Loveliest of the old houses is Todmorden Hall, built over three centuries ago by Saville Radcliffe, and now the post office. Just withdrawn from the busy streets, it has gables and mullioned windows, and is as charming as we could wish. The room where we buy stamps is finely panelled, and its splendid chimneypiece of 1603 has a coloured coat-of-arms.

It is now wholly in the West Riding, but half a century ago Todmorden belonged to both Yorkshire and Lancashire, and the old boundary passed through the Town Hall, a fine stone building of 1875 on an island site. Pilasters and columns climb to its cornice, and the fine pediment has sculpture representing the staple industries of Lancashire and the trades and agriculture of Yorkshire, with two figures symbolising the two shires. The 19th century Christ Church has eight bells and a carillon. St Mary's is an 18th century building with a tower perhaps 300 years old and a chancel of 1896. It has a painted china communion cup used in 1810 (now in a glass case), a 17th century chair, and an oak screen with a pulpit growing from it; it is a War Memorial. The Unitarian chapel built by the Fieldens at a cost of £50,000 is a handsome building with a tower and spire rising nearly 200 feet.

The novelist William Holt, who has used near-by country in his novels, and who has ridden many thousands of miles on horseback selling his books, lived in a fine Elizabethan house here.

Two miles east, on Stoodley Hill, is an obelisk built in 1856 in place of a tower which stood as a thankoffering for peace in 1815 till it was blown down about the time of the Crimean War.

Todwick. The old manor house is by the church, which has a Norman story, though its chancel is 14th century and the tower is a hundred years younger. The ancient porch has its original round arch and old roof beams, and the simple Norman doorway has a door with old hinges. One Norman doorway is blocked in the north wall. The altar rails and a chair are Jacobean, and the box-pews a little younger. There are rough-hewn roof beams, fragments of old glass, and a Bible of 1611. A tiny brass portrait of 1609 shows Thomas Garland kneeling, and pointing to the motto, "After darkness, the light of hope."

Tong. In this unspoiled village near Bradford is no hint of the industrial world about it.

There are trim little stone houses, and the imposing hall (now a hall of residence for Bradford University) built by Sir George Tempest in 1702 and standing amid spacious lawns and magnificent trees, is famous for its beautiful rooms with carving by Grinling Gibbons. From the pretty lodge at the entrance to the drive a green sward stretches to the church and the Lantern House—a stone house with mullioned windows and the date 1615 at the tip of the gable. It was an inn, and takes its name from the stone lantern in which a light used to shine for the guidance of travellers.

For over a century the village pump has stood near the old forge, which is now deserted, although some of the smith's tools remain.

The old stocks and the mounting-stone are by the churchyard wall. The church is a formal building made new in 1727, its windows startlingly white with painted lattice. The east window is in the style of the 15th century, but there is little else to disturb the Georgian air. There are high box-pews for the squire (one with a fireplace) and low box-pews for the people, still with their iron latches. Rising above them is the three-decker pulpit with a big square sounding-board. There are two old chairs and a row of wooden hat pegs. The chief monument is an ornate marble and alabaster arch in the chancel; it is to two of the Tempests of last century and two of this, and has a great display of carving, a dozen small shields, and figures of Fortitude and Justice.

Totley. It lies on the highway climbing up from Sheffield (to which it now belongs), at the mouth of the famous tunnel which runs through the heart of Totley Moor. In a leafy hollow, below a road of lovely trees leading to the great house, now a Training College, is the charming little church, stone-walled and stone-roofed, so hidden that it is easily missed. New in 1924 and unusual in style, it is a light and pleasing place of simple lines and curves. It has round arches everywhere, 18 of them, and the stone of round and square-headed windows, deeply splayed, contrasts with the plastered walls. The chancel has an apse with a domed ceiling and five tiny lancets. The chancel screen and the pulpit are both in one, the stout pillars of the screen simply carved with a pattern suggesting trees from root to branch. On the big square font, with a heavy oak cover, are the happy words, "The children gave me".

Towton. Over a mile from its cottages, farms, and barns, is a cross on a hill, standing in a field by the road to Saxton. The cross, which has a new shaft, marks the place where one of the terrible battles of the Wars of the Roses was fought in the snow one Sunday in 1461. The cause of it all was of little account, but over 30,000 men died for it that day.

It is said that in the silence before the two armies met the tinkling of the church bell at Saxton could be heard. As the armies came face to face a light fall of snow blinded the Lancastrians who were facing the wind, the Yorkists snatching up the arrows which fell short and sending them back with deadly aim. The battle raged for hours, but the appearance of the Duke of Norfolk with reinforcements for the Yorkists sent the men of the Red Rose running down the hill in a panic. They retreated towards Towton, and in the stream, too deep to ford, perished a host of Lancastrians, among them Henry Percy, of whom Shakespeare wrote that a braver man ne'er spurred a courser to a trumpet's sound.

Treeton. Collieries have robbed it and the valley below of their beauty, but the old church on the hill is still charmingly odd with a long 14th century chancel and a short 15th century aisle and a tower at the west end of the other aisle. Its story goes back to the 12th century, told by the lower part of the tower with its sturdy arch, two round-arched bays of the north arcade, and the doorway in the porch, which has a tiny child's coffin in its wall. The chancel arch, the south arcade, and an aisle piscina are 13th century; from the 14th come the font, the sedilia, and the piscina in the chancel; and the top of the tower is 15th century. Across the wide arch to the mediaeval south chapel is a fine old screen with a new top; one of the old bench-ends has an inscription to a parson of four centuries ago; and there are old roofs. The preacher stands with his back to a fine old coffin lid with a cross and a sword, and the congregation turn their backs on a battered stone knight upright in the wall.

Upper Poppleton. Old and new mingle in this village near the Ouse, pleasant with two greens, a fine maypole, and a church with a bell turret and shingled spire supported by a row of three tall arches across the nave. Of the old church it replaced only a few fragments are left. The round arch and stiff leaf capitals of the south doorway are the work of the Normans and the font may be as old; the vestry has a mediaeval window, and several panels in the oak lectern have delicate pierced tracery carved in mediaeval days.

Waddington. Gateway to a wonderful moorland ending in the fells, Waddington is a trim village near the Lancashire border. A stream running along the main street dives under the road and comes out in a wayside garden, where a striking wheelhead cross stands on a rocky base, a tribute to those who died for peace. Facing the garden is the Old Hall, and at the other end of the village is the hospital founded in 1700 by Robert Parker and since rebuilt, the dwellings, with timbered gables and their tiny chapel, gathered round a spacious lawn.

The Old Hall is the home of a remarkable family and has memories of a melancholy king. A charming house in a lovely garden, its gateway has the inscription, "I will raise up his ruins and I will build it as in the days of old." In spite of much change, there is still the air of other days in the stone stairway, the rooms enriched with old panelling and furniture, and the four-poster bed where the poor King Henry VI is said to have slept.

His bedroom is much as it was in 1464, and in it is his portrait and the chair he sat in. Here, too, is the secret room where he crouched when strangers came, and the desk at which he would write. Among the treasures of the house is a cupboard with panels showing the king's flight, a curious piece of 16th century craftsmanship.

The church, with arcades running from the east to the west wall, was made almost new in 1901, but the tower and the south doorway are 15th century, and the chancel has some of its ancient walling, with the head of a doorway shaped from a single stone. Carved on the font are Instruments of the Passion; there are three old carved pews; and in old glass is the quaint figure of a man. A gallery of saints in the windows adds to the modern attraction of the church, with its splendid nave roof, stalls with rich tracery, a chancel screen with fine rood figures, and a beautiful oak reredos with a canopied Nativity, the striking feature of which are the tall pinnacles enriched with angels. There are old fragments in the screen between the north aisle and the chapel.

The Waddingtons have been a remarkable family since they appeared on the stage of history over a thousand years ago. Their founder, Duke Wada, is said to have built Mulgrave Castle in the eighth century and to be buried there between two rocks. The name of Waddington has spread about the world and is on the maps of three continents, for there are towns named after them not only in England but in Australia and the United States, as well as a harbour in Canada and a square in Valparaiso.

Wadworth. Its crooked streets are on a hill, and where the road widens below the church is a maypole. Quaint outside, the church is charming within, its lofty arches in great array. Much of it comes from the 12th century, the south doorway and its sheltering porch being of that time. The simple doorway in the other porch is Norman, and so is the arcading in the south aisle wall, its round arches on detached shafts with simple capitals. The chapels were made new in the 14th century, and windows are of the three mediaeval centuries. From the 15th come the clerestories of the nave and chancel, and the tower standing between the aisles. The sedilia and several piscinas, the font and a huge carved chest, are all mediaeval relics.

On an alabaster tomb with angels lie Edmund Fitzwilliam of 1430 and his wife, their son Edmund of 1465 having a tomb enriched with quatrefoils. A 14th century gravestone shows parts of a praying figure, as if through a coffin lid, and a sculptured figure in hunting attire has a bugle and a sword. It is 14th century, the only one of its kind in the county, and may represent one of the Chaworths.

Wakefield. It is an ancient place, dating back to pre-Roman times, but redevelopment of the city, and in particular the city centre, has removed almost everything of any age. Neolithic implements have been found in the neighbourhood, there are many evidences of Roman occupation, and on the site of the cathedral stood a Saxon church, a cross-shaft from which is in York Museum. Mentioned in the Domesday Book, it had become a centre for the weaving of woollen cloth by the 13th century, by the end of which it was the biggest cloth-producing centre in the West Riding. We still have something living of mediaeval days in the so-called Wakefield Cycle of Mystery Plays; there can be few who have any pretensions to knowledge of English Literature who do not know the famous story of Mak the sheep-stealer, told in the Wakefield Second Shepherd's play. The cycle was translated recently by a lecturer at nearby Bretton Hall Training College, where it was once performed in its entirety; a shortened version was also presented commercially at the Mermaid Theatre in London. A more unhappy memory of these times is the sacking of the town and Sandal Castle in 1460;

2000 men were slain in an hour on one day, and the town suffered considerably at the hands of the victorious soldiery. The town also suffered in the Civil War, but otherwise grew to be a place of considerable importance.

It is now a city of surprises, an industrial city with some old things left, quiet squares and dignified Georgian buildings. The centre of the city is the Bull Ring from which the old "Gates" of the past lead off: Northgate, Westgate, and Kirkgate. This area is occupied with modern shops, room for which has been made, unfortunately, by the destruction of some picturesque old properties. Wood Street is near by, leading off in the Bradford direction, and here we find many civic buildings. The City Museum is housed in the Mechanics Institute, where we find sections devoted to natural history, local "bygones", and period costume; there are also period shops—of the apothecary, newsagent, milliner, barber, and sweet seller. A small subsidiary museum has also been established at Newmillerdam. Next door is the Town Hall with a tower nearly two hundred feet high; beyond this is County Hall, the Headquarters of the West Riding County Council, which has a fine array of sculpture and paintings: between the two is the 19th century courthouse. Also in this street are the headquarters of the West Riding County Police Force and the extensions to the Technical and Art College. A little farther out in the same direction is the City Art Gallery, which houses sculpture by Henry Moore, Barbara Hepworth (who was born here) and Jacob Epstein; it has paintings by Paul Nash and Graham Sutherland of the modern age, and water-colours by Peter de Wint, David Cox, and John Sell Cotman as well as paintings by Gainsborough and English, Italian and Spanish masters. The West Riding Artists' Exhibition is held here once every two years. St John's Square, containing tall Georgian houses, is a beautiful corner in the vicinity.

The city is fortunate in having several parks for the recreation of its people: Clarence Park was given to the city in 1893; Holmfield Park has rose gardens, a nursery, and an alpine garden, and Thornes Park also provides ample space for the playing of games. The Corporation also own the Sandal Castle grounds and a municipal golf course at Lupset, where the clubhouse is the 18th century Lupset Hall.

The crowning glory of Wakefield is its cathedral church of All Saints, begun in Norman days, rebuilt in 1329, given a clerestory in 1470 and raised to the standing of a bishopric in 1888. It has been extended, beyond the high altar, in this century, and it has hence regained the shape of a cross. The nave arcades show signs of their

285

reconstruction, some of them crooked through having been leaning before they were raised. Traces of the Norman church are seen in bases and pillars in the North arcade, and of the 13th century in the south arcade. The tower (of 247 feet and hence the tallest in Yorkshire) has a stone vaulted roof, and its splendid arch soars to the nave's fine panelled roof with golden bosses. The aisles have similar roofs, and those of the old chancel and its aisles are painted in mediaeval style.

Stone-vaulted roofs with flower bosses crown the 20th century transepts and the aisled chapel. A rare gem is this chapel, a lantern of light with fine windows, and particularly charming is its east wall outside, where there are two canopied niches at each side of the east window, and a niche in the traceried gable, sheltering a statue of Archbishop Melton who consecrated the 14th century church.

Beautiful stone carving is seen in the three sedilia in the sanctuary, and the stone seats on the opposite wall. At each side of the chancel are restored 15th century screens; the chancel screen has mediaeval remains in the base, but the upper portion comes from 1634. The stalls with misericords are old and new. The 17th century font has a domed canopy with cherubs and a dove. The canopied throne was brought here in 1888 for the first bishop of Wakefield, William Walsham How, who is seen on a tomb with tracery and shields.

On a classical monument in the south chapel, Sir Lyon Pilkington is a reclining figure wearing the long curly wig of the early 18th century. Set in the floor below the monument is a stone, a memorial to Charles and Elizabeth Pilkington, who both died in 1698.

On the front of the high altar are saints in niches. The elaborate oak reredos, about 20 feet high and richly gilded, has scenes of the Crucifixion and the Last Supper and in Kempe glass we read the story of Our Lord's life and there are portraits of saints with scenes from their lives. An interesting thing is a replica of Wakefield's Saxon cross and in a show-case are a handful of Roman coins dug up hereabouts, and an Elizabethan Latin primer.

Two bridges cross the Calder, joining at one end, one built in 1933 and the other a lovely 600-year-old bridge of nine arches. We come to it to see another Wakefield treasure, the famous chantry chapel of St Mary (one of four remaining in England—the others being at Rotherham, St Ives and Bradford-on-Avon). This gem of the 14th century was restored by Sir Gilbert Scott who gave it a new west front, and it has been given yet another in more recent years; the original one was moved at the time of the restoration to the grounds of Kettlethorpe Hall a few miles away. In three of the five bays of the arcaded base are dainty doorways with rich mouldings; between the arches are pinnacled buttresses, and the wall above is enriched with tracery. At each end of the embattled parapet is a canopied niche crowned with a leafy spirelet, and below are carved scenes of the Annunciation, the Nativity, the Resurrection, and Pentecost. At the north-east corner of the chapel rises an embattled turret, entered by a small doorway leading to a stairway climbing to the roof and descending to a tiny crypt. The seven windows lighting the chapel have beautiful flowing tracery; an elaborate piscina has a fine traceried panel below it and a charming niche by the east window has a vaulted canopy.

St John's church is also worth the attention of the visitor, for it is a fine Georgian building, designed in 1791, with a tower crowned with a cupola, a parapet adorned with vases and inside richly moulded ceilings and carving in the manner of Grinling Gibbons.

There is evidence that there was a school connected with the parish church here as early as 1275, and Queen Elizabeth's Grammar School was founded in 1591. Now in more modern buildings facing the Clayton hospital, the school has had many famous old boys; a school for girls was founded in 1878 and is the Wakefield Girls' High School.

Famous men connected with Wakefield include John Radcliffe, founder of the Radcliffe Library at Oxford, Christopher Saxton, the map-maker of Shakepeare's day, and the novelist George Gissing who was born in Westgate in 1857.

Wales. We hardly expected to find Wales in Yorkshire, but here it is near the Derbyshire border, one of the southernmost villages with a church both old and new. The simple church, built by the Normans and altered in the 15th century, is now the north aisle of a modern one in 500-year-old style, with an outside wall of the mediaeval tower now in the new nave. The beautiful Norman chancel arch has zigzag and cushion capitals, and the old doorway, set in the new walling, has rich ornament, strange faces, and a tympanum with chessboard pattern. The massive font is a Norman relic. The old nave has a fine 15th century roof with floral bosses, and among fragments of old glass are two women at desks.

Walton. It is in the peaceful country by the River Wharfe, with the Roman road called Rudgate close by. Among the farms and barns are houses old and new, one of the 17th century serving as the vicarage. Old Hall, a creepered stone house, was the home of the Fairfaxes, and still has the original oak staircase. Here is remembered Robert Fairfax, no warrior but a musician of Henry VII's

287

day, whose church music is still loved. Standing much as it has been for six centuries, the church (into which we come by a heavy door on its old hinges) is full of light from fine windows, through which we see wide views of the pastoral countryside. The slender tower has its Norman base and the original arch opening to the nave, but the rest of it is 15th century. There is a mediaeval font, a Jacobean pulpit with 19th century panels, a peephole by the tilting chancel arch, and a scratch dial on a buttress. In the chancel is a niche in which lies a 14th century knight in armour, his rich belt adorned with roses, one leg broken but one foot still on a lion.

Walton. It is the Walton near Wakefield, the place where one of the strangest of all Englishmen was born, and where he sleeps. He was Charles Waterton the naturalist.

The village itself is attractive, but we enter another world when we cross the canal to the park, where for half a century birds and beasts found sanctuary. It is a fascinating spot, with the woods coming down to the edge of a beautiful lake. On an island at one end of the lake, reached from the gardens by a delicate iron bridge, is the great house, almost modern as we see it, but standing where the Watertons built a fortified house soon after the Conqueror's day. The old place and the drawbridge were pulled down by the naturalist's grandfather, but by the bridge is a fragment of the old gateway crowned with a crucifix, and in one of the massive doors is part of a bullet fired by the Parliament men in the Civil War.

The house, which Charles Waterton described as a stone box, has reminders of him—the chapel where he prayed half the night and read a chapter from Francis Xavier and *Don Quixote* every morning, and the room where he slept on the bare floor with a block of wood for his pillow. Over a doorway is an old stone panel of a Madonna; we see his sundial, telling the time in all the capitals of the world, the fragment of a cloister he built, and a cross in memory of his daughter. It is now a maternity hospital.

Walking in these fine gardens we liked to think of Charles Waterton standing at the doorway of his island home, and looking over his little kingdom. He was six feet tall, had white hair, and wore an old-fashioned swallow-tailed coat. He had walked barefoot through Brazilian forests, escaped the plague in Spain, climbed up St Peter's and put his glove on the lightning conductor, and had a ride on the back of an alligator. It is said he had only to open his front door and cross the bridge to be welcomed by flocks of birds flying to meet him. He would see from his window great flights of wild duck, widgeon, teal, pochard, coots, and Canadian geese.

Warmsworth. The bell calls us to church from the small ivied tower with Norman masonry and a wooden top, standing by the lawn at the old entrance to the Hall, a fine house of 1702 with a Tudor wing. The church is modern, in the new village half a mile away. There was born at the rectory here in 1720 Francis Fawkes, who grew up to be widely known as a poet as well as a preacher—so widely known that it was worth a publisher's while to buy his name for a serial issue of the Bible in 60 weekly numbers. He was a great scholar, full of good humour, and with a host of friends, but he appears to have been lazy in spite of all the work he did. We read of his fondness for social gaiety and love of ease, and it seems fitting therefore that the best known of all his works today should be the song of *The Brown Jug*.

Wath. A charming bit of Nidderdale, it is a place in which to linger. It is said there are few neighbourhoods in Yorkshire with a greater variety of ferns, and in Watch Woods are sycamores, oaks, and firs. A delightful path brings us to Gouthwaite reservoir, one of the finest engineering feats in Yorkshire; the arches and the parapet are exceedingly imposing. Near by is a packhorse bridge said to have been built by the monks of Fountains Abbey 600 years ago. Doubergill and Merryfield Glen are places worthy of a visit in the vicinity. At a near-by hemp mill is to be seen the largest working waterwheel in Yorkshire.

Wath-on-Dearne. It was a son of this small mining and manufacturing town who helped to speed up the business-world—William Addy, a pioneer of shorthand and author of a shorthand Bible published about 1687.

Its striking church has much work of Norman days, including the base of the tower and the north arcade of the nave and chancel. The rest of the tower and its spire are 15th century, the south aisle and arcade and some windows are 600 years old, and the doorway in the old porch is a little older. So is the big chapel, with an aisle and some Elizabethan bench-ends. One of two old chests has ironwork and chain handles, a bell of Armada year stands under the tower, and one of several piscinas is in a pillar of the chancel, which has a modern screen and an east window with rich memorial glass. In an earlier pulpit Henry Partington preached for 64 years of last century, a remarkable record of service.

Wentbridge. It has grown about a pretty hollow where the Great North Road came steeply down to the two-arched stone bridge spanning the River Went. Very attractive is the wooded valley hereabouts. Charmingly set on a green bank, watching from its quiet retreat all who go by, is the church with red roofs of 1878, wearing a red cap on its central tower.

Wentworth. Its memories are of a family bearing its name and living here four centuries without a break. It has part of their old home in a magnificent park, and part of the old church where many of them lie. There are collieries in the valley, but the village with its trees, the old cross, and the 19th century church near the old one, is all we could wish.

We come to the old church for its interest, to the new one for its beauty. Built by the children of the fifth Earl Fitzwilliam in memory of their parents, it was designed by J. L. Pearson RA in the mediaeval fashion showing the 13th century style passing to the 14th. From its central tower a spire soars to 195 feet, and the porch with lovely doorways prepares us for the splendour within. Graceful arches richly carved are everywhere. The tower has an arcaded balcony and lantern windows. The stone reredos, commemorating the golden wedding of the sixth earl, has rich sculpture of the Last Supper, under a canopy supported by pillars with eight saints in niches.

Of the old church there remain the 15th century tower, a ruined nave, and a chancel and chapel altered in the 17th century, but divided by a mediaeval arcade. Some old glass is 17th century, there is a fragment of Norman carving in a wall, and fragments of Norman capitals are lying about. A floorstone with a bow may be to a mediaeval forester, and one of 1635 is to a steward of the famous first Earl of Strafford. By a 15th or 16th century alabaster knight of the Gascoign family are the head and shoulders of his wife; a sculptured fragment on a wall, showing two knights, may have belonged to their original tomb. A brass plate has portraits of Michael Darcy of 1588 and his wife Margaret Wentworth.

Thomas Wentworth of 1587 lies in rich armour on his tomb, with his wife in a Paris hat and dainty ruff, both a little battered. Sir William Wentworth has a canopied wall-monument with a family group kneeling at prayer, the parents at a desk, their eldest son alone, the rest of the children below. It is the figure of the eldest son on which our interest centres, for he was Thomas Wentworth, the great Earl of Strafford who stood by Charles I on the eve of the Civil War.

His richly carved monument in Wentworth church shows him at

prayer, and his epitaph tells us that his memory will never die. It is not quite certain whether he lies here or not, for some years ago three skeletons were found in the chancel of Hooton Roberts church, where his widow is known to lie, and one of the three appeared to have had the head cut off, so that it was presumed that this might be the earl, the others his wife and daughter. In Wentworth church his son William, the second earl, has a memorial on which he is kneeling with his wife. Their home, Wentworth Woodhouse, now a college for teachers, was much enlarged in the middle of the 18th century by the Marquess of Rockingham, and is a wondrous sight, standing in a park of 1500 acres. With its courts it covers over three acres, and is now the seat of Earl Fitzwilliam. There are ancient oaks, stately avenues of elms and beeches, lakes and lawns, and many of those monuments the 18th century landscape gardeners loved to set up in their parks. Among the monuments is Keppel's Column, over 100 feet high, and the Hoober Stand, odd name for a structure resembling a lighthouse, celebrating the Peace Treaty of Aix-La-Chapelle in 1748. From a balcony up 155 steps we see the towers and spires of 50 churches in Yorkshire and Derbyshire. Almost as high stands the mausoleum, in which is a statue of Rockingham surrounded by busts of six friends, including Edmund Burke, who wrote his epitaph.

Down the Long Walk, resplendent with rhododendrons in due season, we come to the great lawn on which the west front looks out. This was built about 1725 and has four great fluted pilasters about the doorway, high above which heraldic beasts support a coat-of-arms, while the pediment is crowned by a colossal statue. Wings with massive masonry framing bay windows give a solid look to the building, but round the corner we come to a handsome gateway believed to have been designed by Inigo Jones. The great Strafford must often have passed beneath it.

But it is the east front, 600 feet long, that is the most striking thing here. Designed by Henry Flitcroft, son of a Hampton Court gardener who had caught the eye of the famous Earl of Burlington, there is simplicity as well as grandeur in the central block of this long front. Eight columns form the spacious portico, which is reached up double flights of steps; and above the pediment stand Minerva, Ceres, and Juno.

Within is the great hall 60 feet square and rising 40 feet high to a panelled ceiling; its walls are enriched by fluted columns supporting a gallery and framing niches with marble statues, lovely doorways, and a mantelpiece by John Gibson. The marble floor is superb, a great achievement in mosaic.

The state rooms seem to vie with one another in their appeal to lovers of the beautiful. They have such names as the Ship Room, the Whistlejacket Room, the Painted Drawing Room, the Marble Saloon, and Clifford's Lodgings.

West Bretton. In its park of a thousand acres are two fine lakes, a stream flowing to the River Dearne, and a grand company of magnificent Spanish chestnuts and old oaks. The hall was the home of the Beaumonts, and here was born Thomas Wentworth Beaumont, one of the earnest Liberals of the days of the Reform Bill, and one of the originators of the Westminster Review, which appeared as the organ of the Reformers. He was a man of great generosity and a benefactor of the fine arts. The hall itself is now a training college for teachers, specialising in music and drama.

West End. Most of this famous "deserted village" now lies under a reservoir, constructed to help supply Leeds with its vast water requirements.

Weston. A road winding from Otley brings us to the old stocks under a big tree. Then a steep lane shaded with trees drops down to an out-of-the-world spot where the little old church is a companion for the great house, both in the park which goes down to the River Wharfe.

Few churches can be simpler. It has a turret instead of a tower, a porch of 1686, and an aisle with one of its two arches blocked. Some of the walling, a window in the nave, and the plain arch to the chancel are part of the Norman building. There are old box-pews, and the pulpit is a three-decker.

Wetherby. It is a famous little place with nothing much to see. Once more important than now, it has a handsome six-arched bridge to stretch over the Wharfe, but it is now by-passed by the new A1 road. There were stirring times here when Sir Thomas Fairfax garrisoned the town for the Parliament, and traces of a castle high above the river tell of great days earlier still; but Wetherby seems content now to be a placid place with a few grey houses, curious streets which seem to lead to nowhere, quaint old inns, and a marketplace. We see it best from the bridge—the broad sweep of the river, the shining weir, the watermill with its wheel no longer turning, and the trees crowding to the water's edge. On the bridge is a winged figure of Victory with a sword and a crown, the town's tribute to those who gave their lives in the Great War.

Whiston. The old part of this neighbour of Rotherham lies in the hollow, but its church is on the hill, reached by a fine oak War Memorial lychgate. Most of its old work is 15th century, but the tower has a Norman base with a 13th century lancet, and a low pointed arch breaking into a Norman window. Three bells are said to be 15th century, an inlaid chest is 18th, a lovely modern chalice is studded with gems, and the portrait of a vicar is cunningly hidden in the folds of an angel's robe in the east window of the aisle.

Whitgift. Quaint and old-fashioned, joining hands with Reedness and looking out on miles of green countryside that was once marshland, Whitgift is very picturesque with its old red brick houses and grey church on one side of the road, and on the other the high embankments of the dykes beside the Ouse, where ships pass to and fro between Goole and the sea. The manor house looks across the river, and here are the great pylons which carry electricity across it.

Except for the 15th century tower and the mediaeval arcades, the low embattled church has seen much change, but it keeps the old font. Sailors on ships and travellers by road can see the clock on the tower with the words on its face in Latin, "Peace on earth".

Whitkirk. Within easy reach of the wonderful park of Temple Newsam, almost part of Leeds, Whitkirk is the village of the greatest of all our lighthouse builders, John Smeaton. Here he was born and here he lies; he never gave up the house he was born in, which our own century has destroyed.

Standing with the busy road on one side and trees and fields on the other is the 15th century church, notable for the big corbels under overhanging parapets, those of the fine tower built so that when we look up we see the sky between the corbels. Above it rises a tiny spire. The chancel has its old arch to the nave, and a new one where the east end has been extended in our own time. There is an old font bowl and a new font, and some windows are renewed. Faint traces of wall-paintings on the clerestory may be three centuries old. One of the good things in the church is the canopied oak pulpit, looking old though it is the work of a skilled craftsman of our day. The south chapel has a gilded oak screen.

A monument of black and white marble, with a man in elaborate dress and a woman in draped headdress and gown, is a memorial to Edward Ingram, Viscount Irwin, of 1688; and another by Nollekens, to Viscount Irwin of 1778, shows a woman bowed over an urn. In a quaint little wall-monument we see Lord William Gordon in his kilt. The finest monument is to Sir Robert Scarsgill and his wife, an alabaster tomb under an arch. One of the best of its kind in York-shire, it is remarkable for its richness of detail and quality of crafts-manship. The knight is in Tudor armour with a double chain round his neck, his wife is charming in a headdress like a gem-studded coronet, and a magnificent cloak clasped with a double chain, an animal on its turned-back fold. Five daughters are round her.

A marble panel on the chancel wall, crowned with a model of the old Eddystone lighthouse he designed, is in memory of Whitkirk's great son John Smeaton, who set his light far above the waves and made a new star by which sailors might steer a safe course to Plymouth. The house in which he was born in 1724, Austhorpe Lodge, has unhappily been pulled down—unhappily because it was an interesting place. Smeaton lived in it all his 68 years; it was his world of ideas, and he built on to it a tower of four turrets, with a forge on the ground floor, his lathes on the first, his models on the second, his study on the third, and at the top a lumber room full of the relics of old experiments.

Whixley. Its houses are gathered about the winding roads and the little green. The Hall and the church are companions, standing above the rest, and just below the pleasant village is a magnificent view of the rich plain stretching to the Wolds beyond York Minster towers. The Hall is a fine old house of mellowed brick behind high walls; for over a century it was used as the hospital founded by Christopher Tancred in 1754. His wish that his body should never be buried underground has been obeyed, and after being for many years at the Hall he lies in his marble tomb in the church.

The big and impressive church was built in the 14th century, but the upper part of the tower is 15th, the chancel has a Norman window among its modern ones, and the porch is new. The tower stands within the church at the west end, and has two flying but-tresses to the aisle walls. Two of its three arches opening to the aisles and having traces of old painting, continue the nave arcades, whose arches are unusually massive for the slender clustered pillars on which they rest. Stone faces adorn the arcades and the old windows. The massive font is over 600 years old.

The church tower has a red cap and a gilded weathercock.

Wighill. The small church on the hill gleams in the sun, looking out on a wooded countryside. It sees the River Wharfe shining in the meadows below.

A long building of nave and chancel with no arch between them, it has a narrow north aisle divided from the nave by an arcade with round arches on clustered shafts, the fine work of the Normans. An old porch with an Elizabethan roof and a door of 1721 shelters what is the glory of this place, a magnificent Norman doorway of three orders. Under a hood of zigzag are beak-heads; then comes a quaint medley of sculpture showing birds, beak-heads, heads of animals, an old man with a goose slung on his back, a man striking a lion with an axe, a dog attacking a boar, and a dragon eating a cockerel. The last order is roll moulding, and in the carvings of the capitals of the shafts on each side we see three figures holding hands and two seated figures. One charming capital has clustered leaves, another has stiff leaves and honeysuckle.

One of the gargoyles on the 15th century tower is playing a guitar, another a trumpet, and others have hands in their mouths. There are many crude old poppyhead benches, a 17th century pulpit, a low chancel screen with balusters which were once in box-pews, an old font, and fragments of old glass. In lovely glass by Christopher Whall, shining blue, green, and crimson, are St Cuthbert and St Margaret, a child at her feet. Built into the south wall is a fragment of stone perhaps carved in Saxon days.

For centuries the Stapletons have slept in this church. The gravestone of Sir William of 1503 serves for Henry Stapleton of 1779, the last of his line. Here too is the stone of Sir Brian of 1518. Sir Robert of 1635, wearing richly patterned armour, lies on a tomb enriched with the Stapleton lion (seen on a boss in the porch), a coat-of-arms with many quarterings, and figures of his six children, one holding a skull. At Sir Robert's feet is a Saracen's head, the crest of the family.

The old home of the Stapletons has vanished, but there are traces of a moated house near Wighill Park, standing in lovely grounds and 100 acres of parkland a mile away. A long avenue of trees from a corner of the village brings us to it.

Winksley. It is off the beaten track five miles from Ripon, looking from its place on the River Laver to the moors rising in the west. Its chief possession is a beautiful 20th century church, with a massive tower standing like a guardian over the small gathering of cottages. At each side of the nave is an arcade of deep arches, making a passage like a tiny aisle and framing the windows. All the windows glow with colour in scenes of Bible story. Beautiful marble sculpture is seen in the font with tracery and niches, in the pulpit (rising from a low screen), and in the reredos of the Last Supper, curious for the ample supply of food on the table. The carving of linenfold and tracery on the prayer desk is the lovely work of Robert Thompson of Kilburn.

The church was built in memory of the first Lord Furness, the remarkable man known to the last generation as Sir Christopher Furness, a prominent Methodist whose business success was one of the industrial romances of his age. His home was Grantley Hall a mile away, a fine house in a splendid park with the River Skell filling its lakes and making waterfalls. It is now an Adult Education College.

Wistow. Lying among orchards not far from the Ouse, it has a fine little church at a bend of the road, with red-roofed cottages clustering round.

Windows of all three mediaeval centuries pierce the stone walls, which are grey outside and warm-tinted within. The 14th century east window has unusual tracery, and the clerestories are as old as the 15th century tower, which has a red cap on its crown of battlements and pinnacles. The rest of the old work is chiefly 14th century. A floorstone engraved with a cross, a sword, and a battleaxe may have marked the resting-place of one of the Templars of Temple Hirst. One of the 14th century has the sculpture of a woman in wimple and flowing robes, and over her rich canopy are heads of a man and a bishop in quatrefoils. Part of a coffin lid is in the arch of the doorway, and built into the chancel wall are mediaeval sculptures of Our Lord seated, and a kneeling woman turning as if to look at the altar.

The handsome pulpit is Jacobean. There are two old collecting boxes and fragments of old glass. The beautiful modern reredos of carved oak has four saints—Oswald, Chad, Hilda, and Cuthbert—and under canopies on the altar are Cecilia with her organ and Caedmon of Whitby, our first English poet.

Womersley. It shelters by the park in which stands the great house. A pleasant picture by the wayside is the mediaeval church, in a churchyard with an old stone coffin, and a fine yew hedge.

The walls of the church are a patchwork of light-tinted stone, its 14th century tower with a stumpy spire resting on the great arches of a central crossing. We go one step down to the stone-ribbed porch and four more to the wide south aisle, which has an arcade from the 14th century between it and the nave. The arcade leading to the narrow north aisle (like a passage) may be 13th century. The windows are 13th and 14th century, and there is none to light the east wall. The roofs are painted in mediaeval style, six candlesticks and a crucifix are of old silver, and an old painting on tiles is a crude picture of the Last Supper, showing a cat sitting behind one of the disciples, a curious animal on a dish, and the bread and wine untouched. In the south aisle lies a cross-legged stone knight with a dog to guard him, a battered little man at his head having a finger on the page of a book.

Woodkirk. Next door to Dewsbury and sometimes called West Ardsley, it has a few old houses, and a church with some remains of one which is said to have belonged to a monastery. Most of it is made new, but the small tower is much as it was at the end of the 12th century (with a later mediaeval arch), and some windows are 14th century, one full of old glass fragments. There is a fine Jacobean pulpit, and the vestry is panelled with carved ends of old box-pews. The old altar table has a carved border and bulging legs, and the 15th century stalls have poppyheads ending in sheaves. Sir John Topcliffe's mediaeval gravestone is here, and on the porch is an old sundial.

Woolley. The march of industry has left Woolley to grow old graciously with its great company of oaks and birches and its gardens full of colour. Below the church is the old home of the Wheatleys, a charming gabled house; and in the park (with copper beeches and great chestnut trees) is the noble hall that was one of the many fine homes of the Wentworths from the sixteenth century.

A fine avenue of trees brings us to a churchyard like a lawn, with the base of an old cross and a curious weeping beech looking as if a giant had sat on it. Here are two ancient tombs built up of stones, covering no one knows whom.

The dignified church, which replaced the Norman church in the 15th century, is charming within, where arcades of high and low arches run east to west. Over the lower doorway of the roodstairs is a Norman tympanum carved with a holy lamb and a border of trailing leaves, and in the wall at the top of the stairway is a Norman twisted pillar under a flat arch. An old screen spans the arch between the south aisle and the chapel, seven old benches have traceried ends, and a few old bench-ends are adorned with tracery, lettering, and shields. There are two chained books of 1711.

A great possession is the lovely old glass in the two chapels, believed to be 15th century. In the three windows of the north chapel are the Crucifixion (with Mary and John under canopies), St George fighting the dragon, and a knight and lady at prayer. The red, blue, and gold Trinity window in the south chapel shows the Madonna and Child, St Catherine with her wheel, and God the Father with Our Lord on His knee, the dove descending.

Worsborough. It has lost priceless possessions, but keeps many treasures for us to see. Here, years ago, was the coat Charles I wore on the last morning of his life, Sir Thomas Herbert's manuscript account of the king's last hours, and the cushion he knelt on when he "bowed his comely head down, as upon a bed".

But not one of these historic possessions is now here. The hall where the relics were kept is an old house refashioned in Elizabeth I's day and still beautiful, with fine woodwork and fragments of old glass.

This is a pleasant patch of a colliery countryside, and in one of its old houses are carved beams supposed to be from the church. In the churchyard, shaded by a great chestnut and sycamore, sleeps George Rushworth who stood guard over Napoleon at St Helena, and William Wagstaffe, of whom we have read that, having been unjustly imprisoned, he died forgiving his enemies.

The 13th century church was given aisles in the 15th, and restoration has made some windows new. One in the chancel is Norman, the east window is 14th century, and the tower is over 400 years old. One of the carved Norman fragments in the vestry shows Sagittarius shooting an arrow at a weird animal. The door within the old porch may be 15th century, the time of the old work in the chancel screen, with an original figure of the Almighty. The font is 1662. A fragment of old glass has a hand outstretched and two faces in a ruby setting; and in lovely modern glass we see the Madonna, the Wise Men, Our Lord sending out the disciples, and missionaries bringing Christianity to England.

A remarkable possession is a splendid oak monument looking like a double-decker bed, enriched round the base with heraldry. On the upper ledge lies a knight, on the lower a skeleton, both carved in wood, covered with linen, and painted. The knight (Roger Rockley of 1534) is in armour, his feet on a cushion, his hands at prayer.

Wortley. It is old enough for the Romans to have had iron mines here, and beautiful enough to reward the climber up above the River Don, with a view over the crags of Wharncliffe Chase, the hunting ground of 2000 acres which is one of the finest bits of Yorkshire. Famous long before Sheffield steel, the Chase lies below great rocks near the village, and from the ridge we see Yorkshire and Lancashire, the river gleaming among the oaks, and the valley where Scott laid the opening scene of *Ivanhoe*.

The church has little old work except in the tower and a 14th century window. Christopher Whall's lovely glass in the east window show Our Lord, a bishop, and a saint. There is a memorial by Flaxman, and Archibald Stuart-Wortley's unusual tribute is an embroidered spray of leaves, over the words and music of "O God our help in ages past". An artist, Stuart-Wortley was first President of the Society of Portrait Painters, and when he died these words of Kipling were put on his gravestone:

When earth's last picture is painted, and the tubes are twisted and dried,
When the oldest colours have faded, and the youngest critic has died;
Each for the joy of the working, and each in his separate star,
Shall draw the Thing as he sees it, for the God of things as they are.

By the church are the gates of the park round the home of the Wortleys, where the Earls of Wharncliffe have long lived.

Wragby. The church, with treasure in wood and glass, is over 400 years old, standing among yews in the park with its fine old oaks and mile-long avenue of elms, a lake of 40 acres, and a handsome great house known as Nostell Priory, said to have a room for every day of the year. Long the home of the Winns, who built it in the 18th century, it is near the site of the Augustinian priory, some few stones of which remain in a nearby farm. Begun in 1733 the house was designed by James Paine, then 19, and contains work by Robert Adam. There is also a fine collection of Chippendale furniture, including an imposing library table for which the maker charged £72.10.0 in 1767. Zucchi and Angelica Kaufmann contributed paintings, and decorative work. Intriguing are the famous Doll's House of 1740 which portrays in great detail fashions of the time, and a clock, made in 1717 by John Harrison. The house, which is now regularly open to visitors, also houses a very comprehensive museum of vintage and veteran motor-cycles.

Among the treasures in the house is a picture believed to have been painted by Holbein, showing Sir Thomas More and his family. We see Sir Thomas in his Chancellor's collar, his wife kneeling at prayer, and his learned daughter Margaret with a copy of Seneca in her hands. There is her sister Elizabeth with a book under her arm, John (the queer boy) with Anne Cresacre whom he married, the family jester, and Sir Thomas's secretary holding a scroll. Behind them is a Dutch clock, and in a room beyond is a young man reading. The artist has written the names and ages over all the portraits in this picture of the most remarkable family in the England of their day.

The church is a spacious oblong with arcades running its length and a tower at the west end, and is entered through a porch with a sundial telling the time in many cities of the world. Two ancient relics are a worn stone in the chancel wall showing traces of a figure under an arch, and the Norman bowl of the font, carved with crude zigzag. It is said to have been brought from Auburn church (near Bridlington) before the sea washed the church away. One of many memorials to the Winns is to John of 1817, a marble monument with beautiful figures of a man and a woman, by Chantrey.

There is much rich woodwork here—the lectern, the squire's pew in the north chapel, the fine screen-work with carved pillars enclosing the south chapel, a carved seat in the sanctuary, and the old dark oak panelling on the east wall. The canopied pulpit is a superb piece of Italian craftsmanship, looking all the more charming because of its suspension from a pillar of the chancel arch. The magnificent old glass must be seen to be believed, for it fills all the windows except in the clerestory, and comes from the 16th to the 18th century. The chancel has restored English glass with saints and bishops, shedding a golden hue; the rest is chiefly Swiss glass in a wonderful mosaic of colour, some windows charming with roundels and panels like cameos, their brilliant little scenes dazzling in colour and detail. There are fifty in one window alone.

At Foulby in this parish in 1693 was born the wonderful clock-maker John Harrison. When the Government, in 1713, offered a £10,000 prize for a chronometer determining longitude at sea to within 30 miles, it was Harrison who responded with success after researches lasting over 20 years. He did what was wanted in 1735, but the Board of Longitude treated him with extraordinary pettiness, and though they recognised his merit by small payments in 1737 it was not till 1773, after petitions to Parliament and the intervention of the king, that he received the remainder of his prize.

Yeadon. A few miles from Leeds, on the hillside north of the River Aire, it is busy now with woollen mills, but was once cut off from everywhere by hills and moors. Hereabouts are still the pack-horse roads along which carriers brought wool and cloth, but of those days little is left except Low Hall. In the 19th century church is a window to those who fell in the Great War, showing the Crucifixion scene with Mary and John, and figures of saints, a soldier, and a sailor in the roots and branches of the tree forming the Cross.

Though Yorkshire has many greater houses, it has few more charming than Low Hall on the fringe of Yeadon, a small grey house in a lovely spot with trees shading the lawns, a mill-pond which has become a sunken garden, and a rockery ablaze with colour half the year. The stones of the 17th century porch are said to have come from Esholt Priory, and over the porch is a delightful room with

300-year-old glass in an oriel. The massive oak door hanging on heavy hinges, all centuries old, is barred with a heavy beam sliding in the wall.

The township has produced many Yorkshire cricketers, but has a curiosity in a street named "Football". The near-by Leeds–Bradford Airport has grown to impressive size from small beginnings and continues to expand.

APPENDIX

Places of interest open to the public

(* Indicates National Trust Property)

(† Indicates Ministry of Public Building and Works Property)

Aldborough: Aldborough Roman Camp.

Barnsley: Monk Bretton Priory.

Batley: Oakwell Hall.

Boston Spa: Bramham Park.

Halifax: Shibden Hall.

Harrogate: Harlow Car Gardens.
  Rudding Park.

Keighley: *East Riddlesden Hall.

Leeds: Harewood House and Park.
  Kirkstall Abbey.
  Temple Newsam

Mexborough: Conisborough Castle.

Ripley: Ripley Castle.

Ripon: Fountains Hall and †Abbey.
  Markenfield Hall.
  Newby Hall.
  The Old Hall.

Rotherham: Roche Abbey.

Sherburn: Streeton Hall Gateway.

Skipton: Skipton Castle.

Wakefield: *Nostell Priory.

It is advisable to check times of opening before visiting any of these places.

Abbeydale Industrial Village, Sheffield.

Bagshaw Museum, Batley.

Cannon Hall, Barnsley.

Cawthorne Village Museum.

Cliffe Castle Museum, Keighley.

Craven Museum, Skipton.

Doncaster Museum.

Kirkstall Museum, Leeds.

Rotherham Museum.

Royal Pump Room Museum, Harrogate.

Saddleworth Museum.

Tadcaster: the Ark.

Wakefield City Museum.

Wakeman's House Museum, Ripon.

WEST RIDING TOWNS AND VILLAGES

In this key to our map of Yorkshire are all the towns and villages treated in this book. If a place is not on the map by name, its square is given here, so that the way to it is easily found, each square being five miles. One or two hamlets are in the book with their neighbouring villages; for these see Index.

Sharow	K4	Stainforth	D5	Thorpe Salvin		Warmsworth	N13
Sheffield	L15	Stainland	G11		N15	Wath	H5
Sherburn-in-		Stainton	N14	Threshfield	F5	Wath-on-Dearne	
Elmet	M9	Stanley	K10	Throapham	N15		L13
Shipley	H9	Starbotton	F4	Thrybergh	M14	Wentbridge	M11
Silkstone	K12	Staveley	L5	Thurnscoe	M12	Wentworth	L13
Silsden	G7	Steeton	G8	Tickhill	N14	West Bretton	K12
Skelbrooke	M12	Studley Royal	K4	Tockwith	M7	West End	J7
Skelton	L5	Swillington	L9	Todmorden	E10	Weston	H7
Skipton	F7	Swinefleet	Q11	Todwick	M15	Wetherby	L7
Slaidburn	C7	Swinton	M13	Tong	J9	Whiston	M14
Slaithwaite	G11			Totley	K15	Whitgift	Q10
Snaith	O10	Tadcaster	M8	Towton	M8	Whitkirk	L9
South Kirkby		Tankersley	K13	Treeton	M15	Whixley	M6
	M12	Temple Hirst	O10			Wighill	M7
South Milford		Thorne	P12	Upper Poppleton		Winksley	J4
	M9	Thorner	L8		N6	Wistow	N9
Southowram	H10	Thornhill	J11			Womersley	N11
Sowerby	G10	Thornton	G9	Waddington	C8	Woodkirk	K10
Sowerby Bridge		Thornton-in-		Wadworth	N14	Woolley	K12
	G10	Craven	E7	Wakefield	K11	Worsborough	L13
Spofforth	L7	Thornton-in-		Wales	M15	Wortley	K13
Sprotborough	N17	Lonsdale	B4	Walton	L11	Wragby	L11
Stainborough	K13	Thorp Arch	M7	Walton (near			
Stainburn	J7	Thorpe	F5	Wakefield)	L11	Yeadon	J8